THE ASHGATE RESEARCH COMPANION TO MEMORY STUDIES

ASHGATE
RESEARCH
COMPANION

The *Ashgate Research Companions* are designed to offer scholars and graduate students a comprehensive and authoritative state-of-the-art review of current research in a particular area. The companions' editors bring together a team of respected and experienced experts to write chapters on the key issues in their speciality, providing a comprehensive reference to the field.

The Ashgate Research Companion to Memory Studies

Edited by

SIOBHAN KATTAGO

Tallinn University, Estonia

ASHGATE

Published by
Ashgate Publishing Limited
Wey Court East
Union Road
Farnham
Surrey, GU9 7PT
England

Ashgate Publishing Company
110 Cherry Street
Suite 3-1
Burlington, VT 05401-3818
USA

www.ashgate.com

British Library Cataloguing in Publication Data
A catalogue record for this book is available from the British Library

Library of Congress Cataloging-in-Publication Data
The Ashgate research companion to memory studies / [edited] by Siobhan Kattago.
    pages cm
 Includes bibliographical references and index.
  ISBN 978-1-4094-5392-5 (hardback) -- ISBN 978-1-4094-5393-2 (ebook) --
ISBN 978-1-4724-0533-3 (epub) 1. Memory--Sociological aspects. 2. Collective memory.
3. History--Psychological aspects. I. Kattago, Siobhan, 1966-

  BF378.S65A84 2015
  153.1'2--dc23
                                                                        2014020763
ISBN 9781409453925 (hbk)
ISBN 9781409453932 (ebk – PDF)
ISBN 9781472405333 (ebk – ePUB)

Printed in the United Kingdom by Henry Ling Limited,
at the Dorset Press, Dorchester, DT1 1HD

Contents

List of Figures

List of Tables

Notes on Contributors

Mieke Bal, a cultural theorist and critic, is based at the Amsterdam School for Cultural Analysis (ASCA). Her areas of interest range from biblical and classical antiquity to seventeenth-century and contemporary art and modern literature, feminism and migratory culture. Her many books include *Travelling Concepts in the Humanities* (2002), *A Mieke Bal Reader* (2006), *Narratology* (3rd edn, 2009) and *Of What One Cannot Speak* (2010). Mieke is also a video artist and occasionally acts as an independent curator. Her new exhibition and film *Madame B* (with Michelle Williams Gamaker) is currently touring.

Stuart Burch is Senior Lecturer at Nottingham Trent University in the School of Arts and Humanities where he teaches public history and heritage management. He has published articles in *Europe-Asia Studies*, *East European Politics and Societies* and *International Journal of Heritage Studies*, as well as chapters in various books, among them *Contested and Shared Places of Memory* (2009) and *National Museums* (2011). His contribution to this volume is the basis for a wider study of London and the politics of memory.

Alexandre Dessingué is Associate Professor of Uses of History and Literacy Studies at the University of Stavanger, Norway, where he teaches cultural memory studies, critical literacy, literary and cultural theory. His research interests focus on cultural and collective memory, cultural representations of the Second World War and the Holocaust, and literary and memory theory (Halbwachs, Bakhtin and Ricoeur). Between 2008 and 2013, he was the leader of the 'Culture and Memory Studies' research project and, since 2014, Dean of Research and Research Education at the University of Stavanger. He is the author of *Le Polyphonisme du Roman: Lecture Bakhtinienne de Simenon* (2012). Together with Jay Winter, he is currently working on a book, *Beyond Memory: Silence and the Aesthetics of Remembrance*.

Alexander Etkind is Mikhail M. Bakhtin Professor of History of Russian–European Relations at the European Institute University in Florence. Before his move to Italy in 2013, he was Professor of Russian Literature and Cultural History at Cambridge University, where he was also a fellow of King's College and leader of the research project 'Memory at War: Cultural Dynamics in Poland, Russia, and Ukraine'. His recent publications include *Internal Colonization: Russia's Imperial Experience* (2011), *Remembering Katyn* (2012, co-author), *Warped Mourning: Stories of the Undead in the Land of the Unburied* (2013) and *Memory and Theory in Eastern Europe* (2013, co-editor). He is working on a biography of William C. Bullitt, the first American ambassador to the Soviet Union.

Peter Fritzsche is Professor of History at the University of Illinois where he has taught modern European history since 1987. He is the author of numerous books including *Stranded in the Present: Modern Time and the Melancholy of History* (2004), *Life And Death in the Third Reich* (2008) and *The Turbulent World of Franz Göll: An Ordinary Berliner Writes the Twentieth Century* (2011). He is currently writing a cultural history of the Second World War.

Julie Hansen is Associate Professor of Slavic languages at the Department of Modern Languages and research fellow at the Uppsala Centre for Russian and Eurasian Studies at Uppsala University, Sweden. She co-edited *Transcultural Identities in Contemporary Literature* (2013) and has published articles on Russian and Czech modernism, exile literature, translingual literature and the theme of memory in literary fiction. Her most recent project applies memory theory in interpretations of recent novels depicting the Communist period in Central and Eastern Europe.

William Hirst is Professor of Psychology at the New School for Social Research, New York His graduate training was at Cornell University, receiving his Ph.D. in 1976. He taught at Rockefeller University, Princeton University and Cornell University before coming to the New School. He has edited four volumes and published over 120 articles on topics as wide ranging as attention, amnesia and social aspects of collective and individual memory. His research has received support from the National Institutes of Health, National Science Foundation and the McDonnell and Russell Sage Foundations. He also directed a programme to revive psychology in Romania after the fall of Communism. He is currently working on a book on collective memory.

Patrick H. Hutton is Emeritus Professor of History at the University of Vermont, where he teaches in the Integrated Humanities Program. In addition to the books mentioned in his chapter here, most notably *History as an Art of Memory* (1993), he has contributed chapters and essays on memory in its relation to history to *Global Encyclopedia of Historical Writing* (1998), *New Dictionary of the History of Ideas* (2005), *International Encyclopedia of the Social Sciences* (2nd end, 2008), *Sage Handbook of Historical Theory* (2013), *Routledge International Handbook of Memory Studies* (2014) and the anthology *The Merits of Memory: Concepts, Contexts, Debates* (2009). He also recently edited a special issue of the journal *Historical Reflections* on 'Nostalgia in Modern France' (Winter 2013).

Siobhan Kattago is Associate Professor of philosophy at the Estonian Institute of Humanities of Tallinn University. Her academic interests include collective memory, philosophy of history, political philosophy and twentieth-century European history. In addition to editing *The Ashgate Research Companion to Memory Studies*, she is the author of *Ambiguous Memory: The Nazi Past and German National Identity* (2001) and *Memory and Representation in Contemporary Europe: The Persistence of the Past* (2012). She is currently writing about the political philosophy of Hannah Arendt.

Daniel Levy is Professor in the Department of Sociology at the State University of New York – Stony Brook. He is interested in collective memory studies and the cosmopolitan foundations for a sociology of the twenty-first century. Among his publications are *The Holocaust and Memory in the Global Age* (2005) and *Memory and Human Rights* (2010), both co-authored with Natan Sznaider. Together with Jeffrey Olick and Vered Vinitzky-Seroussi he co-edited *The Collective Memory Reader* (2011).

Angelica Nuzzo is Professor of Philosophy at the Graduate Center and Brooklyn College (City University of New York). She has been recipient of a Tow Professorship (2012–13), an Alexander von Humboldt Fellowship (2005–6), and has been a fellow at the Radcliffe Institute for Advanced Studies at Harvard (2000–2001). Among her recent books are *Kant and the Unity of Reason* (2005), *Ideal Embodiment: Kant's Theory of Sensibility* (2008), *Hegel and the Analytic Tradition* (2009, editor), *History, Memory, Justice in Hegel* (2012) and *Hegel on Religion and Politics* (2013, editor).

Jeffrey K. Olick is Professor of Sociology and History at the University of Virginia. His research focuses on collective memory, critical theory, transitional justice and postwar Germany. His recent publications include *In the House of the Hangman: The Agonies of German Defeat, 1943–1949* (2005), *The Politics of Regret: On Collective Memory and Historical Responsibility* (2007), *The Collective Memory Reader* (2011, co-editor) and *The Sins of the Fathers: Governing Memory in the Federal Republic of Germany* (forthcoming).

Luisa Passerini is part-time Professor at the European University Institute, Florence, Italy; Visiting Professor at Columbia University; former Professor of Cultural History at the University of Turin and Principal Investigator of the European Research Council Project 'Bodies Across Borders: Oral and Visual Memory in Europe and Beyond'. Among her recent books are *Fascism in Popular Memory* (1987), *Autobiography of a Generation: Italy 1968* (1996), *Europe in Love, Love in Europe* (1999), *Memory and Utopia: The Primacy of Intersubjectivity* (2007), *Sogno di Europa* (2009) and *Women and Men in Love: European Identities in the Twentieth Century* (2012).

Eva-Clarita Pettai is a Senior Researcher at the Institute of Government and Politics, University of Tartu, Estonia. She obtained a Ph.D. in political science from the Free University Berlin. Living between Berlin and Riga during the 1990s, she was a close witness to the post-Soviet contentions over the ownership of the past. Her most recent books include *Memory and Pluralism in the Baltic States* (2011, editor) and *Transitional and Retrospective Justice in the Baltic States* (2014, co-author). In addition she has also published on the politics of Holocaust and Second World War remembrance in Europe.

Hans Ruin is Professor of Philosophy at Södertörn University, Stockholm. He specialises in phenomenology, hermeneutics and ancient philosophy. His recent publications include *Frihet, ändlighet, historicitet: Essäer om Heideggers filosofi* (2013) and the co-edited volumes *Re-Thinking Time: History, Memory, and Representation* (2011) and *Ambiguity of the Sacred: Phenomenology, Aesthetics, Politics* (2012). He is president of the Nordic Society for Phenomenology, co-editor of Nietzsche's Collected Works in Swedish and director of the research programme, 'Time, Memory, and Representation' (<www.histcon.se>).

Charles B. Stone is an Assistant Professor of Psychology at John Jay College of Criminal Justice of the City University of New York. He earned his doctorate in cognitive science at the Macquarie Centre for Cognitive Science at Macquarie University in Sydney. His research generally focuses on understanding how autobiographical, collective memories and individuals' confidence in said memories are shaped through social interactions. He is currently the lead editor of a forthcoming book entitled *Contextualizing Human Memory: An Interdisciplinary Approach to Understanding How Individuals and Groups Remember the Past*.

Marek Tamm is Associate Professor of Cultural History at the Estonian Institute of Humanities and senior researcher in medieval studies at the Institute of History, both in Tallinn University. His primary research fields are cultural history of medieval Europe, theory and history of historiography, and cultural memory studies. His recent publications include an edited volume on the current state of humanities, *Humanitaarteaduste metodoloogia: uusi väljavaateid* (Methodology in the Humanties: New Perspectives, 2011), a companion to the *Chronicle* of Henry of Livonia, *Crusading and Chronicle Writing on the Medieval Baltic Frontier* (2011, co-editor), *Monumentaalne ajalugu: Esseid Eesti ajalookultuurist* (Monumental History: Essays on the Historical Culture of Estonia, 2012), *Keskaja kirjanduse antoloogia* (Anthology of

Medieval Literature, 2013), *Afterlife of Events: Perspectives of Mnemohistory* (2014, editor) and numerous articles in various anthologies and journals.

Vered Vinitzky-Seroussi is Professor of Sociology at the Hebrew University of Jerusalem. She is the author of *After Pomp and Circumstance: High School Reunion as an Autobiographical Occasion* (1998), *Yitzhak Rabin's Assassination and the Dilemmas of Commemoration* (2009) and the co-editor of *The Collective Memory Reader* (2011). Her papers have appeared in *American Sociological Review, Social Forces, Sociological Quarterly, Qualitative Sociology* and others. She is currently Dean of the Faculty of Social Sciences and conducting research on home museums.

Bradford Vivian is an Associate Professor of Communication and Rhetorical Studies at Syracuse University. He is the author of *Being Made Strange: Rhetoric beyond Representation* (2004), *Public Forgetting: The Rhetoric and Politics of Beginning Again* (2010) and co-editor of *Rhetoric, Remembrance, and Visual Form: Sighting Memory* (2011). His work has appeared in such journals as *Quarterly Journal of Speech, Philosophy and Rhetoric, Rhetoric and Public Affairs, History and Memory* and *Journal of Speculative Philosophy*. He is a recipient of the Winans-Wichelns Award, the Karl R. Wallace Memorial Award and the B. Aubrey Fisher Award, and his research grants include a National Endowment for the Humanities Summer Stipend.

Acknowledgements

This volume would not have been possible without the assistance of many people. I am very grateful to Claire Jarvis, for her enthusiastic editorial guidance as commissioning editor at Ashgate Publishing. Likewise, Gemma Hayman was an enormous help at the production stage. My gratitude to our departmental secretary, Anni Handi for her administrative assistance. Research for the volume was supported by the European Regional Development Fund (Centre of Excellence in Cultural Theory) and by ERC grant IUT3–2. Julie Hansen, Patrick Hutton, Francisco Martinez, Eva-Clarita Pettai, Johanna Söderholm and Marek Tamm were careful readers and provided insightful criticism. I wish to thank my sister, Deirdre Murphy, for her thoughtful artwork on the cover of the volume. Mieke Bal, Daniel Levy, Luisa Passerini and Vera Zolberg have been tireless sources of intellectual support throughout the entire project. In addition, I wish to acknowledge Jeffrey Olick. Without our dinner conversation at an interesting spring conference, 'Towards a Common Past: Conflicting Memories on Contemporary Europe' held in Lund in 2012, I would not have arrived at the idea to take companions so literally. If Proust had his infamous madeleine moment, this modest Companion originated with an elusive meatball. As we searched, but never found those famous Swedish meatballs in the old town of Lund, Jeff encouraged me to ask authors to write about their formative interests in memory. It was from this heated conversation that I began to think seriously about intellectual companions. But, it is, above all, to the authors, who have contributed to *The Ashgate Research Companion to Memory Studies* that I am most grateful. The edited volume entailed a long process of correspondence across different countries and time zones. I am thankful to the authors for their creative insight, patience and reflection on the research companions who accompany their ongoing work on memory.

Introduction:
Memory Studies and its Companions

Siobhan Kattago

Memory has long been a subject of fascination for poets, artists, philosophers and historians. When recalling the past, it is impossible to fully capture the complexity of memory. Instead, as Walter Benjamin noted, the process of remembering seems to unfold like a fragile and unending fan.

> *He who has once began to open the fan of memory never comes to the end of its segments; no image satisfies him, for he has seen that it can be unfolded, and only in its folds does the truth reside; that image, that taste, that touch for whose sake all this has been unfurled and dissected; and now remembrance progresses from small to smallest details, from the smallest to the infinitesimal, while that which it encounters in these microcosms grows even mightier. (Benjamin 1978: 6)*

According to Greek mythology, Mnemosyne was the mother of the nine muses, one of whom was Clio, the muse of history. And yet, remembrance also includes what is forgotten – either deliberately or accidentally.[1] Indeed, forgetfulness played a very important role in the political life of ancient Greece. If the altar to Lethe on the Athenian acropolis symbolised the importance of forgetting for the political unity of the polis, the river Lethe embodied the importance of forgetfulness in the afterlife. How past events are remembered, mis-remembered, understood, contested, forgotten, learned from and shared with others is the subject of this volume.

Research Companions

The Ashgate Research Companion to Memory Studies stems from two sources: the insights of the first historian Herodotus and the etymology of the word 'companion'. In *Travels with Herodotus*, Ryszard Kapuściński reminds his readers that for Herodotus, the purpose of history was to keep the memory of both the Greeks and non-Greeks alive. Indeed, his famous quotation, 'To prevent the traces of human events being erased by time' (Herodotus 1998: 3), was a motif that Kapuściński kept with him on his voyages and reportages around the world. Herodotus understood that the desire to preserve glorious events of the past was not simply a generous gesture but also a double-edged sword. The injunction to remember and

---

1   For important works on forgetting, see Connerton 2008; Ricoeur 2006; Vivian 2010; Weinrich 2004.

prevent time from erasing the memory of hostilities can just as often become the cause of future violence. 'Without memory one cannot live, for it is what elevates man above beasts, determines the contours of the human soul; and yet it is at the same time so unreliable, elusive, treacherous' (Kapuściński 2004: 75). Following in the footsteps of Kapuściński and Herodotus, the interdisciplinary field of memory studies includes those scholars who emphasise the continuity of heritage and tradition and those who focus on the memory of hostilities, traumas and painful events.[2]

In this volume, chapters are devoted to companions who have inspired authors currently writing about memory. Herodotus was one such companion for Kapuściński during his many travels. In its most simple meaning, a companion is one who shares with another (*com* – with + *panis* – bread). Which thinkers and conceptual ideas inspire the growing and diverse field of memory studies? Who are some of the thinkers that accompany contemporary intellectuals as they think about how and why the past is remembered, represented and reconstructed? This volume offers an opportunity for authors to remember and reflect on some of the companions by whom they have been inspired and perhaps troubled. In the spirit of Kapuściński, companionship is understanding and dialogue across different cultures, languages and time periods. Taking its cue from Reinhart Koselleck's conceptual history, chapters reflect on formative thinkers and concepts. Companions who have inspired authors in this volume include Arendt, Jan and Aleida Assmann, Ariès, Bakhtin, Benjamin, Chateaubriand, Derrida, Freud, Halbwachs, Hegel, Heidegger, Koselleck, Lotman, Nietzsche, Nora, Warburg and Yates. Corresponding concepts include collective memory, mentalities, cultural memory, *lieux de mémoire*, monuments, museums, tradition, trauma, nostalgia, historical consciousness, forgetting, silence, commemoration, cosmopolitanism, narrative, mnemohistory, myth, event, modernity and hauntology.

Given the amount of writing and research networks devoted to how and why the past is remembered, this volume tries to guide readers through the labyrinth of the contemporary 'memory boom'.[3] Moreover, it aims to complement the growing amount of literature devoted to the study of memory. Anthologies and readers provide excellent and welcome excerpts of canonical texts. Likewise, handbooks map out important debates and themes.[4] Our volume, however, makes different demands on its authors, because each one has been asked to reflect on his or her academic companions.

How authors interpret companions and choose to write about them is an entirely individual choice. Reflections and memoirs have their own history, and today's world more than borders on the confessional. From Facebook, Twitter and Instagram, we are saturated with indulgent self-promotion. This is certainly not the intention of our volume. Rather, by highlighting the link between memoir and memory, it participates in a far older tradition of self-reflection. St Augustine's writing on the nature of time and memory continues to fascinate readers of his *Confessions*. Likewise, Nabokov's memoir, *Speak, Memory* weaves reflections

---

2   For a helpful Ashgate volume outlining major themes of heritage, tradition and identity, see Graham and Howard 2008; see also David Lowenthal's influential, *The Past is a Foreign Country* (1985) and *The Past is a Foreign Country Revisited* (2014). Hobsbawn and Ranger's *Invention of Tradition* (1983) remains a powerful critique of the political construction of tradition and commemoration.

3   Book series on memory include Ashgate's Memory Studies: Global Constellations; Berghahn's Making Sense of History; De Gruyter's Media and Cultural Memory; Palgrave's Memory Studies; Peter Lang's Cultural Memory; Rowman Littlefield's Place, Memory, Affect; and Stanford University's Cultural Memory in the Present.

4   For anthologies and readers, see Erll and Nünning 2010; Olick, Vinitzky-Seroussi and Levy 2011; Rossington and Whitehead 2007; Wood and Byatt 2009. For general handbooks, see Bal, Crewe and Spitzer 1999; Berger and Niven 2014; Radstone and Schwarz 2010; Tota and Hagen 2015. For introductions to memory studies and cultural memory, see Erll 2011a; Misztal 2003; Whitehead 2009.

on memory with the story of his life. Philosophical memoirs are a genre in themselves: from Rousseau's *Confessions* to Nietzsche's *Antichrist* and Derrida's *Monolingualism of the Other*. By asking authors to write about their intellectual companions, what seems to be emerging is a kind of *ego-histoire* of memory studies.

Pierre Nora's concept of *ego-histoire* (1987) is intriguing because he asked French historians to reflect not only on their historical research but also on themselves as historians within a particular generation. His project thus reflects the interests of certain French historians during the 1970s and 1980s. *Ego-histoire* is connected with a history of the present in which the historian reflects on him- or herself within the present.[5] It is 'neither a philosophical history nor a philosophy of history, but an interior investigation into the object of history itself' (Nora 2011: 140). While there are few free-standing departments of Memory Studies, each author in this volume has been asked to reflect on his or her research as a scholar who studies memory. One might ask whether memory studies is ready for such an enterprise – after all, the discipline of history is far older than that of memory studies. This volume can be seen as a kind of *ego-histoire* because it reflects on the discipline as a whole through the individual reflections of its authors. *Ego-histoire* blurs the line between subjective and professional engagement (ibid.). Pierre Nora's collection of essays has the elegant uniformity of examining the single discipline of history. However, his book is limited to senior French historians of a particular generation. Our volume is broader because it is international, interdisciplinary and includes both senior and junior scholars from different generations.[6] Taken as a whole, the *Ashgate Research Companion to Memory Studies* connects why authors write about memory with their theoretical companions and the larger socio-historical reasons for the memory boom. Each chapter entails a degree of self-reflectivity traditionally bracketed out of scholarly research. What has emerged is a loose *ego-histoire* with a variety of approaches – some more personal than others. However, each chapter provides a self-portrait along with reflections on a particular aspect of memory.

What is Collective Memory?

Although the term 'collective memory' (*la mémoire collective*) was first coined by Maurice Halbwachs in 1925, the study of memory has much in common with historical consciousness, nostalgia, tradition and myth.[7] The idea of historical consciousness is decidedly older than the concept of collective memory, with roots in German philosophy of history and time. Likewise, Durkheim's conscious collective and collective representations have interesting overlaps with the Annales school of mentalities, because both emphasise representative images of a group as well as the continuity between past and present (Durkheim 1995: 207–35; Bloch 1961). As Hutton and Fritzsche highlight in this volume, nostalgia evokes deep longing for a past that has been lost. In addition, collective memory shares much with tradition and myth, particularly in the way that foundational events are remembered as sources of

---

5 My gratitude to Patrick Hutton for calling my attention to the nuances of Nora's *ego-histoire*.

6 In an interesting *ego-histoire* of European historians born between 1935 and 1950, Luisa Passerini and Alexander C. T. Geppert write: 'Ego-histoire, as we understand it, is a mainly methodological enterprise, aiming to establish a ground of meta-historical reflection' (2001: 8).

7 Alon Confino suggests that the field of memory studies is connected not only with the work of Warburg but also with the Annales school of mentalities (2006). Ricoeur writes at length about the important contribution of mentalities to the study of memory (2007: 182–233). See also Burke 1990; Hutton 1993: 91–105; Ch. 1 below. For memory and historical consciousness, see Rüsen 2006; Sexias 2006.

collective identity (Hobsbawn and Ranger 1983; Bell 2003). As Pettai argues in this volume, political myth is 'a simplified narrative' that is not necessarily false. Rather political myth 'describes a form of collective memory' visible in state policy and public commemoration.

In response to academic and popular interest in memory, Susan Sontag and Reinhart Koselleck criticise the very notion of collective memory as a meaningful concept. Sontag writes: 'What is called collective memory is not a remembering but a stipulating: that *this* is important and this is the story about how it happened, with the pictures that lock the story in our minds' (2003: 86). Granted her examples are visual ones and based primarily on documentary photographs, but Sontag's critique is well-worth thinking about.

> *Photographs that everyone recognizes are now a constituent part of what a society chooses to think about, or declare that it has chosen to think about. It calls these ideas 'memories,' and that is, over the long run, a fiction. Strictly speaking, there is no such thing as collective memory – part of the same family of spurious notions as collective guilt. But there is collective instruction. (Sontag 2003: 85)*

It makes no sense to say that remembering is collective – only individuals are able to remember, not groups. However, 'collective instruction' is only possible when individuals speak the same language and can understand one another.

Similarly to Sontag, Koselleck argued against the salience of collective memory. 'I can only remember what I myself have experienced. Memory [*Erinnerung*] is bound up with personal experience' (2004: 3). As a German prisoner of war, he witnessed the liberation of Auschwitz by the Red Army. When reflecting on International Holocaust Remembrance Day (27 January), he distinguished collective memory as the ritualised commemoration of historical events. 'As day of remembrance, as *re-commemoration*, it is semantically a fully different memory from that which I have kept in my memory as a witness [*Augenzeuge*] of the initial news' (ibid.). The larger framework of days of remembrance and commemorative reflection are 'semantically' different from his lived experience. Likewise, Koselleck asks who is the subject who remembers? Individuals are influenced by: 'the 7 P's': professors, priests, preachers, PR specialists, the press, poets and politicians (ibid. 5). 'There are as many memories as there are people and each collectivity, convinced they are the only one, is, in my opinion, *a priori* ideology or myth' (ibid. 6). Arguing against the concept of collective memory, he claims that there are 'collective conditions' enabling individual memory. 'There is thus no collective memory; there are collective conditions [*kollektive Bedingungen*] which make memory possible' (ibid.). And it is precisely here, that he comes closest to the formative ideas of Maurice Halbwachs and Aby Warburg in the first half of the twentieth century because such 'collective conditions' are what enable individuals to understand one another.

As Chiara Bottici suggests, Wittgenstein's argument against private language provides the strongest philosophical support for the existence of collective memory (2010: 341). Experience can only be shared through a common language. In contrast, as Wittgenstein demonstrates in his *Philosophical Investigations*, a private language denotes an inner experience that is utterly impossible to share with others (2001). Hence, if one considers Koselleck's argument that he cannot share his personal experience of witnessing the liberation of Auschwitz, this experience remains a private and individual memory. However, some aspects can be shared through imagination, empathy and, above all, language. Part of Koselleck's individual memory remains a private language – but not all of it. Moreover, Sontag's belief in 'collective instruction' and Koselleck's 'collective conditions' for shared memories are both predicated on language. Halbwachs emphasised the intersubjective or shared space between individuals and the collective; hence, his careful emphasis on frameworks (*les cadres*) in the plural. Collective memory is neither a singular representation of the past, nor an essential substance genetically encoded into human beings. As Halbwachs writes, 'it is language, and the whole system of social conventions attached to it, that allows us at every moment to reconstruct our past' (1992: 173).

From his earlier *Social Frameworks of Memory* (1925) to posthumous book, *La mémoire collective* (1940), Halbwachs argues that it is individuals, as members of a group who remember: 'While the collective memory endures and draws strength from its base in a coherent body of people, it is individuals as group members who remember' (1980: 48). As Alexandre Dessingué points out in this volume, Halbwachs' original insight was to emphasise the intersection of the individual and the collective. Moreover, if one reads Halbwachs within the intellectual context of early twentieth-century writers – such as Proust, Freud, Heidegger, Bloch, Benjamin, Saussure and Wittgenstein – one can trace how the idea of collective memory is accompanied by scholarship in psychology, philosophy of language, phenomenology and the history of mentalities. Collective memory is not the same as Durkheim's conscious collective. Nor does Halbwachs argue for the existence of a primordial Jungian collective unconscious. 'There is no universal memory. Every collective memory requires the support of a group delimited in space and time' (ibid. 83–4). Likewise, his concept of collective memory is not about national memory or *Volksgeist*. Instead, because individuals belong to many social groups, what and how they remember is framed by membership within those groups.

It is worth recalling that the first English-language journal devoted to the study of memory includes both collective memory and historical consciousness as stated objects of academic research: '*History & Memory* explores the manifold ways in which the past shapes the present and is shaped by present perceptions. The journal focuses on a wide range of questions relating to the formation of historical consciousness and collective memory' (*History and Memory* n.d.). Hence, the study of memory is not opposed to history, but a companion to it. The emphasis is on the past–present link, rather than the opposition between history and memory. Moreover, the emphasis is on 'the manifold ways' of interaction between past, present and future.[8] The first article published in *History and Memory*, 'Collective Memory and Historical Consciousness' by Amos Funkenstein, reminds the reader of the close relationship between memory, history, time and narration. '"History," comments Hegel in *Philosophy of History*, "combines in our language the objective as well as the subjective side. It means both *res gestae* (the things that happened) and *historica rerum gestarum* (the narration of the things that happened)"' (Funkenstein 1989: 5). Funkenstein does not see a contradiction here, rather an important connection that Hegel observed: 'without memory of the past, there is no history, in the sense of events that are meaningful to the collective, events experienced by a collective that is aware of them. Collective consciousness presumes collective memory, as without it there is no law or justice, no political structure, and no collective objectives' (ibid.). Both historical consciousness and collective memory refer to communities, whether in the form of tribe, people, nation, religion or civilization. However, as Funkenstein cautions, 'this is confusing, as consciousness and memory can only be realized by an individual who acts, is aware and remembers' (ibid. 6). Moreover he argues, Hegel was the first philosopher to argue that 'self-consciousness *requires* a social context' (ibid.). As Angelica Nuzzo carefully traces in her chapter in this volume, prior to Hegel, self-consciousness tended to posit either a universal view or sacred religious consciousness. Both

---

8   The second English-language journal, *Memory Studies* (since 2008) does not mention historical consciousness at all. Rather the journal 'examines the social, cultural, cognitive, political and technological shifts affecting how, what and why individuals, groups and societies remember, and forget' (*Memory Studies* n.d.). In this sense, the two journals complement one another without overlapping.

historical consciousness and collective memory share an emphasis on the social interaction between individual and community.

A few years earlier than Halbwachs, the German art historian, Aby Warburg wrote about social memory and the afterlife of pagan images in art. In his incomplete 'Atlas Project', entitled 'Mnemosyne', he chronicled symbolic images from the past that radiated a kind of energy, or what he called 'pathos formula'. Warburg argued that certain classical images leave distinctive traces in the present. Such visual remains are not dead or disconnected from the present – rather, they radiate an afterlife or *Nachleben* (Warburg 1999). In particular, he was interested in how images from the past survive and transform within the present. He envisioned his memory project, Mnemosyne as a kind of ghostly presence or '"a ghost story for truly adult people"' (Warburg, quoted in Agamben 1999: 95).

Astrid Erll elaborates on Warburg's idea of afterlife with her theory of 'travelling memory'. For her, the study of memory has travelled between different time periods and countries, as well as within different departments of the humanities and social sciences. 'What Warburg focuses on is the movement, the migration or travel, of symbols across time' (Erll 2011b: 11). If the historical background for the first phase of memory studies were two world wars, during the second phase in the 1970s and 1980s, earlier definitions of culture were reduced to particular cultures. 'What was studied was *the* culture, and *the* memory, of *a* social formation: a religious group, a social class, an ethnicity' (ibid. 6). Beginning in the 1980s, public discussion turned increasingly to the politics of memory represented in national monuments, museums, memorials and commemorations. It is in this second phase that dramatic social transformations converged: the end of colonial empires, the generational change of those who lived through the Second World War, the increased interest in the Holocaust both academically and in popular culture, the fall of the Soviet Union and Communism enabling comparative research into two dictatorships, migration, globalisation and the digitalisation of mass media. In the early twenty-first century, Erll suggests, we seem to be moving away from the 'cultural turn' of the 1980s, towards a 'transcultural turn' in the new millennium that is at the intersection of globalization, migration and the mass media.[9]

The Afterlife of Collective Memory

Since memories are fluid and change over time, what is remembered or forgotten follows different paths, trajectories and vectors. In its various permutations as cultural memory, mnemonic practices, multidirectional memory, politics of memory, postmemory, prosthetic memory, remembrance, social memory and transcultural memory – the reception and interpretation of Halbwachs is a dramatic example of Warburg's concept of the afterlife. Likewise, one might ask whether collective memory qualifies as a 'travelling concept'?[10] Within what Olick terms, the 'complex inheritance of "collective memory"' and Erll's 'travelling memory', the legacy and afterlife of Halbwachs is most visible in Jan Assmann

---

9   Taking her cue from Edward Said and James Clifford, who first analysed travel as a metaphor for the fluid transformation of ideas in time and space, Erll argues that the very activity of remembering is in transit (see Said 1983; Clifford, 1997). For the transcultural turn in memory studies, see Bond and Rapson 2014.

10   For further research on travelling concepts, see Neuman and Nünning 2012. Bal presents a 'rough travel guide' to the interdisciplinary analysis of concepts (2002).

and Aleida Assmann's theory of cultural memory (*das kulturelle Gedächtnis*) and Pierre Nora's *lieux de mémoire*.[11]

Unlike communicative memory, which lasts for approximately three generations, cultural memory has a longer time-span and encompasses all aspects of cultural life. 'What communication is for communicative memory, tradition is for cultural memory' (J. Assmann 2006: 8). In conjunction with Aleida Assmann, Jan Assmann emphasises both the conscious and unconscious importance of culture. The concept of cultural memory corresponds to what Derrida calls "archive" and Bernstein "tradition" and, like them, it is indebted to the psychohistorical dimension and the dynamics of cultural transmission' (ibid. 27). Assmann's concept of *Gedächtnisgeschichte* or 'mnemohistory', bears a family resemblance with Patrick Hutton's idea that 'history is an art of memory'. Influenced by many thinkers, among them Gadamer, Warburg, Halbwachs and Freud, Assmann acknowledges that both the historian and the historical event are affected by time.[12] Moreover, he argues for a 'mnemohistorical logic' focusing on the following questions: 'who is telling the story, how is it being told, and with what underlying intentions?' (2010: 117). Whether written text, mass media image, ritual or monument – memory is based on traces from the past. 'The present is "haunted" by the past and the past is modeled, invented, reinvented, and reconstructed by the present' (J. Assmann 1997: 9).

If Jan Assmann is associated with the concept of cultural memory, Pierre Nora is synonymous with *lieux de mémoire*. Moreover, his contribution to memory studies includes reflections on the era of commemoration, acceleration of time and democratisation of history. Patrick Hutton's chapter in this volume has a substantial and nuanced discussion of Nora's work and legacy.[13] Sites of memory contain the remains, traces, ruins and fragments of the past. As ciphers they not only point to the afterlife of something that occurred in the past, but also frame and shape the content of what is remembered. For Nora, 'modern memory is, above all, archival. It relies on the materiality of the trace, the immediacy of the recording, the visibility of the image' (1996: 8). The work of Jay Winter, George Mosse and James Young on memorials in a media age, in conjunction with Reinhart Koselleck's reflections on war memorials and remembrance of the dead have been important for those studying memorials as places of modern memory. In a similar vein, David Lowenthal's work on heritage, patrimony, historical tourism and nostalgia have inspired numerous studies of landscapes, monuments and relics. 'A mass of memories and records, of relics and replicas, of monuments and memorabilia, lives at the core of our being' (Lowenthal 1985: xxv). Mass tourism, digital history museums, heritage sites and commemorative events raise many questions related to Nora's seminal work on the national symbolism of *lieux de mémoire*.

While Nora elucidated the symbolic places of memory, Marc Augé calls attention to non-places (*non-lieux*) of memory and oblivion (2009). In addition, Aleida Assmann's distinctions between archive, museum and waste, complement the work of Nora and Augé. Each representative 'place' or 'site' has its own logic and is related to a particular ordering and representation of the past (A. Assmann 2011). However, Nora's contribution to memory studies is by no means limited to his writings on French national memory. In addition to

---

11   For a detailed overview of the 'complex inheritance of "collective memory"' in the fields of psychology, sociology and philosophy of history, see Olick, Vinitzky-Seroussi and Levy 2011: 22. There are many influential thinkers writing about memory; however, Nora and the Assmanns are arguably the most wide-reaching and prolific. For discussions of cultural memory and a helpful discussion of *lieux de mémoire*, see Erll and Nünning 2010. For European *lieux de mémoire*, see Majerus 2014.

12   For more on mnemohistory, see Tamm 2013, 2015.

13   See Hutton 1993: esp. 147–53. For his helpful discussion of changing concepts of time with Nora, Hartog, Halbwachs and Benjamin, see Hutton 2000.

his edited seven-volume work (1984–92), Nora's reflections on time and commemoration intersect with the historical scholarship of François Hartog, Henry Rousso and Reinhart Koselleck. Moreover, he seeks to understand the increasing pre-occupation with memory in politics, the academy and popular culture. 'This upsurge in memory intersects, it seems to me, with two major historical phenomena which have marked the age, one temporal and one social' (Nora 2002: 4). It is to these phenomena that we will now turn.

The Memory Boom: Why Such a Pre-Occupation with the Past?

What distinguishes today's pre-occupation with the past from earlier ones? Since Herodotus, historians have chronicled the deeds of their ancestors. Likewise, the frustration of not being able to capture and represent past experience has its origins in Plato's *Phaedrus*. As soon as one tries to write down past experience, it becomes distant and removed. But, it was above all, Nietzsche in his *Untimely Meditations*, who cautioned against the excessive tendency to monumentalise, venerate and criticise the past. He, however, did not use the language of trauma. As the growing literature illustrates, Freud bequeathed a new vocabulary of trauma, repression and the unconscious to the study of the past. Some authors support arguments for cultural trauma while others, are more critical of transposing trauma from the individual to the collective.[14] Nonetheless, acute attention to traumatic rupture distinguishes today's pre-occupation with the past from former ones. 'Trauma … is not only an unfortunate by-product of modernity, but a central feature of it' (Olick and Demetriou 2006: 75).

The memory boom arose from significant events in the twentieth century – two world wars, the Holocaust, the end of colonialism and the fall of Communism. 1989 is a particularly important date for the interest in memory as ideological narratives unravelled and new, predominantly national and ethnic ones emerged. In addition, the crimes of Communism are often compared to those of the Holocaust. Why though has the study of trauma become a kind of subfield of memory studies? Moreover, how and why did trauma emerge and possibly replace tradition as a central category of historical and social understanding? Similar to hermeneutics, which emphasises tradition and the continuity of the past, early theorists of collective memory, such as Halbwachs and Warburg, linked collective identity with collective memory. Indeed, collective memory provided the group with 'a self-portrait that unfolds through time, since it is an image of the past, and allows the group to recognize itself throughout the total succession of images' (Halbwachs 1980: 86).[15]

In their Introduction to *The Collective Memory Reader*, the authors provocatively ask 'did the Holocaust cause memory studies?' (Olick, Vinitzky-Seroussi and Levy 2011: 29–36). The largest shift occurred when the Holocaust became the universal symbol of moral evil and a meta-narrative (Diner 2003; Dubiel 2003; Levy and Sznaider 2006, 2010). At the 'Holocaust Forum', Yehuda Bauer's speech described this sea change: 'In recent decades, actually in most recent years, we have witnessed an amazing development. A catastrophe that had befallen a specific people at a specific time, in a specific place, has been accepted, all over the world, as the symbol of ultimate evil' (Bauer, quoted in Dubiel 2003: 61). Hence, it is the memory of the Holocaust as a symbol of evil that is connected to human rights, a universal conception of human dignity and the desire to prevent future genocide.

---

14   For important work on cultural trauma and memory, see Alexander 2012; Caruth 1995; LaCapra 1994. For more critical approaches, see Kansteiner 2002, 2004; Radstone 2007.

15   On might even argue that 'memory' and 'culture' seem to have replaced the older categories of 'society' and 'class' (Burke 2004; Confino 2006).

From the 1960s onwards, memory studies has been influenced first by German discussions, linking democratic renewal to the recognition of a negative past and then to comparative scholarship examining the Holocaust, postcolonialism and post-Communism.[16] When Halbwachs and Warburg reflected on the past, they emphasised continuity, not trauma – even if this continuity was fragmentary. Likewise, Benedict Anderson's discussion of Ernst Renan's thesis that national sorrows unite more than victories, did not engage with the vocabulary of trauma and mourning (1983). One distinct consequence of historical experience viewed through the prism of trauma is an intertwining of *ressentiment* and trauma into a 'politics of regret' (Olick 2007). It is perhaps the recognition of a traumatic past, combined with a sense of the enormity of twentieth-century violence that distinguishes the memory boom most of all. It is as if Ernst Nolte's phrase during the German *Historikerstreit* (historian's debate) of the 1980s, 'the past that will not pass' (*die Vergangenheit, die nicht vergehen will*), is constantly present (Nolte 1987; 1993).[17] Likewise, Henry Rousso captured a similar sentiment with the omnipresence of the Vichy past (*Vichy, un passé qui ne passe pas*) (Rousso 1994; Conan and Rousso 1998).

In addition to increased attention to traumatic rupture, the memory boom is related to democratisation and the growing importance of the witness. As Annette Wieworka observed, the late twentieth century became the era of the witness (2006). Historians tend to be cautious of solely relying on first-hand witnesses, as they no longer seem to have privileged access to the past. Moreover, François Hartog argues that the centrality of the witness as a survivor or victim is transforming our experience of time (2014a, 2014b). Far more than the heroic soldier or resistance fighter, it is the witness who has become the authoritative voice of the past, represented in museums, memorials, films, survivor stories and commemorations. Jay Winter echoes Hartog and Nora when he writes: 'Thus a new form of collective remembrance was born, that of the witness, understood in both senses of the term' (2006: 30). The witness to war and the Holocaust was both a moral truth-teller and a witness for the legal record. 'Holocaust witnesses took on therefore a liminal, mediating, semisacred role since the 1970s' (ibid.). The importance of the witness as a moral truth-teller called into question the delicate relationship between historical truth, justice, aesthetic representation and political commemoration. Moreover, the important role of the witness is connected to waves of democratisation in Europe, Latin America and South Africa. Historical commissions, recognition and redress for state-sponsored crimes within the growing field of transitional justice demonstrate the moral, political and legal contours of the memory boom.

Haunted by the Past or Stranded in the Present?

In addition to the central role of the witness and development of universal human rights, memory studies lies at the intersection of new configurations of time and rapid technological change. Conceptions of time are visible in the very language used to characterise the present – as postmodern, posthistorical – or even simply modern. According to Koselleck, it was not until the eighteenth century that consciousness of modernity as a new time (*Neuzeit*) emerged. Modern time is experienced as faster and accelerating towards the

---

16   In this respect, Rothberg's *Multidirectional Memory* (2009) has been very influential for comparative studies of the Holocaust and postcolonialism, as has the work of Craps on postcolonialism (2013) and Etkind's comparative analysis of postcolonialism and post-Communism (2013); for comparative East European memory, see Blacker, Etkind and Fedor 2013.

17   For the main articles of the *Historikerstreit*, see Augstein 1987; Knowlton and T. Cates 1993; see also Maier 1988; Diner 1987.

future. 'Acceleration, initially perceived in terms of an apocalyptic expectation of temporal abbreviation heralding the Last Judgment, transformed itself – also from the mid-eighteenth century – into a concept of historical hope' (Koselleck 1985: 36–7). Likewise, his distinction between the past as a space of experience and the future as a horizon of expectation helps one to visualise how the temporalities of past, present and future differ from one another. The space of experience (*Erfahrungsraum*) encompasses both positive and negative aspects of the past. The horizon of expectation (*Erwartungshorizont*) includes all types of expectations for the future: hopes, fears, dreams and nightmares (ibid. 269). Koselleck's space of experience is broader than Nora's *lieux de mémoire* but also employs the metaphor of topology or a map.

The emphasis on trauma results in a blurring of past and present – or a constant presence and haunting of the past. Rousso recalls Nietzsche's warning about nineteenth-century insomnia and feverish attention to the past. The problem arises when the past prevents individuals from paying attention to the present or imagining the future. 'In fact, these are simply inverted symptoms of the same difficulty – in accepting the reality of the past. Consequently, we are unable to confront the present or imagine the future' (Rousso 2002: 12). In contrast, Hartog maintains that contemporary society is less haunted by the past, and more defined by, what he calls, 'presentism' (2003). Influenced by Koselleck, he argues that the memory boom is connected with a new regime of historicity, focused increasingly on the present rather than the future. Since the future no longer seems to offer certainty, individuals either turn towards the past or remain in ever-expanding present. Likewise, Peter Fritzsche characterised modern society as one that is 'stranded in the present' (2004). One can neither return to the past nor go forward. Instead, one remains stranded in a seemingly endless and porous present. What unites the various viewpoints is the acceleration of time, hesitancy towards the future and burning interest in the past. To conclude, the reasons for the memory boom are numerous and 'operate at different wavelengths' (Olick, Vinitzky-Seroussi and Levy 2011: 35). Some have a longer duration than others. Nonetheless, the growing interdisciplinary interest in memory is inseparable from social and temporal transformations.

***

The Ashgate Research Companion to Memory Studies offers an opportunity for authors to reflect on their work within the context of their intellectual and conceptual companions. The volume consists of 17 chapters, divided among four parts, and roughly follows the chronology of Erll's travelling memory. It is by no means exhaustive and leaves out many important themes. However, a conscious effort has been made to balance the insights of philosophy, history, sociology, psychology, politics and cultural studies.

Memory, History and Time

Part I begins in the areas of history and philosophy with reflections on experience, historical consciousness and time. Our volume opens with Patrick Hutton's chapter, which revisits themes from *History as an Art of Memory* (1993). Given that his book was one of the first written in English to discuss collective memory, tradition, hermeneutics and the philosophy of history, it is fortunate that he reflects on his formative companions during the writing of that book and afterwards. Francis Yates' art of memory is a rhetorical technique that inspired his early analysis of the relationship between history and memory. Long before Nora, Yates considered location as a 'point of intellectual departure for interpreting larger cultural realms'. Hutton's two most influential companions are Nora and Benjamin because both questioned the traditional linear narrative of history. Nora's genealogy collected 'a layered repertoire of topical planes' that localised French national memory in key symbolic places. Likewise, Benjamin's work on the redeeming power of memory as a 'profane illumination' 'offered a perspective on the reinvention of the art of memory germane to the troubles of those times'. When reflecting on the current popularity of memory, Hutton suggests that it is 'memory's protean instability that has inspired the burgeoning field of memory studies'.

Peter Fritzsche's chapter begins by observing how his daughter located changes in time with moving from one house to another. 'What once was, but is no longer' became a motif for his reflections on his companions: nostalgia, Chateaubriand, ruins and time. For Fritzsche, nostalgia is 'a portal into the historic nature of conceptions about discontinuity, periodization, and loss and of different ways of relating to and assembling the past'. The distinction of 'was' and 'is' remains influential for his book, *Stranded in the Present* and subsequent research. One image that captures the passing of time is a walk up the stairs to the attic. Different textures of the past are most visibly seen in the attic-like writings of exiled Chateaubriand. 'Man does not have a single, consistent life: he has several laid end to end, and that is his misfortune' (Chateaubriand, quoted in Fritzsche Ch. 2 below). Chateaubriand revealed that the French Revolution not only divided the old world from the new, but that 'ruptures would continue to manifest themselves so that the present would be antiquated just as had the past'. Fritzsche notes that Chateaubriand prefigured Benjamin when he 'remarked that memory was not the sure "instrument for exploring the past", but more resembled the "theatre" of the past, a ceaseless exchange of scenes and characters'.

In her chapter, Angelica Nuzzo illuminates the extent to which memory plays a constitutive role in Hegel's thought, and his formative influence on Durkheim and Halbwachs. Nuzzo highlights her own travels across Hegel's philosophy with an analysis of what she calls 'dialectical memory'. Although there are three words for memory: *Erinnerung*, *Gedächtnis* and *Andacht*, it is only *Erinnerung* that refers to inner self-reflection and interiorization. Memory is both a 'function of the subject's individuality' and the 'collective and intersubjective dimension within which individuality' emerges. 'Hegel is a demanding companion' because he was the first to posit an identity between philosophical thought and the history of philosophy. 'Philosophy is one's own time apprehended in thought' (Hegel, quoted in Nuzzo Ch. 3 below). In many ways, memory is a dialectical process, continually subject to change. She argues that the subject who remembers is not the condition, but the result of memory. In discussing the Hegelian roots of the concept of collective memory, Nuzzo agrees with Funkenstein's claim that that 'collective consciousness' presupposes 'collective memory' (Funkenstein, quoted in Nuzzo Ch. 3 below).

Hans Ruin examines Derrida's category of the phantom and Heidegger's emphasis on the existential importance of death. What kind of responsibility do we have towards the deceased? In reflecting on Derrida's claim that the spectral is an 'indeterminate space between the dead and the living', Ruin argues that recent interest in ghosts, revenants and hauntology requires one to address Heidegger's influence on Derrida's *Specters of Marx*. He demonstrates how Heidegger's account of historicity deals with ethical and political relations with the dead and what Ruin terms, 'the ancestral'. Memory and historical consciousness are part of an obligation to the past. Spectral phenomenology is linked with tradition and cultural memory. Although Derrida calls our attention to 'the politics of memory, of inheritance, and of generations', Heidegger was the first to address existential questions of death and finitude. Similar to Etkind (Ch. 17 below), Ruin is interested in how the dead, as ancestors, remain in our memory. What kind of presence or existence do they have? Ruin's reading of Heidegger and Derrida, as companions in memory studies emphasises 'the peculiar lingering on of the past in the present'.

Social, Psychological and Cultural Frameworks of Memory

Part II shifts the focus to the disciplines of sociology, psychology and cultural studies. How is memory framed and narrated? In what ways are memories, shaped, contained, mediated and reproduced? Chapters in this section demonstrate the growing importance of oral history, history from below, psychology and, above all, culture.

Luisa Passerini reflects on numerous companions including Bakhtin, Vansina, Halbwachs and Yates. Beginning with her interviews with Italian factor workers, who had lived through the Fascist period, she writes: 'Only Bakhtin made it clear that the horizon within which the testimonies of jokes should be understood was a century-long cultural tradition'. It was Philippe Joutard who became important for the study of informal memory by emphasising the link between historical research and collective mentalities. Halbwachs is a crucial figure for his link between collective memory, location and emotion. And yet, Passerini remains critical of the implicit structuralism within his work. It is at this point that the concept of intersubjectivity becomes increasingly important to her work on memory. Like Hutton, she is influenced by the mnemonic places of memory described by Francis Yates. Passerini understands memory as 'a dynamic process, in which changes take place all the time, but not in a causal and inexplicable way'.

Alexandre Dessingué's chapter compares Bakhtin's metaphor of the polyphony of a text with Halbwachs' collective memory. 'Texts do not talk; it is the reader who makes texts talk. In the same way: groups do not remember; it is the individual who remembers'. The term collective is 'far from unitary or homogeneous'; rather, Halbwachs emphasised the collective as 'the crucible of an ongoing discussion with and between *Social Frameworks of Memory* and *The Collective Memory*. Through a reading of Bakhtin, Dessingué emphasises the dialogic and interactive aspect of Halbwachs' relationship between individual and collective. The individual is a 'collectiveness' who carries a multitude or polyphony of voices, not a unitary self. Like Stuart Burch in this volume, Dessingué highlights that we are never alone, but carry a number of persons 'with and in us'. Collective memory is polysemic, integrating the collective as a 'collectivity' and as an internal 'collectiveness'. Halbwachs and Bakhtin are companions to Dessingué's work because both emphasise that 'memory acts, like speech acts, are complex and intricate phenomena without any fixed material meaning'.

William Hirst and Charles B. Stone introduce the concept of the 'extended mind' as a companion to memory studies. In their chapter, they seek 'to find a place for the study of collective memory that builds on the extensive work in experimental psychology'. Indeed, psychology is not merely 'a separate endeavour' unrelated to memory studies, but 'a close companion'. The idea of the extended mind overcomes memories located 'in the head' as collective memory or 'outside the head' as collected memory. Instead, they emphasise how remembering certain events is influenced by what is communicated and to whom. When individuals tell stories, they select certain aspects and forget others, depending on their audience. The extended mind is intersubjective because remembering occurs between people in a particular social environment. Likewise, they suggest that students of memory studies require such an intersubjective approach for understanding examples of collective forgetting and mnemonic silence. If trauma focuses on how people cope with painful events, experimental psychology emphasises particular mechanisms of memory retrieval and retrieval-induced forgetting.

Vered Vinitzky-Seroussi's companion is the sociological problem of generations. Inspired by Mannheim's work, she reflects on her life as an Israeli sociologist on events that were formative for her generation. As Mannheim writes, 'individuals who share the same year of birth are endowed ... with a common location in the historical dimension of the social process' (quoted in Vinitzky-Seroussi Ch. 8 below). While many of Vinitzky-

Seroussi's companions are scholars of memory who appear in this volume, she writes about Mannheim 'because he took our historical position seriously'. Moreover, his work on generations influenced her scholarly work on high-school reunions and commemorations of Yitzhak Rabin's assassination. Weaving the biography of Mannheim with reflections on her own life, the author discusses pivotal moments that influence and constrain how individuals construct their lives. Both Marianne Hirsch and Alison Landsberg 'push the borders of Mannheim's experience' by examining the role of the mass media for creating shared memories which individuals did not live through. Nonetheless, Vinitzky-Seroussi maintains that Mannheim is a formative companion because 'we are all born into a historical moment and go through time'.

Marek Tamm's chapter presents Juri Lotman as an important companion in cultural memory. The majority of Lotman's work as a leading semiotician and cultural theorist is only available in Russian. Tamm's chapter traces his formative influence not only on semiotics, but also on the Assmann's theory of cultural memory. Culture is defined as 'the sum of all nonhereditary information and the means of its organisation and preservation' (Lotman, quoted in Tamm Ch. 9 below). Moreover, Lotman emphasises 'the mnemonic character of culture'. Tamm underscores how 'memory, both individual and collective, is first and foremost a semiotic phenomenon'. Indeed, the term 'cultural memory' first appears in Lotman's writing in 1977 and is subsequently elaborated in the 1980s. Tamm suggests that Lotman's distinctions between informative and creative cultural memory are similar to those made by Jan Assmann and Aleida Assmann between storage and functional memory, canon and archive. The chapter reminds us that Lotman wrote during the Soviet regime, 'where in-depth study of culture and memory was no mere academic pursuit but inevitably entailed an ethical and political stance'. Moreover, he emphasises the nuanced importance of Lotman as one of the first thinkers 'to identify memory as a major subject of cultural studies'.

Acts and Places of Memory

Research into concrete places and realms of memory has become more prominent in recent times, and attention to how past experience is symbolically represented both nationally and internationally is the focus of Part III. Contributions to this section range from the areas of comparative literature and museums studies to philosophy and are empirically grounded in film, art, literature and monuments.

In her contribution, Mieke Bal reflects on her many travelling companions. As the author of *Travelling Concepts in the Humanities* (2002), she argues against the idea of memory as a travelling concept. Memory is not an object that travels. Nor is it a subject. Rather, one needs to distinguish between a word and a concept. Highlighting movement, agency and action, Bal suggests the phrase, 'acts of memory'. Similar to Olick's 'mnemonic practices', memory is something that we do, not have. Memory, then, 'is a verb, a transitive one, and its mode is active; it is something we do'. The world of art is a very important companion for her work on memory. First, with video installation and then with film, she shows how memory is dialogic and social – rarely linear and more often a kind of anachronism. Similar to Hutton, Bal is influenced by Benjamin's redeeming power of memory and discusses two contemporary artists. If Eija-Liisa Ahtila's video-work figuratively foregrounds responsibility in the present, Doris Salcedo shuns representation and even, problematises it. Both artists foreground the political importance of recognising and remembering the past in the present. While Bal's travelling companions might be numerous, art offers her constant companionship.

In Stuart Burch's elegiac chapter, Big Ben provides inspiration for reflections on memory, companionship and loss. The tolling of Big Ben after the death of his mother, in a hospital room facing the clock tower marked a 'public pronouncement of a private tragedy'. The chapter reflects on the many ways that we are still accompanied by those, who are no longer living. As Halbwachs wrote, 'we are never alone'. Indeed Burch reminds the reader of Halbwachs' walk in London: 'only in appearance did I take a walk alone' (quoted in Burch Ch. 11 below). Westminster is a kind of 'palimpsest', in which the face of the Clock Tower and chiming of Big Ben accompanied Burch while he sat vigil for his mother. The monument represents standardised time and yet, the chimes differentiate between inner duration and clock time. Big Ben becomes a 'mnemonic device' and a *lieu de mémoire* of private and public remembrance. Since Burch collects miniature Big Bens, he asks: 'Do they equate to a coming to terms with loss, a retranscription, a screening or an effort to control the past?' Recalling Halbwachs, families provide a framework for collective memory and certain members play a more central role than others. The chapter is a memorial to Burch's mother and ends with the birth of his daughter, who is named in her memory.

In my own chapter, I examine how monuments are written and re-written in stone. If Communist monuments throughout post-Communist Europe are removed, destroyed or relocated, war memorials rarely are. As Passerini and Hutton indicate in this volume, Pierre Nora provides a framework for thinking about the material and symbolic power of *lieux de mémoire*. Likewise, Reinhart Koselleck is an important companion because he traces a genealogy of war memorials, with emphasis on the designs of European monuments commemorating the two world wars and the Holocaust. Both Koselleck and Jay Winter analyse the seminal importance of Tombs of the Unknown Soldier as sites of memory. If such tombs symbolise the democratisation of death in the name of the nation, Holocaust memorials express the utter limit of representation. Finally, Winter's research foregrounds the important relation between the sacred and the profane. As 'sites of memory, sites of mourning', war memorials represent a reconfiguration of the sacred in modern life.

Julie Hansen's chapter asks what fiction contributes to our understanding of memory that we do not already know from science and philosophy. Since memory is linked to identity and imagination, she argues that fiction can 'help us understand the past and define our relation to it'. Literature exists in a grey zone between memory and history, between lived and imagined experience. Since imagined pasts allow the reader to conjure alternatives and to question accepted historical truths, Hansen claims that 'literature also has the potential to shape collective memory'. Contemporary fiction from Central and Eastern Europe are companions for her research in memory studies. 'Much recent fiction about the Communist period interrogates memory itself, reflecting critically upon its functions and limitations'. Literature has the distinct advantage of allowing one to think about memory metaphorically. From Plato's mind as a wax block to Freud's 'mystic writing pad', the inscription of memory onto the mind is an important motif recurring in the humanities and social sciences. Moreover, metaphors of the archive, writing and reading are frequently found in post-Communist fiction.

Politics of Memory, Forgetting and Democracy

The volume concludes with discussions of how memories of the past influence the political imagination of the future. Here the focus is on learning from the past and preventing future hostilities. It is in this section that politics, sociology and history overlap most fruitfully. It is also here that questions of democratisation, justice, human rights, cosmopolitanism and the ethics of memory are addressed.

Daniel Levy maps out his reflections on cosmopolitanism and memory studies through the companionship of three sociologists: Jeffrey Olick, Natan Sznaider and Ulrich Beck. Olick shares Levy's interest in German political culture, memory and social theory. As co-authors of articles and most recently, *The Collective Memory Reader*, their 'main conceptual point centred on the processual quality of memory-making' and its 'historical trajectories'. In their first co-authored book (Levy and Sznaider 2006), they examined how cosmopolitan memories affect old, national narratives. Cosmopolitanism does not contradict the nation; instead methodological cosmopolitanism acts as a kind of 'analytical tool kit' for examining transformations of the nation-state. Levy foregrounds the encounter between global and local in his examination of how memories of the Holocaust became a universal code for human-rights abuses. Moreover, the Holocaust has become a 'symbol of transnational solidarity'. Finally, in conjunction with Beck, who coined the term 'methodological cosmopolitanism', Levy's more recent work focuses on cosmopolitanism as a 'heuristic for the global age'.

Bradford Vivian reflects on Hannah Arendt and Thomas Paine as intellectual companions who have accompanied his research on 'public practices of forgetting'. As 'companions in remembering anew', both examine how members of political communities liberate themselves from past tradition. Arendt influences Vivian's research on 'forgetting as a transformative property of public remembrance'. Moreover, Arendt's attention to promising and forgiving is linked with public remembrance and forgetting. By arguing for independence from Britain, Paine asked British subjects in America to end their 'memorial existence as royal subjects'. Vivian warns that commemoration as public remembering 'in the company of others' can just as easily further conservative as well as transformative civic ends'. Arendt and Paine are formative companions because both demonstrate how 'modes of organised remembrance' may constitute or constrain shared political life. Recalling Proust, Vivian suggests that memory is like a rope that can just as easily bind individuals to the past as rescue them from it.

Eva-Clarita Pettai's chapter focuses on historical truth commissions and reconciliation. Important companions for her work are the public sphere, myth and the politics of history. As a political scientist, she identifies historical truth commissions as 'semi-state actors that emerge in particular situations of memory-related conflict'. The fall of Communism meant the end of old narratives and re-discovery of memory and history. Pettai examines these commissions through the conceptual lens of memory studies, thus highlighting the interaction between different forms of collective memory and democratic politics. Using examples from Lithuania, Estonia and Switzerland, she examines the different outcomes of three historical truth commissions with a mandate to examine the Holocaust. Inspired by Elazar Barkan, she asks whether history might facilitate or hinder reconciliation? She argues that such commissions either open up space for critical reflection of political myths or offer a reductive reading of history. Commissions are potential mediators, fact-finders or myth-makers – depending on their mandate.

The last chapter is Alexander Etkind's, 'Post-Stalinism, Memory and Mourning'. His companions are melancholy, mourning and ghosts. Reflecting on the differences between memories of Nazi Germany and Communist Russia, he argues that post-Soviet memory is characterised by 'warped mourning'. In addition to the social framework of nations and classes, Etkind suggests the role of associations. Inspired by Tocqueville, he sees a link between civic associations such as Memorial in contemporary Russia and the democratisation of memory. Russian citizens are not suffering from amnesia nor prone to nostalgia, rather they are melancholic and fail to distinguish between the past and present. Moreover, he distinguishes three types of memory: hardware, software and ghostware. Derrida is a formative companion for Etkind. Because Russia's dead have not been acknowledged, they have a ghostly presence haunting contemporary society. Even before Derrida, Edmund Burke invoked the 'great primeval contract' between the living, the dead and the unborn. Unlike Derrida, however, Etkind does not argue for justice but recognition. 'Ghosts do not want us to repay our debts; all that they want is recognition'.

The volume concludes with an afterword by Jeffrey Olick in which he reflects on his intellectual and personal companions. Recalling his first encounter with the work of Maurice Halbwachs, Olick discovered not only the term 'collective memory' but also a theoretical way in which to link his interest in storytelling and identity. As in my own case, Hutton's *History as an Art of Memory* had a formative influence on his academic interests. However, it was in the work and personal mentorship of American sociologist, Barry Schwartz that Olick truly found a kindred spirit. Ranging from professional and personal companions to friendly antagonisms, the field of memory studies has itself become a companion in Olick's thought-provoking work.

On the one hand, memory is a fleeting activity that changes quickly. And yet, certain recognisable patterns do emerge. The artwork of Deirdre Murphy for the cover of the *Ashgate Research Companion to Memory Studies* represents both aspects in her depiction of migrating bird flocks. Travelling and migrating are not necessarily without purpose, but often return to a particular and meaningful source. Likewise, her painting portrays the ephemeral aspects of memory in which distinct patterns are visible in the landscape, but often remain blurry and far away.

References

Agamben, G. 1999. *Potentialities*, trans. D. Heller-Roazen (Stanford, CA: Stanford University Press).

Alexander, J.C. 2012. *Trauma: A Social Theory* (London: Polity).

Anderson, B. 1983. *Imagined Communities: Reflections on the Origin and Spread of Nationalism* (London: Verso).

Assmann, A. 2011. *Cultural Memory and Western Civilization: Functions. Media, Archives* (Cambridge: Cambridge University Press).

Assmann, J. 1997. *Moses the Egyptian* (Cambridge, MA: Harvard University Press).

— — 2006. *Religion and Cultural Memory*, trans. R. Livingstone (Stanford, CA: Stanford University Press).

— — 2010. *The Price of Monotheism*, trans. R. Savage (Stanford, CA: Stanford University Press).

Augé, M. 2009. *Non-Places: An Introduction to Supermodernity*, trans. J. Howe (London: Verso).

Augstein, R. 1987. *Historikerstreit: Die Dokumentation der Kontroverse um die Einzigartigkeit der nationalsozialistischen Judenvernichtung* (Munich: Piper).

Bal, M. 2002. *Travelling Concepts in the Humanities: A Rough Guide* (Toronto: University of Toronto Press).

— — J. Crewe and L. Spitzer (eds) 1999. *Acts of Memory: Cultural Recall in the Present* (Hanover, NH: University Press of New England).

Bell, Duncan S.A. 2003. 'Mythscapes: Memory, Mythology and National Identity', *British Journal of Sociology* 54/1: 63–81.

Benjamin, W. 1978. 'A Berlin Chronicle', in *Reflections*, trans. E. Jephcott (New York: Schocken Books), pp. 3–60.

Berger, S., and B. Niven (eds) 2014. *Writing the History of Memory* (London: Bloomsbury).

Blacker, U., A. Etkind and J. Fedor (eds) 2013. *Memory and Theory in Eastern Europe* (Basingstoke: Palgrave).

Bloch, M. 1961. *Feudal Society*, trans. L.A. Manyon (Chicago: University of Chicago Press).

Bond, L., and J. Rapson (eds) 2014. *The Transcultural Turn: Interrogating Memory Between and Beyond Borders* (Berlin: De Gruyter).

Bottici, C. 2010. 'European Identity and the Politics of Remembrance', in K. Tilmans, F. van Vree and J. Winter (eds), *Performing the Past* (Amsterdam: Amsterdam University Press), pp. 335–59.

Burke. P. 1990. *The French Historical Revolution: The Annales School 1929–1989* (Stanford, CA: Stanford University Press).

— — 2004. *What is Cultural History?* (Cambridge: Polity).

Caruth, C. 1995. *Trauma: Explorations in Memory* (Baltimore, MA: Johns Hopkins University Press).

Clifford, J. 1997. *Routes: Travels and Translation in the Late Twentieth Century* (Cambridge, MA: Harvard University Press).

Conan, E., and H. Rousso 2013. *Vichy, un passé qui ne passe pas* (Paris: Fayard and Pluriel).

Connerton, P. 2008. 'Seven Types of Forgetting', *Memory Studies* 1/1: 59–71.

Confino, A. 2006. *Germany as a Culture of Remembrance: Promises and Limits of Writing History* (Chapel Hill: University of North Carolina Press).

Craps, S. 2013. *Postcolonial Witnessing: Trauma out of Bounds* (Basingstoke: Palgrave).

Diner, D. (ed.) 1987. *Ist der Nationalsozialismus Geschichte? Zu Historisierung und Historikerstreit* (Frankfurt am Main: Fischer).

— — 2003. 'Restitution and Memory: The Holocaust in European Political Cultures', *New German Critique* 90: 36–44.

Dubiel, H. 2003. 'The Remembrance of the Holocaust as a Catalyst for a Transnational Ethic?', *New German Critique* 90: 59–70.

Durkheim, E. 1995. *The Elementary Form of Religious Life*, trans. K.E. Fields (New York: Free Press).

Erll, A. 2011a. *Memory in Culture*, trans. S.B. Young (Basingstoke: Palgrave).

— — 2011b. 'Travelling Memory', *Parallax* 17/4: 4–18.

— — and A. Nünning (eds) 2010. *A Companion to Cultural Memory Studies* (Berlin: De Gruyter).

Etkind A. 2013. *Warped Mourning: Stories of the Undead in the Land of the Unburied* (Stanford, CA: Stanford University Press).

Fritzsche, P. 2004. *Stranded in the Present: Modern Time and the Melancholy of History* (Cambridge, MA: Harvard University Press).

Funkenstein, A. 1989. 'Collective Memory and Historical Consciousness', *History and Memory* 1/1: 5–26.

Graham, B., and P. Howard (eds) 2008. *The Ashgate Research Companion to Heritage and Identity* (Farnham: Ashgate).

Halbwachs, M. 1980 [1950]. *The Collective Memory*, trans. F.J. Ditter Jr and V. Yazdi Ditter (New York: Harper Colophon).

— — 1992 [1941]. *On Collective Memory*, trans. L. Coser (Chicago: University of Chicago Press).

Hartog, F. 2014a. 'The Modern Regime of Historicity in the Face of Two World Wars', in C. Lorenz and B. Bevernage (eds), *Breaking up Time: Negotiating the Borders Between Present, Past and Future* (Göttingen: Vandenhoeck & Ruprecht).

— — 2014b. 'Time of the Victims', <http://www.interior.ejgv.euskadi.net/contenidos/nota_prensa/12_ponencias/es_ponencia/adjuntos/Francois_Hartog_en.pdf> (accessed 15 Feb. 2014).

— — 2003. *Régimes d'historicité* (Paris: Points).

Herodotus 1998. *The Histories*, trans. R. Waterfield (New York: Oxford University Press).

History and Memory n.d. 'Publication Information', <http://www.jstor.org/page/journal/histmemo/about.html> (accessed 14 Feb. 2014).

Hobsbawn, E., and T. Ranger 1983. *The Invention of Tradition* (Cambridge: Cambridge University Press).

Hutton, P.H. 1993. *History as an Art of Memory* (Hanover, NH, and London: University Press of New England).

—— 2000. 'Recent Scholarship on Memory and History', *History Teacher* 33/4: 533–48.

Kansteiner, W. 2002. 'Finding Meaning in Memory: A Methodological Critique of Memory Studies', *History and Theory* 41: 179–97.

—— 2004. 'Genealogy of a Category Mistake: A Critical Intellectual History of the Cultural Trauma Metaphor', *Rethinking History* 8/2: 193–221.

Kapuściński, R. 2004. *Travels with Herodotus*, trans. K. Glowczewska (London: Penguin).

Knowlton, J., and T. Cates (trans.) 1993. *Forever in the Shadow of Hitler? The Dispute About the German Understanding of History* (Highlands, NJ: Humanities Press International).

Koselleck, R. 1985. *Futures Past: On the Semantics of Historical Time*, trans. K. Tribe (Cambridge, MA: MIT Press).

—— 2004. 'Gibt es ein kollektives Gedächtnis?', *Divinatio* 19/2 (Spring): 1–6.

LaCapra, D. 1994. *Representing the Holocaust: History, Theory, Trauma* (Ithaca, NY: Cornell University Press).

Levy, D., and N. Sznaider 2006. *The Holocaust and Memory in a Global Age*, trans. A. Oksiloff (Philadelphia, PA: Temple University Press).

—— and — 2010. *Human Rights and Memory* (University Park: Pennsylvania State University Press).

Lowenthal, D. 1985. *The Past is a Foreign Country* (Cambridge: Cambridge University Press).

—— 2014. *The Past is a Foreign Country Revisited* (Cambridge: Cambridge University Press).

Maier, C.S. 1988. *The Unmasterable Past: History, Holocaust and German National Identity* (Cambridge, MA: Harvard University Press).

Majertus, B. 2014. '*Lieux de mémoire*: A European Transfer Story', in S. Berger and B. Niven (eds), *Writing the History of Memory* (London: Bloomsbury), pp. 157–71.

Memory Studies n.d. <http://mss.sagepub.com> (accessed 15 Feb. 2014).

Misztal, B.A. 2003. *Theories of Social Remembering* (Maidenhead: Open University Press).

Neuman, B., and A. Nünning (eds) 2012. *Travelling Concepts for the Study of Culture* (Berlin: De Gruyter).

Nolte, E. 1987. 'Vergangenheit, die nicht vergehen will', in R. Augstein (ed.), *Historikerstreit: Die Dokumentation der Kontroverse um die Einzigartigkeit der nationalsozialistischen Judenvernichtung* (Munich: Piper), pp. 39–47.

—— 1993. 'The Past that will not Pass: A Speech that Could be Written but not Delivered', in J. Knowlton and T. Cates (trans.), *Forever in the Shadow of Hitler? The Dispute About the German Understanding of History* (Highlands, NJ: Humanities Press International), pp. 18–23.

Nora, P. (ed.) 1984–92. *Les Lieux de mémoire*, 7 vols (Paris: Gallimard).

—— 1987. *Essais d'ego-histoire* (Paris: Gallimard).

—— 1996. 'General Introduction: Between Memory and History' in *Realms of Memory*, trans. Arthur Goldhammer (New York: Columbia University Press), pp. 1–20.

—— 2002. 'Reasons for the Current Upsurge in Memory', *Transit* 22, <http://www.eurozine.com/articles/2002-04-19-nora-en.html> (accessed 5 Feb. 2014).

—— (ed.) 2011. *Présent, nation, mémoire* (Paris: Gallimard).

Olick, J.K. 2007. *The Politics of Regret: On Collective Memory and Historical Responsibility* (New York: Routledge).

——— and C. Demetriou 2006. 'From Theodicy to *Ressentiment*: Trauma and the Ages of Compensation', in D. Bell (ed.), *Memory, Trauma and World Politics: Reflections on the Relationship between Past and Present* (Basingstoke: Palgrave), pp. 74–98.

——— V. Vinitzky-Seroussi and D. Levy (eds) 2011. *The Collective Memory Reader* (Oxford: Oxford University Press).

Passerini, L., and A.C.T. Geppert 2001. 'Historians in Flux: The Concept, Task and Challenge of Ego-histoire', *Historien* 3: 7–18.

Radstone, S. 2007. 'Trauma Theory: Contexts, Politics, Ethics', *Paragraph* 30/1: 9–29.

——— and B. Schwarz 2010. *Memory: Histories, Theories, Debates* (New York: Fordham University Press).

Ricoeur, P. 2007. *Memory, History, Forgetting*, trans. K. Blamey and D. Pellauer (Chicago: University of Chicago Press).

Rossington, M., and A. Whitehead (eds) 2007. *Theories of Memory: A Reader* (Edinburgh: Edinburgh University Press).

Rothberg, M. 2009. *Multidirectional Memory* (Stanford, CA: Stanford University Press).

Rousso, H. 1994. *The Vichy Syndrome*, trans. A. Goldhammer (Cambridge, MA: Harvard University Press).

——— 2002. *The Haunting Past: History, Memory and Justice in Contemporary France*, trans. R. Schoolcraft (Philadelphia: University of Pennsylvania Press).

Rüsen, J. (ed.) 2006. *Meaning and Representation in History* (New York and Oxford: Berghahn).

Said, E. 1983. *The World, the Text and the Critic* (Cambridge, MA: Harvard University Press).

Sexias, P. (ed.) 2006. *Theorizing Historical Consciousness* (Toronto: University of Toronto Press).

Sontag, S. 2003. *Regarding the Pain of Others* (New York: Picador).

Tamm, M. 2013. 'Beyond History and Memory: New Perspectives in Memory Studies', *History Compass* 11/6: 458–73.

——— (ed.) 2015. *Afterlife of Events: Perspectives on Mnemohistory* (Basingstoke: Palgrave).

Tota, A.L., and T. Hagen (eds) 2015. *The Routledge International Handbook of Memory Studies* (London: Routledge).

Vivien. B. 2010. *Public Forgetting: The Rhetoric and Politics of Beginning Again* (University Park: Pennsylvania State University Press).

Warburg, A. 1999. *The Renewal of Pagan Antiquity*, trans. D. Britt (Los Angeles: Getty Research Institute).

Weinrich, H. 2004. *Lethe: The Art and Critique of Forgetting*, trans. S. Rendall (Ithaca, NY: Cornell University Press).

Whitehead, A. 2009. *Memory* (London: Routledge).

Wievorka, A. 2006. *Era of the Witness*, trans. J. Stark (Ithaca, NY: Cornell University Press).

Winter, J. 2006. *Remembering War* (New Haven, CT: Yale University Press).

Wittgenstein, L. 2001 [1953]. *Philosophical Investigations*, trans. G.E.M. Anscombe (Oxford: Blackwell).

Wood, H.H., and A.S. Byatt (eds) 2009. *Memory: An Anthology* (London: Vintage).

PART I
Memory, History and Time

History as an Art of Memory Revisited

Patrick H. Hutton

On Historians Writing Memoirs

It has been twenty years since *History as an Art of Memory* was published, my wide-ranging historical inquiry into the workings of memory. Upon completing the typescript, my wife Lee and I took a vacation in Bermuda. The idea was to put a little distance between ourselves and the project. But it was not a complete escape. Most afternoons I sat in the sunshine by the sea and sketched a preface to my book. My essay was not unlike the exercise that we have been asked to undertake here. The French historian of memory Pierre Nora labelled such writing *ego-histoire*. Mine consisted of two parts.

One part was a condensation of my argument, distilled from what had been lengthy discussions of the idea of memory by a gallery of philosophers, ancient and modern. I cast this precis of my interpretation as a historical reflection on the notion of memory's eternal return. I reviewed the four phases of the memory cycle, as first limned by Aristotle deep in antiquity and later given more elaborate substance by Giambattista Vico in his *Scienza nuova* in the mid-eighteenth century. The cycle they envisioned proceeded from imagination to recollection, then to historicisation, before passing into forgetfulness. The closing of the cycle evoked nostalgia for its renewal. Today we autopsy such memory cycles from a critical historical perspective. Our sense of emotional distance from once valued traditions has been a factor prompting today's fascination with the relationship between collective memory and historical understanding.

The other was a personal sketch of influences from my own heritage that had set me on my intellectual journey toward these reflections on memory in the middle of my life-journey. Rereading this passage today leaves me slightly embarrassed by its transparent candour. Having laboured so long in realms of historiographical abstraction, I must have wanted to convey the concrete beginnings of the project through memories drawn from my own life-world. The substance of my book, by contrast, marked a time and place in my maturation as a scholar, and, as I would later come to recognise, my witness to a sea change in thinking about the nature of history in its relationship to memory.

Nora attributed the phenomenon of historians writing memoirs to the breakdown of personal identification with well-defined historiographical traditions (2003). His observation correlates closely with philosopher Jean-François Lyotard's thesis concerning the demise of scholars' allegiance to the idea of a unified, continuous narrative of history, conceived as the rise of modern Western civilisation through the agency of the nation-state (1979). Most contributors to Nora's edited collection, *Essais d'ego-histoire* (1987), attested to the constraints of having written under the tutelage of a master historian articulating a well-established historical narrative. As historians, each had a different tale to tell about their entry into the profession, and, for readers, all of their stories were absorbing for their personal reflections on the routes by which they sought a measure of intellectual autonomy from the historiographical traditions in which they had been apprenticed.[1] My favourite is Michelle Perrot's account of her audience in the early 1960s with the eminent doyen of studies in the French revolutionary tradition, Ernest Labrousse, her thesis advisor as a graduate student. When she proposed a study of the feminist movement, he suggested that she try something more current. He set her to the task of investigating workers' coalitions in the face of economic crisis in the early nineteenth century, a topic, he allowed, not yet filled in the broad canvas of social history that he was painting. Perrot complied, but eventually found her own path into women's history (1987: 275–8).

At the time, I conceived of my preface as a rhetorical strategy. As an editor, I had learned to be attentive to the pragmatics of writing in ways that might draw in readers beyond professional specialisation. Moreover, I was attuned to the 'rhetorical turn' in contemporary historiography. I had read Hayden White's study of the poetics underpinning historical narrative and Michel Foucault's rhetorical inversion of the knowledge–power relationship for interpreting the meaning of public discourse. These scholars confirmed my understanding that the past as history is not encountered transparently but rather through the narratives we devise to set forth its meaning. I began each chapter of my book with a place of memory taken from a passage by the author under review. Each localised an argument in a mnemonic scheme. My preface was a walkway toward the portals of these 'memory palaces' of my thinking about history among the arts of memory.

Sources of the Idea of History as an Art of Memory

I initially conceived of my project on the art of memory as a study within the genre of the history of ideas. The principal concept underpinning its method is that of associative displacement. The ancient art was a hermeneutical exercise: familiar places anchor less familiar ideas.[2] Working from easily remembered spatial designs, mnemonists devised a method for organising their thoughts as their knowledge widened. Their art was the first studied formulation of artificial memory, permitting a distinction between spontaneous recall and conscious recollection. Not surprisingly, its invention was related to the rise of manuscript literacy in ancient Greece and Rome. The realm of artificial memory – memory as exported into archives and memory banks – has since expanded and diversified exponentially, and so the practical uses of the art for rote memorisation have been marginalised. Our current passage from print into media culture has been a major incentive behind all of the recent historical scholarship on like transitions in the invention of new technologies of communication in times past (Ong 1982: 3, 79–81, 135–8).

Some see mnemonics as a lost skill, one that if revived as a technique could strengthen one's powers of recollection. Since the early twentieth century, books on mnemonics as a remedy for weak or failing memory have regularly appeared to renew that promise.[3] My sense is that this is a fundamentalist interpretation of the resources of the art of memory.

---

1   See biographer François Dosse's interesting comment on Nora's difficulties in inducing his invited colleagues to overcome their reservations about such autobiographical writing. Nora noted, however, that most either agreed to write chapters for his edited collection or later published memoirs of their own separately (Dosse 2011: 389–96).

2   My understanding of the hermeneutics of tradition was deepened by my reading of Hans-Georg Gadamer (1989). His argument is too complex to precis here, but I discuss his ideas at some length in Hutton (1993: 23, 157–60).

3   The most recent and skillfully composed is that by Joshua Foer (2011).

Instead I went in search of learned uses of mnemonic schemes, notably those that might enhance our understanding of cultural history. This ancient art remains of historical interest, because it has survived in so many disguises. Its changing uses can be traced over time. My question as I embarked on my research was: in what guise has the art of memory been dressed in modern times?

In making my way into this field, the English historian Frances Yates served as a guide, and she provided me with a model for proceeding on my own. During the 1950s and 1960s, she wrote a series of studies concerning radical (mostly arcane) intellectual movements of the Renaissance. A scholar of considerable originality, she had the good fortune in mid-life to become involved in the scholarly work of the Warburg Institute in London, a centre where studies in art history were conjoined with those in philology and cultural history (Yates 1984; Jones 2008). The institute's founder, the German exile Aby Warburg, had been fascinated with the persistence throughout history of certain kinds of iconic representation and wondered whether he might identify archetypal images that gave form to a collective unconscious available to all humankind (Gombrich 1986: 221–3). Yates never subscribed to this notion of free-floating collective memories unbounded by time and place, but she was especially interested in the way images localized in specific contexts may be read for their historical meaning.

Yates sketched the origins of the art of memory as a useful rhetorical technique in Graeco-Roman antiquity. But her larger interest was to explain the ways the art had been put to use by the idealist philosophers of the Renaissance in their efforts to fathom the design of the universe. They conjured up ornate memory palaces to portray correspondences between their frameworks of earthly philosophy and what they imagined to be God's providential plan (Yates 1966). Yates studied the art, architecture and learning of the Renaissance on these historical margins – inquiries of passionate interest during those times but since relegated to intellectual obscurity. Thereby she found a place for this lost learning in her interpretation of the Renaissance as a more pluralistic intellectual milieu than modern scholars had imagined. Among the many topics of magic, the occult and spiritualism that she examined, that of the art of memory would be the one her readers would find most intriguing.

Yates' work on the art of memory played into her method for understanding history. For her, places of memory are points of intellectual departure for interpreting larger cultural realms. The art of memory exemplified in rudimentary fashion the method she would come to employ as cultural historian. She recognised that the art, invented to facilitate accurate recall, contained the ancient beginnings of the modern technique of philological investigation. Philologists reconstruct intellectual traditions. They locate cultural images in their time and place, then study the way they are revised as they are used and reused in changing cultural contexts. Yates' method presupposes that in their beginnings there was a transparent correspondence between image and artefact. Words and things mirrored one another. Over time, the divide between them widened. Their initial connection was eventually forgotten, as ideas conceived in particular places took on a life of their own as they were remembered in unrelated contexts. Philologists reconstruct these lost connections, revealing the way the meanings of ideas are modified (and almost always idealised) over time as they come to be appreciated in new cultural settings. Out of this chain of ongoing revision, one may read the history of the way in which they have been remembered. In closing, Yates speculates briefly about what uses of the art of memory might be worthy of study in modern times, noting in particular its visible applications in the scientific writings of Frances Bacon and Gottfried Leibniz during the seventeenth century (Yates 1966: 368–9).

I saw possibilities for exploring other vocabularies of mnemonic association in times closer to our own, as in the case of the poet William Wordsworth or the neurologist Sigmund Freud. My strategy at the time was to further extend Yates' project by exploring modern uses of the ancient art of memory in this paradigmatic way. Along the way, I had also come to see that mnemonic schemes took on a historical cast in the early twentieth-century studies by the sociologist Maurice Halbwachs. He showed how the influence of collective memory is intimately tied to the realities of social power. The construction, vitality and decay of the commemorative sites in which such memory was localised could be plotted historically. I read widely in his writings and especially appreciated his historical study of the imaginary topography of the Holy Land as it was constructed and reconstructed over the course of the Middle Ages according to the vicissitudes of the encounter between Christian pilgrims from Europe and indigenous people in Palestine (Halbwachs 1971). Though written in the 1930s, Halbwachs' study was recalled to serve as the prototype for the new interest in the history of commemorative practices, the first foray of historians into memory studies during the 1970s.

Eventually, I came to appreciate Yates' approach to memory less as a matrix for understanding the memory phenomenon in contemporary historiography and more as an application of the uses of memory in manuscript culture. There were other sources for my inquiry, notably the workings of collective memory. This interest grew out of a larger and earlier historiographical context, that of the history of collective mentalities as it developed as a field of historical scholarship during the 1960s and 1970s (Mandrou 1968; Ariès 1988). Work on mentalities proposed new approaches to cultural history, putting the accent on popular mores as opposed to learned high culture. Leading the way in these investigations was the highly respected French Annales school of historical scholarship. Its founders, Lucien Febvre and Marc Bloch, and their successors, Fernand Braudel and Robert Mandrou, were famous for their ambition to write a synthetic history that encompassed not mere politics and statecraft but also the largely anonymous social, economic and geographical processes that shape the deep structures of historical change. Annales scholarship was grounded in evidence supplied by material culture, and it evinced a deterministic view of history. It leaned heavily on accounts of slow-moving impersonal forces whose impact was barely perceptible at any moment but sure and certain when considered *à la longue durée* (Pomian 1986).

The take among Annales scholars on mentalities as a problem of collective memory, therefore, emphasised the weight of tradition. In their research, they gravitated toward the early modern era so as to expose the way tradition acted as a break upon innovations in the natural and social sciences and as an opposing force to the moral imperatives of political reform that we have come to identify with modernity. Progress was made against the stubborn resilience of tradition-bound custom and the habits of mind of ordinary people in their everyday lives. The entry of memory into scholarship on mentalities, therefore, came through their interpretation of tradition as a bulwark against the erosive forces of historical change. The topic of the dynamics of tradition was the basis of my interest in the historian Philippe Ariès, whose nostalgia for old France inspired his highly original studies of the cultural history of attitudes toward the life cycle in the modern world (1986: 33–43). Ariès, I soon discovered, was as interested in innovations that updated or supplanted custom as he was in stubborn resistance to change. Drawn to his insights into the relationship between continuity and change in explaining the nature of tradition, I decided to write his biography (Hutton 2004). Ariès' historical scholarship is an exegesis of the collective memory of the tradition into which he had been born and continued to cherish. Hence it would be a stretch of the imagination to portray him as a pioneer of memory studies as we have come to understand the interpretative perspectives they advance today.

After researching and writing my study of Ariès as historian, I returned to the larger topic of memory within contemporary historical scholarship, prompted by requests to write encyclopaedia articles on the relationship between memory and history (esp. Hutton 2013). By the turn of the twenty-first century, what had first been perceived to be a transitory 'memory boom' in historical scholarship had become a well-established field of cultural history. In this new milieu of scholarly endeavour, my thinking about the topic turned from the workings of memory to the implications of memory studies for historiography. Two questions preoccupied me. How does collective memory influence the rhetoric of historical writing? To what degree is it possible to recapture the experience of the past in our present imagination? Two authors especially have helped me to address these questions and to think through this reorientation in historical understanding in light of all the interest in memory: the French historian Pierre Nora and the German literary critic Walter Benjamin. I valued the first for the way he had placed the memory/history puzzle in a historiographical context germane to the needs of the present age and the second for his insight into memory's power to rekindle the human imagination.

Pierre Nora on History and Memory Reconfigured

I have studied and appreciated the work of French historian and publicist Pierre Nora for a long time. His *Les Lieux de mémoire* (1984–92) is the most imposing work by an historian within the emergence of memory studies, and it helped me to see the historiographical implications of the new interest in memory. He conceived, planned and edited this complex study of commemorative conceptions of the French national memory. I dealt with him only briefly in *History as an Art of Memory*: he was the final figure in my discussion of the memory cycle in the historiography of the French Revolution. His project, which over the course of the 1980s ran to three volumes, appeared about the time of the celebration of the bicentenary of the Revolution. As a pioneering work in memory studies, it became the seminal historical study of the moment, diverting attention from books about the Revolution itself. Nora and his contributors canvassed the varied sources of the national memory, of which the Revolution was but one. Like Foucault during the 1980s, Nora became an intellectual celebrity for the first decade of the twenty-first century, at least in French circles. In 2002, he was elected to the Académie Française. More recently, he has published an anthology of his most important essays on memory and history (Nora 2011a). An admiring scholar has written a highly sympathetic biography of him (Dosse 2011).

I was first intrigued by what I perceived to be Nora's application of the art of memory as a method of framing his historical inquiry. In abandoning the linear sequencing of conventional historical narrative in favour of a spatial design of a genealogical tree of memory, he returned to the multitude of places that had contributed to the making of the modern French national identity with a method not unlike that employed by Halbwachs. He visited sites of memory in a retrogressive perspective, turning attention to a vast array of formative influences in the construction of the national memory, including sites that had become obscure or that localised lost causes. Cultural sites were juxtaposed to those that were political. Like Yates, he pointed to the pluralism of the past when viewed not as an ascent from origins but as a descent into the complex mix of collective memories issuing from the past.

In recent years, Nora has reflected frequently on *Les Lieux de mémoire*. Since the last volume appeared in 1992, he has devoted much time to writing articles and giving lectures that place his project within the context of a changing historiography. He has offered what has struck me as the most convincing explanation of the concept of the 'end of history', a notion that captured the media's attention at the end of the Cold War. The deep issue, Nora contended, lay not in a new conception of politics but rather in a changing conception of historical time – what he and his colleagues referred to as a 'new regime of historicity' different from modern history, indeed from all such regimes that had gone before (Hartog 2003: 26–30). Citing the present (as opposed to the past or the future) as the privileged moment of historical time, historical inquiry no longer proceeded out of the subjective impulse of a generative matrix of memory. Now it turned back to interrogate objectively the myriad collective memories that had contributed to the making of the French national identity. His argument might be summarized as follows.

The late twentieth century, more specifically the crucial decade 1975–85, witnessed the demise of what Nora characterized as *memoire/histoire*, the naive intertwining of unconsciously held notions about the French national memory and consciously constructed interpretation of modern French history. This historiographical orientation had served as the foundation for professional historical scholarship through the nineteenth and well into the twentieth century. Collective memory, particularly notions about the origins of the modern nation-state in the French Revolution, served as a point of departure for historical analysis. In other words, this idea of history was indebted to the promptings of tacitly held convictions concerning the future course of history. The historian evaluated and corrected aspects of these assumptions by testing them against evidence in the archives of state papers, which tended to confirm the larger paradigm. This stance on history was future-oriented. One looked to origins, but anticipated ongoing development toward a presumed destiny.

In our times, Nora contended, that harmonious relationship between memory and history has unravelled, in large measure because the collective memory of the ways of modern French politics no longer speaks to the dilemmas of France in an age of globalisation. The passion that once animated the French revolutionary tradition was a forgotten resource for the sclerotic French Communist Party. The memory of Charles de Gaulle as avatar of French nationalism has been subtly transformed into de Gaulle as symbol of the French heritage (Nora 1990, 1992b). Cut free from the anchor of past assumptions about their integral relationship, memory and history have gone their separate ways. Rather than the source of history's inspiration, memory has become the object of its critical inquiry, in effect a history of collective memory. Even as history has laid its claims on memory, however, memory has reasserted its autonomy in the intense revival of commemorative practices, testimony and personal memoir. Nora labelled the present age an 'era of commemoration' (Nora 1992a).

Nora had launched his project on the sources of the French national memory during the late 1970s. It was a time of opening to new ideas about French historiography. The Marxism of the intellectuals, so popular in the post-war era, had lost its enthusiasts. Some of them now wrote memoirs about their emancipation from their youthful flirtations with its ideological conceptions (see esp. Le Roy Ladurie 1982). Even the famous Annales school of historical scholarship had lost its reputation as avant-garde historical writing (Boutier and Julia 1995). As an editor at Gallimard, Nora was ideally situated to grasp current trends in historical scholarship. His contacts among scholars in the social sciences were legion. While never an insider as an Annales researcher, he played a key role in editing collections on method in the Annales tradition, with particular attention to the 'new cultural history' (Le Goff and Nora 1974). Nora was on the lookout for an innovative way to write about the history of France in a comprehensive way. Newly elected in 1976 to the École des Hautes Études, the prestigious French graduate school, he decided to offer a seminar that would investigate the nature and sources of the French national memory. He later claimed that the venture was experimental and open-ended (Nora 1984–92: vol. 1, p. vii). The scope, fame and impact of his project over the following years achieved a magnitude about which he could only marvel as he looked back later.

It is significant, I think, that Nora's research and writing decades earlier concerned the historiographical role of Ernest Lavisse, an eminent figure in the professionalisation of historical scholarship at the turn of the twentieth century. He was also a patriotic spokesman for the civic virtues of the Third French Republic. His work, and one might say self-conception as a historian, made it possible for Nora to draw a sharp contrast between ideas about the historian's craft then and now. Lavisse approached French history as if the story of the rise of the French republic as the embodiment of high political ideals could be told as a seamless narrative. At the same time, he aspired to move history from the milieu of *belles lettres* to that of science. In practice as in theory, he taught the importance of archival research and hard evidence as a foundation for historical writing. He supervised his graduate students closely, leading them into the archives to share in his work. He was a prolific author, producing a nine-volume grand narrative history of France from its foundational origins and later another of corresponding scope on modern France from the Revolution to the First World War. He was keenly interested in pedagogy and his history became the principal manual for public education in French primary and secondary schools. Thanks to his connections with the statesmen of the day, he contributed to the formulation of public policy in education. Lavisse, Nora claimed, helped to build a historical consensus that ratified the assumptions of the statesmen of the Third French Republic about the nature and meaning of the role of the modern French nation-state. His ability to write a grand narrative of the development of French history from medieval origins was made possible by the unity of the national memory that sustained it. For Nora, Lavisse's magisterial project had become dated. To study it was to recognise how far removed it was from the writing of a history for the present age (Nora 1986, 2009). Nora's project, therefore, opened the way for the differentiation of approaches to the writing of French history, recalling forgotten ideas contributing to the French identity that had been there all the while if one went looking for them.

As historiographer, Nora came to see his role as analogous to that of Lavisse. He was shaping a new paradigm for historical scholarship in his own time in history. But a grand narrative of French history in the manner of Lavisse was no longer possible. In so many ways, France had become a nation of plural allegiances for its citizens, among which the nation-state was but one. He proposed therefore to inventory the many places that had contributed to the rich and diverse heritage of French culture. The question was whether the history of the nation conceived as heritage could provide a sense of unity comparable to the one once provided by Lavisse in his history of the rise of the nation-state. The framework Nora introduced here was no longer a linear narrative but rather a spatially conceived scheme, assembled as a layered repertoire of topical planes, which localised memories of the places identified with the republic, the nation and the cultural heritage (including the culture of its politics). Nora may have reconstructed French history as a map of memory. On the historiographical plane, though, one might argue that he does not abandon linear sequencing. One may situate his project within a plotline of the ways in which French history has been conceived. He notes that French history has been framed and reframed four times since the era of the French Revolution in light of a changing stance on its relationship to memory (Nora 1993, 2011c).

Nora is not without his critics. The philosopher Paul Ricoeur has questioned whether Nora has done justice to the resources of memory apart from those of history (Ricoeur 2000: 522–35; 2002). Writing an op-ed piece for *Le Monde*, media critic Laurent Gervereau has argued that Nora's model of history merely recomposes elements of the old history in new ways (not unlike the uncanny images of a Surrealist artist such as René Magritte). Nora's conception of history, he contends, offers no insight into what the future may hold (Gervereau 2011). Put more philosophically, it is subversive without being revisionist. Gervereau challenged the utility of Nora's model as a means of preparing French youth for the world in which they must make their way. In this respect, Nora has his own worries about recent directions in French historical scholarship. Having become separated from its once solid grounding in a broadly conceived collective memory, French history in our times, he laments, has become a prey to identity politics. Special interest groups – particularly those with grievances – now wish to feature their memory as a basis for a history that showcases their claims for attention (Nora 2002, 2008, 2011b). In a larger perspective, social theorist Daniel Levy has argued persuasively for the limitations of Nora's exclusive focus on the French experience. The memory boom in our times, he explains, is a global phenomenon, signifying the degree to which a nationalist perspective on memory is better appreciated in relation to a cosmopolitan one (Levy Ch. 14 below). Nora does not relate his project to those in memory studies elsewhere in the world that have reshaped our thinking about history. Still, he has given us an extraordinary accomplishment. In the originality of his initiative, his project is comparable to that of Philippe Ariès on collective mentalities, whatever its shortcomings. Nora's model has been widely imitated by a generation of scholars in memory studies, in France and beyond.

Walter Benjamin on Memory's Redeeming Power

In 1993, the very same year that my book on memory was published, I discovered the writings about memory and history by the German-Jewish literary critic and essayist Walter Benjamin. My incentive to do so was prompted by my reading of Lutz Niethammer's chapter about Benjamin's idea of history in his stimulating *Posthistoire*, a review of theorists who speculated about a posthistorical future beyond the conventional understanding of modern history as the saga of the bourgeoisie in its struggle to refashion the good society in its own image. Niethammer directed attention to Benjamin's last essay, 'Theses on the Philosophy of History', hastily composed in 1940 on the eve of his flight from Paris, for it contained messianic aphorisms about the dashed promise of modern history (Niethammer 1992: 4–5, 101–34). In his plight as an exile on the run from Nazi persecution, Benjamin looked to the past for some intimation of the possibility of the future redemption of missed opportunities for making the world a better place. Fascinated with Benjamin's retrospection on historical time, I turned to in-depth reading of the writings of his Paris exile during the 1930s, where he addressed with urgency the topic of memory's relationship to history. In Benjamin, I found an approach to memory that complemented and deepened ideas in my *History as an Art of Memory*. I regretted that I had not discovered his work earlier. He was the mid-twentieth-century scholar on memory and history that I had been looking for back then, for he offered a perspective on the reinvention of the art of memory germane to the troubles of those times.

By the 1990s, Benjamin was on his way to becoming a cult figure for scholars in the humanities, analogous to, if not quite of, the celebrity stature that Michel Foucault had enjoyed during the mid-1980s. He was lionised among students of literature as one of twentieth-century Germany's most sophisticated literary critics. I had been vaguely aware of his standing as the 'last European' man of letters, carrying forward the humane tradition of the German Enlightenment in the midst of his homeland's subjection to Nazi tyranny. Beyond his writings, the story of his failed attempt at escape from France in the face of German occupation had by then captured the popular imagination. Benjamin had come to personify the ordeal of that cohort of Central European Jewish intellectuals who sought refuge in the United States on the eve of the Second World War. Reflection on the meaning of his story was all the more poignant because he perished en route to his destination.[4] Eventually, his scattered writings were collected, edited and assembled by his former colleagues. His closest intellectual friends, Gershom Scholem and Theodor Adorno, published his collected correspondence (Benjamin 1978). A Zionist and a Marxist respectively, they had been rivals in life for Benjamin's intellectual affections. Now they joined in seeing to the posthumous publication of everything that he had ever written. The subtext of their own memoirs about him convey the tragedy that a life of so much intellectual promise had been cut short amidst the atrocities of the Holocaust (Scholem 1981).

Benjamin produced a great deal of original material germane to memory and history during the last years of his exile. His writings took a new direction as he faced Hitler's impending invasion of Paris, his last refuge. Literature was still important to him but history even more so. In scanning the tragic failure of democratic politics in his native Germany, he took the longer view by dismissing the idea of history as a story of ongoing progress. In light of his dire circumstances, he judged the idea of continuity between past and present an intellectual contrivance. Between them he saw only stretches of empty time. Benjamin envisioned leaps across these intervals to moments in the past that might provide guidance for facing the problems of the 'now time' of history – history from the vantage point of the dynamic present (Benjamin 1940b: 696–7). Here he introduced the idea of eternal return to memory's inspiring sources. With dim prospects for his own future, he sought consolation in remembering moments out of the past in which kindred spirits had reckoned with dilemmas like his own. Nostalgia for such moments, he believed, was a resource for creativity. His conception of the power of memory involved the idea of time travel, prompted by the re-awakening of collective memory in unrelated moments of time. The task, he proposed, was to import quickening memories that help us to understand our present dilemma. As Benjamin characterised them, they were like 'heliotropes turning toward that sun that is rising in the sky of history'.[5] He labelled such memories moments of 'profane illumination'.[6]

Benjamin wanted to rethink the meaning of history for his present age. He had come to see that the promise of modern history for the making of a better world had been broken. His idea of history is famous for his evocation of the image of an Angel of History looking back in sadness on the debris of dashed hopes and lost causes strewn across the reaches of modern history (Löwy 2005). Like the angel, Benjamin saw in the near past only ruins of well-intentioned projects for the improvement of the human condition. His hopes for humankind lay in memory's revitalising power to rescue ideas that had aspired but failed to be reified back then, a resource for a future time and place he knew he would never see.[7]

---

4   The safeguarding of Benjamin's most valued unpublished papers, hastily confided to friends and acquaintances while he was on the run, is a fascinating story of its own. There is a memorial dedicated to Benjamin at the cemetery at Port Bou, France, where he was anonymously interred. I like Jay Parini's novel, *Benjamin's Crossing* (1997), an imagined narrative of Benjamin's life journey as he moved toward his last days.

5   Benjamin took the angel motif from the painting by Paul Klee, *Angelus Novus*, which Benjamin purchased and took with him into exile. Today it hangs in the Israel Museum, Jerusalem (Benjamin 1940b: 694–5).

6   Benjamin's notion of profane illumination may be construed psychologically as an example of involuntary memory. Benjamin garnered many of his ideas about memory from his reading of Marcel Proust, for whom a chance visit to a physical place of memory could bring forward an entire remembered milieu (Benjamin 1934).

7   Benjamin's own time-travel led him to the discovery of the writings of the early nineteenth century scholar Carl Gustav Jochmann. Like himself, Jochmann was a wanderer, a refugee from the oppressive politics of Eastern Europe. Jochmann's ideas about history confirmed his own. Like Benjamin, Jochmann was a writer of modest reputation, a voluntary exile from his native land, a champion of unrequited progressive cause, and, most importantly, a writer whose hopes for the future were embedded in the secrets of the past (Benjamin 1940a).

Benjamin's angel metaphor has exercised a powerful appeal upon scholars in our own times. It has acquired such fame, I think, because it provides a metaphor for our own disappointment with the expectation of modern historical thought about fulfilling the moral imperatives of the Enlightenment. It was as if Benjamin were importing into his present age his longing for what might have been.[8] The imagined future, he suggested, was to be found in the poetics of the past. Modern history had been cast in a developmental pattern and so has been manipulated to confirm a conception of historical inevitability (Benjamin 1940a: 693). But Benjamin was sensitive to history's contingencies. The art of memory as reconceived in his thinking lay in making connections between memories of lost opportunities in the past and present possibilities for their retrieval. Time and again across the span of history like-minded thinkers rediscovered the force of such memories in what he thought of as the circle of return to inspiring precedent (Cohen 1993: 3–6).

Benjamin's most concrete formulation of history as an art of memory is revealed in his research project on the material culture of Paris during the mid-nineteenth-century age of high capitalism. He informally called it *Das Passagen-Werk* (translated into English as *The Arcades Project*), alluding to those once fashionable commercial passageways that structured the map of Parisian commerce and industry. These were corridors among the places of memory of the material culture under construction in that city. New ideas circulated through this labyrinth of arcades as well. They made possible what Benjamin called the 'phantasmagoria' that characterised the imagination of capitalist culture. Benjamin elaborated repertoires of these places by topical category. He was more interested in the imagination generated by this culture than he was in its economics. But he was sufficiently sympathetic to Marx's method to position his rubrics so as to reveal the dialectical interplay of forces of economic innovation and political resistance. Arcades were paired with barricades in the topical organization of his project. Arcades facilitated commerce; barricades obstructed it. Benjamin identified cascades of such places of memory. Each place generated an elaborate chain of memory, and each link within set the imagination soaring. Places marked dreams of the future urban landscape as designed by engineers such as Georges Haussmann and of harmoniously planned societies by social theorists such as Charles Fourier. He noted as well the disenchanted reflections of alienated youth, such as that of the poet Charles Baudelaire.[9]

Noteworthy for me in the *Arcades Project* was Benjamin's discovery of and attention to the infamous insurrectionist Auguste Blanqui, the revolutionary gadfly who troubled a succession of nineteenth-century French political regimes with his incessant (if ineffectual) plotting to overthrow them by instigating popular upheavals in imitation of the revolutionary days of 1789 and 1792. I had devoted a fair portion of my early years as a scholar to researching and writing a book about Blanqui and his followers as practitioners of a politics of commemoration (Hutton 1981). As I explained, they created a cult of the revolutionary tradition, mimicking its methods in ways that were self-defeating and as political strategy ultimately futile. As an *habitué* of the Bibliothèque Nationale, I could identify vicariously with Benjamin's research on the veteran insurrectionist, for I had consulted many of the same sources as had he in my effort to understand Blanqui's appeal to the French revolutionary tradition. We agreed that Blanqui for all the drama of his political interventions was fighting a rearguard action. Yet he was a fascinating figure all the same for his faith in memory's inspiring power. For Benjamin, Blanqui's struggle resonated with his own. Like Blanqui, he

---

8   Acknowledging an intellectual debt to Benjamin, Svetlana Boym takes up this theme of 'reflective nostalgia' in her *Future of Nostalgia* (2002: 27–32).

9   Benjamin, *Arcades Project* (1999), esp. Convolutes A (Arcades), D (Eternal Return), E (Haussmannization, Barricades), J (Baudelaire), N (Theory of Progress), V (Conspiracies), W (Fourier).

aspired to revisit those places of memory that had roused the people of Paris to insurrection time and again despite the repeated frustration of their cause. Blanqui, Benjamin concluded, could not break free of the phantasmagoria of the culture in which he was immersed and so could see no way out of his dilemma. Neither could Benjamin, as he witnessed the inability of the Left in France as in Germany to stay fascist aggression. That is why he was partial to Blanqui's speculation on the eternal return, a pamphlet written in late-life in his prison cell entitled *L'Eternité par les astres* (1872). Blanqui may have failed in his objectives, but Benjamin was willing to believe with him that the remembrance of that struggle provided hope for redemption in circumstances as yet beyond their ken (Benjamin 1938; 1999: 111–19).

The *Arcades Project*, like that of the life of Benjamin himself, was an unfinished venture. My sense is that its published version was a provisional draft. Benjamin was a terrible procrastinator. His text might be construed as notes preparatory to the writing of an integrated narrative. But in our times, attuned to the fragmentation of the grand narrative, the tentative nature of the text of the *Arcades Project* – notes arranged topically as quotations or precis with commentary – has a postmodern appeal. Historian Vanessa Schwartz has observed that Benjamin's map of an imagined culture springing from places of the memory of nineteenth-century Paris prefigures the method employed by Pierre Nora in his study of the places of the French national memory (Schwartz 2001: 1723). That may be so, but Benjamin did so with more confidence in memory's power to renew the human prospect. His writing conveyed a religious sensibility in his search for the redemption of a lost cause. He referred to his faith in such a possibility as a mild messianism (Benjamin 1940b: 703–4). In today's parlance, his thinking on the subject might be characterised as an expression of religious atheism.

Why the Memory Phenomenon and Why Now?

My teaching has been one practical route through which I have come to understand why the memory phenomenon has attained such prominence today. Since the 1980s, I have regularly taught a course at the University of Vermont on contemporary history. Teaching that subject can be tricky, for its overall interpretation is continually vulnerable to unanticipated contingencies. Over the past 30 years so much has my conception of our time in history changed that the organisation of the course with which I began is unrecognisable in the way I teach it now. Back then, I conceived of it as an extension of the narrative structure of modern history, told as the story of the rise of Western civilisation. I focused on the politics and statecraft of the Cold War with some attention to the domestic politics of leading nations. The superpowers, the United States and the Soviet Union, each drew on different interpretations of the Enlightenment's conception of our destiny. With my students, I witnessed the drama of the revolutions of 1989–91 in Eastern Europe, marking the precipitous collapse of ideological rivalries dating from the end of the Second World War. But more than the closing of a particular narrative, the date symbolised a changing way of conceptualising our place in the historical continuum – a move from thinking of our time in history as an extension of the modern age toward thinking of it as an age apart.

These days, the future of history is as often forecast in terms of cultural as in political trends, for the former provides both consolation and opportunity. One notes that since the 1970s more and more historians have redirected attention from the old political to the new cultural history. They have redesigned the curricula of history departments, disaggregating the conceptual unity once ascribed to 'Western civilisation'. Amidst the fractured elements of the old and grand historical narrative of the rise of the West, memory has re-surfaced in a new relationship to history in narratives more modestly designed around cultural topics in a range of global settings. I no longer structure my course around an advancing timeline but rather proceed from topics that travel together in the making of the history of the present age. My course features such topics as the globalisation of consumerist culture, the politics of gender identity, the cultural effects of the media revolution, advances in biotechnology, robotics in our future and the consolation of the pursuit of happiness in private life. Politics has its place less for its statecraft, more for its culture. Such topics cannot be studied in linear sequence but only in parallel track or, better, as places on today's map of memory. This reversal recast the relationship between memory and history in contemporary historiography – from well-remembered events placed on a single narrative timeline to a pluralism of topics from which particular narratives proceeded in a way I had not anticipated when I wrote my book on the art of memory during the late 1980s.

It is noteworthy that the rise of the memory phenomenon is coeval with these transforming historical changes. My sense is that the current scholarly interest in collective memory, moving beyond its initial association with time-bound tradition, suggests a reorientation in contemporary historiography driven by historians' greater understanding of memory's place in the rhetoric of historical writing. Ironically, it has not been the stability of tradition, as emphasised in studies of the history of collective mentalities, but rather memory's protean instability that has inspired the burgeoning field of memory studies. Whereas the Annales historians had emphasised the constancy of memory, today's scholars point to its fragility in its endless reconfigurations. As Benjamin presaged, the rise of the memory phenomenon is symptomatic of the vanishing faith in a particular conception of the idea of progress as a framework for a historical understanding of the present age. Scholars have expressed the notion differently over the course of the past half-century: such evocative notions as the end of ideology, the end of history, *posthistoire* and the disintegration of the grand narrative of Western civilisation. All signal the denouement of a conception of history that framed the relationship between past and present as a continuum emanating from well-defined origins and tending toward a preconceived destiny. Far from striving toward an endpoint, history as an art of memory might be likened to a never-ending story.

Historiography has its fads and fashions. That of the present age is no exception. The lively interest in memory across the curriculum, though, would seem to denote more than a passing fancy (Rosenfeld 2009). Clearly the memory phenomenon in contemporary scholarship has come to encompass more than a field of specialised historical interest. It has had its effect on the way we understand history and the place of history among the arts of memory. The subject matter has led to critical thinking about the relationship between memory and history that has no precedent. One context is historical, the other historiographical.

As for historical understanding, we may interpret this interest in terms of the contribution of memory scholarship to cultural history. These studies suggest why historians have redirected attention from political to cultural history in the choice of subject matter for research. As sociologist Jeffrey Olick has explained, we have come to appreciate collective memory as the constituent glue of culture. As an approach to cultural history, the concept of memory has proven more useful than its cognate predecessors: myth, tradition and heritage. Memory studies have enabled us to trace continuities in the modulations of collective memory in all of their complexity as they have contributed to the making of culture (Olick 2007: 17–35).

As for historiography, memory studies have prompted us to revisit age-old notions about circular versus linear patterns in history with new-found critical insight into the differences between memory and history, the resources of each, as well as their complex interactions. The evocation of memory is emotional and mythical. Historical interpretation, by contrast, is rational and analytical. Each has its logic, which plays out differently.

34

Memory with the passage of time tends to move through stages of modification – from testimony to storytelling to historical reconstruction to idealised nostalgia before passing into forgetfulness. But memory as a resource of the human imagination may at any time break free of this pattern to revitalise present experience. A memory out of the past may be awakened time and again. The narratives of history, by contrast, are grounded in historical evidence of events that transpire but once and for all time. Their interpretation tends to play out in sequential patterns. Still, memory and history impinge on one another, as today's historiographical discussions reveal. The memory phenomenon in contemporary historiography points toward our changing expectations of history for the time in which we live. The current favour accorded present-oriented historical interpretation in some ways mimics memory's operations in its topical organisation and its importation of the past into the present randomly.

Even though memory and history will always display sharp differences as approaches to our understanding of the past, our inquiry into their relationship has led us to recognise how the patterns of historiography – considered as the history of historical writing – paradoxically lie closer to those of collective memory. Movements in historical writing tend to play out the inspiration behind their construction, much like the dissipation of energy in the process of entropy. They carve out new domains of scholarship, flourish, then fade away as they are displaced by new enthusiasms more in keeping with the realities of changing times. In this way, collective memory may be said to subtend traditions of historical writing. For historians, that may be the main lesson derived from the preoccupation with memory in our times. However one evaluates the importance of all the recent scholarship on memory, our understanding of its relationship to history will never be the same again.

References

Ariès, P. 1986 [1954]. *Le Temps de l'histoire* (Paris: Seuil).

— — 1988. 'L'Histoire des mentalités', in J. le Goff (ed.), *La Nouvelle Histoire* (Paris: Éditions Complexe), pp. 167–90.

Benjamin, W. 1934. 'Zum Bilde Prousts', in Benjamin 1974–89: vol. 2, pp. 310–24.

— — 1938. 'Während der Commune war Blanqui', in Benjamin 1974–89: vol. 1, pp. 1153–4.

— — 1940a. '*Die Rückschritte der Poesie* von Carl Gustav Jochmann', in Benjamin 1974–89: vol. 2, pp. 572–98.

— — 1940b. 'Über den Begriff der Geschichte', in Benjamin 1974–89: vol. 1, pp. 693–704.

— — 1974–89. *Gesammelte Schriften*, 7 vols, ed. R. Tiedemann and H. Schweppenhauser (Frankfurt: Suhrkamp Verlag).

— — 1978. *Briefe*, ed. G. Scholem and T.W. Adorno (Frankfurt: Suhrkamp Verlag).

— — 1999. *The Arcades Project*, trans. H. Eiland and K. McLaughlin (Cambridge, MA: Harvard University Press).

Boutier, J., and D. Julia. 1995. 'A Quoi pensent les historiens', in eid. (eds), *Passés recomposés* (Paris: Editions Autrement), pp. 23–8.

Boym, S. 2002. *The Future of Nostalgia* (New York: Basic Books).

Cohen, M. 1993. *Profane Illumination: Walter Benjamin and the Paris of Surrealist Revolution* (Berkeley: University of California Press).

Dosse, F. 2011. *Pierre Nora: Homo Historicus* (Paris: Perrin).

Foer, J. 2011. *Moonwalking with Einstein: The Art and Science of Remembering Everything* (New York: Penguin).

Gadamer, H.G. 1989 [1960]. *Truth and Method* (Cambridge, MA: MIT Press).

Gervereau, L. 2011. 'Pourquoi canoniser Pierre Nora?', <LeMonde.fr/ides/articles/2011/11/01> (accessed 9 Aug. 2013).

Gombrich, E.H. 1986. *Aby Warburg: An Intellectual Biography* (Chicago: University of Chicago Press).

Halbwachs, M. 1971 [1941]. *La Topographie légendaire des évangiles en Terre Sainte* (Paris: Presses Universitaires de France).

Hartog, F. 2003. *Régimes d'historicité; présentisme et expériences du temps* (Paris: Seuil).

Hutton, P.H. 1981. *The Cult of the Revolutionary Tradition: The Blanquists in French Politics, 1864–1893* (Berkeley: University of California Press).

— — 1993. *History as an Art of Memory* (Hanover, NH: University Press of New England).

— — 2004. *Philippe Ariès and the Politics of French Cultural History* (Amherst: University of Massachusetts Press).

— — 2013. 'Memory: Witness, Experience, Collective Meaning', in N. Partner and S. Foot (eds), *The Sage Handbook of Historical Theory* (London: Sage), pp. 354–77.

Jones, M.G. 2008. *Frances Yates and the Hermetic Tradition* (Lake Worth, FL: Ibis).

Le Goff, J., and P. Nora (eds) 1974. *Faire de l'histoire*, 3 vols (Paris: Gallimard).

Le Roy Ladurie, E. 1982. *Paris-Montpellier* (Paris: Gallimard).

Löwy, M. 2005. *Reading Walter Benjamin's 'On the Concept of History'* (London: Verso).

Lyotard, J.F. 1979. *La Condition postmoderne* (Paris: Éditions de Minuit).

Mandrou, R. 1968. 'L'Histoire des mentalités', in *Encyclopédie Universalis France* (Paris: Encyclopédie Universalis France), vol. 8, pp. 436–8.

Niethammer, L. 1992. *Posthistoire: Has History Come to an End?* (London: Verso).

Nora, P. (ed.) 1984–92. *Les Lieux de mémoire*, 3 vols (Paris: Gallimard).

— — 1986. '*L'Histoire de France* de Lavisse', in Nora 1984–92: vol. 2, pp. 317–75.

— — (ed.) 1987. *Essais d'ego-histoire* (Paris: Gallimard).

— — 1990. 'L'Historien devant de Gaulle', in Nora 2011a: 278–88.

— — 1992a. 'L'Ère de la commémoration', in Nora 1984–92: vol. 3, pp. 977–1012.

— — 1992b. 'Gaullistes et Communistes', in Nora 1984–92: vol. 3, pp. 347–93.

— — 1993. 'Les 'Lieux de mémoire,' sont-ils exportable?', in Nora 2011a: 373–84.

— — 2002. 'L'Histoire au second degré; réponse à Paul Ricoeur', *Le Débat* 122: 24–31.

— — 2003. 'L'Ego-histoire est-elle possible?', in Nora 2011a: 138–46.

— — 2008. 'Les Lieux de mémoire, ou comment ils m'ont échappé', *L'Histoire* 331: 32–5.

— — 2009. 'Pourquoi lire Lavisse aujourd'hui', in Nora 2011a: 193–204.

— — (ed.) 2011a. *Présent, nation, mémoire* (Paris: Gallimard).

— — 2011b. 'Recent History and the New Dangers of Politicization' (24 Nov.), <www.eurozine.com> (accessed 14 July 2013).

— — 2011c. 'Les Trois Pôles de la conscience historique contemporaine', in Nora 2011a: 7–29.

— — 2013. *Esquisse d'ego-histoire*. Paris: Desclée de Brouwer.

Olick, J.K. 2007. *The Politics of Regret* (New York: Routledge).

Ong, W.J. 1982. *Orality and Literacy: The Technologizing of the Word* (London: Methuen).

Perrot, M. 1987. 'L'Air du temps', in *Essais d'égo-histoire*, ed. P. Nora (Paris: Gallimard), pp. 241–92.

Pomian, K. 1986. 'L'Heure des *Annales*', in Nora 1984–92: vol. 2, pp. 377–429.

Ricoeur, P. 2000. *La Mémoire, l'histoire, l'oubli* (Paris: Seuil).

— — 2002. 'Mémoire: Approches historiennes, approche philosophique', *Le Débat* 122: 51–6.

Rosenfeld, G.D. 2009. 'A Looming Crash or a Soft Landing? Forecasting the Future of the Memory Industry', *Journal of Modern History* 81: 122–58.

Scholem, G. 1981. *Walter Benjamin: The Story of a Friendship* (New York: New York Review of Books).

Schwartz, V. 2001. 'Walter Benjamin for Historians', *American Historical Review* 106/5: 1721–43.

Yates, F. *The Art of Memory* (Chicago: University of Chicago Press).

—— 1984. 'Autobiographical Fragments', in *Collected Essays* (London: Routledge), vol. 3, pp. 303–22.1966.

Chateaubriand, Selfhood and Memory

Peter Fritzsche

We were still in the old house (but already no longer in the old old house), when my daughter, Lauren, who must have been about seven or eight years old, said, 'Isn't that the way we used to do things?' I don't remember what she was referring to, maybe the use of an old screwdriver or handsaw, at a time when we were generally working with power tools, or a typewriter, but I was struck by her attentiveness to 'what once was, but is no longer'. I have been to enough seminars on memory with psychologists and neuroscientists to know how many scholars assume that the distinction between 'was' and 'is' is constituted in language templates anchored in the structure of the brain. Yet what I heard was evidence that the sense of time passing and even a nostalgic sentimentality about that passage was learned, perhaps sometime between the move from the old old house to the old house. In other words, I leaned toward the idea that the learning of language does much to create the structures of cognition so that different languages, tenses and attentions work themselves out to elaborate different kinds of structure, which consequently cannot be regarded as anthropological constants. In my view, much of the amplitude of tense, duration, rupture and the work of memory that attends to them are learned in and vulnerable to culture.

At the time, in the old house, I was working on what I, in the late 1990s, had conceived as a history of nostalgia. For me, nostalgia was not simply an unexplored phenomenon of modern life long held in condescension and misunderstood but a portal into the historic nature of conceptions about discontinuity, periodization and loss and of different ways of relating to and assembling the past. I was trying to write a history of the practices of memory, which finally emerged in somewhat different form as *Stranded in the Present: Modern Time and the Melancholy of History* (Fritzsche 2004), which focused on the French revolutionary period. I argued for the importance of the French Revolution but also for the emergence of drastic description that enabled contemporaries to see things as revolutionary in ways that radically realigned the relationships between 'was' and 'is'. I was interested not so much in the content of memories, whether or not they were exculpatory, admonitory or adversarial, or in the destination of the work of memory: what interested me was the history of the shapes and forms of time (Fritzsche 2013). Exactly what weight to put on the decades around the turn of the nineteenth century (and I would say lots) was secondary to suggesting the overall historical nature of those shapes and forms.

One of the most compelling images I found to guide me was an imaginary history of the walk up the attic stairs. At least in colonial New England, the garret had traditionally been a 'lumber room' or a storage place for 'meal, flour, and dried food stuffs'. Until the hard freezes of winter, the dry heat of the attic was well suited to preserving apples, squashes and onions. William Pyncheon of Salem, Massachussets, for example, noted in his diary at the end of October 1788, that the weather had turned surprisingly, 'excessively cold' and that 'people's roots were frozen in the garret' (Nylander 1993: 97). Otherwise the attic was an unfinished loft where boys and girls were bedded down. One hundred years later, however, the scenery in the attic and the things people did there had changed dramatically. 'What a museum of curiosities is the garret of a well-regulated New England house', wrote one novelist, Thomas Bailey Aldrich in 1870:

> *Here meet together, as if by some preconcerted arrangement, all the broken down chairs of the household, all the spavined tables, all the seedy hats, all the intoxicated-looking books, all the split walking sticks that have retired from business (weary with the march of life). The pots, the pans, the trunks, the bottles – who may hope to make inventory of the numberless odds and ends collected in this bewildering lumber-room? But what a place it is to sit of an afternoon with the rain pattering on the roof? What a place in which to read Gulliver's Travels. (Nylander 1993: 14)*

The attic, one might remember, was also Jo March's favourite reading place in Louisa May Alcott's *Little Women*. A few decades in the nineteenth century sufficed to turn parlours and attics into 'mini-museums, filled with heirlooms, mementos, and souvenirs of family' (Gillis 1996: 16). The house with old things was not so much the remnant of the past, but its theatricalisation, a ceaseless exchange of scenes and characters, of disappearances and reappearances, an 'airy structure ... open to the wind of time', in the words of Gaston Bachelard (1994: 54).

These American moments suggest that the new texture to the past was not the simple result of the French Revolution but part of a much broader, trans-Atlantic configuration of time which depended as much on new knowledge about movements around the globe and about the nature of historical change as it did on political transformations and westward expansion. If at the beginning of the eighteenth century, scholars measured the age of the earth in thousands of years, by the end, they did so in millions of years – indeed tens of millions of years. Georges Buffon, Jean-Baptiste Lamarck and Georges Cuvier not only extended time backward along an unprecedented scale, but they chopped it up into distinctive prehistoric epochs in which characteristic forms of life were not necessarily present in preceding or succeeding periods. The 'discovery of time' was accompanied by the discovery of a new order of difference over time (Rossi 1984), and current events seemed to replicate ancient geological stratification. For many contemporaries, the French Revolution validated the insights of Buffon's *Les Epoques de la Nature* (1778) or Cuvier's *Discours sur les révolutions de la surface du globe* (1822) which could be applied to the much shorter, but still highly varied, history of human society. The demolition of the 'old regime' gave a heart-felt poignancy to the ideas of periodicity which broke apart what had once been assumed: the basic similarity of society in ancient Greece, fifteenth-century Florence or eighteenth-century France. These places became increasingly ontologically differentiated through the advance of chronological supersession as we can see in the displays of natural history museums to this day. Even individual lives were increasingly measured according to revolutions of abrupt leave-takings and sudden arrivals: 'There is always a time when we possessed nothing of what we now possess, and a time when we have nothing of what we once had', François-René de Chateaubriand concluded in his acclaimed memoirs in 1811: 'Man does not have a single, consistent life: he has several laid end to end, and that is his misfortune' (Chateaubriand 1961: 73). New ways of remembering proliferated in the kinks and folds of these newly mobilised public and personal histories, which made Thomas Bailey Aldrich's walk up the attic stairs in 1870 so different from William Pynchon's in 1788.

Chateaubriand (1768–1848), who as a child lived for a time in a kind of attic, an 'isolated cell at the top of the turrett' at his father's Combourg Castle, served me as an excellent guide because his extraordinary memoirs (and other essays on revolution, Christianity and ancient societies) reflect but also comment on and both argue for and against the 'discovery of time'. Precisely his social position as a nobleman and his political fate as an émigré during the Revolution and his role at once as a democratic and royalist dissenter during the Restoration made him alert to what he considered to be mutable and also irreconcilable in the course of current history.

Chateaubriand's vocabulary is replete with nautical terms that have an eighteenth-century feel about them, but they act with the revolutionary forcefulness of the nineteenth century. He opened the *Essay on Revolutions* (1797), which he wrote in English exile: 'We are sailing along an unknown coast, in the midst of darkness and the storm.' These maritime metaphors assisted Chateaubriand in describing a totally mobilised landscape in which the jeopardy of shipwreck loomed always on the horizon. 'No one can promise himself a quiet moment', he admitted, 'the friend is now torn from the friend', the age 'resounds with the fall of thrones' (Chateaubriand 1815a: 4–5). But on reflection in the memoirs, which Chateaubriand began to write in 1811, the 'unknown coast' became more historiographically sensible. 'I have seen a world end and a world commence', he wrote during the wars of the revolution. 'Old Europe thought it was fighting only France; it did not perceive that a new age was marching upon it' (Chateaubriand 1902: vol. 3, p. 46). While Chateaubriand eventually returned to France after seven years of exile, he continued to feel like a 'foreign soldier':

> *I am writing, like the last of the Romans, to the sound of the Barbarian invasion. By day I compose pages as agitated as the events of the day; at night, while the rolling of the distant cannon dies away in my solitary woods, I return to the silence of the years that sleep in the grave and to the peace of my youngest memories. (Chateaubriand 1902: vol. 3, pp. 47–8)*

There would be no restoration, the old society would not revive: this was Chateaubriand's message, even as he clung to the old regime, believing even when he witnessed the disinterment of Marie Antoinette from the old Cimetière de la Madeleine in January 1815 that he 'recognized the Queen's head by the smile which that head had given me at Versailles' some 30 years earlier (Chateaubriand 1902: vol. 3, p. 103). It is through his nostalgic bearing that he accounted his losses.

Moreover, the revolution did not just divide one world from another, the lesson of periodisation, but posited the principle of historical change, the lesson that ruptures would continue to manifest themselves so that that the present would be antiquated just as had the past: 'Ever the revolution recommences', he wrote in 1832 with the effect that in the shadow of the French Revolution, Chateaubriand made the world look completely different by scattering across its face the ruins of people (Chateaubriand 1902: vol. 5, p. 306). He was fascinated by the wrecks of old empires in Rome, Athens and Jerusalem, yet he also recognised the wrecks of the present, Louis XVI's France, of course, but also Danton's or Robespierre's, where, when he returned from his London exile early in 1800, the walls were still 'smeared' with 'Republican inscriptions … already grown old: LIBERTY, EQUALITY, FRATERNITY, OR DEATH' (ibid., vol. 2, pp. 155–6). In Canning's London where 'new buildings … cover up memorable events' that had taken place but 30 years earlier – the 'old meadows' now constituted Regent's Park (ibid., vol. 1, p. 187) or even in the forests of a brand New World, where the young traveller, who confidently believed he would find nothing old or decrepit, stumbles across abandoned mounds littered with 'fragments of vases and various utensils' (Chateaubriand 1828: vol. 1, p. 181). 'What nation was this?', he demanded, 'What revolution has swept it away?' (ibid. 157). It was with the eyes of an archaeologist that Chateaubriand came to see the world revealed as disenchanted so that this revolution had forever made things after-revolution.

The effect of the French Revolution was to dramatise the world history that Chateaubriand assembled in his essays and commentaries. He often held out the itinerant nature of all things so that the writer's fantastic detonation of the French Revolution across all of time and space actually naturalised it in overarching the operations of endless rhythm of return and departure: rise and fall. Indeed, in the *Génie du Christianisme* (1802), he argued that 'God created a world that was at once old and new' (see Sainson 2005: 57), the 'scathed oak' and scarred rock were manufactured 'marks of antiquity' that lent the original state of nature its charm (Chateaubriand 1856: 136–7), the old man was manufactured in order to cringe at the adolescent (Vial 1963: 7). Yet it seems very clear that the French Revolution and not the Creation was the point of origin of this mobilised landscape of ashes, rubbish and dust. Chateaubriand's writings themselves are scarred with the unprecedented force of 1789, which ruptures any ongoing cycle of rupture, of degeneration and rejuvenation, decay and advance. In particular, for Chateaubriand, what marked the quickened, chaotic time of the post-revolutionary era was the ongoing production and the ceaseless effacement of ruins. This is in fact the driving power behind the production of the memoirs themselves. The precedent in the cycle of ruination is deployed to indict the self-sufficiency of the present. The unprecedented in the ancient cycle is allowed to emerge to dramatise the new quality to destruction.

Chateaubriand's melancholy possessed a special intensity whenever he contemplated the possibility that the monuments of the past might no longer remain visible in the future. If the 'scathed oaks' or the scarred rocks of history were to disappear, creatures would live in a perpetually simulated present that offered no notice of other lives and other ways. The distinction is well drawn in *A Letter from Rome*, written in 1804 after his final break with Napoleon. There are two kinds of ruins, Chateaubriand maintained, 'the one the work of time; the other of man'. In the first instance, 'nature acts in unison with time', so that the crevice that appears is quickly filled with the nest of a dove and the rubbish that gathers is enwreathed with flowers. Human ruins, by contrast, are out of joint with time. They are the 'effect of calamity' rather than of time, a violence that leaves the scene of devastation 'without any reparative power' (Chateaubriand 1815b: 18–20): and this calamity can be given temporal specificity. 'The old men of former times', and here Chateaubriand reflected on the society of his childhood, 'were less unhappy and less isolated than those of today: if, by lingering on earth, they had lost their friends, little else had changed around them; they were strangers to youth, but not to society'. It is all different 'nowadays', that is, since the French Revolution, 'a straggler in this life has witnessed the death, not only of men, but also of ideas: principles, customs, tastes, pleasures, sorrows, opinions, none of these resemble what he used to know. He belongs to a different race from the human species among which he ends his days' (Chateaubriand 1902: 38–9). Chateaubriand makes a claim for the special weight of this time, 'nowadays', which depart from the models of the past, however much these models continue to bear on Chateaubriand's thinking. And what was particularly calamitous about the French Revolution was not so much that it destroyed worlds and created ruins – killing a king or washing up émigrés such as himself on foreign shores – but it destroyed the monuments of the past. Chateaubriand's readers are taken again and again to the Abbey of Saint-Denis, outside Paris, where in August 1793 the royal tombs were plundered and the bones of kings smashed and thrown into a rubbish basket (Chateaubriand 1856: 524–5, 730–31). To take away 'the bones of their fathers', he wrote in another context, 'you take away their history', you rob them 'of the proofs of their existence and of their annihilation' (Chateaubriand 1902: vol. 1, p. 231). It was the ruin of the ruin that distinguished the destruction of modern people from the destruction of eternal time. Later, Victor Hugo would push the point further; in *Notre Dame de Paris*, he observed that it was fashion and good taste that threatened Notre Dame more than natural erosion or political and religious struggles.

Moreover, it was the French Revolution of 1789 that cast Chateaubriand into the difficult, unwelcomed role of émigré. The émigré came upon new, unexpected perspectives. It allowed Chateaubriand to see others as 'stranded in the present' as he himself was. When he encountered American Indians in his travels through the United States in 1792 he found himself. North of Albany, along the Hudson River, Chateaubriand stumbled on 'a sort of barn' in 'the midst of a forest'. He peered inside and found 'a score of Savages', 'their bodies half bare, their ears slashed', but also a 'little Frenchman, powdered and frizzed'; he was 'making the Iroquois caper to the tune of Madelon Friquet' – this was 'an overwhelming thing for a disciple of Rousseau' (Chateaubriand 1902: vol. 1, pp. 218–19). Instead of hearing the 'shouts of the Savage and the braying of the fallow-deer', Chateaubriand walked through the Adirondack forests only to make out 'the habitation of a planter' which lay just beyond 'the hut of an Indian' (Chateaubriand 1828: vol. 1, pp. 123–4). By the time he made his way down the Ohio River, Chateaubriand had grown weary at the sight of new settlers pressing into Kentucky from Virginia. In 'wilds where man [once] roved in absolute independence,' he asked, 'will not slaves till the ground under the lash of their master … will not prisons … replace the open cabin and the lofty oak'. Chateaubriand recognised the poignant signs of destruction in the New World: the tragic figure of the Indian who 'is no longer a Savage in his forests, but a beggar at the door of a factory' (ibid., vol. 2, p. 101). And Chateaubriand identified his own fate with that of the Indian: both he and they had suffered a historical defeat and were condemned to live amidst the ruins of what once had been a noble existence. In a flash of recognition, Chateaubriand on the Ohio River approached the Indians on the far shore as fellow victims of historical transformations that had destroyed traditional habitations. Colonialism and mercantilism stood as the confirmation of the obsolescence of both the nobleman and the 'noble savage'.

Although Chateaubriand despaired over the humiliations endured by the American Indians in this first American century, he ultimately fixed his identity to his status as a fallen nobleman, as an émigré who belonged neither here nor there, as a 'foreign soldier' or 'shipwrecked mariner'. 'I shall continue to relate my shipwreck', he concludes, a continuation which was the 30-year work of the memoirs from 1811 to 1841. 'I believe in nothing except religion', Chateaubriand announced at one point, and so 'I distrust everything' (Chateaubriand 1902: vol. 2, p. 95). In the affairs of this world, he was a non-believer: he made an awkward republican in America, cut a poor figure as an émigré in England and infuriated his fellow legitimists during the Restoration. He repeatedly described himself as a swimmer in the course of events who refused to try to reach the banks on either side despite turbulent conditions. 'Each age is a river that carries us off according to the whims of the destiny to which we have abandoned ourselves', he explained.

> *There are those (the republicans) who cross it headlong and throw themselves onto the shore opposite. The others are perfectly happy to remain where they are, without plunging in. Trying to move with the times, the former transport us far from ourselves into an imaginary realm; the latter hold us back, refusing to enlighten themselves, happy to be men of the fourteenth century [at the end of the eighteenth] (quoted in Barbéris 1976: 107–8).*

For his part, Chateaubriand preferred to remain castaway. Wreckage swirled around the swimmer, who abandoned any attempt to gather up the debris and found solace in hanging on to this or that piece. 'It will depend but on myself to knot together again the two ends of my existence, to blend far-distant periods, to mingle illusions of different ages', he wrote

(Chateaubriand 1902: vol. 4, p. 188). Indeed, the dislocations of the Revolution provided Chateaubriand with a kind of thematic coherence: he described his delivery as an infant to a wet nurse as 'my first exile', compared life changes to 'revolutions' and referred to his well-paged memoirs as his 'orphan' (ibid., vol. 1, p. 17; Conner 1995: 1). (The very idea of 'my orphan' suggests how identity was shaped by loss in the modern era).

Chateaubriand's self-apprehension as an émigré or 'orphan' enabled him to be more attentive to rupture and dislocation, provided him with new perspectives from which to witness and made it possible for him to conceive of assembling or reassembling the various parts of his life. It also extended to make him conscious of the destabilisation of the authority of his sightfulness. He fretted constantly about the unfaithful nature of his memory. The work of meditating over 'the wreck of empires' was impaired by the fact that the meditator himself considered himself to be a wreck, what with 'his lukewarm hope, his wavering faith, his limited charity, his imperfect sentiments, his insufficient thoughts, his broken heart'. For Chateaubriand, memory was a slight impression that crumbled at the touch into 'dust and ashes' (1815b: 23). It was so feeble that the 'unforgettable' ended up crushing the 'not-yet-forgotten'. After seeing the spectacle of Niagara Falls, for example, Chateaubriand realised with horror that he would never again experience either the memory of earlier waterfalls or encounter later waterfalls except in terms set at Niagara, which 'eclipses everything' (1902: vol. 1, p. 229). 'My memory constantly counterposes voyages with voyages, mountains with mountains, rivers with rivers', he explained. 'My life destroys itself' (quoted in Richard 1967: 110). This was so because past memories governed present experiences and later encounter erased previous recollections. Chateaubriand anticipated Walter Benjamin, who remarked that memory was not the sure 'instrument for exploring the past' but more resembled the 'theater' of the past, a ceaseless exchange of scenes and characters (1978: 25). In this sense, souvenirs called forth the instability of representation as forcefully as they recalled the otherness of the past.

Chateaubriand described his memoirs as an edifice, 'which I am building up out of ruins and dead bones', but the effacement of those ruins and bones would have caused the disintegration of the self (1902: vol. 1, p. 189). If the self was a wreck, its integrity would be threatened by the wreck of the wreck, the ruin of the ruin. Exile was thus constitutive of Chateaubriand's identity.

The notion of exile is central to my reading of how Chateaubriand located himself in the period of post-revolution. His nomadism corresponded well to a century that devoured biographies and autobiographies, thousands of itineraries which lost their way. One exile, Mme de Fars Fausselandry, proclaimed the nineteenth century a 'century of memoirs' already in 1830, on the first page of her own autobiography. Indeed, the French Revolution generated an outpouring of memoirs equalled only by the survivor literature of the Second World War, notes Marilyn Yalom (1995: 10–11). The spectacle of dispossession lingered well into the twentieth century. Portraying his own royalist family circle, Philippe Ariès recalled that 'the passages that were read to me were either touching statements of loyalty or declarations of the happiness to have lived back then' (1988: 12). Yet the particular misfortunes of the exiles resonated with a much wider range of readers for whom 'hybrid chronicles that track[ed] the convergence of an individual destiny with national destiny' corresponded to a general sense of displacement in what quickly became known as 'the age of revolution' (Yalom 1995: 10).

Chateaubriand thus introduces the general theme of dislocation in time and space. Exile, displacement and diaspora have become central categories in the work of anthropologists, literary critics and historians. A veritable publishing industry has grown up in response to the work of Anthony Giddens (1991) and Ulrich Beck (1993), examining the post-traditional aspect to late modernity in which individuals have been largely 'disembedded' from social milieus, such as region, religion, ethnicity and even family; find less applicable the experience that those milieus had attempted to transmit; move about among a variety of social settings; and quite self-consciously construct for themselves morally autonomous life trajectories. Arjun Appadurai refers to this condition as 'modernity at large' (1996). James Clifford, for example, cites the wonderful example of the anthropologist Amitav Ghosh. Over the course of fieldwork in small village outside Alexandria in the early 1980s, Ghosh expected to find a 'settled and restful people'. As it turns out, however, he found quite the opposite: 'The men of the village' – and it is *the men* – 'had all the busy restlessness of airline passengers in a transit lounge. Many of them had worked and travelled in the sheikdoms of the Persian Gulf, others had been in Libya and Jordan and Syria, some had been to the Yemen as soldiers, others to Saudi Arabia as pilgrims, a few had visited Europe' (Clifford 1997: 1–2). Even their parents and grandparents had travelled since last names betrayed origins in the Levant, Turkey and Nubia. Born in India, trained in England and having worked in Egypt, Ghosh himself embodies the transnational mobility he studied. In similar fashion, in *The Black Atlantic*, Paul Gilroy (1996) reveals a much travelled Atlantic Ocean where the back-and-forth movement of slaves, former slaves, labourers, writers and musicians over the nineteenth and twentieth centuries has created a distinctive modern black culture that is not African, not American, not British, not Caribbean, but insistently diasporic. The image of the transit lounge or the concept of the 'black Atlantic' indicates that place and identity are as much the result of displacement as they are of stasis. Home is not just a location from which one takes leave and to which one might return, it is a place very much in motion. In this context, Chateaubriand's shipwreck, his lives 'end to end', his travel to America and his exile in England, his suspicions about identity and duration, looks much more familiar.

There is a certain conceit to the notion that we are all exiles or the idea that dispossession provides the thematic unity to modernity. Chateaubriand as an orphan only takes us so far. There have been a series of massive re-solidifications, which have, to switch metaphors, corralled in much of Appadurai's 'modernity at large'. Both the catastrophes of the two world wars had the effect of remaking the history of the preceding decades into the sentimentalized homes that were subsequently then lost. Old photographs 'before the deluge' verge on the pastoral (Friedrich 1972). 1968 and 9/11 may have had similar effects. Modern times have created any number of containers of memory, which resist easy dissolution. In Liisa Malkki's study of Burundian (Hutu) refugees (or exiles) in Tanzania, *Purity and Exile* (1995), for example, the refugees in the town conform very much to the ways of being embroidered in the transit lounge or the black Atlantic. They worked hard to assimilate, to speak Swahili, to procure Tanzanian identity cards and to receive government benefits. They hardly talked about the murderous past in the midst of negotiations and business deals. But when Malkki went to a refugee camp, about 200km from the town, she found something completely different, an 'extravagant self-consciousness' about being Hutu (Malkki 1995: 197). In the camp, which occupied a space that had been cleared out of the forest, a dark, dense, towering mass surrounding the perimeter, hundreds of people who spoke as if with one voice which recollected an obsessive, violent history of the subordination and suffering of the Hutu people and outlined a future of redemptive return to a purified Hutu nation. They were exiles, but felt deeply attached to the idea of a Hutu home, which they lived in the mythic history they embroidered. Malkki reminds us that the town does not necessarily or logically supersede the camp, as the camp does not displace the fact of the town.

A final guide. In her acclaimed travelogue of pre-war Yugoslavia, *Black Lamb and Grey Falcon*, Rebecca West includes a scene, which suggests the strong affiliation between the experience of loss and attachment to the nation. On her visit to Sarajevo just before the start of the Second World War, West entered a graveyard. Not far from the cemetery gates she saw 'a new grave, a raw wound in the grass'. It is the likely consequence of a military skirmish because 'a young officer' stood at its edge. 'He rocked backwards in his grief, though very slightly', she observes. All at once, 'he tore open his skirted coat as if he were about to strip', but just as quickly 'his hand did up the buttons'. In this brief gesture, as the still uniformed mourner avoided giving way to private grief, West recognized the 'discipline' of the soldier who understood and accepted loss in the name of the nation. 'His hand did up the buttons', although it was tempted to cast off the uniform. 'This was a Slav, this is what it is to be a Slav', West concluded: 'He knew only that in suffering or rejoicing he must not lose that control of the body which enabled him ... to defend himself and his people' (West 1943: vol. 1, p. 390). There is no mistaking the enormous pain of the individual, who then, on second thoughts, accepted the demands of the nation and the redemptive commemoration it offered the dead. The officer chose to see the 'raw wound' as a site of national memory. This recognition is not imperative or unconditional, we know the soldier wavered and 'rocked backwards in his grief', but it is compelling because it gives collective meaning to individual suffering and restores 'discipline' and 'control'. West herself is, of course, in control of the scene, but she sets it to reveal how national history is made at the side of the grave and how gravesites replenish national history. In the face of loss, the soldier stepped back from the new grave to embrace the epic of the nation. But he did waver, as Chateaubriand repeatedly did, and he could have stripped off his uniform and entered a less fearsome, less judgemental, more easy-going world, embraced perhaps by Malkki's town, which is not cast in the terms of the cry of 'liberty or death' which echoes in the camp. There is movement in both directions, toward the grave or back into town. Each enables, and each disables.

References

Appadurai, A. 1996. *Modernity at Large: Cultural Dimensions of Globalization* (Chicago: University of Chicago Press).

Ariès, P. 1988. 'Ein Kind entdeckt die Geschichte', in *Zeit und Geschichte*, trans. P. Duttke (Frankfurt: Athäneum), pp. 9–20.

Bachelard, G. 1994. *The Poetics of Space*, trans. Maria Jolas (Boston, MA: Beacon).

Barbéris, P. 1976. *Chateaubriand: Une réaction au monde moderne* (Paris: Larousse).

Beck, U. 1993. *Die Erfindung des Politischen: Zu einer Theorie reflexiver Modernisierung* (Frankfurt: Suhrkamp Verlag).

Benjamin, W. 1978. 'A Berlin Chronicle', in *Reflections: Essays, Aphorisms: Autobiographical Writing*, ed. P. Demetz (New York: Harcourt, Brace & Jovanovich), pp. 3–60.

Chateaubriand, F. 1815a. *An Historical, Political, and Moral Essay on Revolutions, Ancient and Modern* (London: Henry Colburn).

—— 1815b. *A Letter from Rome*, trans. W.J. Walter (London: Keating, Brown, and Keating).

—— 1828. *Travels in America and Italy*, 2 vols (London: Henry Colburn).

—— 1856. *The Genius of Christianity*, trans. C.I. White (Philadelphia: J.P. Lippincott).

—— 1902. *The Memoirs of François René Vicomte de Chateaubriand*, 6 vols (London: Freemantle).

—— 1961. *The Memoirs of Chateaubriand*, selected and trans. R. Baldick (New York: Knopf).

Clifford, J. 1997. *Routes: Travel and Translation in the Late Twentieth Century*. (Cambridge, MA: Harvard University Press).

Conner, T. 1995. *Chateaubriand's* Mémoires d'outre-tombe: *A Portrait of the Artist as Exile* (New York: P. Lang).

Friedrich, O. 1972. *Before the Deluge: A Portrait of Berlin in the 1920s* (New York: Harper & Row).

Fritzsche, P. 2004. *Stranded in the Present: Modern Time and the Melancholy of History* (Cambridge, MA: Harvard University Press).

—— 2013. 'The Ruins of Modernity', in C. Lorenz and B. Bevernage (eds), *Breaking Up Time: Negotiating the Borders Between Past, Present and Future* (Göttingen: Vandenhoeck & Ruprecht), pp. 57–68.

Giddens, A. 1991. *Modernity and Self-Identity: Self and Society in the Late Modern Age* (Stanford, CA: Stanford University Press).

Gillis, J. 1996. *A World of Their Own Making: Myth, Ritual, and the Quest for Family Values* (New York: Basic Books).

Gilroy, P. 1996. *The Black Atlantic: Modernity and Double Consciousness* (Cambridge, MA: Harvard University Press).

Malkki, L. 1995. *Purity and Exile: Violence, Memory, and National Cosmology Among Hutu Refugees in Tanzania* (Chicago: University of Chicago Press).

Nylander, J. 1993. *Our Own Snug Fireside: Images of the New England Home, 1760–1860* (New York: Knopf).

Richard, J. 1967. *Paysage de Chateaubriand* (Paris: Seuil).

Rossi, P. 1984. *The Abyss of Time: The History of the Earth and the History of Nations from Hooke to Vico* (Chicago: University of Chicago Press).

Sainson, K. 2005. 'Revolutions in Time: Chateaubriand on the Antiquity of the Earth', *French Forum* 30/1(Winter): 47–63.

Vial, A. 1963. *Chateaubriand et le temps perdu: Devenir et conscience individuelle dans 'Le Mémoires de d'outre-tombe'* (Paris: Julliard).

West, R. 1943. *Black Lamb and Grey Falcon: The Record of a Journey through Yugoslavia in 1937*, 2 vols (London: Macmillan & Co.).

Yalom, M. 1995. *Blood Sisters: The French Revolution in Women's Memory* (New York: Pandora).

Dialectical Memory:
The Intersection of Individual and
Collective Memory in Hegel

Angelica Nuzzo

The Elusiveness of Dialectical Memory

Memory is dialectical. It is an act of spiritual activity and creativity as much as it is a state of passivity and dependence; it constitutes one's identity as much as it changes and distorts such identity. Memory seems to be the act of retrieving something buried in the past, but it is instead the action coming from the present that institutes something past for the first time. Although memory is a journey in the inner dimension of the self, it is also, at the same time, the highest act of alienation and exteriorization – *Er-Innerung* is, dialectically, *Ent-Äusserung*. This is the first lesson of Hegel's philosophy. But memory is also the fundamental 'methodological' function through which dialectic articulates its processes – its formal thought processes as well as the real historical processes taking place in the social, collective and institutional world of *Geist*, or 'Spirit'. This is the second lesson of Hegel's philosophy. And yet, to tease out these apparently simple claims from his complex philosophical system is no easy task. This explains, at least in part, why readers and interpreters have generally failed to appreciate the extent to which the concept of memory plays a constitutive role in Hegel's thought, surfacing at so many levels in his system and assuming so many forms – individual and collective forms, logical, phenomenological, psychological, artistic forms.

My task in this essay is to give an account of my own 'travels' across Hegel's philosophy – but also back and forth and around in a circle again – chasing the elusive but deeply pervasive idea of what I call 'dialectical memory'. To reflect on or better to recollect such an (interpretive) itinerary is ultimately to discover that, in the end, in order to travel this path, dialectical memory has always already been mobilised. The process that one recollects is the very process of dialectical recollection. Or, to put the point differently, that which one is in search of has been always already there, for that which one searches for is the very action one performs in that searching. This is the 'trick' that Hegel plays on his readers – or, at least, on those readers who are patient and perseverant enough to follow him through the complex and meandering structure of his philosophical system. But this is also, far more generally, the 'trick' of memory itself, that which betrays and reveals the properly dialectical nature of memory.

For a long-standing tradition of interpreters, Hegel is the philosopher of history – alternatively, of 'world history', of historical progress, of historical consciousness, of *Geist* as a fundamentally historical reality. On this point critics and supporters agree as on no other issue of Hegel's widely debated philosophy. Hardly, however, do interpreters recognise the central role that the concept of memory plays in the development of his thought.[1] On the other hand, given the connection between memory and history that has come so prominently to the forefront in our time and is generally taken for granted, one seems to implicitly embrace the conclusion that, if the concept of memory does in fact appear in Hegel, then it must have a connection with the idea of history and become thematic in the philosophy of history. What this connection is, however, and what is its basis is neither questioned nor examined in the literature. My contention, by contrast, is that while the concept of memory is indeed central for Hegel, its link to the issue of history is not as direct and straightforward as we are accustomed to have it in our contemporary discussion. For, the basis of such connection is, on Hegel's view, his idea of dialectical logic as the foundation of history. This is, in sum, the conclusion to which my own journey through Hegel's system has led (Nuzzo 2012). Now, by recollecting the itinerary of my past research, the present chapter shall argue, yet again but from a different perspective, in favour of the thesis that memory fulfils a variety of different functions for Hegel: it constitutes the 'subject' in its individual and collective identity, it animates the creation of works of art and religious practices, but it does not (and perhaps should not) directly itself make history (*res gestae* as well as *historia rerum gestarum*) despite its fundamental link with the historical reality of Spirit. Ultimately, I consider it worthwhile for us today to reflect on the significance of this conclusion as well as on the broader context in which Hegel's idea of dialectical memory is developed.

But why has it been historically so difficult to concentrate critical attention on the theme of memory in Hegel's philosophy? Why has dialectical memory always been so elusive? One general reason is an indirect confirmation of my main thesis. It is the assumption that the systematic connection in which memory should be sought is first and foremost Hegel's philosophy of history. However, as suggested above, this is not the case – or, at least, it is not immediately and unproblematically the case. Moreover, I see three additional interconnected reasons for the interpreters' usual blindness to the topic of memory in Hegel's philosophy. First, memory is present in Hegel's discourse even where it is not directly thematised and where the concept is not explicitly invoked. It is the interpreter's task to tease out of Hegel's argument the conceptual constellations in which the idea of memory is differentially inscribed. Second, Hegel articulates the notion of memory in a broad conceptual spectrum that both harkens back to – or re-collects, as it were – the historical tradition, Plato and Aristotle in particular, and is functional in the systematic articulation of the concept of *Geist*, whereby Spirit is successively developed in its individual subjective forms, in its collective, objective and institutional manifestations and finally in its 'absolute' productions in art, religion and philosophy. Terminologically, memory is, alternatively, *Erinnerung*, *Gedächtnis*, *Andacht*. These terms, in turn, display different uses and associations: among them the reflective and intransitive movement of interiorization – the movement of *sich erinnern* and *Innerlichkeit* – and even the activity of (subjective) thinking – *Denken* in its connection to *Gedächtnis* (Hegel 1986: vol. 10, §464; Grimm and Grimm 1862). The consequence of this terminological differentiation is that in order to follow the development of the theme of memory in Hegel, one is required to follow the inner articulation of his entire system of philosophy. This is the challenge of dialectical memory. Memory is not contained within one spiritual manifestation or within one form of consciousness only. By its very nature, memory is pervasive and contradictory. It belongs to one aspect of spiritual life and to its very opposite. It is a function of the subject's individuality but is also the collective and intersubjective dimension within which individuality first becomes what it is. While it is the individual who remembers, she remembers only on the basis of the collective memory

---

1   For discussions of Hegel's idea of *Erinnerung*, see Bloch 1962; Marcuse 1968: 73–9; Verra 1992; for
     bibliographical references, see Nuzzo 2012.

in which she participates and which she always already presupposes. Collective memory, however, is in turn and reciprocally formed through the recollecting activity of individual consciousness. It is here that we find the systematic point of connection of Hegel's three levels of Spirit's reality: subjective, objective and absolute.

Finally, the third reason for the elusiveness of dialectical memory: the highest level – or, as Hegel occasionally says, 'the most proper meaning' (1986: vol. 10. §454) – in which the activity of memory is present in his philosophy is the methodological level of the making of dialectical philosophy itself: to philosophise is to mobilise dialectical memory. There is a sense in which memory is the proper 'method' of dialectical thinking: it is the circular movement that advances and produces the new by sinking regressively back to the ground (Hegel 1986: vol. 6, p. 570). Moreover, the system of philosophy is constituted through the activity of dialectical memory as Hegel's system is the dialectical recollection of all the systems of the past – or of the history of philosophy – but also, at the same time, a radically new chapter in that history. This accounts for the fact that memory is not easily 'seen' as a topic since it is the key or the dimension in which all topics taken up by dialectical thinking are always necessarily inscribed. Memory does not provide the content that philosophical thinking assumes as its object; dialectical memory is rather the form within which philosophical thinking inscribes whatever it thinks.

In what follows, I shall present a recollecting reflection on my itinerary through Hegel's philosophical account of memory. In this itinerary I can now, retrospectively, rethink the unfolding of the work that has led to my book *Memory, History, Justice in Hegel* (2012). In engaging in this process of recollection (and self-reflection), I implicitly address the problematic points concerning the issue of dialectical memory just mentioned. The thesis concerning the complex relation – or the severed link – between history and memory is the end result of this itinerary. Moreover, this reflection will bring to the fore the link between the practice of memory and the activity of philosophising – it will present a new claim regarding the task of philosophy with regard to both its historical present and its historical past. Finally, the account of this journey will reveal, at the same time, what kind of 'companion' Hegel can be for anyone interested today in the theme of memory from a philosophical perspective. I shall begin with some remarks in this direction. They will open the way for the reflection on my path through Hegel's concept of dialectical memory.

Hegel as 'Companion': The Demands of Memory

Hegel is a demanding companion. But then, perhaps, it is not so much Hegel who is demanding as the theme of memory itself. What is at stake is the recollection of the entire history of philosophy; that is, the conviction that to do philosophy or to begin philosophising one has to go back to philosophy's own history and appropriate this history yet again, thereby fundamentally transforming it. To engage in this project, however, is precisely the first demand that Hegel makes on us. This is also the idea that we must embrace if we want to begin the journey through Hegel's philosophy. To accept this premise, however, is already to accept engagement in an exceptionally vast and demanding act of philosophical memory or recollection. This is Hegel's famous thesis that posits the identity of philosophy and the history of philosophy (Nuzzo 2003). While the activity of philosophising as rational comprehension of one's own present is deeply rooted in the contemporary world (philosophy, Hegel claims, is 'one's own time apprehended in thought'[2]), such activity

---

2   My translation.

is made possible by the historical progression that has led thinking or reason (Hegelian *Vernunft*) to the standpoint of the present (Hegel 1986: vol. 7, p. 26). It is such a historical progression that has equipped the philosopher with the rational tools that now allow her to carry on the project of presenting or translating in concepts the actuality of the world of Spirit. In other words, it is the activity of memory that connects philosophy to its present time conferring on it a properly historical dimension.

It is on the basis of this same argument that Hegel also claims that there is really nothing new in the concepts of his dialectical logic, that all the concepts developed in his logic are nothing but the appropriation of the 'categories' of traditional formal logic – the categories first introduced by Aristotle and used most recently by Kant (Hegel 1986: vol. 6, p. 243). And yet, Hegel does admit that there is something new in his logic, and this is precisely what makes it a distinctively dialectical logic. He suggests that what distinguishes dialectical logic from traditional formal logic, as well as from Kant's transcendental logic is not so much the 'content' but the 'method', that is, the way in which the content is dealt within the exposition itself, or the way in which the logical forms of the tradition (the 'content') are framed anew and presented in their immanent and necessary succession (Hegel 1986: vol. 5, p. 48). In particular, Hegel argues that while traditionally logic has treated its content as a 'dead', unmoved material and therefore has arranged it in a merely arbitrary and external way (the latest of which being the rigid and unmoved 'table of the categories' of Kant's *Critique of Pure Reason*),[3] Hegel's task is to 'infuse life in the dead limbs of logic', hence to treat those 'limbs' according to their own 'spirit',[4] showing how they can move on their own if left to their own devices. This is, on Hegel's view, the new strategy of dialectic, the new 'method' inaugurated by his logic.

From this twofold general presentation of the nature and task of Hegelian philosophy, it follows that Hegel's demand on us is accordingly also double. We must 'remember' the philosophical history of the categories he presents – lest we take them to be new inventions when they are instead historical products. But we must also be willing to let ourselves be carried on by the immanent rhythm of dialectical thinking without imposing on those categories our own way of thinking them (which is subjective, historically shaped and biased by our own standpoint). Thereby we are required to show our openness to an utterly new way of appropriating them, which is precisely the dialectical method. To be sure, the duplicity that characterises dialectic as well as its demand on us – namely, to be the recognition and repetition of an established tradition as much as its fundamental renewal – is the very duplicity of memory. While memory seems to be the retrieval and repetition of the past, it is also the fundamental alteration of it – it is that which introducing the 'new' in the process of immanent progression first constitutes the dimension of the present in its historical character.

Once we have accepted the fundamental premise of Hegel's idea of philosophising – that is, the premise that entails accepting the task of retrieving the memory of philosophy's long-standing past – Hegel, who has thereby begun appearing more as our 'companion', teaches us the virtue of patience. He appeals to the 'patience of the concept' when what is at stake is 'the work of the negative' characterising dialectic. He opposes dialectical thinking and its slow unfolding processes to the impatience of 'intellectual intuition', which instead is content only with results or with an instantaneous, all-consuming grasp (Hegel 1986: vol. 3, §19; see Lebrun 1972). Patience is the human virtue needed in order to fulfil the task posed by memory. Memory works slowly – in fact, it excavates its tunnels similarly to a patient

---

3   See Hegel's criticism in the Preface of the *Phenomenology* (Hegel 1986: vol. 3, §53).
4   Hegel (1986: vol. 5, p. 48). The claim is repeated in the introductory pages of the *Begriffslogik* (ibid., vol. 6, p. 243) and is in the preface of the *Phenomenology* (ibid., vol. 3, p. 37).

'mole'. And in this regard memory seems to work just like history. Using a Shakespearean allusion, Hegel presents history itself as the patient subterranean work of a mole (the 'old mole' that is Spirit), which, however, just as dialectic, is responsible for the big momentous conflagrations that change the course of the process (the course of logical and historical processes).[5] To be sure, patience is the virtue required from all those who set out on long travels – from all those who value the path as much as (if not more than) the results to which the path supposedly leads. Hegel sets us on the philosophical journey that is, explicitly, the *Phenomenology of Spirit* (1807) – the journey into the 'experience of consciousness' that leaves us at the threshold of the *Logic*.[6] But later on he also sets us on the systematic journey that starting in the *Logic* progresses through the 'Philosophy of Spirit' in order to return back to the *Logic* in the circular structure of the *Encyclopedia* (in its three editions: 1817, 1827, 1830).

The Journey of Memory Begins: Logical Memory and the Absent Subject

The study of Hegel's *Logic* has marked the beginning of my travels in Hegel's philosophy – the beginning of my engagement with the topic of dialectical memory even before I was aware that this was really my topic. I was coming to this study from the deeply rooted Hegelian tradition of European and in particular Italian historicism. In this tradition, the preliminary claim of Hegel's philosophy discussed above, namely the convergence of the acts of philosophising in the present and of retrieving philosophy's own historical past, was an easily accepted tenet. In this tradition, the historical memory of the past is, albeit often unconsciously, a ready available and indeed a much used tool in the philosopher's arsenal. My project was a study of the 'method' of Hegel's *Logic*. At stake at the most general level was an investigation into the question of the status of Hegel's dialectical logic: What is Hegel's logic properly *about*? What kind of theory is it, given the striking difference that separates his dialectical logic from the logic of the tradition? For, to the dismay of so many generations of interpreters, Hegel's *Logic* poses peculiar difficulties as a logic since it encompasses traditional categories such as 'substance', 'cause', 'necessity' and so on, as well as metaphysical concepts such as 'being', 'essence', the 'absolute' and so on, but it also takes on concepts that do not seem to have any legitimate place in a logic – notions such as 'measure', 'life', 'mechanism', 'chemism'. Hence my chief question: What kind of theory is Hegel's *Logic*? And assuming that the 'method' plays a fundamental role in making it the logic that it is: How does it proceed in its presentation of the logical forms; that is, what is its immanent method? In setting out in this investigation, I thought I was the farthest possible from the theme of memory. I had no idea I was deeply involved in it already from the outset.

Hegel describes the process of the *Logic* as the movement of descent in the 'realm of shadows' of pure thinking. This is, to be sure, a strange otherworldly journey in several respects. For one thing, at stake in the logical 'realm' are those 'abstractions' – or the 'shadows', as it were – that are the logical categories: pure, disembodied forms of thinking that maintain, however, a virtual link to the absent content which in reality corresponds to them – just like the shadow, in its being a shadow, maintains a link to the object that casts it. Hegel claims, 'the system of logic is the realm of shadows, the world of the simple

---

5   Hegel appeals famously to the ghost of Hamlet's father, the 'old mole' that is spirit – a reference taken up later on by Marx in the *Eighteenth Brumaire of Louis Bonaparte* (Hegel 1986, vol. 18, 454; Marx 1960: 196).

6   'Science of the Experience of Consciousness' is the subtitle of the 1807 work.

essences, free from all sensible concretion' (Hegel 1986: vol. 5, p. 55). Thinking's engagement with these logical shadows is an apparently estranging business far removed from sensible intuition, feeling and the common representation of things. And yet, it is through the discipline learned by dwelling among these shadows that thinking conquers its first sense of freedom and independence and gains the capacity of capturing the real in the dimension of truth, namely, the capacity of recognising rationality at work in it. It is immediately striking how the logical process described in this way comes close to being an account of the process of memory and reminiscence – albeit a disembodied and purely 'logical' memory, a memory still operating outside of time and space (and yet, as I will soon learn, this is precisely the nature of memory: it is memory itself that first institutes 'its own time and its own space' (Hegel 1986: vol. 10, §452). Memory does not presuppose them). Memory concerns virtual 'objects' – or properly 'shadows' – which it then makes 'real'. Memory is *Er-Innerung* – the process of 'interiorisation' whereby thinking (or Spirit) descends deeper into itself. In this interiority, memory 'finds' those estranging shadows, which it then projects out of itself, making of them real objects and real events taking place in the past. Thus, truly, it is memory itself that first makes those shadows real, positing them in the concreteness of a newly invented exteriority constituted by a subjective time and space. Interiorisation, dialectically produces the highest form of alienation or exteriorisation – *Ent-Äusserung*. This polarity characterises the journey into the 'realm of shadows' – both the journey of memory and that of pure logical thinking. Finally, the logical process advancing through the 'realm of shadows' may recall – and indeed may recollect – the Platonic itinerary back into the cave (although, perhaps, moving in the opposite direction: for Hegel it is the ideas or the logical forms taken in their truth, not the notions of common sense that display the reality of shadows).

The second peculiarity we encounter in Hegel's idea of the *Logic* as the itinerary through the realm of shadows is that this is a journey that, paradoxically, lacks the subject who journeys. Here we meet the crucial difference between the process of the *Logic* and that of the *Phenomenology*. The *Phenomenology* is the 'science of the experience of consciousness'. It is the experiential process that has consciousness as its 'subject' (and as its 'object' as well). The *Logic*, by contrast, is the pure immanent process that first and only in its conclusion institutes thinking as 'subjective' thinking. At the beginning of the *Logic*, however, there is no presupposed, substantial or psychological subject doing the thinking that is developed in this work through the succession of logical categories. Rather, Hegel claims that thinking is here properly 'objective thinking' – it is the rationality immanent in all things insofar as they posses 'truth'. It is not an activity inhering in an independently given 'subject' (Hegel 1986: vol. 10, §25). Hegel's suggestion is that it is only by dwelling in the disembodied and purely abstract realm of shadows that the activity of 'objective' thinking emerges as a properly 'subjective' thinking. It is only under the condition of enduring the journey through the realm of shadows that a thinking subject or thinking as a subject first emerges. Yet, before the end of the *Logic* there is no 'subject' at all – neither a psychological 'I think', nor an 'I think' in the sense of Kant's transcendental unity of apperception, nor a metaphysical *res cogitans* such as the Cartesian meditator, 'I think, I am', nor a phenomenological subject such as the experiencing consciousness of Hegel's own early work.[7] In other words, the logic shows, with a dialectical inversion, that the story precedes the subject whose story it is. While the story develops on its own, that is, immanently, without presupposing a subject whose story it is, once the story reaches the end it reveals who is the subject—the subject who can now claim the story as her own.

---

7   See Hegel 1986: vol. 5, p. 61.

It is at this point of my investigation that I realised what I was truly dealing with, that I became aware of what my topic really was. What we have here, I understood, is the process of memory once memory is taken as a pure activity that works on its own, without depending – metaphysically, psychologically, phenomenologically – on a presupposed and pre-constituted 'subject' who is exercising the activity and claiming such activity as her own. The suggestion of Hegel's logic is that memory is, at the most original level, an 'objective' and 'impersonal' activity. At this level, memory may be considered the natural organic process of evolution (the memory of genes) as much as the spiritual activity of conscious individuals and collectives. This, I soon realised, is an incredibly interesting and fruitful perspective allowing for an unprecedented insight into the nature – in fact, the dialectical nature – of memory. What is the process of memory – the very activity of remembering and recollecting – when the 'subject' who remembers is not presupposed as the condition of such activity but is seen instead as the very result, or end-product, of such an activity? What is the structure of memory when the 'subject' in its determinate existence, concrete constitution and authoritative position is not taken for granted? How does the problem change when the process of recollection is not made dependent, as we usually assume it to be, on the presupposed identity of the subject who recollects but it is instead the 'subject' who is constituted in its identity by the very activity of memory thereby depending on it? As Hegel shows in the 'Psychology' of the 'Philosophy of Subjective Spirit', for example, the individual in her identity is itself the result and the product of spiritual recollection – *Erinnerung* (Nuzzo 2012: 82–102; Hegel 1986: vol. 10, §§452–4). In other words, the suggestion is that it is memory that first makes us who we are, it is not who we are that determines the type of memories we have. Now, conceiving of memory in this way, free from its inhering on a presupposed subject, opens up the possibility of conceiving of different types of 'subjects' that are first constituted and determined by such activity – the individual, to be sure, but also the collective, social subject, political institutions, history itself and works of art are among a few examples. The point is that these entities count indeed as 'subjects' that can perform the activity of recollecting because they are, in turn, first constituted by the more original – 'impersonal' and 'objective' – activity of recollecting in which logical rationality is actualized in the world.

Thus, in the perspective disclosed by Hegel's dialectical logic, memory is the process that progressively and immanently weaves together the story that, once it is remembered or re-collected as a 'story' first institutes the subject who can then claim the story as her own. On this account, the subject does not pre-exist her story but is instead directly identical with the story itself, once this story is appropriated – or re-collected, as it were. Hegel's dialectical logic shows that in fact the relation between memory and the subject who remembers is the reverse of what common sense assumes. Hegel's logic, I realized at this point, is the logic of dialectical memory. This answer to my initial questions – what is the status of Hegel's logic, what kind of theory does this logic provide and what is its 'method' – was surprising. But then also not that surprising: just as the inversion (the journey makes the subject who journeys and not vice versa) reveals, in fact, the dialectical nature of pure logical thinking, it also reveals the fundamentally dialectical nature of memory, its inner, objective logic. The topic of memory was now at the centre of my investigation. This is, to be sure, a peculiar kind of memory: it is memory that works under the most estranging conditions. Not only is dialectical memory a process of recollection without a subject who recollects. Dialectical memory (and the thought process developed in the *Logic*) is also memory working without anything pre-existing and presupposed to be remembered. Logically, memory works without a presupposed subject as much as without an intentional object. It is rather the working of memory that first institutes both the recollecting subject and the recollected object. It is only by the act of remembering that the subject who remembers is produced. It is only by the act of remembering that the object, which is remembered, first arises – neither of them was there before the activity of memory took place. Memory is the radical creation of the new: it creates the subject in its – individual as well as collective – identity; it creates the object as an – individually and socially – appropriated (object of) memory. This is, however, an act of creation that immediately revokes and effaces itself, presenting itself under the 'semblance' (*Schein*) of repetition, as being the retrieval of something already existing by someone already existing (Hegel 1986: vol. 10, §445). This is the complex 'logic' of memory, the way in which dialectical memory presents itself to common sense.

The Memory of Spirit: The Intersection of Individual and Collective Memory

The importance of this dialectical concept of memory is far-reaching. In particular, the dialectical reversal – whereby memory seems to be the act of a presupposed subject searching for an intentional existing object while it is, instead, the very activity that first posits both the subject and the object for what they are – this reversal is at the heart of the relation between 'individual memory' and 'collective memory'. This is the relation that Hegel explores throughout his 'Philosophy of Spirit'. While I had already dedicated quite a bit of work to this topic before coming to the logic project, only now I could see how the two issues (logical and spiritual memory) were closely related. It was now clear to me that I had been working on the same topic of memory all along. And yet, the fact of approaching the issue of memory in the 'Philosophy of Spirit' coming from the *Logic*, allowed me to frame the relation between the individual and collective memory of spirit in a new perspective. *Geist*, which is a fundamentally historical and dynamic reality, is first and foremost a product of logical memory. This is the meaning of Hegel's claim that the *Logic* is the first sphere of the system and the foundation of his 'real' philosophy (or *Realphilosophie* comprising the 'Philosophy of Nature' and the 'Philosophy of Spirit').

Hegel articulates the complex and manifold reality of spirit across three main systematic spheres. *Geist* is first caught in its 'subjective' reality whereby it manifests the successive anthropological, phenomenological and psychological constitution of its individual identity. Directly thematised here for the first time, memory – *Erinnerung* and *Gedächtnis* – plays a crucial role in the transition that leads 'theoretical intelligence' to the incipient still subjective freedom of 'practical' spirit. The latter, in turn, prepares the systematic transition to the sphere of 'objective' spirit. It is at this more advanced level that *Geist* is manifested in the social and political institutions that ultimately constitute its collective identity in the nation state. On Hegel's view, this is the distinctive subject or the main actor of world history. Finally, on the basis of the development of world history, Hegel introduces the concluding forms of 'absolute' spirit: art, religion and philosophy. These spiritual productions are systematically positioned beyond world history and yet, in actuality, they are always and necessarily within history, within the collective reality of objective spirit.

The question that I needed to examine at this point is: At which of these successive systematic levels does dialectical memory play a role for Hegel? In examining this question it became very clear to me that while Hegel explicitly thematises 'memory' as *Erinnerung* and *Gedächtnis* in the 'Psychology' of the 'Philosophy of Subjective Spirit', the concept plays a constitutive role throughout the development of *Geist* in all three systematic spheres. This is the point so easily and so generally overseen by the interpreters. The analysis of the notion of *Erinnerung* in the 'Psychology' already led me to ascertain that next to the properly 'psychological' notion of recollection Hegel mobilises the 'methodological' – or indeed, logical – function of memory which is responsible for carrying on the development of 'theoretical spirit' (Nuzzo 2012: 82–102). The general idea here is that spirit constitutes its individual reality and subjective identity as it 'recollects' itself from its interiority. Thereby, however, spirit makes itself actual by coming out of such interiority in the opposite movement of 'exteriorisation'. Again, *Er-Innerung* or the interiorisation of memory is, at the same time, *Ent-Äusserung* or memory's movement of exteriorisation. Throughout this process spirit begins to gain a sense of its freedom. As spirit makes itself objective in the world, a world that is progressively formed in its institutional and historical reality, and as spirit's task is to form an identity that is, this time, a collective identity, we may expect memory to play a role analogous to the one encountered within subjective spirit, namely, to repeat for the collective subject what it was doing for the individual, personal subject. This, however, is not the case.

At this point the lesson of the *Logic* proves itself momentous. The idea that the logical process of dialectical memory is the foundation of the development of spirit's forms led me to the insight into the reversal that structures the relation between the individual and the collective memory of spirit. To be sure, this is a notion that Hegel had already explored in the early *Phenomenology of Spirit* (Nuzzo 2012: 20–49). Now, if memory is the process and dialectical activity that constitutes spirit's identity as a 'subject', and if we apply, yet again, the dialectical reversal implicit in the workings of memory, then we reach the conclusion that the collective memory and consequently the collective reality and identity of spirit is truly the foundation of spirit's individual and subjective identity. In other words, memory inverts the systematic relation between subjective and objective spirit. What the individual truly is (for Hegel: in her 'truth' and 'actuality'), she is on the basis of her collective participation in the social and political structures of spirit's objective world. Hence, what one as individual remembers, and what thereby constitutes her personal memories and identity is originally formed, shaped and determined by the collective memory of the social whole to which she belongs as an active member. Thus, what common sense posits as the first is, in truth, the last. Our personal memories are made possible only by the collective memory in which all our spiritual, conscious and unconscious activities are always already inscribed.

At this point in my investigation, an examination of Maurice Halbwachs' anti-psychologistic and anti-individualistic notion of *mémoire collective* proved crucial (Halbwachs 1925, 1950). I could now see the Hegelian root of the concept of 'collective memory' – a concept that has become so current in the contemporary discussion as to lose the awareness of its distinctive philosophical origin. Indeed Halbwachs is a necessary historical reference when the issue of collective memory is invoked. In his seminal *Les Cadres sociaux de la mémoire* (1925) and then in the posthumous *La Mémoire collective* (1950), contrasting the view that only individuals can remember and that collective memory can be at the most only a metaphor of dubious validity, Halbwachs famously claimed that individual memory depends on and is structured according to the social frameworks in which all individual activity is inscribed. 'Collective memory' is a social reality transmitted and sustained by the conscious efforts and institutions of the group. It is only to the extent that the individual is placed within a social context that she is able to remember. Significantly, this holds true not only for communal and communally shared contents but even – and in the first place – for utterly personal and apparently private events. Individuality is itself the product of 'collective memory' and cannot exist or have meaning without a social framework. If memory is crucial to personal identity, personal identity is necessarily built out of references to and interactions with social objects, institutions and events. Thus memory itself is, in the first instance, a collective activity and a collectively constituted endeavour. But even self-consciousness, on this view, is never entirely (and it is not originally) personal but rather social.

This view is carried a step forward by historian Amos Funkenstein. Establishing an intriguing connection with Hegel – a connection that I extensively explore in *Memory, History, Justice in Hegel* (2012) – Funkenstein claims that 'collective consciousness' presupposes 'collective memory'. He sees this position expressed in a paradigmatic way in Hegel's view of history. 'Collective consciousness presumes collective memory', claims Funkenstein, 'as without it there is no law and justice, no political structure, and no collective objectives' (1989: 5). Collective memory is the condition for the constitution of the (collective) agent of history. And it is, on Halbwachs' premises, the condition for the constitution of individual personal memory.

Working within a different disciplinary and historical constellation this discussion reproduces Hegel's account of the relation between the individual memory of subjective spirit and the collective memory operating within the different institutions of objective spirit. The latter is what the *Phenomeology* already indicated as the intersubjective spiritual 'we', a product, significantly, of the dialectical process of 'recognition' whereby the 'I' and the 'we' are mutually constituted: spirit is 'the *I* that is *we* and the *we* that is *I*' (Hegel 1986: vol. 3, §177). However, the relevant point to my present purposes is that this crucial thesis, so successful in Hegel's aftermath, is in turn the consequence of Hegel's idea of dialectical memory as an activity or a process that on the basis of its immanent logic produces that on which it seems to depend. Memory is the recollecting process that first institutes both its subject and its object.

Conclusion

I want to conclude with a brief remark on the challenge and the lesson that we find in Hegel's account of dialectical memory. So far, I have dwelt for the most part on the logical aspect of this concept, which may have been frustrating for many readers, who coming from the contemporary discussion of the issue of memory (in history, sociology, political science and so on) are used to and hence expect much more 'concrete' topics to be at issue. Yet, I believe that the dialectical logic of memory is precisely the main lesson that the contemporary reader should learn to patiently appreciate in Hegel. I am convinced that the power of this lesson consists in its 'applicability' to many constellations in which the discussion currently flows. As for my own itinerary, I can point to two directions in which my work on the logic of memory has been leading. On the one hand I have begun construing the 'intersection' of individual and collective memory as the work of what, for Hegel, are the forms of absolute spirit. I have concentrated my attention in particular on art. The artwork is the individual and at the same time collective expression of spirit's own historical memory (Nuzzo 2012: 136–64). In the artwork we find crystallised what Pierre Nora has called *lieux de mémoire*. On the other hand, I have ascertained the fruitfulness of Hegel's perspective in the possibility of connecting the issue of collective memory dialectically construed with the contemporary discussion on 'social epistemology' (Nuzzo 2013). Inserting Hegel for the first time into this debate, I have claimed that he provides us with a 'dialectical' social epistemology where truth is indeed the fundamental aim of science and yet it is a historical and collective construction of spirit.

References

Bloch, E. 1962. 'Hegel und die Anamnesis', *Hegel Studien* 1: 167–81.

Funkenstein, A. 1989. 'Collective Memory and Historical Consciousness', *History and Memory* 1/1: 5–26.

Grimm, J., and W. Grimm. 1862. *Deutsches Wörterbuch* (Leipzig: Hirzel).

Halbwachs, M. 1925. *Les Cadres sociaux de la mémoire* (Paris: Alcan).

— — 1950. *La Mémoire collective* (Paris: Presses Universitaires de France).

Hegel, G.W.F. 1986. *Werke*, 20 vols, ed. E. Moldenhauer and H.M. Michel (Frankfurt: Suhrkamp Verlag).

Lebrun, G. 1972. *La Patience du concept: Essai sur le discours hégélien* (Paris: Gallimard).

Marcuse, H. 1968. *Hegels Ontologie und die Theorie der Geschichtlichkeit* (Frankfurt: Klostermann).

Marx, K. 1960. *Eighteenth Brumaire of Louis Bonaparte*, Werke 8 (Berlin: Dietz Verlag).

Nuzzo, A. 2003. 'Hegel's Method for a History of Philosophy: The Berlin Introductions to the Lectures on the History of Philosophy (1819–1831)', in D. Duquette (ed.), *Hegel's History of Philosophy: New Interpretations* (Albany: SUNY Press), pp. 19–34.

— — 2012. *Memory, History, Justice in Hegel* (London: Palgrave Macmillan).

— — 2013. 'The Social Dimension of Dialectical Truth: Hegel's Idea of Objective Spirit', *Social Epistemology Review and Reply Collective* 2/8: 10–25.

Verra, V. 1992. *Letture hegeliane: Idea, natura e storia* (Bologna: Il Mulino).

Spectral Phenomenology: Derrida, Heidegger and the Problem of the Ancestral

Hans Ruin

Introduction

At the beginning of his essay *Specters of Marx*, published in 1993, Jacques Derrida recalls how the existential imperative to live also implies an imperative to address death (Derrida 1994: xvii). Learning to live is learning to exist between life and death, in the existential stretch constituted by one's own life span, from not yet being born to no longer existing. But it is also to learn to live in relation to those no longer there. In order to describe this situation, this existential in-between, Derrida here suggests that we think about it in terms of 'the phantom' (*le fantôme*). It is a category connected to ghosts, spectres and spirits and the different forms of beings that occupy this ontological threshold. To learn to live would then partly amount to learning to live with and among spectres, as also – as he writes – a 'politics of memory, of inheritance and of generations' (ibid. xviii). It is a politics, but perhaps even more an ethics, since it concerns how we comport ourselves in relation to those who are no longer there. There is a peculiar kind of responsibility for and toward the deceased, which marks and constitutes the living in their self-understanding. Or perhaps we should speak of it as responsiveness, rather than responsibility, since the latter could be taken to imply that we already know what our obligations are. The point here is precisely that there is no certainty on this ground. We do not know what we owe the dead – nor what they owe us.

For Derrida the 'spectral' designates the indeterminate space between the dead and the living, but also a distance or difference within time itself, as that which is never fully itself, but always divided, carrying a past and anticipating a future. In a footnote to the essay he also indicates the possibility of what he calls a 'phenomenology of spectrality', that should be carried out, as he writes, 'with good Husserlian logic, cutting out a limited, relative field within a regional discipline' and that should explore systematically the 'original experience of haunting' (Derrida 1994: 237). But in the end, it is more than just a regional ontology that is at stake here. The problem of the 'spectral' points to the fundamental phenomenological theme of ideality and the so-called intentional object (the *noema*). The latter does not belong to the world nor to the mind but to a third, indeterminate space of meaning. With such a radicalisation of the phenomenological enterprise, Derrida writes 'the possibility of the other and of mourning' would be written into the very phenomenality of the phenomenon (ibid. 238). In the book on Marx all of this remains a tentative anticipation of something yet to be developed. Husserl is mentioned in the footnote, and Heidegger is recalled only in passing. As it stands the book leaves open the question how and to what extent the question of the spectral is possible to develop more closely in phenomenological terms.

Partly as a direct consequence of Derrida's book, the last two decades have witnessed a literal invasion of 'ghosts', 'revenants' and 'hauntings in cultural theory'.[1] Yet, throughout this upsurge of 'hauntological' discourse there has been no real attempt to develop further Derrida's own idea of a 'phenomenology of the spectral'. It is in response to this unfulfilled promise that I will here try to take the question back again to Heidegger and his existential analytic, in order to probe the extent to which we can still give a more systematic meaning to the phenomenon of the spectral, by expounding, as a partly hidden stratum within his ontological project, the attempt to account for the space in-between the dead and the living as a space of survival and visitation but also of tradition, memory and of history.

In my own work on the theory of history and historicity from a Heideggerian perspective, a concern has been to try to understand and articulate this peculiar ontology of being-with-the-dead. Through Derrida's analysis of 'spectrality', 'hauntology' and the 'ghostly', a trajectory is opened up that, I think, permits us to read Heidegger's account of historicity as in fact dealing with the ethical and political relation to the dead and thus with the general question of what I also prefer to speak of as 'the ancestral'. Here memory and historical consciousness are articulated in terms of standing under an obligation and of being summoned by the past, rather than holding it in our hand and under our gaze. In what follows I will move from Derrida and the problem of history as spectrality back to Heidegger's existential analytics and then return again to outline the deeper significance of thinking through the problem of ancestrality as a task for memory studies and theory of history, thus tracing also what has been a long inner dialogue in my own work. I will concentrate on two sections of *Being and Time* that in different ways approach the being of the dead as this is lived and experienced in mourning and the formation of historical consciousness. Before doing so, however, I want to outline in more general terms what is at stake when approaching something like the phenomenology of the spectral.

I

In his book Derrida develops a beautiful and meandering analysis that ties his reading of Marx to an interpretation of Shakespeare's *Hamlet*. The ghost of the father calling for revenge and restitution is linked to a ghost that in the form of Communism moves through Europe, as stated in the *Communist Manifesto*, but also to the different aspirations that run through the work of Marx, to exorcise ghosts and superstitions. The text circles around the idea that justice is somehow always tied to a relation to the dead, and that it thereby works according to what we could call a 'spectral logic'. Justice, the claim of justice, is something that speaks to us from the past, with a testimony of how 'time is out of joint', demanding that it be resurrected and reinstated for a future to come. But even though the call for justice and the inner necessity to work towards its fulfilment is a future-directed aspiration, its orientation issues from the past, not an abstract past, but from a demand of those no longer there.

---

1   The examples could be multiplied, but for an excellent survey of the thematic and the literature, see Davis 2007, which brings together the work of Derrida and the French psychoanalysts Nicolas Abraham and Maria Torok with analyses of contemporary popular cultural interest in ghosts, vampires and zombies. For a Marxist approach, with contributions from some of the leading neo-Marxist thinkers such as Jameson, Eagleton and Negri, see Sprinker 2008.

As Derrida himself notes, the question of 'ghosts' and 'spectres' is not what traditional 'scholars' are expected to deal with. Their ethos is defined rather by the prerogative precisely to separate the real from the phantastic or phantasmatic (1994: 12). But, as his book demonstrates in a convincing way, the compulsive rejection of the ghostlike, of revenants, spirits and other questionable apparitions, tends to recoil against science itself for a convinced rationalist like Marx and not just in his metaphors, as in the 'ghost' (*Gespenst*) of Communism haunting Europe at the outset of the *Communist Manifesto*. In a concluding passage, Derrida quotes *Hamlet* and the passage where Marcellus, at the sight of the ghost of Hamlet's father, calls out to Horatio: 'Thou art a scholar, speak to it Horatio.' Speak to the dead, listen to the dead, let the voices of the dead be heard and resonate, and let life be touched by that non-life which has already from the beginning addressed it: thus one could tentatively summarize its credo and its ethos.

This appeal from Marcellus to a 'scholarly' ability to speak with the dead in the fictional world of Shakespeare could also be seen to touch a basic dimension of what we normally, if yet inadvertently, take to be central to our scholarly identity as historians and interpreters of past intellectual achievements, namely precisely an ability to speak with, about, to, for and from the perspective of the dead. Much work in the humanities – or the 'spiritual sciences', *Geisteswissenschaften*, as they are called in German – is concerned with this spiritual telecommunication with those no longer there. Much of what we are doing in all our conferences and lecture rooms all over the globe amounts to comparing our understanding of those no longer with us, in order to do them justice, to speak for them against others who claim to speak for them as well, to enact them, to bring them back to life, to celebrate their birthdays, to give of our life blood to let them live and speak again. The art of interpretation is presumably the ability to somehow communicate with those no longer present, through the medium of their remains. It is, as Dilthey and hermeneutics once taught, the ability to somehow relive in oneself the life of the other. In this way we can see how Derrida with his speculative terminology also brings out an implicit thematic and logic in the whole historicist culture, the compulsion and the ambition, to permit the dead to speak and to live on.

The task of a spectral phenomenology thus also points to the more general question of understanding the very emergence and maintenance of something like 'tradition' or 'cultural memory'. As Derrida says in a passage quoted earlier, the spectral concerns in the end also a 'politics of memory, of inheritance, and of generations'. Cultural memory studies is concerned with the formation and maintenance of tradition, as precisely a politics, ethics and technics of memory. Jan Assmann speaks of it as the study of memory with a focus on the function of how individual and collective cultural continuity is shaped. For him it is a question of studying the 'connective structures' whereby a culture maintains itself over time through practices of 'repetition' (Assmann 2011: 2). Assmann does not address this topic explicitly in terms of the ghostly or the revenant. Yet, at the heart of the 'connective structures' explored by cultural memory studies is the passage from the dead to the living in the forms of institutionalised memory practices, of rituals and technologies that can be said to work according to a logic of the revenant. The connective structures are practices through which the dead are contained and kept 'alive' through their remains and thus are permitted to return and revisit the living under restricted circumstances, to speak again as it were, including philosophy conferences devoted to the 'actuality' of this or that personage from the great columbarium of thought.

Through archives, legal documents, constitutions, dogma, doctrine and through art in general, we continue to live and to experience the life of those once living. But as Derrida also indicates, this is always also a contested space. What the dead demand from us, what we owe them, in terms of living their hopes and phantasies, often border on the question

✗ of justice, not just of doing justice to them, but of being just as such. From this brief survey of our problem it is possible to sense how the topic of a 'spectral phenomenology' also touches deep chords in contemporary concerns in cultural memory studies and its attempts to understand tradition and collective memory as transmissions of inheritance, ultimately pointing to questions of justice and the formation of an ethical orientation in the present.

II

A few years after the book on Marx, Derrida returned to the theme of death and revenants again in the book entitled simply *Apories*, a series of mediations on death, partly motivated by a reading of Philipe Ariès monumental *L'Homme devant la mort*. Here he does devote an explicit critical analysis to Heidegger and the existential analysis of death, concluding that 'the existential analytic does not want to have anything to do with the revenant and with grief' (Derrida 1993: 60). The remarks echo the critical analysis of Heidegger's analysis of death that Levinas had developed in his last lecture course in the mid-seventies (Levinas 1993). In these lectures he criticises Heidegger precisely for reducing the role and meaning of the death of the other in favour of the problem of personal finitude.

Both Levinas and Derrida point to a lacuna, and maybe even a structural limit, in Heidegger's articulation of death. Still it should be noted that it was from the perspective of his existential analytic that the phenomenological question of death and finitude was initially posed in such a way as so as to make their critical interventions possible. Also when it comes to the problem of 'spectrality' and the presumed possibility of giving it a more precise phenomenological meaning, I think that it is necessary to return to the Heideggerian analysis of mortality, not in order to simply rehearse and affirm it, but to activate its analyses against the background of Derrida's work and critical questions.[2]

The problem of the dead other is not a central theme in *Being and Time*. Where it surfaces, it is more as a fringe topic. Still the deeper reverberations of it reach the heart of Heidegger's project in its attempt to think from within the experience of the historicity of thought. The first time where the dead other makes its appearance in the existential analytic is in a discussion of the finitude or mortality of human existence or *Dasein* and its being-toward-death in the first chapter of the second part of the book. Later in the book when the dead other is recalled again (this time more implicitly) it is precisely in conjunction with a discussion of history and historicity, where the issue is to determine how *Dasein* exists historically, so as to make history in the common sense possible.

The overall argument of *Being and Time* rests on the premise that even though human existence, *Dasein*, is closest to itself simply by being itself, it is nevertheless estranged from itself and will tend to misrepresent its own being when it conceptualises its own mode of being. It is for this reason that Heidegger will also argue that the constructive enterprise of developing an existential analysis must run parallel to a destructive dismantling of the tradition of metaphysics and of inherited theories of human being and existence. In short, a genuine, authentic conceptual grasp is possible only by turning away from the tendency to represent ourselves from the viewpoint and with the help of that which is not ourselves

---

2 My dissertation from 1994 was devoted to an in-depth survey and analysis of the emergence, meaning and development of the topic of 'historicity' (*Geschichtlichkeit*) in Heidegger's works. Already then it was clear to me that the question of the dead other marked some kind of inner limit within Heidegger's thinking, and I even signalled it out as a possible theme for further study, unaware at that point of the analyses of Levinas and Derrida that had been published some years before its completion. See Ruin 1994: 131.

and thus to move beyond the alienated and alienating objectification of existence into a comprehension of our being on the basis of concepts elicited from existence itself as lived in and through its possibility.

Throughout the different stations of the book, a similar argument is repeated again and again, whereby objectified and objectifying misconceptions of existence are countered with new concepts that supposedly permit *Dasein* to grasp itself more 'authentically'. Human existence tends to represent itself through alienating categories, elicited from types of non-human being. It is as a consequence of this self-alienating tendency that the constructive attempt to forge a more adequate existential-ontological terminology must run parallel with a 'destruction' of the history of metaphysics and inherited modes of designating life. A more genuine or 'authentic' grasping of human existentiality requires that *Dasein* is able to tear itself lose from this tendency of 'falling prey' to inherited modes of discourse. *Being and Time* is an attempt to secure such a more appropriate terminology for the exploration of the being and movement of life.

One and the same argument is thus rehearsed in new constellations, according to which objectified and objectifying conceptions of existence are contrasted with new concepts through which *Dasein* can supposedly grasp itself in a more 'authentic' way. Already at the outset of the book, Heidegger differentiates what is simply given as a present object (*Vorhanden*) as ontologically primary by showing how it presupposes the primordial givenness of meaningful and useful things to hand (*Zuhandenheit*). In a similar way objective physical space is reinterpreted as in fact secondary to lived spatial structures where *Dasein* orients itself in de-distancing (*Entfernung*) and directionality (*Ausrichten*), furthermore he shows how the experience of being an 'ego' rests on a structure of 'self' and of 'being-with'. Perhaps most importantly he challenges the conventional ways of designating and understanding time as the objective framework of events. In its place he develops the account of existential temporality (*Zeitlichkeit*), as the most fundamental or primordial level of meaning-formation and thus also as the theoretical peak of the book.

The persistent challenge throughout the book is thus to conceptualise life from the perspective of its potentiality rather than through the categories of its objective being. And nowhere is this challenge more acute than in the sections that explicitly try to think the nature of finitude and mortality (Heidegger 2007: §§47–53). Here the issue at stake is to think human existence or *Dasein* as a whole. After having determined its essence in the first part of the book as being-in-the-world and as care, Heidegger opens the question again of how this presumed totality could be conceptually grasped and articulated. Existence is delimited by birth and death, thus constituting what appears as a finite stretch of life. In order to really think its totality, however, we cannot simply rest with an understanding of it as a life-process, delimited by death, as if death were somehow outside life or simply its outer limit. For death belongs to life, and life is a being-toward-death permanently open to the possibility of its non-possibility. But what could a proper and supposedly authentic conceptual mastery of death then amount to? We think that we know death, simply because we experience it all around us. But what we experience is in fact the death of the other, not death as our death or as my death. We should not take the medical, biological and social 'fact of death' for granted as our source of knowledge and reflection for understanding mortality. For death, as he says, is ultimately a phenomenon of 'Dasein as possibility' (ibid. 250[3]). Somehow death should be grasped and conceptualised as a phenomenon of life, from the viewpoint, as it were, of the living, indeed as the 'possibility of im-possibility' as his definition reads (ibid. 262).

---

3   All references to *Being and Time* are to the original German pagination (Heidegger 2006), which is given in the margin of the English translation (Heidegger 2007).

In order for this analysis to be carried out it still needs first to address the experience of the dying and dead other, as its phenomenal negative correlate and contrast. This takes places in §47, which is of particular importance here, since it marks the only place in Heidegger's work that provides us with a rudimentary phenomenology of the being of the dead other and therefore indirectly with the precursor to what Derrida will speak of as the 'spectral', despite his voiced criticism quoted above that Heidegger fails to think the revenant.

When it has reached its completion (*Gänze*), the other *Dasein* becomes a no-longer-being-in-the-world. This is the first phenomenal aspect of its being as dead. But how should we understand its leaving the world? In one sense it is no longer here, but in another sense it is here, but now as the apparent thing of a being no-longer-alive. In the dying of others, Heidegger writes, a 'remarkable' phenomenon occurs, the sudden transition or reversal (*Umschlag*) of *Dasein*, or (as he adds in a parenthesis) of *life* – to a 'no-longer' *Dasein*. It is as if the end of *Dasein* were suddenly the beginning of another type of being or entity, now in the order of a purely present entity, namely as corpse. But, he says – and this is especially important here – this conventional description of what takes place at the moment of death does not really capture the phenomenal character of this event. More precisely it fails to capture the sense in which this being, as he says, 'is still remaining' (*nochverbleibende*) and as such not really represented by the purely corporeal. It is 'more' than lifeless (*leblose*), instead it is something 'unliving' *Unlebendiges*. As such it can be the object of multiple concerns, he writes, precisely as in funeral rites and cults. The mourners are still with the other, in the mode of a care that is characteristic of being-with others and not the kind of care we devote to objects. A dead body is not taken care of in the same way that we take care of artefacts. We continue to be with them, in a world that continues to give meaning and significance to our peculiar mode of being with those no longer there, even though they have, as it were, left it behind (*zurückgelassen*).

These reflections basically sum up what Heidegger has to say in this particular part of the book concerning the dead other. As already stated, the primary purpose of the analysis is not to provide a separate phenomenology of the deceased but rather to serve as an introduction to the taking up of the question of the nature of mortality from a new angle. Still, his analysis brings us up against the irreducible phenomenon of what could be called precisely spectral existence, which here makes its appearance in the existential analytic under a different name. The dead are not only possible objects of concern for *Dasein*. They have a peculiar mode of being, what we can speak of as the 'still-remaining' and 'un-living'. Yet, the further implication of this mode of being is not treated at this stage of the existential analytic. What more could we then say about this mode of being, this form of presence of the no longer?

In order to pursue this question, I will now turn now to another section in the book where the dead other appears from a different angle and with far reaching implications. In chapter five, in the second part of the book, Heidegger turns to the existential problem of history as a problem of how to understand the 'stretch' or interconnectedness of life, as played out between birth and death. A phenomenological task is to understand better the possibility of this dynamic in-between as an origin and foundation for historical being and awareness, what he refers to as its occurrence or way of happening, its *Geschehen*, as another word for its 'historicity', or *Geschichtlichkeit*.[4]

Following the general pattern of critical-destructive hermeneutics, he states that for such a pursuit we cannot base our understanding on actual observed history, its artefacts, remains or narratives. Just as the death of the other could not ultimately provide the key to what it means to die, neither can objective history account for the possibility of the historical happening of human existence. Instead the articulation of this possibility must be sought as

---

4   For the definition of historicity, see Heidegger 2007: 383–4.

a kind of critical self-explication of the *historising* that we ourselves are. This is what it means to have an 'ontological understanding of historicity' or of the existential a priori of history.

The first question that opens the analysis of historicity in §73, concerns what makes something historical? Usually we would say: its 'pastness' or 'being past', but what is then the phenomenal content of being something 'of the past'? 'History' in the conventional sense is taken to refer to all that was. What is the relation between history in this general sense and human existence? Is it the case that we simply belong to history, as somehow contained in it, and therefore that our becoming part of history is something that comes to us so to speak from the outside, as we are situated in the great river of history? Or is there a more intimate relation between the historical and human existence that we could explicate so as to account for the very possibility of there being a history in the first place? Is there also an existential historical a priori? In order to begin to answer this question Heidegger invites us to contemplate a historical artefact, a household utensil of the kind of which our so-called 'historical museums' are full. As buildings devoted to 'presenting the past' or of 'showing history', they rely to a great extent on material remains, preserved and taken out of their original context, placed in cases as objects of historical contemplation and learning. But what is the source of this phenomenal meaning 'historical'? In other words, how do certain things become historical? Heidegger's response is that this meaning relies entirely on them being perceived as being part of a world once lived, a world that is no longer. But what is the nature of this world that is no longer? Should we say that it is simply past? Then it too would be taken to be just an objectified entity, among other entities in a chronological sequence of things. Then we would also have taken for granted precisely what was to be clarified, namely the very possibility of appearing as historical, as carrying or marking a past. From where does its meaning of 'past-ness' emerge? This, he says, is the real 'philosophical enigma' that we are facing: 'on the basis of what ontological conditions does historicity belong to the subjectivity of the "historical" subject as its essential condition?' (Heidegger 2007: 382).

The no-longer-being of human existence is here described as 'having-been-there' (*da-gewesen*), the perfective version of *Da-sein*. He himself does not make the connection to the problem of the dead other as previously addressed, but he could just as well have said: *Da-sein* as un-living. For the questions are inextricably connected. The dead – as the having-been-there – are the source of the meaning of the historical, precisely by not being simply past, but by somehow lingering on in that ghostlike region of perfective being. It is this region that I would name the 'ancestral' in Heidegger.

He himself does not himself speak of 'ancestry' or 'ancestral', the standard German words for which would be *Abstammung* or *Vorfahren*. Yet at the outset of his analysis of history as historicity he suggests that 'the past' does not simply mean that which is located in another temporal region, but rather carries the meaning of 'derivation', *Herkunft*. The word *Kunft* or *Kumft* is an older German word for *coming* and thus also for the arrival or simply future. The *Her-kunft* thus means that from which something has come or originated, in other words its ancestry, that which 'comes before' (*ante cessor*). As such it is also closely aligned with the term finally chosen to capture the history inherent in *Dasein*, the 'having-been', *Da-gewesen*.[5]

---

5   I should add a few words about the term 'ancestral' and the new interest it has received recently in the phenomenological, or perhaps we should say the anti-phenomenological, literature, as it was picked up by Quentin Meillasoux in his influential book *After Finitude* (2008). There he takes phenomenology and all different versions of transcendental philosophy to task for having failed to overcome what he calls 'correlationism', by which he refers to the idea that the real is only available through a constituting subjectivity. In its place he refers to the ancestral as that which precedes subjectivity and human cognition. In this criticism, the word 'ancestral' is thus meant to point to those traces of a past that stretches beyond the reach of present humanity and thus

The guiding concern for him is to find a way to describe the reality and happening of past-ness in terms of its existential meaning for existing *Dasein*. He wants to remain true to the basic phenomenological imperative that we seek the meaning of a phenomenon on the basis of its lived futural projection of understanding. However, when it comes to the meaning of the past, he is nevertheless compelled to recognise that the very meaning of past-ness somehow invites the past-ness of the other, not as an entity from a presumed objective past somehow preserved in the present but rather as a strange past-ness in the present, of which we are somehow a part and in and through which we are united in acts of understanding, repetition and action with the ones no longer there. It is as if he is both affirming the irreducibility of this mode of being and at the same time trying to dispel it, in a kind of fundamental-ontological exorcism, only to see it return again. This is, at least, one way of reading and interpreting what goes on in the key §74 of *Being and Time* that deals with 'the essential constitution of historicity', to which I now turn.

The idea here is to examine a kind of micro-situation where the historical happens (*geschehen*) in and through the movement of living *Dasein*. The point is to describe historicity as the general event-structure of human existence without taking any historical framework, any specific narrative, calendar or archive for given. Rather the different ways in which history can be lived and conceptualised should ideally be seen as variations on a more general matrix, an a priori of historical existence and experience. In order to isolate a basic interpretative domain, Heidegger recalls the description of human existence as a temporal finite and thrown projection. Earlier he has defined 'resoluteness' as that projection toward the future that takes place in the most lucid awareness of one's personal mortality, in the clarity of seeing one's basic existential predicament. But death – or finitude – does not provide any specific possibilities. Mortality has nothing concrete to teach about how to live one's life. Instead the resoluteness with which *Dasein* comes back to itself, he writes, discloses its own possibilities in terms of a 'heritage' that it takes over. The 'thrownness' of *Dasein* means that it is always thrown into a world with others in a more or less illuminated 'taking over' of existential possibilities. This is what he here designates as heritage (*Erbe*) (Heidegger 2007: 383). It is from within a handed-over set of existential possibilities that *Dasein* orients itself and projects itself toward a future.

There is something compelling in Heidegger's idea of the original historical happening as a moment of action where history emerges as that which both lays a claim on us, and in relation to which we constitute ourselves and our own being. Since this being is always also a being-with-others, the constitution of ourselves through the affirmation of an inheritance is also carried out in a shared space of meaning. In acting, he says, we act with our 'generation', taking over an inherited possibility in the moment of decision. This whole movement he then summarizes under having a 'fate', the collective modality of which is 'destiny' (Heidegger 2007: 384).

In his ambition to stay within the framework of the existential analytic, Heidegger creates this idealised situation of how the happening of *Dasein* and thus the manifestation of historicity takes place. At the core of this phenomenon we find human existence as possibility, projecting itself toward a future in such a way as to permit history to happen

supposedly beyond what any constituting subjectivity can master. My motivation for bringing the term 'ancestrality' into the discussion is very different, namely in order to point to the persistent challenge for a phenomenology of history to give an account of the possibility of the historicity of an event or artefact as precisely a present absence in the present. Unlike Meillasoux, the ancestral does not refer simply to the naively conceived 'objective past' but instead to the phenomenological quality of that which in the present recalls and reaches back into what which presents itself as 'past'. It is in this sense it can be said to capture the core problem of a phenomenology of history, namely the meaning of present-past, or in Heidegger's terms *Herkunftigkeit* or *Da-gewesenheit*.

through the repetition of an inheritance, assumed as a project for the future. An example that comes to mind when one reads these passages is revolutionary political action. In moments of decision, when human beings are pushed to the limit of their existence and are forced to act by choosing sides, history as it were becomes real in a more concentrated sense. It is no longer a question of taking an interest in this or that nor of knowing about what has been in general but of living toward an uncertain future in the necessity of collective choice that places belonging, inheritance and commitment in focus. Who we are and what we become are determined by the way that we permit the possibilities of the past to resound and to whom we profess loyalty. Do we speak or do we remain silent, do we join or do we resist, do we act or do we refrain from action, do we go to war or do we seek another solution, do we cling to the other or do we let go? These are decisive choices, painful choices, where history is enacted in and through a space of conflicting loyalties.

The suggested idea that individual (and collective) *Dasein* could generate its distinct and authentic direction by moving towards its own mortality nevertheless ultimately distorts the full complexity of its phenomenal character. We could phrase it in the following way: as we are called to act and to assume a situation, we are ultimately alone with our decision in relation to the inheritance handed over to us. But in seeking the right action, in seeking the measure or simply the just, we are often forced to confront a conflicting set of voices, directives and imperatives, where truthfulness and betrayal are not always easy to disentangle and where the very idea of there being one 'right' course may even be detrimental to the possibility of making a fair and wise decision.[6]

The dilemma of historical belonging and existential choice can be illustrated from a moving sequence in the cinematic adaption of Dee Brown's classic study of the physical and cultural destruction of the Native American population during the later part of the nineteenth century, *Bury My Heart at Wounded Knee* (1970).[7] The young protagonist, a Sioux boy has been left by his father in the hands of the American school authorities in order to learn 'the white man's trade' and avoid becoming a poor wreck in the reservation. He learns English, but he refuses to compromise about his cultural identity, wanting to preserve loyalty to his ancestors and his roots. Even though he knows the answer to the teacher's questions and raises his hand to answer, he never gets to speak, because he refuses to be called by a 'Christian name'. The requirement for being permitted to speak is to give up his Sioux identity. So he remains silent in class. But when the teacher tells a lie about one of the Sioux chiefs he can no longer keep quiet. Under great anguish he permits her to call him 'Charles' in order to be able to say how it really was, namely that the chief really did not want the war. The will to be true to himself and true to his origin places him in the situation of having to tear himself apart and betray his commitment not to be subjugated. Through his choice of adopting an American identity, he is gradually integrated and achieves success, but when he retells the story of this necessitated betrayal to a lover and friend much later he is still shivering with anguish over what he had to do precisely in order to be 'true' to his past. The example illustrates the general dilemma of entangled, and hybrid identities, often discussed not least in postcolonial literature and cultural theory, where the issue of authentic belonging and commitment often become the source of more complex and sometimes interminable negotiations.

Heidegger's somewhat idealising attempt to close the existential space of the happening of history through repetition of past possibilities for the future through the hope of a single authentic resolve does not discharge the fundamental relevance of his basic point;

---

6   For a more extended critical discussion of the theme of destiny in Heidegger's work, see Ruin
      2007. The text has also been published in Danish and Swedish, but not yet in English.
7   The film adaption by Daniel Giat (screenplay) and Yves Simoneau (director) was released in 2007.

namely, that what we think of as history, tradition and collective memory is constituted in this ambiguous in-between of freedom and destiny in relation to inherited existential possibilities. In the constitution of historical time, we are open to the future through the enactment of a 'past' that makes its appearance as an ancestral inheritance in and through which our thoughts and actions are enacted in relation to the dead. *Dasein* lives its historicity in this openness toward an address that has always already reached it from *Dasein* already having been, or from having-been-ness as such.

It is important here to note the words he uses to qualify the peculiar from of 'repetition' that characterizes genuine historising, namely that 'repetition responds [*erwidert*] to the possibility of existence that has been-there' (Heidegger 2007: 386). It is not a question of blind repetition nor of refusing the historical in the present but of somehow letting it happen through an affirmative response. The historical in *Dasein* thus appears as an ambiguous middle ground where it first emerges as an inner opening in the direction of the demand of the dead other. It is not properly a dialogue, for the situation lacks genuine reciprocity. Historical *Dasein* relates to an address that reaches it both from the outside and from inside itself, in relation to which it is called to respond and to take responsibility and which thereby contributes to constituting it in its own sense of continuity and identity.

In the age of post-totalitarian and postcolonial politics and in the era of multiplying trans-linguistic and trans-ethnic identities, we need to take seriously, like never before, the existential meaning of human historicising as a reciprocal being-with-the-dead and ancestrality. This is especially true for memory studies, as it concerns the attempt to capture the workings and inner logic of how tradition is maintained through the lives of individual subjects. In the end I think it is correct to see it as a theme before which Heidegger ultimately recoils but which he nevertheless permits us to think in a very profound and perhaps still unsurpassed way.

Through his analysis, he invites us to contemplate the peculiar lingering on of the past in the present that can mark certain things present as also things past and that can thus open the historical as a kind of breach or lacuna in the solid fabric of the present. By articulating the problem of *Dasein* as *da-gewesene*, he has pointed the way toward a deeper exploration of this phenomenology of the non-present other for an understanding of the historical. His analysis of historicity has shown how the circular and projective temporality of existence is a prerequisite for historical understanding and awareness.

More generally he has signalled the need to explore the existential roots of history in its reflective, scientific form, the supposedly true account of 'how it really was'. To understand the past, and to live meaningfully in relation to the past, is not something that requires the existence of history as a scientific or academic enterprise. On the contrary, the scientific pursuit of the truth about the past is a later and secondary event in the evolution of something like the phenomenon of history in the sense of *Dasein*'s historicising. Before and beyond history as the presumed existence of an objective past, we therefore need to explore the different ways in which the human being comports itself in response to those who no longer there and who are yet here, the ghosts and the spectres that rely on us to remember them and which come back to haunt us when we believe that we have laid them to rest.

References

Assmann, J. 2011. *Cultural Memory and Early Civilization* (Cambridge: Cambridge University Press).

Brown, D. 1970. *Bury My Heart at Wounded Knee* (New York: Henry Holt and Co.).

Davis, C. 2007. *Haunted Subjects: Deconstruction, Psychoanalysis and the Return of the Dead* (New York: Palgrave).

Derrida, J. 1993. *Aporias*, trans T. Dutoit (Stanford, CA: Stanford University Press).

— — 1994. *Specters of Marx: The State of the Debt, the Work of Mourning and the New International*, ✗ trans. P. Kamuf (New York: Routledge).

Heidegger, M. 2006. [1927]. *Sein und Zeit* (Tübingen: Niemeyer Verlag).

— — 2007. *Being and Time*, trans. J. Macquarrie and E. Robinson (Oxford: Blackwell).

Levinas, E. 1993. *Dieu, la mort et le temps* (Paris: Grasset).

Meillasoux, Q. 2008. *After Finitude*, trans. R. Brassier (London: Continuum).

Ruin, H. 1994. *Enigmatic Origins: Tracing the Theme of Historicity Through Heidegger's Works* (Stockholm: Almqvist & Wiksell).

— — 2007. 'Ein geheimnisvolles Schicksal: Heidegger und das griechische Erbe', *Martin Heidegger Gesellschaft Schriftenreihe* 8: 15–34.

Sprinker, M. (ed.) 2008. *Ghostly Demarcations: A Symposium on Jacques Derrida's Specters of Marx* (London: Verso).

PART II
Social, Psychological and Cultural Frameworks of Memory

Continuity and Innovation in the Art of Memory

Luisa Passerini

Guides

The texts that accompanied me along the first steps of my journey through the study of memory were more than companions. They were guides showing the way: often examples far in front of me, but very visible in the distance.

A decisive early beacon was the work of Mikhail Bakhtin. At the end of the 1970s, I conducted interviews with about 70 factory workers in Turin, both male and female, who had been born between 1884 and 1922 and had lived through the Fascist period. I asked them general questions to elicit narratives about their lives, followed by more detailed questions on their experience of Fascism. I was struck by the inconsistency between the testimonies I collected and the accepted histories of Fascism, which generally did not deal with subjective experiences of the regime. Some of the responses seemed irrelevant: silences, anecdotes, jokes. Most striking of all was the insistent recurrence of jokes about the regime.

The work of Sigmund Freud was an important influence on my interpretation of the psychic mechanisms operating within those memories, as I have written elsewhere (Passerini 2012), but only Bakhtin made it clear that the horizon within which the testimonies of jokes should be understood was a centuries-long cultural tradition. In fact, parts of the testimonies I recorded could be assigned to the category Bakhtin referred to as 'comic-serious', which includes such genres as mime, fable, dialogue and satire, since the comic and the spectacle were particularly prominent (Passerini 1987). Later, I came to understand the prevalence of the body and the animal world, especially their 'low' aspects, in the popular memory of Fascism.

It became evident to me that the self-representations of the subjects took similar narrative forms and included stereotypes about themselves. Following Bakhtin, I took the common-place elements in these self-representations as expressions of cultural attitudes and views of the world and history. The narratives included formalised anecdotes as well as experiences from daily life. Bakhtin was crucial in understanding this distinction, thanks to his highlighting of the relevance of conventional forms in stories passed on by word of mouth.

More specifically, Bakhtin made it clear that various literary genres or at least some elements within them are older than writing and have maintained to some extent their sonorous nature. His work opened my eyes to the distinction between oral and written that could be still perceived in spite of the blurring of the borders between the two. He insisted on the prominence of genres in interpretation, particularly of genres based on laughter, pointing to the original ambivalent nature of laughter as both creative and destructive at the same time, and the fact that it could retain its strength, at least partially, when transferred from one historical context to another. According to his interpretation, laughter has the strength to make its object – including power and authority – very close to the subject and thus to turn it upside down, to dismember and decompose it, to destroy any fear from or respect towards it, becoming the basis of a realistic attitude to the world rather than a heroic and epic one (Bahktin 1970).

Jokes are examples of such an attitude, and their importance can be understood if they are not only referred to their immediate context but also seen against the background of a larger and much older culture. The jokes I collected concerned daily transgressions against the discursive Fascist regime and emphasised 'the baseness' of the regime and its representatives through references to the lower or baser parts of the body and low animals like rats and pigs. This symbolic system can be interpreted using Bakhtin's analysis of the tradition of the grotesque, in which the individual body represents the social body, which is destroyed in the metaphorical world of cursing and swearing. Thus the complex vision of popular tradition presented by Bakhtin in his work on Rabelais (which became available in Italian in 1979) made the memories of the older workers understandable in a wider historical context. Often these memories centred on how Fascist squadrons in the period of Mussolini's ascent to power (1921–22) made their victims drink castor oil (a strong purgative). This torture, although not lethal, put people at the mercy of nature in the lowest sense, causing shame and humiliation through the scatological aspects of the sufferings inflicted, which dissuaded them from speaking about the violence they had undergone. However, the memories of it – 50 years on – were integrated into the image system of the ancient popular comic tradition.

In his analysis of the carnivalesque, Bakhtin interpreted comic culture as a systematic whole and illustrated the historical fortunes of the comic genre over the course of centuries, showing how 'baser' concerns became private and how laughter was reduced to sneering or to the level of political and moralising satire. However, even the loss of the symbolic character of the comic and its transference from the cosmic to the level of the individual's mind and body were to him signs that comic culture was not in the danger of becoming frozen and static.

I was struck by the fact that some of my interviewees, both women and men, presented themselves – within the context of the Fascist regime – as funny characters, capable of being objects of laughter but also, at the same time, creators of laughter, playing various tricks on representatives of the regime. Bakhtin's work clarified for me how the mask of the fool and the buffoon, representing the privilege of immunity, has deep popular roots linked to the culture of the piazza and the theatre. A very ancient function of this mask, according to Bakhtin, is to make public the private spheres of life, such as the sexual one, which becomes evident for instance in carnival (Bakhtin 1975).

Moreover, the use of dialect by the interviewees evidenced the popular derivation of the culture which was being recalled. Significantly, the change from dialect to standard Italian often reflected a change from the private to the public sphere. Bakhtin suggested that there are non-public spheres of language that contaminate the public sphere, and they are particularly apt to be impressed on memory. According to his analysis, the comic tone was based on a similar contamination and carnival had been the public sphere of the poor.

I concluded that, if the comic genre adopts low tones, turns things upside-down and opposes the dominant order, in the popular memory of the twentieth century it has lost its previous cosmic dimension but retained to some extent the character of daily resistance to the existing order. I think now that this type of interpretation was still possible when I collected those testimonies in the late 1970s, in a country like Italy, where old people still kept and transmitted popular comic culture. This common discursive background would not have been available later or in other contexts. In other cases, different traditions, such as television serials and popular films, provide the background discourses and allow for their transmission from one generation to another. I realise that in these cases even the meaning of the term 'generation' would be different, and therefore the application of Bakhtin's insights might also have to change, but I am still convinced of the importance that his work could have for many projects engaged in recording collective memories, and I believe that the anachronism that I had to engage with in adapting an analysis of the mediaeval and Renaissance traditions of laughter, carnival and feasts to a modern situation could still be of inspiration to many researchers.

Crystallisation and Fluidity

That first oral history research of mine, in the late 1970s, had started as a collective project on the memory of Fascism among working-class women and men in Turin (Levi, Passerini and Scaraffia 1977). In the course of that project, my colleagues and I noticed that parts of the narratives of the interviewees reappeared in successive interviews, even if sometimes with different meaning, always expressed in the same way and often in the same words. They were anecdotes or short stories that were claimed to have happened to the interviewee and that illustrated a specific part of his or her personality or attitudes. While the life-story was variable in words and priorities, the anecdotes remained relatively fixed, or 'crystallised', and could be arranged in different contexts, while retaining much of their original meanings. Sometimes they were part of family or small-group traditions, within which they had been repeated many times, while the life-story in its entirety had probably never been recounted before the interview. We concluded that collecting biographies as spontaneously as possible produced narratives with a recurrent structure: what we called a 'duration', the autobiographical narrative of a life as a whole, and what we recognised as 'episodes', a specific phase of life, historical period or self- image. The links between the various parts of the life-story were not necessarily chronological or causal: they could be by association or to reinforce a previous point.

These recurrences raise a serious problem for interpreting a collection of memories conducted with a common methodology – especially if no questionnaire is used – that of individual variations on a collective theme and where they come from. In other words, it raises the question of the existence and nature of collective memory.

This question receives different answers in different contexts. The principal and most inspiring case has been for a long time the study of African oral traditions, and a major guide in this field is the work by Jan Vansina on the ancient kingdoms in tropical Africa, especially Rwanda, Burundi and the Congo. His book *Oral Tradition: A Study in Historical Methodology* (1965), originally published in French in 1961, was seminal in establishing the dignity of anonymous oral traditions (for instance, royal genealogies or slogans and stock phrases which expressed the commonly accepted ideals of a culture) as historical sources, suggesting the methods by which their reliability could be assessed. He did this on the basis of a careful distinction of various types of testimony (historical tales, aetiological myths, poems, proverbs, songs and so on), with different value for the historian, and of a classification of the principal forms and causes of distortion. The book was very instructive for me, particularly its reflections on the combination of crystallisation and fluidity in oral traditions.

A similarly good companion was the research by Iona Opie and Peter Opie on the language of children (Opie and Opie 1959). In the 1950s, the authors interviewed 5,000 children aged between 6 and 14 in Britain (from a total of some 7 million), collecting rhymes, binding formulas, incantations and various forms of slang. The result was a fascinating corpus of oral memory, transmitted by word of mouth from child to child, generally of ages less than five years apart. This complex corpus had a remarkable continuity, and some rhymes could be shown to be more than 130 years old, passing through 20 generations of schoolchildren: some traditions of children's lore were several centuries old. Oral lore, the authors state, is subject to a continual process of wear and repair in order to survive: for instance, in the passage from rural to urban environments. This extraordinarily rich repertoire was very suggestive for my understanding of the close relationship between a formalised text and its variations through time and space.

However, both Vansina and Opie and Opie dealt with highly formalised or crystallised forms of memory, while I needed company on the route to understanding a more informal memory. For me, a decisive companion along this road was Philippe Joutard's *La Légende des Camisards* (1977), which recounts the history and memory of the revolt of the Protestant population of the Cévennes under Louis XIV against the persecutions following the 1685 revocation of the Edict of Nantes, which had guaranteed the rights of the Calvinist Protestants, or Huguenots, in a predominantly Catholic country. The revolt broke out in 1702, with the worst of the fighting in 1704 followed by scattered outbursts of violence until 1710, and concluded with the peace of 1715. The term Camisard is derived from *camisa*, a type of shirt worn by the peasants, in contrast with the uniforms of the soldiers.

La Légende des Camisards combines analysis of the written historiography and of unpublished manuscripts. Joutard also conducted a 'ethnological search' in 1967 in order to collect the oral traditions of the revolt. He stated clearly that he was not trying to produce a sociological inquiry based on a representative sample: for instance the number of Catholics in the group of interviewees was higher than that of Protestants. His was a qualitative search, which included individual interviews but also his own participation in gatherings on winter evenings organised by pastors, aiming to record the collective memory of the Cévennes region. Thus an inventory of testimonies was collected that often included the memories of the contributors' grandfathers.

The inventory was not merely of qualitative relevance: Joutard collected 221 historical traditions, of which more than three-quarters concerned the Camisards, even if they did not refer only to the precise period of the revolt. In fact, it emerged from the research that a sort of 'camisardisation of history' had taken place, in that everything of importance that happened in the Cévennes ended up being attributed in some way to the Camisards. Altogether 168 events were attributed directly to the Camisards, and the records of them were claimed to have been transmitted orally: quite a consistent corpus of memory, which Joutard analysed in detail. He classified the stories into four themes: the celebration of the victory of the Camisards, the resistance of the ancestors who refused to be re-baptized, their skill and cleverness in resisting and the suffering because of the persecutions. The resulting self-image was one of Cévenols as fiery lovers of freedom, very jealous of their independence. Collective memory was organised around this self-image, which Joutard defined as the 'cultural personality of the country'.

Joutard discovered a conjunction of historical culture, biblical interpretation and oral tradition. The written and oral sources throw light on one another. A number of *lieux de mémoire*, sites of memory, such as the caves where important events of the legend happened, recur throughout the oral narratives. This is remarkable in itself, but also in view of the fact that the volumes on *lieux de mémoire* edited by Pierre Nora started to appear in 1984. A final interpretative hypothesis by Joutard was that the dialectics between the internal and the external was a crucial factor in the survival of a collective memory. In the end, his conclusion was that, on many topics, historical research could not be separated from the examination of collective mentalities.

Joutard's work inspires admiration for its great care and precision in dealing with oral, printed and manuscript sources, as well as for the depth and cleverness of his interpretation. It also shows eloquently that oral memory transforms itself into oral tradition through a process that I have defined as crystallisation, a fixation of memory around the original nucleus adapted to the needs of the present. As indicated in the title of this chapter, a double process is at play: the continuity of tradition and the innovation of the transmitted repertoire. All this is to be understood not in a psychological or physiological sense, but discursively, as a narrative memory shared by generations both diachronically and synchronically.

I must distinguish this definition of collective memory, at least to a certain extent, from that used by Maurice Halbwachs. Like other historians of memory, I owe a great deal to Halbwachs, who taught us to look for the various forms of social remembrance, such as the shared memory of a nation, a family, a couple or a group of peers, friends or relatives. It can be the memory of an encounter, a relationship or an anniversary, and it can concern primarily the public or the private sphere or the connections between the two. All these cases can be interpreted as forms of intersubjectivity, as I have argued, suggesting the primacy of intersubjectivity over subjectivity, as the latter cannot exist without the former. This is evident first of all in the very formation of language but also in its transmission (Passerini 2007). In *Les Cadres sociaux de la mémoire* (1925) and *La Mémoire collective* (published posthumously in 1949, a few years after he died in the Nazi concentration camp of Buchenwald), Halbwachs argued convincingly that while memory and history can converge or diverge, memory connects the past and the present. He also insisted on the links between memory and place and memory and emotion, two decisive elements for understanding what is remembered and why and how.

In *La Mémoire collective*, Halbwachs discussed a famous anecdote by the philosopher Charles Blondel, his contemporary and friend. One of Blondel's childhood memories involved visiting an abandoned house where he accidentally fell into a deep hole full of water. The child was so scared that the memory remained with him for his whole life. Halbwachs questions the individuality of such memory, observing that, although this remembrance did not seem to imply the presence of anybody else, since the child was alone at the time, he was immersed in the current of thoughts and feelings that connected him to his family. Thus he was momentarily isolated, but the thoughts and feelings relating to his family were with him (Halbwachs 1980: 36–7). These constituted what Halbwachs called 'les cadres sociaux de la mémoire', the social frameworks of memory. Individuals remember by taking on the perspective of a group: family memory is a good example of collective memory, given the social and emotional value of the family environment. As a consequence, social relationships can crystallise around events or places and give rise to collective memory. Therefore, although the past does not recur as such, we can say that we have a contact with the past on the basis of such crystallisation. We could add to the picture the impact of the affective sympathy or empathy that we can experience in reading or listening to stories of this kind.

This discussion is useful for reflecting on the connections between the individual and the collective, and it explains the term 'collective representations', which originated in Emile Durkheim's sociology. Maurice Halbwachs stated that the memory of the group realises and manifests itself in individual memories. While I considered his work an indispensable companion in my work on memory, I could not accept the primacy of collective memory, except in certain examples of narrative memory. I was very critical of Halbwachs on this point, as I wrote on various occasions, believing that his approach was too strongly influenced by Structuralism and clashed with ideas that I had derived from the reading of Marx proposed by the Frankfurt school, which gave a central relevance to subjectivity understood as the product of human activity.

Therefore, while I found a companion in Maurice Halbwachs, inevitably my relationship to his work was one of challenge and struggle. In fact, from the beginning my aim in the study of memory has been to promote the idea of individual subjectivity and to understand forms of intersubjectivity. My work has been centred on considering memory as a type of subjectivity and more specifically of intersubjectivity.

Memory of Self and Others

In the second half of the 1980s, I gave a public format to some of my own memories, which I had originally written down as private diaries, and I combined them with those of a number of my contemporaries that I had interviewed about the international political protests of 1968 and their effects on their lives. The resulting collage was *Autobiography of a Generation* (Passerini 1996). I had no direct companion for this book and no real model, but in the preliminary work that led to it, I received inspiration from many texts. Among these, Ernst Bernhard's *Mitobiografia* was the most important. He was a paediatrician born in Berlin in 1896, who underwent Freudian and then Jungian analysis. Obliged to leave Berlin by the Nazis, he found refuge in Italy, where however in 1938 the racial laws stopped all activities by Jews, including his own as a psychoanalyst. He was held in a concentration camp in Calabria from 1940 to 1941. His book of notes was published posthumously in 1969 (he died in 1965) with the title based on a term he had coined: 'mythbiography'. Dreams are an integral part of the diaries and memories collected in his book.

Bernhard's idea was that the basis of each individual's biography is a 'mythologeme', which uses the repertoire of the common cultural heritage in different ways: blindly, like the Germans who enacted the myth of Hagen killing the hero Siegfried out of envy and misguided loyalty, or consciously and critically. This means that there is a close connection between the psychic and cultural. The task of individuals is to understand the myths on which their 'destiny' (not in the sense of predetermined fate) is based. In Bernhard's case, it was the story of the diaspora of the Jewish people, chased and persecuted, that had a decisive influence on his mind and psyche. He tried to reach a dialectical position between this heritage and radically new ways of imagining it. For instance, he decided consciously that his attitude to the guards in the concentration camp would not to be that of a victim but of a saviour. To recognise one's myth requires a similar approach to interpreting one's dreams: some detachment together with passion and the refusal of any moralistic attitude. It is not a merely individual task, since the communication of elements of one's own mythbiography to others can have a snowball effect that can transform the collective consciousness.

I think now that these ideas resonated in my mind and inspired the construction of an autobiography that was both individual and collective. This process was not fully conscious at the time, but during those years I was aware of the relevance that Bernhard's text had had for my intellectual development (Passerini 1990).

On a different note, I had found it suggestive to read (with a certain degree of criticism) Philippe Lejeune's *Le Pacte autobiographique* (1975) and *Je est un autre* (1980). Lejeune poses the question of the grammatical person used in the autobiographical narration: 'I', 'You' or 'He' (1989). (Lejeune didn't acknowledge inclusive language, although feminism was in full swing at the time. *Autobiography of a Generation* went the opposite way: I deliberately took gender as a central point of my narration ('Responses' 2012).) Lejeune's reflection on both the position of the narrator when the narrator and the principal character are identical and on the retrospective point of view of the narrative was useful, since I would later occupy both these positions. He also paid attention to the reproduction of or allusions to oral discourse in written form, a topic I was very interested in. The very idea of the autobiographical pact (distinct from the fictional pact) was important, as this type of contract between the author and the reader is a way of reaffirming in the text the identity of the author and the person named on the cover of the book. I found out later how embarrassing it can be if the contract is understood literally, as if the autobiography were faithful to what actually happened to the author. However, I thought that some points of relevance for history, such as how can a text 'resemble' a life, were not discussed deeply enough or were treated too formalistically; but I liked the chapter on Sartre's *Les Mots*, particularly on the absence of chronological order and the dictatorship of meaning, by which Sartre questions the existence of a past in itself and the identity of the relationship of succession and the relationship of causality.

Lejeune pays much attention to oral sources (for instance, to radio interviews), particularly when discussing the autobiography of 'those who do not write', providing many examples and quotations – mainly from a French context. In the French version of his writings there are many interesting observations on the processes of transcription and montage in oral interviews. He rightly stresses the relevance of the literary montage resulting from oral autobiographies based on extensive interviewing, while he is critical of the scientific quality of such work, which often does not make clear which operations have been done by the collector–author. I agree with this, as I do on another point he makes: that any effort to fix and preserve the memory of an 'oral' society alienates, recovers and reifies it, an ambiguous operation that does not give a voice to the interviewees but rather takes it from them. However, I do not believe that 'the person who is asked to remember in front of the tape recorder does not realize that listening to his memory answers to a strategy other than his own participation in the act of memory' (Lejeune 1989: 214). Altogether, in spite of some disagreement, I found the reading of Lejeune's books very helpful.

Finally, a more personal companionship: in June 1984 I was in London for a meeting of an oral history project on the protests of 1968, which involved several people from various countries and led to a book, to which the whole group contributed but that was written by Ronald Fraser. Ronnie, author of *Blood of Spain*, an oral history of the Spanish Civil War, was also a friend with whom I exchanged ideas on oral history and psychoanalysis. On the occasion of the London meeting he gave me a copy of his book *In Search of a Past* (1984), the story of his childhood (largely based on interviews with those who had been his family's servants in a manor house in England) and of his psychoanalytical experience.

The author narrates in the first person some of the dialogues with his psychoanalyst, punctuated by heavy silences and his own thoughts. The same grammatical person is used for reporting the results of the interviews, but in this case the author also adopts the second person singular, as if talking to himself and thus reflecting on his memory of the past as well as on his actions in the present (such as plugging the tape recorder in). He justifies this habit by telling his analyst that he never had a clearly defined 'I', and the analyst retorts that probably he had two, one for his mother and one for his nanny, who was like a mother to him. This conflict is developed from childhood to the present, together with the conflict with his father and his relationships with friends.

The author transcribes some of his own questions to the former household staff, starting with Ilse, who was not a servant but his German nanny. He also uses the impersonal form when reporting the testimonies for instance of the cook and the gardener. The book includes some pages of a memoir by the author, dated three and a half years after the beginning of his search for testimonies. Again, long excerpts from the analysis are presented, interspersed with the writer's memories and conversations with his brother on their shared past. Significantly, on the last page the author's aim is spelled out: to be both the subject and the object of the book. But the very last words tell us that his analysis will continue next week, and he takes his leave, staring into the impassive face of the analyst.

There are political and social meanings in the interstices of the narrative: the servants were poorly paid for long hours of work; the father was a staunch conservative who did not allow them to vote Labour and who devoted his life to hunting; the mother's family despised her husband for his social origins, despite his wealth; the two parents had an unhappy relationship and were divorced when Ronnie was 15 and his brother 9.

I am sure now that this book influenced me deeply, although I had no clear awareness of it as a model when I wrote *Autobiography of a Generation*. This may seem astounding, but I believe it is deeply true and significant, because how Fraser's book acted as a companion was subterranean and to some extent unconscious or more precisely semiconscious. I read the book in mid-1984 and re-read it only recently, after Ronnie died and I wrote an obituary for him. The extent to which I had forgotten his book surprised me, but it is a good example of how memory works.

Symbols

In the 1990s and the 2000s, I worked on the cultural memory of Europe, including symbols and myths. The main influence in my understanding of the symbolic nature of memory was the work of Frances Yates. While I owed the interpretation of symbols in memory to Carl Jung and Kàroly Kerényi as well as Jacques Lacan, it was Yates who opened my mind to the historical articulation of the cultural and the psychological in memory.

The Art of Memory allows the reader to discover the ancient techniques of impressing 'places' and 'images' on memory, an art known as 'mnemotechnics' from ancient Greece to the Renaissance (Yates 1966). This art consisted of remembering a speech or a poem by establishing associations between its various elements on the one hand and the components of a temple or a house on the other. Yates' book starts with the ancient tradition on the origin of this technique. At a banquet given by a nobleman of Thessaly, the poet Simonides of Ceos – who lived between the sixth and fifth centuries BC – sang a poem in honour of his host, half of which however was in praise of the divine twins Castor and Pollux. In reaction, the host retorted that he would pay the poet only half his compensation, while the gods would have to pay the rest. Shortly after, Simonides was called out of the house because two young men had requested to see him. However, nobody was there to meet him. During his absence the roof of the hall collapsed, killing the host and all the other guests. Although their corpses could not be recognised by their relatives, Simonides remembered where they were sitting, and on this basis he was able to identify them. Thus mnemotechnics was invented, the art of connecting names and places, mental images and sites, an art indispensable to anyone who had to memorise a speech or a poem. This famous anecdote made it evident that the faculty of sight is essential to the art of memory.

Yates' approach was another indication of the connection between the collective and the individual dimensions of memory. She showed how a body of knowledge could be transmitted through generations by associating memories and images – or things – that assumed the role of symbols. The art of memory was transmitted from antiquity to the Renaissance and the following centuries, giving rise to artificial memory systems like the ones by Giulio Camillo and Giordano Bruno.

Figure 5.1 shows the artificial memory system created by Giulio Camillo, called the 'Memory Theatre'. Camillo was born about 1480, had a professorship at the University of Bologna and travelled to France at the invitation of King Francis I. He devoted his life to building a theatre of wood, large enough to be entered by two people at once, marked with many images and full of little boxes. Its plan, as presented by Frances Yates, illustrates the

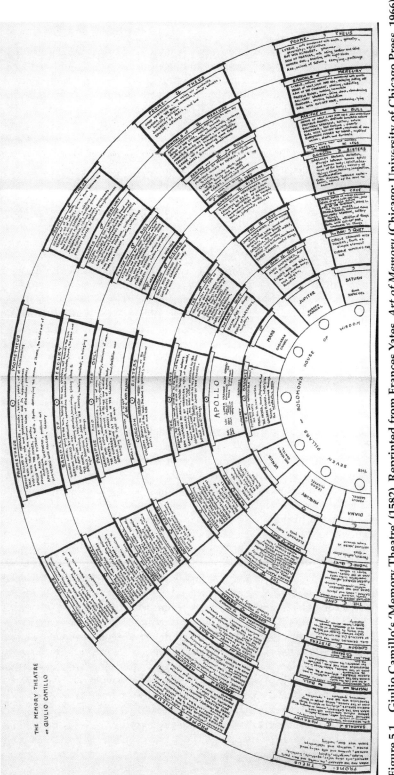

Figure 5.1 Giulio Camillo's 'Memory Theatre' (1582). Reprinted from Frances Yates, *Art of Memory* (Chicago: University of Chicago Press, 1966)

universe expanding from First Causes through the stages of Creation. The theatre, resting upon the Seven Pillars of Wisdom, conserved all the things, words and arts of value to humanity. Its basic images are those of the planetary gods, and its centre is an idea of a memory organically geared to the universe so that the microcosm can fully understand and remember the macrocosm. Such a memory would have the magic power of unifying its contents by basing it upon images drawn from the celestial world. Camillo was a Christian Hermetist, trying to relate the Hermetic teachings on the divine and demonic powers of the universe to Christianity. His 'Memory Theatre' was not fully perfected at his death in 1544, after which it was completely lost.

Figure 5.2 shows the 'Wheel of Memory' invented by Giordano Bruno in 1582 and recreated by Frances Yates on the basis of his book *De umbris idearum*, 'On the Shadows of Ideas'. Bruno was born in 1548, became a Dominican friar and was celebrated for his work in the art of memory. However, he was obliged to leave the order after being accused of theological errors and travelled to France (where he was well received by King Henry III), then to England and Germany. When he returned to Italy, he was imprisoned by the Venetian Inquisition and, after a trial of seven years, found guilty of heresy and burned at the stake in Rome in 1600.

Bruno's wheel is a memory system of five concentric rings divided into 30 segments, giving 150 sub-divisions in all. The rings are marked with the letters A to Z, followed by some Greek and Hebrew letters to make up the 30 segments. This heavily inscribed wheel is an astral power station, containing, among other things: the signs of the zodiac; the planets; the various aspects of the life-cycle; lists of birds, animals, stones and metals; artefacts and other objects; the names of inventors in the fields of agriculture, trapping, hunting and fishing; the inventors of instruments and procedures, pottery, spinning, weaving, cobbling and so on: in fact, all the inventors of the fundamental technologies of advanced civilisation, of magic and religion, of letters and writing, astronomy, astrology and philosophy. Significantly, the final name in the wheel is Melicus, indicating Simonides, the inventor of the classical art of memory.

The wheel is a system for memorising universal knowledge – we could call it a map of global collective memory. It is a product of highly systematised magic. It could be the memory of a magus with powers in harmony with the cosmic powers, according to the principle of the reflection of the universe in the human mind.

Yates observes that an art requiring the manipulation of images in memory must always to some extent involve the psyche as a whole. Therefore the term 'mnemotechnics' seems inadequate to cover all the expertise from the scholastic virtue of prudence to the magical or occult memory systems of the Renaissance. Again, I found myself transposing a lesson on memory from the past to the present, although this time less literally than in the case of Bakhtin. Some of Yates' observations on the art of memory in the Middle Ages and the Renaissance have been of inspiration to me even in very recent times, after I started working on the visual – and not only the oral – memory of migration. Yates drew analogies, between the blossoming of new imagery in religious art and the importance given to metaphors and symbols in the study of memory, during the age of Scholasticism. She herself was inspired by comparisons like the one drawn by Erwin Panofsky between a scholastic summa and a gothic cathedral, both arranged according to a system of homologous parts and parts of parts. This calls to mind the correspondence between the sections of an orator's speech and a complex building and between memory pictures and texts. I find it highly suggestive that, while art proper and the art of memory, which is an invisible art, must be distinguished, their frontiers must be seen as overlapping. The art of memorising groups of objects and places associated with one another was itself a creator of imagery. Indeed, I have personally

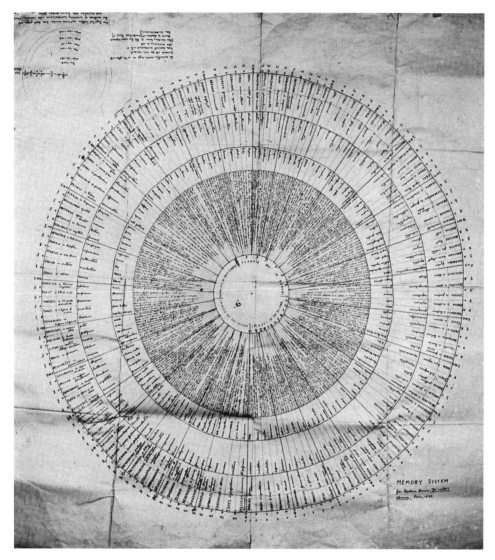

Figure 5.2   Giordano Bruno's 'Wheel of Memory' (1544). Reprinted from Frances Yates, *Art of Memory* (Chicago: University of Chicago Press, 1966)

come to question the 'invisibility' of the art of memory, when I started to try to discern what connections memory has with the visible and in which way.

Some of Yates' findings can be used to establish a contrast between past and present forms of memory, like the capacity of memory in the past to be organically geared to the universe and affiliated to the proportions of world harmony. Indeed two acts of memory in two different circumstances and times can be far apart and not even comparable in strict terms: such would be for instance the fact that Dante's *Inferno* can be regarded as a kind of memory system (the *Divine Comedy* being a great example of converting an abstract summa into a summa of similitudes and examples) and the fact that some migrants today represent their itineraries of migration – from various parts of the world to Europe – on the basis of connections between various steps of their travel and names or places or words. In the second case, the relation between memory and the formation of imagery does not mean that the migrants use an artificial memory in the literal sense, but that they adopt a series of devices and associations to evoke their movements. Many of Yates' observations resonate with this: for instance, her mention of Quintilian's saying that one may form memory places – *lieux de mémoire* – when on journeys, and her insistence on the emotional or affective appeal of a good memory image. Once more, these examples from the past do not provide literal models but suggestions and invitations.

Short Term/Long Term

In recent years, my best memory companion has been the autobiography of the Nobel Prize winner Eric Kandel, *In Search of Memory: The Emergence of a New Science of Mind* (2006). I keep going back to some passages of this text, and I have often used it in my courses on memory.

Kandel's efforts to find links between personal memory and the biology of memory storage resonate with my own preoccupations, although in a different way, and has enriched my understanding of my own memory. Kandel has written about memory not only as a way of recalling something, but also as an emotional experience. In fact, he chose as the starting point of his autobiographical narration his own experience of the Nazi invasion of Austria and his flight to the United States. His early interests were in becoming a historian and then a psychoanalyst, before he embarked on his career as a biologist of mind and a cognitive neuroscientist. This is the opposite itinerary to the one followed by Freud in turning from a neuroanatomical researcher into a psychoanalyst, but I always appreciated that Freud continued to believe that the neurological bases of the psyche could be found. Of course I cannot venture into this field of research myself, but it has been illuminating for me to follow the path of Kandel's experiments and discoveries.

Thanks to his reconstruction of the localisation of different memories in different regions of the brain, I finally have some idea of what was meant by the numerous efforts at various points in history to distinguish different kinds of memory, efforts that were enigmatic to me. On the basis of Kandel's book, 'conscious memory' and 'unconscious memory' have become more meaningful terms, in the sense that the first indicates a type of explicit or declarative memory (such as the conscious recall of people, places and events) and the second an implicit or procedural memory, underlying habituation and conditioning as well as perceptual and motor skill (such as riding a bicycle or hitting a tennis ball). All this did not have a direct impact on my research but contributed indirectly to my vision of the various forms of memory that I could experience myself and encounter in other people.

This reading satisfied my curiosity in various ways. For instance, I was interested to learn that the cellular mechanisms of learning and memory reside not in the special properties of the neuron itself, but in the connections it receives and makes with other cells. I was impressed by the fact that the process of memory storage requires the synthesis of new proteins and modifies the synaptic connections, thereby producing anatomical changes. And I was fascinated by the story of *Aplysia californica*, the giant marine snail which can be both male and female, with different partners at different times, on which Kandel experimented as he became a cellular neurobiologist of behaviour and learning. The nerve cells of *Aplysia* were so large and identifiable that they allowed him to study something he called 'biochemical identity', explaining that this type of identity – new to me, who had studied all sorts of other identities, connected with gender, generation, nations and continents – had to do with how one cell differs from another at the molecular level and what actually happens at the level of the synapse when behaviour is modified by learning.

By 1985, after more than 15 years of research, Kandel and his collaborators had shown that a simple behaviour in *Aplysia* could be modified by various forms of learning and, more specifically, that short-term memory could be converted into long-term memory. They identified specific motor neurons in *Aplysia* that controlled a specific behaviour, and discovered that training could convert a short-term memory into a persistent, self-maintained long-term memory, and, after a certain amount of time, this process results in memory consolidation, a state that is stable for a long time and can be less easily disrupted.

I found all this extremely suggestive as a general indirect indication of what could have happened with the process of crystallisation of anecdotes. I will not try to reproduce here Kandel's clear but specialised descriptions of tracing the transient changes in the strength of synaptic connections between sensory and motor neurons. All this is helpful to understand how memory is a dynamic process, in which changes take place all the time but not in a causal and inexplicable way. Nor do I mean that the discoveries made through the study of *Aplysia* can be transferred automatically to the study of memory in human beings, but I am convinced that it would be blind to negate the value of neurobiology for the cultural study of memory. At the same time, Kandel's book illustrates the fluidity required or induced in animals by changes in the environment and their adaptation to it.

Viaticum

Viaticum in Latin means the provision for a journey, and the term is still used in Spanish and Italian to indicate the final wishes before a trip, real or metaphorical. Sometime between 1298 and 1314, Giovanni di San Gimignano wrote verses on the best memory companions: order, passion (*passione*, inadequately translated into English as 'affection'), association and meditation. His advice can still be of use to us today, as a viaticum on our way through memory:

> *There are four things, which help a man to remember well.*
>
> *The first is that he should dispose those things, which he wishes to remember in a certain order.*
>
> *The second is that he should adhere to them with affection.*
>
> *The third is that he should reduce them to unusual similitudes.*
>
> *The fourth is that he should repeat them with frequent meditation. (San Gimignano, quoted in Yates 1966: 85–6)*

References

Bakhtin, M. 1970. 'Epos i roman (O metodologii issledovanija romana)', *Voprosy literatury* 1: 95–122; It. trans.: 'Epos e romanzo: Sulla metodologia dello studio del romanzo', in *Problemi di teoria del romanzo*, ed. G. Lukács and C.S. Janovič, trans. M. Bakhtin et al. (Turin: Einaudi, 1976), pp. 179–221.

—— 1975. *Voprosy literatury i estetiki* (Moscow: Chudožestvennaja literatura); It. trans.: *Estetica e romanzo*, trans. C.S. Janovič (Turin: Einaudi, 1979).

Bernhard, E. 1969. *Mitobiografia* (Milan: Adelphi).

Fraser, R. 1984. *In Search of a Past* (London: Verso).

Halbwachs, M. 1925, *Les Cadres sociaux de la mémoire* (Paris: Alcan).

—— 1949. *La Mémoire collective* (Paris: Presses Universitaires de France).

—— 1980. *The Collective Memory*, trans. F.J. Ditter Jr and V. Yazdi Ditter (New York: Harper & Row).

Joutard, P. 1977. *La Légende des Camisards: Une sensibilité au passé* (Paris: Gallimard).

Kandel, E. 2006. *In Search of Memory: The Emergence of a New Science of Mind* (New York and London: Norton).

Lejeune, P. 1975. *Le Pacte autobiographique* (Paris: Seuil).

—— 1980. *Je est un autre* (Paris: Seuil).

—— 1989. *On Autobiography*, trans. K. Leary (Minneapolis: University of Minnesota Press).

Levi, G., L. Passerini and L. Scaraffia 1977. 'Vita quotidiana in un quartiere operaio di Torino fra le due guerre: L'apporto della storia orale', in *Oral history: Fra antropologia e storia*, special issue of *Quaderni storici* 35 (May–Aug): 433–49.

Opie, I., and P. Opie 1959. *The Lore and Language of Schoolchildren* (Oxford: Oxford University Press).

Passerini, L. 1987. *Fascism in Popular Memory* (Cambridge: Cambridge University Press).

—— 1990. 'Mythbiography in Oral History', in R. Samuel and P. Thompson (eds), *The Myths We Live By* (London: Routledge), pp. 49–60.

—— 1996. *Autobiography of a Generation: Italy 1968* (Hanover, NH, and London: Wesleyan University Press).

—— 2007. *Memory and Utopia: The Primacy of Intersubjectivity* (London: Equinox).

—— 2012. 'An Eclectic Ego-Histoire', in S. Alexander and B. Taylor (eds), *History and Psyche: Culture, Psychoanalysis, and the Past* (New York: Palgrave Macmillan), pp. 305–24.

'Responses' 2012. 'Responses to Luisa Passerini's *Autobiography of a Generation: Italy, 1968*: Taking Gender Seriously: Luisa Passerini's Quest for Female Subjectivity between the Self and the Collective', *European Journal of Women's Studies* 19/3: 371–89.

Vansina, J. 1965. *Oral Tradition: A Study in Historical Methodology*, trans. H.M. Wright (London: Routledge & Kegan Paul).

Yates, F. 1966. *The Art of Memory* (Chicago: University of Chicago Press).

From Collectivity to Collectiveness: Reflections (with Halbwachs and Bakhtin) on the Concept of Collective Memory

Alexandre Dessingué[1]

The theoretical influence of Mikhail Bakhtin and Maurice Halbwachs has been consistently important for my work during the last 15 years. Although I have been interested in each theorist separately, I quickly realised that they shared much in common, and it became more and more interesting to explore them in relation to each other. Reading Halbwachs and his concept of collective memory accompanied by Bakhtin has been very fruitful throughout the last few years and this is what I propose to discuss in my chapter.

First of all, Bakhtin and Halbwachs share the fact that they experienced, ideologically and physically, twentieth-century barbarism. Halbwachs died in Buchenwald concentration camp in 1945. In 1929 Bakhtin was arrested by the Stalinist regime, sentenced to exile to Siberia and then to Kazakhstan until 1936. Their ideas and theories face authoritarian ideological contexts both on the right and left. Given the extreme ideological Manichaeism that Fascism and other totalitarian regimes have put in place from the beginning of the twentieth century, the two theorists adopt the same scientific posture: they reflect on the complexity of the formation of the thought and thereby analyse the interrelation and interconnection that a person has with his social and cultural surroundings. My assumption is that the statement made by Gary Saul Morson and Caryl Emerson in *Mikhail Bakhtin: Creation of a Prosaics* could also easily be used in the case of Halbwachs:

> *Books about thinkers require a kind of unity that their thought may not possess. This cautionary statement is especially applicable to Mikhail Bakhtin, whose intellectual development displays a diversity of insights that cannot be easily integrated or accurately described in terms of a single overriding concern. Indeed in a career spanning some sixty years, he experienced both dramatic and gradual changes in his thinking, returned to abandoned insights that he then developed in unexpected ways, and works through new ideas only loosely related to his earlier concerns. (Morson and Emerson 2002: 1)*

1   I would like to thank Steffi Hobuss and Siobhan Kattago for their critical and constructive reading of this chapter.

The Bakhtinian and Halbwachian theoretical attitudes are similar. Their theories and reflections are linked to life experiences that they develop in a philosophical and temporal continuum. Thinking and living are inseparable. In other words, the dynamic of their concepts and theories also reflect a dynamic way of thinking. Secondly, another similarity between Halbwachs and Bakhtin is that the main concepts they shaped and used can primarily be regarded as metaphorical notions:

> *It must be noted that the comparison we draw between Dostoevsky's novel and polyphony is meant as a graphic analogy, nothing more. The image of polyphony and counterpoint only points out those new problems which arise when a novel is constructed beyond the boundaries of ordinary monologic unity, just as in music new problems arose when the boundaries of a single voice were exceeded. But the material of music and of the novel are too dissimilar for there to be anything more between them than a graphic analogy, a simple metaphor. We are transforming this metaphor into the term 'polyphonic novel', since we have not found a more appropriate label. It should not be forgotten, however, that the term has its origin in metaphor. (Bakhtin 1984: 22)*

Peter Novick expresses the same kind of considerations concerning the work of Halbwachs: 'When we speak of "collective memory", we often forget that we are employing a metaphor – an organic metaphor – that makes an analogy between the memory of an individual and that of a community' (Novick 1999: 267). It is obvious that using concepts like 'polyphony' in the case of the text, which does not have 'voices', or 'collective memory' in the case of groups, who do not have the organic ability of remembering, may seem problematic. Texts do not talk; it is the reader who makes texts talk. In the same way: groups do not remember; it is the individual who remembers, groups create collective and cultural reconstructions of the past that can eventually become acts of collective remembrance, as for instance, in the case of commemorations.

On the other hand, one could say that it is because of these concepts' metaphorical nature, because of the distance between the signifier and the signified they introduce, that they have been so much used and that they still need to be defined and discussed today. The understanding of these concepts is unconfined and not narrow, as is their usage. Neither Halbwachs nor Bakhtin propose a clear categorisation or an operationalisation through their respective concepts. Using metaphorical concepts tell us something about the fact that we are dealing with questions that cannot be reduced and delimited through words. Writing and reading, as well as remembering, are dynamic processes, but which, at the end, depend on the action of the individual influenced by socio-cultural surroundings and by cognitive processes, attitudes and abilities.

Thirdly and finally, both theorists and their works could, in many respects, also be regarded as 'generators' of new concepts, as a kind of conceptual toolbox. Bakhtin's theories on dialogism and polyphony have largely inspired, for instance, the notion of 'intertextuality' in the work of French Structuralists, such as Julia Kristeva (1967) and Tzvetan Todorov (1981) but also the structural notions of hypertextuality, paratextuality, architextuality and metatextuality in Gérard Genette's *Palimpsestes* (1982: 7–19). Kristeva and Todorov were very clear about the fact that intertextuality was delimitation and concretisation of the notion of the dialogic, which has been very fruitful in analytical contexts and especially in the field of literary studies during the last 50 years.[2]

---

2   In her introduction to the French edition of *La Poétique de Dostoïevski* (1970), Kristeva writes that the notion of dialogism in Bakhtin is linked to the dual dependence of the speech to the 'I'

In the same way, in recent decades, there has been an enormous production of new concepts related to the notion of collective memory. This terminological process has contributed to definitions of an international and interdisciplinary new research field accompanying a process that has been called a 'memory boom' (Winter 2000). We can still regret the fact that the concept of collective memory in itself has sometimes worked as an accepted global framework without critical discussion about the epistemological dimension and evolution of the notion in the work of Halbwachs and, in particular, between the elaboration of *The Social Frameworks of Memory* published in 1925 and *The Collective Memory* published posthumously in 1950.[3]

In this chapter, I propose first to discuss different approaches to the concept of collective memory that have been proposed within the interdisciplinary field of memory studies during the last decades. I will then go back to the 'source' and look closer at the epistemological dimension of the concept of collective memory and discuss its semantic evolution within the work of Halbwachs. The complexity and variability of the notion of collective memory is a central characteristic of Halbwachs' work, and it is part of this Halbwachian complexity and variability that I will reveal, thereby presenting some methodological issues and challenges for memory studies as a research field.

Halbwachs' Heritage

In Michael Rothberg's work, the term 'multidirectional memory' is used and linked to the problem of the subjectivity of the system of representation and group identification. In his book *Multidirectional Memory*, Rothberg studies, under the same rubric, both Holocaust and postcolonial studies. The aim of this common term is mainly to draw a different picture of the relationship between the formation and re-formation of collective memory and collective representations. According to Rothberg, acts of remembrance as well as cultural representations of the Holocaust can, among other things, be considered as influenced by cultural memories from colonialism and slavery. In turn, representations and cultural memories of the Holocaust have influenced the way in which the postcolonial period has been depicted (Rothberg 2009: 13). Rothberg's multidirectional memory has to be seen in

---

and to the 'other'. She links the notion of the dialogic to the *Spaltung* of the subject and to the psychoanalytical approach referring, for instance, to Lacan and his works on typologies of the subject (Kristeva 1970: 14–15). In other words, intertextuality in Kristeva has to be considered as a limited 'operationalisation' of the notion of the dialogic in Bakhtin. This precision on the notion of the dialogic is closer to the definition of the concept by Bakhtin: 'The polyphonic novel is dialogic through and through. Dialogic relationships exist among all elements of novelistic structure; that is, they are juxtaposed contrapuntally. And this is so because dialogic relationships are a much broader phenomenon than mere rejoinders in a dialogue, laid out compositionally in the text; they are an almost universal phenomenon, permeating all human speech and all relationships and manifestations of human life – in general, everything that has meaning and significance' (Bakhtin 1984: 40). Todorov is a bit more ambiguous but still recognises the link that exists between the notion of the dialogic and 'the conception elaborated by Bakhtin of the human being' (1981: 95, my translation).

3   It has to be noted that the work by Lewis A. Coser titled *On Collective Memory* (1992) includes selected and translated chapters from *The Social Frameworks of Memory* and from another work of Halbwachs published in French in 1941 titled *La Topographie légendaire des évangiles en Terre Sainte: Études de mémoire collective*. But paradoxically *On Collective Memory* does not include parts of the work *La Mémoire collective*. This has created some confusion and misunderstanding in the way that the notion of *mémoire collective* has been used in research, some authors referring to *On Collective Memory* thinking that it was a translation of *La Mémoire collective*.

relation to his concept of *noeuds de mémoire*, influenced by Pierre Nora's *lieux de mémoire*. Going beyond the 'framework of the imagined community of the nation-state' (Rothberg 2010: 7), Rothberg reaffirms through this concept the necessity of considering acts of remembrance as, referring to Deleuze, 'rhizomatic networks of temporality and cultural reference that exceed attempts at territorialisation … and identitarian reduction' (ibid.).

We find another example of a concept directly influenced by the notion of collective memory in Alison Landsberg's idea of 'prosthetic memory'. The new media technologies of the twentieth and twenty-first centuries and the possibilities they offer are important factors in the transmission and uses of memory that 'make possible a new relationship to the past' (Landsberg 2004: 47). The term 'prosthetic memory' is used to describe the way in which the mass media and digital communications make it possible for some individuals to treat an event as if it was part of a their memory, despite the fact that they did not experience it. Landsberg goes even further, stating that the new context of mass culture, 'the forces of modernity and the changes … have made Halbwachs's notion of collective memory inadequate' (ibid. 8).

The differentiations introduced by Jan Assmann between communicative and cultural memory are also inspired by the Halbwachian concept of collective memory (J. Assmann 2008: 109). Communicative memory is considered as a 'living and embodied memory' transmitted through vernacular communication and interaction, while cultural memory is regarded as the mediated and objectified memory through cultural artefacts or manifestations such as 'texts, icons, dances, rituals and performances of various kinds; "classical" or otherwise formalized language(s)' (ibid. 117). Communicative memory can be regarded as an immediate and spontaneous autobiographical memory, while cultural memory should be considered as a reconstruction of a past event, a cultural and retrospective elaboration of a remembered event in a given social and historical context.

Jeffrey Olick has another approach to the term 'collective memory' introducing a differentiation between 'collected memory' on the one hand which concerns the 'aggregated individual memories of members of a group' (Olick 1999: 338) and 'collective memory' on the other which 'emphasizes the social and cultural patternings of public and personal memory' (ibid. 333). While collected memory concerns the individual and the way individual remembering is dependent on and structured by the social structures which are around us, collective memory, for Olick, concerns all the different representations of the past that are present in the public sphere that might contribute to establishing a shared memory within a specific group.

Finally, we should also mention the terminological differentiations made by Avishai Margalit between 'common memory' and 'shared memory'. Margalit defines the notion of 'common memory' as 'an aggregate notion. It aggregates the memories of all those people who remember a certain episode which each of them experienced individually' (Margalit 2002: 51) and 'shared memory' as a memory that 'integrates and calibrates the different perspectives of those who remember the episode' (ibid.).

The concepts introduced by Rothberg, Landsberg, Assmann, Olick and Margalit can be seen as fruitful reflections on the notion of collective memory and the challenges they face regarding their mediation. At the same time, their work indicates clearly to what extent the notion of collective memory is complex to define and to delimitate. With reference to Rothberg (and Deleuze), one could say that the notion of collective memory today has become a starting point for a 'rhizomatic network', where it becomes more and more difficult to understand the meaning of the original notion or, more precisely, the meaning of each of the components which constitutes the Halbwachian paradigm: the collective and the memory.

All five scholars are very clear about the necessity of considering the interdependence or interaction of the individual and the collective spheres in the acts of remembering. In this sense, they keep exploring and renewing the Halbwachian tradition where memories are considered as simultaneously individual and collective. None of them wishes to replace the concept of collective memory; however, their theoretical goals are quite different. While Assmann, Rothberg and Landsberg focus on the mediation of collective memory presenting different *modi memorandi* or 'ways of remembering' (J. Assmann 2008: 110), Margalit and Olick try to establish a differentiation in the apprehension of the term collective memory. Olick, in particular, wants 'to inquire into the value added by the term, to specify what phenomena the term sensitizes us to as well as what kind of a sensitivity this is' (1999: 334), talking about 'two cultures' or two traditions in the way the term has been understood and used.

Looking closer at the different uses and understandings of the concept of collective memory, what also seems obvious is that memory has been seen both as the result of an individual act of remembering and as the result of a cultural reconstruction of a past event. This second use of the memory concept does not include a process of remembering as an organic activity but contributes to establishing a past event in a collective canon, to use the notion of Aleida Assmann (2008: 97), and in this way it participates in shaping a cultural community.[4]

In the same way, all five scholars have a different understanding or interpretation of the collective. The collective is considered both as a group in a particular socio-cultural context but also as the aggregation of individuals considering the collective as the consequence of this aggregation forming an interrelation from the collective sphere to the individual sphere and from the individual sphere to the collective sphere. In other words, it is clear that today there is no common understanding and use of the concept of collective memory.

In a previous article, I pointed out that the term 'collective' has sometimes contributed to misunderstandings, leading one to consider collective memory as a unified memory while the term 'collective', in my opinion, necessarily indicates a certain internal dualism or even pluralism (Dessingué 2011: 172) as demonstrated in the different uses and understandings of the concept (Table 6.1). Like the majority of scholars today, my assumption is that the concept of collective memory is far from unitary or homogeneous, but I also suggest that the way the collective is apprehended in Halbwachs has to be considered as the crucible of an ongoing discussion within and between *The Social Frameworks* and *The Collective Memory*.

Above all, in the work of Maurice Halbwachs, it is necessary to differentiate between the concept of collective memory, which seems to defend a certain ideological Durkheimian stance where the subject disappears or even drowns in a collective, and the collective memory concept, which seeks to integrate a thorough reflection about the nature of the relationship between the 'I' of the individual and the 'we' of the collective to which the individual is supposed to belong in a given space and at a given time.

Further on, I propose to discuss the concept of collective memory related to three elements that I believe are essential to the overall understanding of this concept in Halbwachs' work. First, the evolution of the concept of collective memory has to be intimately related to an authorial position. The concept of collective memory evolves as Halbwachs' ideological positioning changes between the contexts of the two world wars. Secondly, I will discuss elements that contribute to perceptions of the collective memory concept as one unitary, authoritarian or monolithic. Finally, I will seek to compare this unitarian approach to a much

---

4   Several works, during the last decade, have emphasised the dynamics of memory in contemporary societies, considering the 'cultural community' as a moving transcultural/transnational entity (see e.g. Erll and Rigney 2009) or as 'travelling memory' (Erll 2011).

more dialogic Halbwachian conception of the relationship between the individual and the collective considering Halbwachs' theories in the light of Bakhtinian theories on dialogism.

Table 6.1   Uses of the collective memory concept

	Collective considered within	**Memory considered as the result of**
Cultural memory (Assmann)	a particular socio-cultural group	a cultural reconstruction of a past event
Communicative memory (Assmann)	a particular inter-generational group	an individual act of remembering
Collected memory (Olick)	a particular socio-cultural group (aggregation of individual memories)	an individual act of remembering
Collective memory (Olick)	a particular socio-cultural group	a cultural reconstruction of a past event
Common memory (Margalit)	a particular socio-cultural group (aggregation of individual memories)	an individual act of remembering
Shared memory (Margalit)	a particular socio-cultural group (calibration and standardisation of individual memories)	an individual act of remembering
Multidirectional memory / *noeuds de mémoire* (Rothberg)	a global network	a cultural reconstruction of a past event
Prosthetic memory (Landsberg)	a global network	an individual reconstruction and internalisation of a past event

Collective Memory in Context

Studies, including those of the sociologist Gérard Namer and the historian Annette Becker, have clearly shown that the concept of collective memory in Halbwachs' work evolved between the two world wars. In this sense, and to a certain extent, the semantic evolution of Halbwachs' concept of collective memory can be considered in relation to the displacement of an ideological authorial position. When Halbwachs began writing *The Social Frameworks*, the First World War had just ended. Halbwachs did not participate in the war as a soldier, because of his profound myopia, but he was attached to the Ministry of Defence, responsible for the production and supply of military equipment. However Halbwachs refers only on very rare occasions to the war in *The Social Frameworks*, excluding any involvement of a more intimate and personal memory. Looking at the correspondence with his wife Yvonne during the war, we see to what extent his non-participation in the conflict as a soldier was in reality a true source of frustration. Annette Becker, Halbwachs' biographer, even defines this frustration as a *refoulement* (denial) of this intimate memory in *The Social Frameworks*

(Becker 2003: 160). Everything happens as if there was a refusal of interference or interaction between the private sphere and the public sphere, between the individual and the collective or, as Annette Becker writes:

> *Halbwachs draws a line that he never crosses: he refuses to speak publicly about commitment in general and military commitment in particular. On one side, his private correspondence, where he fully expresses each of his thoughts; on the other side, his work, where any reference to contemporary and political surroundings, or to the ongoing war, have to disappear. (Becker 2003: 170)[5]*

The editorial context of *The Collective Memory* is, in itself, much more difficult to identify, because it covers a period of almost 20 years, between 1926 and 1944. It must also be noted that this work actually appeared in the form of several manuscripts and other notebooks that not only changed over the years by the hand of the author, but also by the hand of relatives who kept the manuscripts after Halbwachs' death. *The Collective Memory* is therefore a collection of articles, mostly manuscripts that are more or less difficult to locate in time and also difficult to include in a more global structure.

At this stage, Gérard Namer's critical edition of 1997 is an essential reference in the field. It is an important fact that from 1938, Halbwachs was firmly committed to the antifascist struggle with all the consequences this had for him as an intellectual and as a man. There is a context of growing personal commitment unquestionable in the work *The Collective Memory* linked, among other things, to the enthusiasm provoked by election of Leon Blum as French President in 1936 (Becker 2003: 304–6).

This personal commitment, which he refused to make explicit in the context of *The Social Frameworks*, led Halbwachs to an a posteriori reflection on the role of the First World War that is present in his notebooks and his private correspondence (Becker 2003: 294). At this particular moment, the shift of ideological position and intention of the author seems to corroborate Gérard Namer's thesis that *The Collective Memory* cannot be read as a continuation or supplement of *The Social Frameworks* but as a theoretical displacement or even a reversal of this work (Namer 1997: 8).

If the shift in Halbwachs' ideological position between *The Social Frameworks* and *The Collective Memory* is an important factor in the overall understanding of his work, however, it seems to me not to be a sufficient to explain Halbwachs' theoretical displacement as Namer suggested. It seems essential to look at the development of Halbwachs' theoretical framework considering the evolution and the nature of the relationship between the 'I' and the 'me' of the individual and the collective 'we' and 'us'. That is to say, one needs to examine the evolution and the nature of the relationship between individual and collective memory. It seems to me that the individual and the collective are already in a relation of permanent tension in *The Social Frameworks*. My main assumption is that *The Collective Memory* can be considered neither as a continuation or supplement of *The Social Frameworks* nor as a theoretical reversal of it, as Namer suggested, but as the continuity of an ongoing internal Halbwachian discussion and tension.

Upon publication of *The Social Frameworks* in 1925 and until his last writings before his arrest by the Gestapo in 1944, there is, I believe, a latent and an ongoing reflection about the way of considering the 'collective', the question of otherness and the positioning of the 'I' related to the 'we'. This question is not explicit in a structured manner in Halbwachs' writings and we can even consider that there are some contradictions or incoherencies in his theoretical approach. But we have to remember that Halbwachs' work was not expected

---

5   My translation.

to be a posthumous one and that is the reason why we have to consider the concept of collective memory as a concept in a permanent and ongoing 'process of development'. There is a clear instability with the position of the 'I' and the 'we.' In addition, the question of the locatedness of the otherness and of the collective in Halbwachs' work seems to be one of the main keys for understanding his work in general and the concept of collective memory in particular.

Halbwachs' Ideological Position as Durkheimian

In *The Social Frameworks of Memory*, Halbwachs' argument seems at first to be proceeding without questioning. The foreword leaves no doubt about that. Memories, according to Halbwachs, are always connected to the outside. The surroundings work not only as a framework but also as a stimulus for the individual memory. The 'we' becomes the global framework within which and through which the individual has the opportunity to rebuild their own souvenirs from the perspective of the others who surround them. The social and collective memory are thus defined initially as the replacement of the self in an exteriority 'it is because our individual thinking is able to situate itself in social frameworks … that we would also be able to remember' (Halbwachs 1994: vi).[6]

The process described here by Halbwachs is very similar to the way that Mikhail Bakhtin describes the process of exotopy, or 'outsidedness'. According to Bakhtin our relationship to the otherness (as a person or an object) on an ethical, cognitive or aesthetic level, depends on the phenomenon of identification-integration: first, identification with the other and, secondly, integration of the other in the self (Dessingué 2003: 130). The individual must be able to take the place of the other, externalizing him or herself, and only then return to the self in order to truly perceive the other in all its complexity (Bakhtin 1984: 46–7).

The fundamental difference between Halbwachs' and Bakhtin's positions is the fact that for Halbwachs the exotopy, at least at this stage, seems incomplete. The 'I' is confronted with otherness, namely the 'we', but there is no reference to the return to the self as Bakhtin pointed it out. By following Halbwachs' argument, this incomplete exotopy therefore leads to a paradigmatic relation between the individual and the collective. At this point, the otherness is only considered in the process of the externalisation of the individual. Collective memory as socio-cultural memory is almost the only framework that matters. In other words, individual memory exists only insofar as it is able to blend into a collective. Collective memory in this case is actually very close to what Aleida Assman chose to define as the 'canon' in her conception of cultural memory (2008) or as Halbwachs states, the recomposition of the image of the past, which corresponds to the dominant thoughts in society (1994: viii).

In the first two chapters dedicated to dreams and language in *The Social Frameworks*, Halbwachs continues to present a paradigmatic relation between the individual and the collective, assuming a fully Durkheimian legacy. Developing a systematic critique of Henri Bergson and of psychology, Halbwachs asserts and reaffirms the importance of the social frameworks in the formation of memories. The dream, he says, is the only event where the individual is truly with him or herself. During the dream, the individual escapes from the temporal and spatial frameworks that govern social life, thereby explaining the incompleteness of the dream. In other words, without social frameworks, the individual is

---

6   All translations of Halbwachs are mine.

unable to remember in a 'correct way' and the dream has to be considered as an absolute proof of this 'incompleteness':

> *The memory operation presupposes a constructive and rational activity of the mind which it is incapable of during sleep: memory takes place in a natural and social environment orderly and coherently, in which we recognize at every moment the overall plan and the main directions. (Halbwachs 1994: 37)*

In the logic of the Halbwachs' argument, the incoherence of dreams has to be compared to the incoherence of language disorder during sleep in which the individual may not be understood by others and to a certain extent by himself (Halbwachs 1994: 57). In order to legitimise this argument, Halbwachs uses the example of aphasia, the inability to remember words. According to Halbwachs, aphasics are unable to remember, because they are unable to externalise their thoughts through language and to communicate with other people (ibid. 76). This last example contains the dominant argument of the first two chapters in *The Social Frameworks* considering that 'there is no possible memory outside frameworks that people living in society use to set and retrieve their memories' (ibid. 79). But we also find this assumption widely discussed in the first chapter of *The Collective Memory*, 'The Collective Memory in Musicians', where the collective rules of language are considered as structuring elements of memory that does not depend on the individual him or herself but on the group to which he or she belongs (Halbwachs 1997: 48).

At an early stage, Halbwachs defines the individual and the collective memory in a paradigmatic way. It seems that this theoretical approach is the result of the individual ideological position of the author as a clear and assumed 'disciple of Durkheim', presenting a frontal opposition with Bergson or Freud and the associative psychology, an opposition which is also clearly and explicitly expressed in *The Social Frameworks* (Halbwachs 1994: 4, 40–41).

Towards a More Syntagmatic Relationship Between Individual and Collective Memory: 'La Société originale'

Nevertheless, this paradigmatic relationship between individual and collective memory is repeatedly challenged in *The Social Frameworks* and this questioning is also intensively present in *The Collective Memory*. In *Memory, History and Forgetting*, Paul Ricoeur criticises Halbwachs for crossing a line (Dessingué 2011: 173). For Ricoeur, Halbwachs goes too far in formulating the interrelation between the individual and the collective, not only saying that 'we cannot remember alone', which is, according to Ricoeur, an acceptable position, but also that 'we are not genuine owners of our own memories' (2000: 149) which is 'unacceptable' because it presupposes that the human will, thoughts and thinking are not free. It is at this point that Ricoeur's critique, accusing Halbwachs of depriving the individual of his own memory, seem unfounded to me.

In *The Social Frameworks*, the relationship between the individual and the collective is often introduced in a self-reflexive way: 'Are memories in our own domain? And when we take refuge in our past can we affirm that we escape from society to retreat into ourselves?' (Halbwachs 1994: 24). Already in the first chapter of *The Social Frameworks* Halbwachs raises explicitly the question of the return to the self that we have earlier outlined in Bakhtin. He also suggests the need to recognize the impact that certain social or cultural events have on individual conscience and individual memory (ibid. 125).

The self-reflexive nature of the Halbwachian language is also present in *The Collective Memory*, especially when he returns to the critique by psychologist Charles Blondel that was formulated right after the publication of *The Social Frameworks*. In his review, Blondel referred to the lack of consideration of what he called the 'sensitive intuition', that is to say the part of free personalisation that occurs in the reconstruction of the past. For the past to keep its personal appearance, says Blondel, and not to be confused with that of someone else, we need to consider the intervention of specific factors related to the individual at the time of the perception of the past event (Halbwachs 1997: 67). This critique from Blondel will lead Halbwachs to recognise the part of the 'sensitive intuition' which is at the very beginning of any memory defined as a recall of a purely individual consciousness (ibid. 66). As mentioned earlier, Halbwachs' work is not characterised by a linear argumentation but by an ongoing recurrent and explorative questioning and self-reflection.

It seems that there is indeed an epistemological shift in the concept of collective memory that is interested in questioning the absolute supremacy of the socio-cultural framework for the individual act of remembering. Chapter 4 of *The Social Frameworks*, 'The Location of Memories' also seems to particularly undermine the more normative reading and understanding of the concept of collective memory. There is a clear recognition and affirmation of not only interaction but also the interdependence between the individual and the collective: 'The people and objects we've seen most recently, those around us, which live and are in our immediate surroundings, form with us a collectiveness at least temporary. They act or can act on us and we on them. They are part of our everyday concerns' (Halbwachs 1994: 136).

Halbwachs seems to go even further when he claims the necessary recognition of what he calls 'the original society' ('la société originale'), that is to say, the collectiveness that 'every individual somehow forms with himself' (1994: 139). The individual is defined here as a collectiveness which means a 'collective insideness', bearing a multitude of voices, to use a Bakhtinian concept. This idea of multivoicedness or polyphony at an individual level, in other words an internal collectiveness, is also quite explicit in *The Collective Memory* when Halbwachs asserts that 'our memories remain collective and are reminded to us by others, even though it is events in which we have been involved alone, and objects that we've seen alone. The truth is that we are never alone. It is not necessary that others are there, others that differ materially from us, because we always carry *with us and in us* a number of persons who are easily identifiable' (1997: 52, my italics).

There is, therefore, indeed a theoretical displacement from a clear paradigmatic conception of collective memory to a much more syntagmatic consideration of the collective memory. This theoretical displacement is not only characteristic of the work on collective memory as it is also present in the work on the social frameworks. This theoretical shift towards a more syntagmatic relation between the 'I' of the individual and the 'we' of the collective requires the recognition of plurality within the same individual, a merger within the self of a multitude of others, in some ways an internal and ontological collectiveness. This also leads directly to the necessary fulfilment of Bakhtin's exotopy.

The interdependence of the 'me' and the 'we' inside the individual, as well as a plural conception of individual identity implies a return to the self. This return to the self is also specifically mentioned by Halbwachs in the work on the frameworks when he states that:

> *Each time we replace one of our impressions in the actual context, the context (or the framework) transforms the impression, but the impression, in turn, changes the context. ... Hence a perpetual work of readaptation, which forces us to return to the impressions that we got from the past events. (Halbwachs 1994: 135)*

This work of perpetual readaptation mentioned by Halbwachs implies the consideration of the dynamic nature of memory in relation to the conception of a moving identity of the self. Paul Ricoeur would speak of the ipse-identity, which corresponds in reality to the part of the self that changes and evolves through time and space (1990: 11).

According to Jan Assmann, memory makes us 'conscious of our self' at both an individual and collective level. He claims that since the 'I' or the 'self' is an unstable and diachronic identity, the synthesis of time and identity needs to be concretized by memory (2008: 109). Looking at the work of Halbwachs, we have to consider a double approach to the question of the links between memory, time and identity. On the one hand, memories can be considered as confirming or unifying the question of the identity of the 'I' as an individual or of the 'we' as a group through time as Assmann also suggests. On the other hand, memories can be considered as challenging the question of identity, by changing the paradigm of identity to the dynamic paradigm of identification. In this sense, memories as a dynamic phenomenon also contribute to the instability of the 'self' and of the conception of 'us'.

Conclusion

There is indeed a necessity to consider the collective memory as a concept in perpetual gestation and discussion in the works of Maurice Halbwachs. The Halbwachian concept is clearly a polysemic one. There is in Halbwachs' work a latent reflection that is related to the nature of the relationship between individual and collective. The response is always in gestation and oscillates along a line defined by a more or less paradigmatic or more or less syntagmatic consideration of the relation between the individual and the collective. The notion of collective memory seems to integrate, in a more or less implicit way, a complex understanding of the collective both as 'collectivity' (a particular socio-cultural group), as a result of an 'aggregation' of individual memories and as an inside 'collectiveness' (Table 6.2), whereby the notion of memory designates both an act of reconstruction of a past event and an act of individual remembering.

This dialogical and dynamic approach of the understanding and use of the past has been a key element in the international research field in memory studies during the last 20 years trying to go beyond a static and linear approach of the 'past-in-present' and of the question of individual and collective identity. Halbwachs and Bakhtin have really been central companions in my work because both authors emphasise that memory acts, like speech acts, are complex and intricate phenomena without any fixed material meaning.

In order for the memory boom not only to become a boom, methodological approaches in the field of memory studies should continue to explore the complexity and instability of the memory processes. This implies discovering deeper structures in our encounter with the other(s) and with the world of representation. Since Halbwachs initiated an awareness that the notion of collective memory is not only working as a transversal and concept (through time and space) but also as an ontological concept within individuals.

Table 6.2   Collective memory as a polysemic concept

The collective as 'collectivity'	The collective as 'aggregation'	The collective as 'collectiveness'
The collective memory as a result of selection through time and space within a particular group, as a culturally established reconstruction of a past event (cultural memory, multidirectional memory, collective memory [Olick], shared memory)	The collective memory as a result of aggregation of individual memories within a particular group (collected memory, communicative memory, common memory)	The collective memory as an inside collectiveness within the individual (ontological collective memory, the Halbwachian 'sensitive intuition' and 'société originale')

References

Assmann, A. 2008. 'Canon and Archive', in Erll and A. Nünning 2008: 97–108.

Assmann, J. 2008. 'Communicative and Cultural Memory', in Erll and Nünning 2008: 109–18.

Bakhtin, M. 1970. *La Poétique de Dostoïevski* (Paris: Seuil).

— — 1984. *Esthétique de la création verbale* (Paris: Gallimard).

Becker, A. 2003. *Maurice Halbwachs: Un intellectuel en guerres mondiales 1914–1945* (Paris: Agnès Vienot).

Dessingué, A. 2003. 'Le Polyphonisme de Bakhtine à Ricœur', *Literary Research / Recherche littéraire* 39–40: 128–44.

— — 2011. 'Towards a Phenomenology of Memory and Forgetting', *Études Ricœuriennes / Ricoeur Studies* 2/1: 168–78.

Erll, A. 2011. 'Travelling Memory', *Parallax* 17/4: 4–18.

— — and A. Nünning (eds) 2008. *Cultural Memory Studies* (Berlin: De Gruyter).

— — and A. Rigney 2009. *Mediation, Remediation and the Dynamics of Cultural Memory* (Berlin: De Gruyter).

Genette, G. 1982. *Palimpsestes ou la littérature au second degré* (Paris: Seuil).

Halbwachs, M. 1994. *Les Cadres sociaux de la mémoire* (Paris: Albin Michel).

— — 1997. *La Mémoire collective* (Paris: Albin Michel).

Kristeva, J. 1967. 'Bakhtine, le mot, le dialogue et le roman', *Critique* 23: 438–65.

— — 1970. 'Une poétique ruinée', in Bakhtin 1970: 5–29.

Landsberg, A. 2004. *Prosthetic Memory: The Transformation of American Remembrance in the Age of Mass Culture* (New York: Columbia University Press).

Margalit, A. 2002. *The Ethics of Memory* (Cambridge, MA: Harvard University Press).

Morson, G.S., and C. Emerson 2002. *Mikhail Bakhtin: Creation of a Prosaics* (Stanford, CA: Stanford University Press).

Namer, G. 1997. 'Un demi-siècle après sa mort', in Halbwachs 1997: 7–18.

Novick, P. 1999. *The Holocaust in American Life* (Boston, MA: Houghton Mifflin).

Olick, J.K. 1999. 'Collective Memory: The Two Cultures', *Sociological Theory* 17/3 (Nov.): 333–47.

Ricoeur, P. 1990. *Soi-même comme un autre* (Paris: Seuil).

— — 2000. *Mémoire, histoire et oubli* (Paris: Seuil).

Rothberg, M. 2009. *Multidirectional Memory: Remembering the Holocaust in the Age of Decolonization* (Stanford, CA: Stanford University Press).

— — 2010. 'Introduction: Between Memory and Memory: From *Lieux de mémoire* to *Noeuds de mémoire*', in M. Rothberg, D. Sanyal and M. Silverman (eds), *Noeuds de mémoire: Multidirectional Memory in Postwar French and Francophone Culture*, Yale French Studies 118/119 (New Haven, CT: Yale University Press), pp. 3–10.

Todorov, T. 1981. *Mikhail Bakthine: Le Principe dialogique* (Paris: Seuil).

Winter, J. 2000. 'The Generation of Memory: Reflections on the Memory Boom in Contemporary Historical Studies', *Bulletin of the German Historical Institute* 27: 69–92.

A Unified Approach to Collective Memory: Sociology, Psychology and the Extended Mind

William Hirst and Charles B. Stone

It says a great deal about the field of memory studies that psychologists interested in memory are the odd-men-out in a volume on the topic. When we first came across the field of memory studies, we were mystified. There seemed to be little interest in individual memory in the field, and what interest existed adopted a psychoanalytic perspective. As experimental psychologists, we felt that a vast wealth of theory and data about human memory was not figuring in the discussion.

We certainly were aware that experimental psychologists did not make it easy for students of memory studies to find the relevant literature. To a large extent, the topic of interest in the field of memory studies is collective memory, but if one turns to the experimental psychology literature, it is rarely discussed as a topic. The reason for this neglect reflects, at least in part, experimental psychologists' strong bent towards methodological individualism and their inclination to strip away social influences on cognition and behaviour rather than study them. As Mary Douglas opined, a bit harshly, psychologists may be 'institutionally incapable of remembering that humans are social beings' (1986: 81). As a result, something as socially encrusted as collective memory is simply not something they, as experimental psychologists, would gravitate toward studying. We understood this line of reasoning, but found it difficult to embrace. Ulric Neisser (1988) trained the first author to study cognitive phenomenon in 'ecologically valid' settings. Stripping away social factors affecting cognition moves away from, rather than towards, ecological validity.

This chapter is about how we, and others, have tried over the last decade or so to find a place for a study of collective memory that builds on the extensive work in experimental psychology. We will not attempt to detail the experiments some pioneering psychologists have done in the last few years. Along with colleagues, we have done that elsewhere (Hirst and Echterhoff 2012; Stone et al. 2012). Furthermore, we suspect that most readers of this volume will find the details tedious. Rather, we will focus on why a psychological approach to collective memory is needed and why the time is ripe to undertake such an endeavour. In doing so, we will illustrate why psychology cannot merely be a separate endeavour, unconnected to the rest of the field of memory studies, but must be a close companion with which there is a constant exchange about ideas and concerns.

In what follows, we will (1) frame our concerns in terms of the distinction between collective and collected memory, (2) consider this distinction in terms of an 'extended mind' and (3) apply the arguments we developed about a psychology of collective memory by examining the experimental psychological work on collective forgetting.

Collective and Collected Memory

In his attempt to bring some coherence to the field of memory studies, Olick distinguished collective memories from collected memories.[1] Building on discussions of culture, he treated collective memory as 'patterns of publicly available symbols objectified by society' (1999: 336). Collected memories, alternatively, are 'aggregated individual memories of members of a group' (ibid. 338). For several reasons, Olick argued that the two captured 'radically distinct ontological orders' (ibid. 336). First, he underscored how collective memories cannot be reduced to individually held memories. As he wrote elsewhere, with Vinitzky-Seroussi and Levy: 'One need not become a metaphysician to believe there is an emergent dimension of collective remembering that is organized without direct reference to individuals' (Olick, Vinitzky-Seroussi and Levy 2011: 21).

Second, he suggested that it might be possible to conceive of collective memories not just as emerging out of but also as independent from individual memories. Olick, Vinitzky-Seroussi and Levy (2012) offered an example: few Americans can say what the Gettysburg Address was about, though many could recite its first phrase. Despite this lack of an individual memory, the sentiments expressed in the Gettysburg Address continue to animate the American spirit and shape its politics. We assume that, for Olick (1997), there is a memory for the address because the sentiment lingers. Moreover, we would further assume that if what is driving this lingering sentiment is the cultural artefact of the speech itself, then the memory might legitimately be called cultural (Assmann 1995). As such, the memory survives not because it is held by individuals, but because of social efforts. Individual memories for the address need not figure in the process.

Third, Olick (1999) appears to argue that the processes underlying the formation and retention of collective and collected memory differ. On the one hand, the processes involved in the formation and retention of collective memories depend on societal efforts and 'societal machinery', that is, cultural and institutional structures, artefacts and practices, as well as political machinations. Sturken's (1997) discussion of the politics surrounding the construction of the Vietnam Veterans Memorial would be a good example of how a student of collective memory might study collective memory from Olick's perspective.

On the other hand, the processes underlying the formation and retention of collected memories depend on individual efforts and the use of the psychological machinery involved in an individual memory's formation, maintenance, transformation and recollection, including the neurological machinery. For instance, to understand the role of the Lincoln Memorial in shaping Americans' memory of Lincoln, the student of collected memory might consider the role visual imagery plays in cementing individual memories (Pavio 1971). They might note that the designers of the memorial were clearly employing the well-known psychological principle that visual imagery is generally a more powerful mnemonic than verbal imagery when they decided to place the dramatic statute of a Zeus-like Lincoln at the centre of the memorial. For a student of collected memory, as Olick conceives it, Americans' memory of Lincoln has the form it does because of the use of this powerful psychological principle.

Finally, as Hirst and Manier (2008) indicated, Olick's (1999) treatment of collective and collected memory suggests that collective memories are 'in the world', that is, 'outside the

---

1   Our focus on Olick should not be viewed as an attempt to diminish his substantial contribution. He has taught students of collective memory a great deal. We concentrate on his writings because he writes clearly and forcefully, placing the perspective held by many of his colleagues in eloquent but bold relief.

head', whereas collected memories are 'in the head.' Given their different spatial locations, their ontological distinctiveness is almost ensured.

The Extended Mind and the Collective/Collected Distinction

Once one adopts the distinction between collective and collected memory, it becomes understandable why psychologists rarely figure in discussions of collective memory. After all, psychology is important to the study of collected memory, not collective memory. However, the ontological claim Olick (1999) makes for his distinction rests on a concept of the mind that recent philosophical work on the extended mind hypothesis has robustly questioned (Clark and Chalmers 1998). Indeed, when the mind is appropriately conceptualised, we would claim, the distinction between collective and collected memories collapses. Just as light can be particle and wave at the same time, so can collective memory be both aggregated individual memories and publicly available symbols. No ontological distinction is needed.

The standard view of the mind, the one implicit in Olick's (1999) distinction, locates it somewhere beneath the surface of the skin. Whereas one need not identify the mind with the brain, the mind is clearly contained within an individual, the argument goes. Philosophers who have recently questioned this conceptualisation have argued for an 'extended mind'. We will not describe here, in detail, the various arguments for what has been called the first and second wave views of the extended mind (Sutton 2006). Rather we will confine ourselves to motivating the general intuition and then apply this intuition to the collective/collected memory distinction.

Consider Bateson's (1979) blind man navigating through the world with a cane. To explain the blind man's navigation, cognitive neuroscientists might investigate cortical activity and treat any input from the outside world in terms of cortical input. Some researchers might want to go beyond an exclusive focus on cortical activity and include in their explanations the origins of cortical inputs, for instance, the activation occurring at the nerve endings of the fingers holding the cane. The configuration of these nerve endings might be important, for instance, inasmuch as different configurations might produce different patterns of cortical input. A proponent of an extended mind would ask: Why not go beyond the surface of the skin and include the cane? Unquestionably, the nature of the cane – for instance, its rigidity – is as much a factor in the blind man's ease of navigation as the configuration of nerve endings or the activities in the cortex. There is no *a priori* reason to exclude the cane from any explanation. For proponents of an extended mind, the most principled approach would include the cortex, the fingertips and the cane.

In a similar way, those postulating an extended mind want to include external influences in their explanations (Wilson and Clark 2009). Even the simple presence of a 'similar other' can, for example, increase the accessibility of memories (Shteynberg 2010). Or consider the conversations in which remembering often takes place (Hirst and Echterhoff 2012). Although one can, in some instances, distinguish between the retrieval of a memory and its conversion into an expression of this memory, often in the form of a conversation (Tulving 1983), in many instances, it is impossible to separate the memory from its expression. Jane's conversation with her mother about her date might differ in content from her conversation with her girlfriend about the same date. Jane may sometimes intentionally censor what she says to her mother, but in many instances, she simply talks to her mother in a free-flowing manner, without any sense of censoring herself. The nuances of the ending of the date may simply not come to mind because that is not what her mother is interested in or asks her about. Alternatively, details about the end of the date may figure centrally in Jane's conversation with her girlfriend. These details may be what the girlfriend is interested in and what she asks Jane about. In her conversations, Jane is simply tuning her remembering to her audience (Echterhoff, Higgins and Levine 2009). From this perspective, what is remembered is governed by what is communicated. If you like, remembering is communicating.

This point extends to considerations of memorising and remembering at the societal level. Tourists may visit the Lincoln Memorial, which evokes memories of Lincoln. What is elicited depends critically upon the memorial – the steep steps one must climb to gain access to the 'inner chamber', the looming presence of the Zeus-like Lincoln and the solemn lighting created by the massive three walls that articulate the inner chamber. It is not that the visitors bring to mind all they know about Lincoln and then consider more thoroughly those recollections that fit into the perspective captured by the design of the memorial. To be sure, there may be some sceptical visitors that make this effort. But, perhaps because humans want to minimise rather than maximise how much they tax their cognitive resources (Kahneman 2011), most people simply want to visit the memorial, not critique it. They surrender themselves to its influences. The result is that the give-and-take between the memorial and the visitor leads to recollections in accordance with the intentions of the designers. In order to capture this give-and-take, researchers cannot focus solely on what is happening in the head of the visitor, the design of the memorial or its socio-history. Rather they must include all of these components in interaction with each other. There is no reason to privilege one explanation or one of these components over the others. An account of the Lincoln Memorial's role in American collective memory would be incomplete if one did.

It seems best, then, to take a systems approach, in which memorising and remembering occurs within a system that includes individuals and the environmental and social context in which these individuals are memorising and remembering (Hutchins 1995; see also Pettai Ch. 16 below). From this perspective, there are not, on the one hand, collective memories involving public symbols objectified by society and, on the other hand, collected memories made up of aggregates of individual memories. Rather there are simply individuals acting in a social and environmental context. The system produces and contains the memories, not the individuals within or the surrounding social and environmental context. There are no separate collective and collected memories, but simply one memory reflecting the interaction between the system's components.

One might wonder when considering the concept of an extended mind, its relation to other concepts that figure more heavily in discussions about collective memory from a memory studies perspective, for instance, notions of intersubjectivity (Passerini Ch. 5 above) or Durkheim's notion of the 'conscious collective'. However, an exploration of this issue would take us far beyond what is possible in this short chapter, but it underscores how the companions of those who adopt a more cognitive psychological approach largely exist in different social networks than those who accompany scholars in the mainstream of memory studies. Clearly, there is a need for the social networks of scholars from different disciplines to intersect more in an interdisciplinary endeavour such as memory studies.

Collective Forgetting

We want to make the previous discussion more concrete by examining how a systems or extended mind approach might work when considering collective forgetting. As any student of memory studies will easily accept, no matter how one defines collective memory, it will involve not just what one remembers, but also what one forgets. Collective forgetting can take different forms (Connerton 2008), but how a community envisions its past will be in part captured by what they forget. In evoking the notion of forgetting, we do not mean to imply that the memory is erased. Rather, at a particular time and place, the memory is inaccessible, or, at least, difficult to access. Cole (2001), for instance, discussed how villagers in Madagascar seemingly 'forgot' their colonial past only to find the memories come flooding back as democratic elections take place. This inability to recollect their initial memories has recently been framed in terms of 'mnemonic silence' (Ben-Ze'ev, Ginion and Winter 2010; Stone et al. 2012; Zerubavel 2006). A critical task for students of memory studies is to understand the origins of collective, mnemonic silence and its consequences.

One might expect that a good starting point would be to understand the social dynamics that govern silence. For decades, for instance, Turks were forbidden to discuss what is often referred to as the Armenian genocide (Lewy 2005). One might try to understand the history of the mnemonic silence surrounding the genocide, the politics that led legal restrictions on public discussion and the nature of any resistance to the prohibition. Such an explanation would be ideal fodder for students of memory studies.

But the claim here, though, is that it is not enough to discuss these societal variables. The effects of mnemonic silence on memory are subtle, as we shall see. Without building on careful psychological research, one might not fully appreciate the nuances and come to inaccurate conclusions about the influence of different cultural artefacts and practices on memory.

Within-Individual Retrieval-Induced Forgetting

Let us start with a purely individual memory phenomenon. Consider a story about a day in the life of John. The day consists of a series of discrete episodes: preparing for the day, shopping for week-end groceries, visiting a friend at a hospital, taking a trip with Mike to Coney Island, and finishing the day with dinner at Mike's. Each episode might, in turn, consist of a series of events. For instance, while at Coney Island, John and Mike might swim in the ocean, ride a roller coaster, and eat a hot dog. A friend, Mary, might learn about John's day, for instance, by reading a written account on Tumblr. What happens to Mary's memory when she tries to recall John's story?

Two responses to this question seem fairly straightforward and do not need sophisticated psychological experimentation to justify. First, what Mary recalls will be selective. People do not recall everything they are capable of remembering in most instances (Marsh 2007). The reasons for this selectivity are multiple, but it is often the case that selective remembering occurs, not just overtly, but also covertly. Mary probably selectively recalls overtly the story about John, with not much more coming to mind covertly. Second, in large part because remembering is selective, Mary will recall some aspects of the memory and not others. The positive effect of rehearsal on memory is perhaps one of the most well-established principles in the psychology of memory.

But what happens to those memories that Mary does not recall, those that remain mnemonically silent. Again, there is a fairly obvious answer: The absence of rehearsal allows the unrecalled memories to decay. However, much more may be transpiring besides decay. Not all mnemonic silences are mnemonically equal. More specifically, after selectively recalling her story about John's day, Mary will be more likely to forget (or at least, fail to remember) unmentioned events related to the recalled memories than unmentioned, unrelated events, a pattern of remembering and forgetting referred to as 'retrieval-induced forgetting' (Anderson, Bjork and Bjork 1994). For instance, Mary might recollect the episode involving Coney Island, but not the episode involving a hospital visit. Moreover, within the Coney Island recollection, she might mention that John went swimming, but fail to mention that he ate a hot dog. Retrieval-induced forgetting occurs when Mary is more likely to forget that John ate a hot dog than any event that occurred while John was at the hospital in that the hot-dog eating is closely related to what Mary talked about, whereas the hospital trip is not.

The usual psychological account of the retrieval-induced forgetting phenomenon involves inhibition (for a review, see Storm and Levy 2012). When Mary remembers selectively that John went swimming, she ends up inhibiting the hot-dog memory. It is not that she is aware of that the memory is inhibited, but successful remembering involves inhibiting competing responses. The inhibition does not extend to the events concerning the hospital visit. There is no reason why trying to remember what John did while at Coney Island should elicit, even covertly, the details of the hospital visit. As a result of the selective inhibition, there is selective forgetting: more forgetting of the unmentioned, related memory than the unmentioned, unrelated memories.

Socially Shared Retrieval-Induced Forgetting

The situation we just described is usually the kind of situation most psychologists study – one person learning about something and then recalling it in isolation. But, as we have emphasised, remembering occurs within a larger social and environmental context, particularly in the form of a conversational interaction. Let us take an extremely straightforward context, one implicit in the situation we just described for Mary. That is, Mary is recalling John's day to another person. This person has their own agency and the relationship between Mary and her listener is rife with social complexity – they may be intimates or not trust each other or have a particular power relationship between them. Does what Mary say in this complex social situation have any effect now, not on Mary's memory, but on the listener's memory? Here we are most interested in the situation where both Mary and her listener already have pre-established memories about John's day. Such situations are fairly common. Not only do people listen to others convey new information, but, in what may be a uniquely human undertaking, conversational remembering frequently involves discussions about events which both speaker and listener already have fairly good memories. College alumni meet to reminisce with each other about their shared experiences; couples sit by the fireside and remember their early dating experiences; faculty get together at meetings and try to remember what was said at previous meetings. Can Mary's selective rendering of John's day induce forgetting not only in her own memory, but also now in the memory of an already knowledgeable listener?

It can. Not only are memories mentioned in a conversation likely to be better remembered subsequently by both speaker and listener, but unmentioned memories related to what was remembered are more likely to be forgotten in the future than unmentioned, unrelated memories, again, for both speaker and listener (Cuc, Koppel and Hirst 2007; for a review, see Hirst, Coman and Coman 2014). Because of her selective remembering, Mary might be more likely to forget that John ate a hot dog at Coney Island, but so will her listener. As a result, selective remembering on the part of one participant in a conversation produces collective forgetting across conversational participants (Stone et al. 2010).

One possible explanation for socially shared retrieval-induced forgetting is that listeners concurrently, albeit covertly, retrieve with the speaker. Consequently, they are selectively remembering in the same manner as the speaker and, hence, manifesting the same pattern of induced forgetting. Such concurrent retrieval takes effort on the part of the listener. What is startling about the now repeatedly observed socially shared retrieval-induced forgetting is that listeners appear to make such an effort.

Does this finding have practical significance for the formation and retention of collective memories? It would suggest, for instance, that George Bush would have been well served to mention the build-up of the Iraq War, while failing in his discussion to mentioned weapons of mass destructions (WMDs). In this way, he would have induced forgetting for his argument that the United States needed to go to war because Iraq possessed WMDs. Collective forgetting of the WMD argument would be less pronounced, the argument goes, if President Bush had simply avoided any mention of the build-up of the war.

The Social in Socially Shared Retrieval-Induced Forgetting

A key point we made when discussing the extended mind is that remembering is a product of individual psychological mechanisms within a larger social context. We began the discussion here on retrieval-induced forgetting by describing a purely individual phenomenon – the selective remembering by one individual leads to selective forgetting for this individual. There is no social context to consider. We then introduced a social context by examining the mnemonic effect of what a speaker says on a listener. In systems language, we created a system that contained two people and their interactions within this system. This interaction led not only to mutual influences on each other's memories, but also to a potential convergence onto a shared memory. But even here one could try to revert to a more traditional approach and view what the speaker says as merely 'input' for the listener.

This mere 'input' argument becomes more difficult to support if the effect of the speaker on a listener's memory can be shown to depend on the social relationship between the speaker and the listener. In such a case, one must discuss more than just input. We are only beginning to understand how the social relationship between speaker and listener matters, but there are some tantalizing suggestions.

For instance, the credibility of the speaker matters. Koppel et al. (2014) found that socially shared retrieval-induced forgetting was less likely to occur when the source of a message was viewed as an expert. It was more likely to occur when the listener was warned that the speaker's memory may be unreliable. They accounted for this finding by first observing, as we just did, that concurrent retrieval takes effort and then referring to epistemic motives that might lead listeners to make such an effort. Specifically, they reasoned that the more credible the source, the more likely the recollection is accurate and the less likely it should be that a listener would make the effort to concurrently remember along with the speaker. Alternatively, the less credible the source, the more likely a listener will make the effort to concurrently remember.

Relational motives may also govern the extent to which listeners concurrently retrieve. When a couple reminisce about their early dating experiences, one member of the pair may be the speaker, while the other listens, but the listener will no doubt be remembering the romance along with the speaker. The listener's motive here is probably not to test the accuracy of his partner, but to form a tight relational bond with his partner. That is, he is relationally, not epistemically, motivated to concurrently retrieve (see e.g. Stone et al. 2014). When might someone be relationally motivated? One possibility is, when one is aware of the characteristics of the speaker and these are generally positive, the listener might be more relationally motivated to concurrently retrieve. In some acts of communication there is a clear and present source of the communication: One can see, for instance, the speaker when listening to a YouTube lecture. In other acts of communication, the communicator is implicit. A journalist may communicate a news story to their readers, but the readers rarely have a clear image of the journalist and, indeed, do not even think about the fact that there is someone behind the communication. Will the level of socially shared retrieval-induced forgetting differ in these two instances?

Fagin, Meister and Hirst (forthcoming) explored this issue in instances in which the communicator was not known to the listener and had no obvious connection to the speaker. Will socially shared retrieval-induced forgetting be more likely to occur if the source is clearly, for instance, visually represented to the listener? Fagin, Meister and Hirst asked participants to first study a story about the day in the life of John and then attend to a selective retelling of the story. In the various conditions they tested, the retelling took the form of a simple narrative presented in different ways: (1) as text on PowerPoint slides; (2) as text, but preceded with a statement that the author was a young man from New York; (3) as text, with a picture of the author by the side; (4) as an audio recording, without a picture of the speaker; (5) as an audio recording, with a picture; and (6) as a video recording, with the audio. Although other conditions are being explored, the results for these six are suggestive: Socially shared retrieval-induced forgetting was only observed in the final memory test when there was a picture present or when the presentation took the form of a video with audio. Neither audio alone nor text alone was sufficient to induce forgetting in the listener, at least in the situations studied by Fagin, Meister and Hirst. One apparently had to 'see' the person responsible for the narrative. Presumably, the communicative situation had to emphasize that there was a person behind the message for socially shared retrieval-induced forgetting to take place. There had to be a person the listener was 'relating to.' A simple audio presentation was not enough.

Coman and Hirst (forthcoming) examined a situation in which listeners not only saw the speaker, but had different social relationships with the speaker. Specifically, they investigated the effect of group membership. Princeton students first studied a story and then listened to an audio paired with a photo and background information of a young person selectively recalling the story. Group membership appeared to matter. Socially shared retrieval-induced forgetting was found when the speaker was identified as a Princeton student, but not when he or she was identified as a Yale student. We do not suspect that the Princeton student thought the Princeton or Yale student speaker was more or less credible. Rather they were more likely to see themselves as related to the Princeton student. This explanation is underscored by the finding that socially shared retrieval-induced forgetting was more likely to be found if the listeners were primed to think about their identity as a Princeton student.

Moving Toward a Politically Relevant Situation

Some students of memory studies may question the relevance of these studies because they examine conversation interactions rather than their usual phenomena of interest: memorials or commemoration, political speeches or history textbooks, cultural artefacts or practices. But conversations can be viewed as a practice that can underlie the formation of a collective memory, albeit not a ritualistic one like a commemoration. Moreover, conversations are known to assist in the formation of collective memories. For example, Lithuanians of Lithuanian descent can recite important historical events relevant to Lithuania, not because they studied them in the Soviet-developed textbooks they used in school (Schuman, Rieger and Gaidys 1994): they did not. Rather they presumably learned about Lithuanian history through informal conversations with friends, relatives and acquaintances. It is also worth noting that computer simulations suggest that conversations within small groups can lead to shared memories across larger groups within a network (Coman et al. 2012). That is, even though socially shared retrieval-induced forgetting has primarily been studied in the lab using small groups, Coman et al.'s simulation study suggests that it may also prove to be a force in the formation of collective memories in larger groups.

Of course, it would be best to show that socially shared retrieval-induced forgetting occurs in the real world and across large populations. With this in mind, we, with some of our colleagues, decided to determine whether listening to a political speech would lead to socially shared retrieval-induced forgetting in the general public (Stone et al. forthcoming). We tested this possibility using, as a case study, Belgium, a country comprised primarily of two opposing social groups (French-speakers and Dutch-speakers). These two groups have been in conflict with each other for decades, at times making it difficult to form a government. Indeed, several years ago (2010–2011) Belgium broke the record set by Iraq for the number of days without a government.

We examined the effect of the biannual speech of the King of Belgium, Albert II, on the public's memory for four politically sensitive topics: (1) the economic concerns of Belgium, (2) the 'linguistic' issue (Belgium is trilingual, composed primarily of French and Dutch speakers with a small contingent of German speakers), (3) issues related to Brussels [a bilingual city – French and Dutch – whose relation to the two linguistically distinct regions of Belgium is contested], and (4) Belgian history (how to frame Belgium's history given the present concerns about the future of Belgium). The king's speech was televised on both French-language and Dutch-language stations and widely discussed in the newspapers serving both linguistic groups. The king delivered it in both French and Dutch (each pre-recorded). With respect to the attitude of the Dutch-speaking and French-speaking public toward the king, it is worth noting that the king's family speaks French at home and that his Dutch is less than perfect. The Flemish (Dutch-speaking) nationalist party Vlaams Belang did not attend the recent swearing-in of the new king, Phillippe, which took place shortly after Albert's recent abdication.

We were interested in whether listening to the speech affected the public's mnemonic accessibility of information relevant to the four political issues. Unlike the other research we have described, this investigation did not first ask the public to study a story or acquire new information about the four political issues. Each member of the Belgium public no doubt came to the speech with knowledge about the political issues. The king would presumably talk about only some of what the general public knew. Would listening to the speech affect the accessibility the general public had to their political knowledge about the issues? Would it facilitate access? Or would it hinder it? And in the case of the latter, would any observed 'forgetting' apply to all four political issues or only the issues that the king discussed? And, finally, would this retrieval-induced forgetting differ for Dutch and French speakers? The French speakers may feel closer to the king and, as a consequence, be relationally motivated to concurrently retrieve along with him, just as the Princeton students concurrently retrieved along with a Princetonian speaker. The Dutch speakers may treat the king as an out-group member, and, as a consequence, not be relationally motivated to make the effort to concurrently retrieve.

From a systems perspective, there is more to the system than the speech itself and the public. The king may be constrained by the prestige of his position, his need to remain dignified and above petty politics, the assurance that every word will be analysed in detail, and the need to vet the speech with his staff. The public will have at most a limited influence on these processes, yet what they hear and in the end how their memory is altered by the speech is a product of each of these 'social components.' Our interest was, however, in the effect of the speech, once written and delivered, on the public, specifically, whether even at such a large, public level, socially shared retrieval-induced forgetting can be observed under certain conditions.

With these considerations in mind, we drafted an online questionnaire that, among other things, asked participants to list six facets of the four political issues and disseminated it to both French- and Dutch-speaking Belgians shortly before and after two of the king's public speeches. As one might expect, the king's speeches were selective. He discussed economic issues and linguistic issues, but did not discuss issues involving Brussels or Belgian history, two topics the king had discussed in the past.

Few participants were able to list six facets for each of the four political issues either in the before-questionnaire or the after-questionnaire. We therefore focused our attention on whether the number of facets listed increased, decreased or remained the same across the two questionnaires. For the French-speakers, it actually decreased for those who listened to the speech, but only for the two political issues discussed. They could list fewer points of concern when it came to the economic and the linguistic issues after listening to the king's speech than before the speech. There was no difference in the length of their lists for the Brussels or historical issues. There was also no difference in the length of the list for the French speakers who did not listen to the speech, now for all four political issues. As for the Dutch speaker, the king's speech had no affect on their ability to recall facets of the four political issues regardless of whether or not they listened to the speech. The length of their lists was the same in the before and after questionnaires for all four political issues. By attending to individual, psychological memory mechanisms, we predicted and confirmed that listening to a political speech can lead the public to know less rather than more about a political issue, but only if they are in a position to want to relate, in some way, to the speaker.

General Discussion

How well then does the claim that one must view collective memory in terms of a system, in which individuals and their psychology plays a large role, hold up? Does it provide interesting insights into the formation, maintenance and recollection of collective memory, the burden we accepted at the beginning of this chapter? It may be better for researchers to include both social and psychological components within the system purely on philosophical grounds, in that the distinction between collective and collected memory may make assumptions about the mind that are questionable. But more to the point, do we learn anything interesting about memory in the real world by merging collective with collected memory?

At the start, we should insist that despite the consequences of separating collective from collected memory, most discussions of what would be classified as collective memory acknowledge certain psychological principles at work. It is just that the principles are so intuitive and straightforward that they seem to almost pass without acknowledgement. For instance, almost every discussion of collective memory we know of assumes that (1) rehearsal reinforces memory, (2) silence leads to decay and (3) memory is malleable. To the extent that these general, widely accepted principles are replaced with more nuanced, detailed mechanisms, the field of collective memory has, as we noted in the beginning, relied on psychoanalytic theories of memory. Once again, we think at least one reason for this reliance on psychoanalytic theories has to do with starting points. As Olick, Vinitsky-Seroussi and Levy noted in their *Collective Memory Reader* (2012), trauma studies has played a central role in the study of collective memory. Psychoanalytic theories of memory were developed in large part to understand how people cope with traumatic events, and, hence, they offer a ready vocabulary for understanding how nations, for instance, might deal with a traumatic past.

The real question, then, is whether the more subtle, less transparent psychological principles of memory add much to the discussion. The answer depends on how relevant one finds the kinds of results we discussed in this paper. Does the phenomenon of socially shared retrieval-induced forgetting speak to those that would, returning to Olick's distinction, be more interested in collective rather than collected memory? The average citizen would probably not predict that listening to a political speech would induce the public to forget memories related to the political issues the politician spoke about. After all, good citizens are expected to listen to political speeches. Moreover, the same citizen might not predict that listening to politicians selectively remember would induce forgetting for material related to what was discussed rather than unrelated material. But it does, and it does so in real world settings. In this regard, it is worth highlighting that retrieval-induced forgetting has been found to be long lasting. Fagin, Meksin and Hirst (forthcoming) have found it lasts for over a month after three exposures to the selectively presented material. Presumably multiple political speeches following well-established talking points would produce even longer lasting and more robust retrieval-induced forgetting. Taken together, the relevant psychological research suggests that socially shared retrieval-induced forgetting is, at least, one means by which groups can come to share a similar rendering of the past.

This brings us to our last point. To the extent that one wants to understand the formation of a collective memory at the micro-level, one must apply general mechanisms that can hold when considering small groups, such as couples, or large groups, such as nations. Halbwachs certainly treated collective memory in this way, in that he discussed collective memories of families as well as collective memories of nations. The umbrella of collective memory must also encompass a wide range of events – from traumatic events to positive, celebratory ones (the signing of the Declaration of Independence, for instance). It must envelope not just events that occurred, but also historically inaccurate events (Washington's demolition of a cherry tree), not just significant events, but trivial ones as well (Jacqueline Kennedy's refurbishing of the White House). This variety almost begs for an account that includes at least one general component that can stretch over each instance. Collective memories might arise out of particular cultural artefacts and practices and specific political efforts, but they also involve individuals who are endowed with distinctly human psychological mechanisms. As a consequence, ideal students of collective memory should have as their companions, both those steeped in general approaches and those concerned with the particular.

References

Anderson, M.C., R.A. Bjork and E.L. Bjork 1994. 'Remembering can Cause Forgetting: Retrieval Dynamics in Long-Term Memory', *Journal of Experimental Psychology: Learning, Memory, and Cognition* 20: 1063–87.

Assmann, J. 1995. 'Collective Memory and Cultural Identity', trans. J. Czaplicka, *New German Critique* 65: 125–33.

Bateson, G. 1979. *Mind and Nature: A Necessary Unity* (New York: Dutton).

Ben-Ze'ev, E., R. Ginion and J. Winter (eds) 2010. *Shadows of War: A Social History of Silence in the Twentieth Century* (New York: Cambridge University Press).

Clark, A., and D. Chalmers 1998. 'The Extended Mind', *Analysis* 58: 7–19.

Cole, J. 2001. *Forget Colonialism? Sacrifice and the Art of Memory in Madagascar* (Berkeley: University of California Press).

Coman, A., and W. Hirst forthcoming. *Perceived Speaker–Listener Similarity Affects Socially-Shared Retrieval Induced Forgetting*.

— — et al. 2012. 'Mnemonic Convergence: From Empirical Data to Large-Scale Dynamics', *Social Computing, Behavioral-Cultural Modeling and Prediction* 7227: 256–65.

Connerton, P. 2008. 'Seven Types of Forgetting', *Memory Studies* 1: 59–71.

Cuc, A., J. Koppel and W. Hirst 2007. 'Silence is Not Golden: A Case for Socially Shared Retrieval-Induced Forgetting', *Psychological Science* 18: 727–33.

Douglas, M. 1986. *How Institutions Think* (Syracuse, NY: Syracuse University Press).

Echterhoff, G., E.T. Higgins and J.M. Levine 2009. 'Shared Reality: Experiencing Commonality with Others' Inner States about the World', *Perspectives on Psychological Science* 4: 496–521.

Fagin, M., A. Meister and W. Hirst forthcoming. *Communication Modality as a Determinant of Socially Shared Retrieval-Induced Forgetting.*

— — R. Meksin and W. Hirst forthcoming. *Massed and Distributed Selective Practice and Lasting Socially Shared Retrieval-Induced Forgetting.*

Hirst, W., and G. Echterhoff 2012. 'Remembering in Conversations: The Social Sharing and Reshaping of Memories', *Annual Review of Psychology* 63: 55–79.

— — and D. Manier 2008. 'Towards a Psychology of Collective Memory', *Memory* 16: 183–200.

— — A. Coman and D. Coman 2014. 'Putting the Social Back into Human Memory', in T.J. Perfect and D.S. Lindsay (eds), *The Sage Handbook of Applied Memory* (Washington DC: Sage), pp. 273–91.

Hutchins, E. 1995. *Cognition in the Wild* (Cambridge, MA: MIT Press).

Kahneman, D. 2011. *Thinking, Fast and Slow* (New York: Macmillan).

Koppel, J., et al. 2014. 'The Effect of Listening to Others Remember on Subsequent Memory: The Roles of Expertise and Trust in Socially Shared Retrieval-Induced Forgetting and Social Contagion', *Social Cognition* 32: 148–80.

Lewy, G. 2005. *The Armenian Massacres in Ottoman Turkey: A Disputed Genocide* (Salt Lake City: University of Utah Press).

Marsh, E.J. 2007. 'Retelling is not the Same as Recalling: Implications for Memory', *Current Directions in Psychological Science* 16: 16–20.

Neisser, U. 1988. 'What is Ordinary Memory Good For?', in E. Winograd and U. Neisser (eds), *Remembering Reconsidered: Ecological and Traditional Approaches to the Study of Memory* (New York: Cambridge University Press), pp. 356–73.

Olick, J.K. 1999. 'Collective Memory: The Two Cultures', *Sociological Theory* 17: 333–48.

— — V. Vinitzky-Seroussi and D. Levy (eds) 2011. *The Collective Memory Reader* (New York: Oxford University Press).

Pavio, A. 1971. *Imagery and Verbal Processes* (New York: Holt, Rinehart & Winston).

Schuman, H., C. Rieger and V. Gaidys 1994. 'Collective Memories in the United States and Lithuania', in N. Schwarz and S. Sudman (eds), *Autobiographical Memory and the Validity of Retrospective Reports* (New York: Springer), pp. 313–33.

Shteynberg, G. 2010. 'A Silent Emergence of Culture: The Social Tuning Effect', *Journal of Personality and Social Psychology* 99: 683–9.

Stone, C.B., et al. 2010. 'Building Consensus about the Past: Schema Consistency and Convergence in Socially Shared Retrieval-Induced Forgetting', *Memory* 18: 170–84.

— — et al. 2012. 'Toward a Science of Silence: The Consequences of Leaving a Memory Unsaid', *Perspective on Psychological Science* 7: 39–53.

— — et al. 2014. 'Forgetting our Personal Past: Socially Shared Retrieval-Induced Forgetting of Autobiographical Memories', *Journal of Experimental Psychology: General* 142/4: 1084–99.

— — et al. forthcoming. 'Public Speeches Induce "Collective" Forgetting? The Belgian King's 2012 Summer Speech as a Case Study'.

Storm, B.C. and B.J. Levy 2012. 'A Progress Report on the Inhibitory Account of Retrieval-Induced Forgetting', *Memory and Cognition* 40: 827–43.

Sturken, M. 1997. *Tangled Memories: The Vietnam War, the AIDS Epidemic, and the Politics of Remembering* (Berkeley: University of California Press).

Sutton, J. 2006. 'Exograms and Interdisciplinarity: History, the Extended Mind, and the Civilizing Process', in R. Menary (ed.), *The Extended Mind* (Cambridge, MA: MIT Press), pp. 189–225.

Tulving, E. 1983. *Elements of Episodic Memory* (Oxford: Clarendon Press).

Wilson, R.A. and A. Clark 2009. 'How to Situate Cognition: Letting Nature take Its Course', in P. Robbins and M. Aydede (eds), *The Cambridge Handbook of Situated Cognition* (New York: Cambridge University Press), pp. 55–77.

Zerubavel, E. 2006. *The Elephant in the Room: Silence and Denial in Everyday Life* (New York: Oxford University Press).

Mannheim and the Sociological Problem of Generations: Events as Inspiration and Constraint

Vered Vinitzky-Seroussi

When I think of humanity,
I only think of those born in the same year as I.
…
You are all brethren to my hopes and companions to my despair.
…
And whoever recalls his childhood more than others is the victor
If there are any victors.
– Yehuda Amichay, '1924'[1]

Let us ponder for a moment the magic of those who were born in the same year as me. Why are they the brethren to my hopes and companions to my despair more than my family, my co-workers, fellow members of my tribe, be it a nation, an ethnic group, gender, race or the city I live in? What Yehuda Amichay (who was born some 30 years after Mannheim) used poetry to convey, Karl Mannheim stated sociologically in his essay, 'The Sociological Problem of Generations': 'Individuals who share the same year of birth are endowed … with a common location in the historical dimension of the social process … . The fact of belonging to the same class, and that of belonging to the same generation or age group, have this in common, that both endow the individual sharing in them with a common location in the social and historical process, and thereby limit them to a specific range of potential experience, predisposing them for a certain characteristic mode of thought and experience, and a characteristic type of historically relevant action' (Mannheim 1952: 290–91).

First memory. 1964. Tel Aviv, Israel. It is the eve of elections. I am 4 years old. Someone knocks on the door of our apartment. My mother opens it. I'm hanging on to her dress or pants – I cannot remember which. The two people standing on the other side of the doorway introduce themselves as representatives of the then ruling party Mapay, an acronym for the Land of Israel Workers Party. They would like to inquire whether the lady of the house will vote for the party in the coming election. The lady, my mother, says 'yes'. She has been their supporter for years and in fact was at the time working for them as a freelancer stenographer. 'Mmm', say the couple, 'and who is your husband thinking of voting for?' My mother quickly answers, 'He has not

---

1 Translated by Ornan Rotem. The poet was born Ludwig Pfeufer in Germany in 1924 and died in Israel as Yehuda Amichay (lit.: 'my people are alive') in 2000.

made up his mind yet.' How diplomatic. How smart for a woman married to a Right-winger who belonged to an underground organization and was a political prisoner during the pre-state years. 'Mom', I chime in, 'don't you know that Papa votes for Gahal?' Gahal, for those not familiar with the Israeli political map (my young Israeli students included), was the name of the Right-wing party, headed by Menachem Begin. The couple look at my mom and say in a nonchalant voice: 'Ma'am, you have to watch your daughter's mouth.' So much for democracy in Israel in 1964, so much for my first political memory.

Why was I attracted to collective memory? What is the memory of my own journey in this field? Who inspired me and in what ways? From my research on American high-school reunions (Vinitzky-Seroussi 1998), I know enough about narratives and the way in which one tells one's own story, one's biography, to know that stories are constructed and biographies are constantly changed in accordance with both past and present circumstances. Only now, in this collection of essays, the stories are themselves about memory, and they are told by those well acquainted with the business of narrating the past, of its possibilities, constraints and meanings. At the same time, we, scholars of memory, are no different from any other people who attend their high-school reunion, prepare their curriculum vitae, go on first dates, attend funerals of long-time friends, or encounter an 'autobiographical occasion' (Zussman 1996). An autobiographical occasion is a more or less critical point from which one can make sense of one's life – in this essay, that point is a collection of essays on our professional lives and the audience is our professional community. Not an easy task.

Second memory: Tel Aviv, Israel. I lost my father in 1969. He died of cancer – which was nothing heroic, nothing to be proud of. At the time people would barely even utter the word 'cancer', so my father died of 'a severe illness.' Israel has been involved for over 60 years in major wars and innumerable skirmishes, attacks and confrontations. Being an orphan of an 'ordinary death' was nothing to write home about. So, at the age of 9, I got my first taste of culturally bound death hierarchy. Only later in life did I learn the hierarchy of the ladder of sorrow: at the top are the fallen soldiers, and beneath them come civilian victims of terrorist attacks, victims of the Holocaust, car accidents and the like. I have to admit that throughout my childhood, I envied my peers whose fathers died in war – in fact, it didn't matter which one, they were all good for the purpose of being a privileged orphan.

Inspiration for an interesting research question, for a new book, for a grant proposal or for enlightening our thinking can come from two major sources: theory and life. An example of the former would be a young graduate student (or any other figure in academic life) reading a book or an article that generates an idea that makes him want to challenge an existing theory, refine it, argue with its premises. An example of inspiration from real life would be a professor (or any other figure in academic life) experiencing an event that generates her curiosity, makes her aware of social circumstances. There are of course other reasons for starting a research project, like pragmatism: 'There is a great fellowship or grant that supports this or that area, I'll submit a proposal because this is where the bucks are' or 'Here is a powerful professor. I'll work for him/her and that will pave my way into academia.' Putting aside institutional circumstances, opportunities and just pure calculation (and we have witnessed all of these), probably the most important impetus for starting a research study comes from reading something or experiencing something. These are ideal types, and like other ideal types they are good for thinking with but rarely represent the reality in which theory-driven research and primarily experience-driven research intertwine and dialogue with each other. And yet, at the end of the day, one can clearly see that one avenue was the main one.

So who were my companions? I can name many, beginning with teachers who opened my eyes and changed the way I perceive the world; the late Gerald Cromer comes to mind, a wonderful, albeit unknown, teacher and scholar whose class on deviant behaviour I attended as a first-year student. Other companions are scholars of collective memory whom I often quote, and whose theories and ideas have inspired me and my work on so many levels. Many of the names appear in the table of contents of this collection, as authors of their own memories, inspirations and lives, and many are the thinkers who influenced all of us. Halbwachs, Nora and Schwartz will probably head the list, but there are many more.

I chose to focus in this essay on Mannheim, a scholar whom I have quoted from time to time, whom I have read but not more than others. I never thought of him as my most important companion until I started thinking about this intriguing project, and then his seminal paper on the problem of generations (1952) came to mind. Mannheim is my hero because he took our historical position seriously. No less importantly, his essay explains better than any other text how I ended up with the research questions I ask, and how I chose the path that I took. Mannheim portrays the way I think and work; he acknowledges the role of experiences, events, history and location in forming one's consciousness. And what is collective memory about, if not about our being in time and our relations with time?

Where Max Weber added status and party to Marx's class as fundamental units of social organisation, Karl Mannheim, who was interested in the sociology of knowledge, introduced the idea of generations as social and cultural rather than biological units. Mannheim took very seriously the time we are born into, especially if that time happened to include major social and political events, ones that left their mark on the mind, body and soul of many. While Mannheim introduced the idea, scholars who followed in his footsteps, whether explicitly or implicitly, solidified the idea that mega-events shape both individuals and collectives: events like wars, the rise and fall of repressive regimes, protracted economic depressions, mass immigrations, violations of human rights, and the like (e.g. Fussell 1975; Wohl 1979).

A few words about Mannheim's biography are in order. Mannheim's biography matters because he wrote about historical location and because his life embodied that of a whole generation that witnessed some of the most difficult moments in human history: two world wars which became the model for and the ultimate expression of mass destruction, cruelty, and atrocious violations of human rights and dignity. These wars left people, to echo Walter Benjamin, 'not only without the conditions of telling stories in the heroic form of the epic or even the redemptive form of the novel, but with experiences that were in fact ultimately incommunicable' (Olick, Vinitzky-Seroussi and Levy 2011: 14).[2] On a different level, Mannheim's life also spanned some of the major milestones in the evolution of collective memory and commemoration, such as the rise of the cult of fallen soldiers, the transformation of individual grief into public mourning (Winter 1995), the prominence of heroic monuments and, later, reflective memorials (Mosse 1991), as well as an increasing focus on victims and trauma over victors (on the history of collective memory, see Olick, Vinitzky-Seroussi and Levy 2011, see also Erll 2011).

Károly Mannheim was born in Hungary in 1893. He immigrated to Germany in 1919, where he changed his name to Karl. In 1933, when the National Socialists came to power, Mannheim, already a known scholar, was fired from his position at the University of Frankfurt and left for England. Compared with other Jews, 'companions to his despair',

---

2   Benjamin made this observation on the First World War, but the same sentiment was expressed, even more strongly, after the Second World War (see e.g. Amery 1980).

he was fortunate to leave in time. Due to the large number of Jewish academics fleeing Germany and for obvious reasons to the same destination, he encountered difficulty finding an academic post, but eventually secured a position at the London School of Economics and Political Science. He died suddenly shortly after the Second World War at the age of 54, relatively young even for that time. Thus, he was not able to comment on the notion of generation in the face of the new challenges – challenges that changed the name the Great War, which stood at the centre of his writing on generations, to the First World War.

Generations, Mannheim states, are constituted by the memory of historical events experienced by those who were in their formative years during the events. Historical times, events and moments are crucial in shaping our time, our understanding, our worldview, our life. 'Social life', for Mannheim, is first and foremost something that 'has an impact on the thoughts of society' (Karacsony 2008: 106). And the way we see things is not timeless but time-bound.

At the end of the First World War, Mannheim wrote his dissertation, in which he first presented his notion of generations. In 1925, he listed the three criteria that would become the building blocks for understanding generations as social and cultural units: (1) Chronological simultaneity, (2) belonging to the same historical-social space and time and (3) participating in the common fate of this historical-social unity (Mannheim 1952). The common historical-social unity can easily be translated into a mega historical event.

Third memory: Tel Aviv, Israel. The weekend of 4 November 1995 was filled with heated debate over attending what would become the fatal demonstration in support of the Israeli-Palestinian peace process being pursued by Prime Minister Yitzhak Rabin (1922–95) and his government. Many of my liberal friends claimed that in a democratic society, people don't take to the streets to support the government. Such social activity, they argued, is saved for other regimes, while in democracies the streets are left to the opposition. Other friends (and I) claimed that the Israeli Left can no longer sit quietly at home and let the streets be taken over by those who object vehemently to the peace process. They argued that the Left was about to lose the upcoming election and that staying home was a luxury no longer affordable or justified. Other friends and relatives from the Right, who saw the government's policies as irresponsible and dangerous, did not call me that weekend; this was probably out of respect for my family – after all, being divided between Right and Left, we always avoided political issues at family gatherings. I decided to attend the demonstration even though I was scared. I was scared of the radicals from the Israeli Right and I was scared of the radicals from the Palestinian side. Between the increasingly vicious demonstrations by Israeli Right-wingers whose dreams were fading fast, and the bombs strapped to the bodies of Palestinians whose dreams were going nowhere and whose despair was growing deeper, there was little hope in the air. 'Happy New Fear' read a card sent around two months earlier. Fear indeed, was what many others and I felt at the time. I decided to take our then five-year-old daughter, our only child at the time, with me. During the afternoon she had kept herself busy preparing a special poster with the word 'peace' and naïve, childish drawings of flowers and butterflies while I caught a nap. I had a terrible feeling that something bad was going to happen. I had this vision that I would spend the rest of the evening trying to contact my husband who was on a business trip to New York to let him know we are okay. We drove to Tel Aviv for the demonstration, singing 'The Song for Peace' (a popular song pregnant with meanings and associated with the peace movement – in fact, the last song Rabin would sing before he was assassinated). Like a responsible parent, I tried to hide my fears from my daughter. We met the 'usual suspects' in the demonstration: old friends and relatives who have protested for years. Some demonstrations do carry a sense of a class reunion. My daughter was bored and I promised her we would leave as soon as the Prime Minister spoke. And that is what we did. Yitzhak Rabin gave a speech – his last one – and we left. A few minutes later, three shots were heard. My nightmare had come true. For the rest of the night – a rather long and dark one – I tried to reach my husband to tell him that we, the micro circle, were okay. Toward dawn, I added the date 4 November to the poster drawn by my daughter. She was 5. I was 35.

She was a bit too young and I was a bit too old for Mannheim's theory about the formative years, a theory that has received much confirmation from Schuman and his colleagues' work (e.g., Schuman and Scott 1989; Schuman and Rodgers 2004). Nevertheless, there are events that are big enough, that are etched deep enough into the national consciousness that they are perpetuated, institutionalized enough, controversial enough, part of the present enough that they spill beyond their 'age group.' Rabin's assassination was such an event.

When Rabin was assassinated, I was busy writing a book on autobiographical occasions and American culture. Issues of collective memories were at the heart of the book, but they had little to do with national memory, let alone with a difficult national past. It is hard to pinpoint the moment when I began to wonder about the issue of how societies deal with a difficult past, one devoid of national honour, one replete with social conflict and ethical and political dilemmas. When such a toxic past can no longer be ignored, what forms can its commemoration take? These and similar questions were at the core of my academic pursuits for a decade or so, but they did not start the night of the assassination. Like many others (sociologists included), I watched with horror the hatred and violence that characterised demonstrations against Rabin and his government that preceded the assassination and could not believe that a political assassination was around the corner. Like many others (sociologists included), I watched young people singing and lighting candles at the site of the assassination in those first days, recalling how I had sat in the very same square some 15 years earlier holding a torch and mourning through the night the killing of a Peace Now activist by a Right-wing radical.

Following Mannheim, Eyerman and Turner (1998) offer us a definition of generation that explains how Rabin's assassination was to remain a pivotal event beyond a specific age group. Moreover, they claim that given the 'right' traumatic event, generational consciousness can transcend even the power of class in affecting social relationships. A traumatic event is always the starting point, but it is not enough. To the magnitude of the event, one must add a number of other factors: powerful and articulate social agents who define the event and clearly state what often appears to be the obvious (especially once they utter it), a dramatic change in the demography of the society, a special time frame 'that connects a generation into a cycle of success and failure', specific places that are associated with the event and can become kind of shrine, and the collective memory and shared culture of those who wish to remember (Eyerman and Turner 1998: 96). But a generation can be born not only through traumatic events and the memorials and rituals marking them but also as a result of socio-economic factors (such as available resources in a specific era). It goes without saying that peers may experience the same tensions yet move in different directions, but we are where and when we are born: our horizons, dreams and knowledge (memory included) are more often than not the result of that accident, and our personal and collective biographies interact and intertwine.

Here, we touch on a sensitive issue: the too common confusion between macro social events and memory and individual ones. Mannheim himself referred to micro social phenomena as well as to macro ones. 'Our culture is developed', states Mannheim, 'by individuals who come into contact anew with the accumulated heritage … a fresh contact …

play[s] an important part in the life of an individual when he is forced by events to leave his own social group and enter a new one – when, for example, an adolescent leaves home, or a peasant the countryside for the town, or when an emigrant changes his home, or a social climber his social status or class … . In all these cases, however, the fresh contact is an event in one individual biography' (1952: 293). Mannheim distinguishes between fresh contacts on an individual level and on a collective-generational level, but the idea is the same. While no one can compare immigration under social hardship, war and the like to a student coming from Israel to study in America for her Ph.D., it was still a major change – a change that, at least in my case, effected my intellectual direction and the kind of sociological questions I was interested in. In many ways it laid the foundation for the rest of my career. In fact, it changed my life.

Fourth memory: New York. I came to America to go to graduate school so I could write a dissertation on political treason. I studied criminology and political science in my home country and found political treason an interesting subject to think about. The Pollard Affair, an American Jew who spied for Israel in the 1980s, was in the air and sparked my curiosity. Moreover, being born in 1960, being 7 during the 1967 war, growing up with the Israeli occupation of the land conquered as a result of that war, coming of age during the 1973 war and its collective and personal trauma, remembering with excitement the historic visit to Israel of Egyptian president Anwar Sadat, in 1977, watching the signing of the peace agreement with Egypt, being disillusioned by the 1982 Lebanon War, it should come as no surprise that the expectations from me, and me of myself, were to write something political. I remember the surprise verging on disappointment of my former professors in Israel when I returned for a visit and told them that I decided to study American high-school reunions. 'Are you sure you know what you're doing?' They could not see what was or could be important about such a non-political, banal topic. I not only found the topic existential – after all, what could be more interesting than using this dramatic event to explore the ongoing construction of identity in American society, of a clash between one's collective and personal past and present. No, it was more; it was about 'fresh contact'. Moreover, studying abroad is much (if not all) about 'fresh contact': the streets, the friends, the challenges, the teachers, the food, trying to get a driver's license, the cultural codes, the whole thing is about fresh contact.

Part of it was the classes that I took. The first year in graduate school I took a class on cognitive sociology taught by Eviatar Zerubavel. The last assignment was to write a paper about collective memory. I was thinking about how to get into the piece when two things happened. The first involves an embarrassing confession: I love watching television. One of those waste-of-time stares at the screen introduced me to two commercials. Both used the theme of high-school reunions as a shared reality between the advertising people and their audiences. Someone actually thought that a class reunion was an important moment for people – a moment they would connect to. Boy, were they right. In one of the ads for a jeep, everybody is surprised that the former class president arrives to his class reunion in a car unlike what they had expected from 'the student most likely to succeed'. Alas, soon enough everybody discovers that the jeep is no less than the best deal and most prestigious thing in town. The star did not disappoint us – he is still on top of his game. The second ad depicted a young woman eating diet yogurt so she can fit into a dress to impress her classmates at the reunion. The yogurt delivers the goods – all ends well, the others (not as beautiful) applaud soundly when they see their young-looking, stunning classmate. While a gender analysis of the ad is called for, it is beyond the scope of my essay; however, it is worth noting this sad reality in which a young man in 1990 middle-class America is evaluated by the size of his car (i.e., the size of his pay check) and a young woman by the size of her dress (i.e., by her looks). Watching the ads made me think that there is something about this social ritual that is so important and central to Americans that the ad agents capitalize on it to sell stuff.

The second occurrence had to do with friends of my mother who had lived in New York since 1974. She had dreams about America for many years. He was desperate to make a change in his life following his six months of military service in the 1973 war. Perhaps they were also trying to protect their son from going to the Israeli army. I don't know. The son was my age when they left Israel and it was clear that compulsory service would still be in effect when we came of age. When I arrived for my schooling she was worried about me losing touch with the homeland ... so she invited me to join her for a reunion in New York for a prestigious Tel Aviv high school. I hadn't graduated from that school, but I had a hunch that I had found the site for a term paper. Imagine the following scene. A reunion of Tel Aviv secular Zionist high-school students in the basement of a synagogue on the upper east side of New York City, to which graduates from Israel who live in North America made a special effort to fly, drive, take trains only to meet people they don't know (graduates from all classes were invited), but who all had made the decision to emigrate from Israel and reside in North America. They were carrying out what was perceived during those years as nothing short of a stigma, a 'betrayal of the Zionist dream'. Israelis who grew up in the '70s remember Prime Minister Rabin calling such émigrés 'contemptible wimps. Thus, a Sunday noon hosted dozens of people who stood at attention for a minute in memory of Israel's fallen soldiers (thus re-enacting an old and common Israeli ritual), sang old Hebrew songs (dated mainly from the 1948 War of Independence), ate what is considered by many as Israeli food (falafel and tahini), and listened to a lecture on the conflict in the Middle East by an Israeli-born professor who had made a big name for himself in America. For a student of rituals, soon to be a student of collective memory and commemoration, it was a gift. I submitted the paper. Zerubavel said, 'You've got to do your dissertation on that topic.' I was still hesitating. It took more than a year to separate from the topic I had brought with me to America and let the fresh contact take hold.

The theoretical questions guiding my writing on reunions focused on the forms of cultural resources and structural constraints people use to construct their biographies, and thereby their personal, situational and social identities. Whereas questions of identity may erupt at various points in the course of an individual's life, moments of personal crisis (divorce, changing jobs, being considered for tenure) and moments of collective reckoning (the jubilee of a state's independence, 30 years after Woodstock) intensify such existential questions. It is precisely these kinds of social junctions that I was interested in and have studied in an effort to understand the resources mobilised by, and the constraints imposed on, men and women who are called upon to tell their life-stories in a social context that shuttles between their past and their present. The high-school reunion brings the ghosts of the past into contact with indices of present achievements. It constitutes a fascinating juncture for those who attend (as well as for those who decide to stay home). It is also a magical juncture of a multitude of theoretical questions, at the centre of which stands memory (both personal and collective) and the notion of 'autobiographical occasion' – a term coined by Robert Zussman (1992), my thesis advisor.

Fifth memory: Givatayim, a town east of Tel Aviv, 1996. My husband is called up for reserve duty. The tank unit in which he served as an officer before we left for the United States has long been dismantled, but he is still eligible for reserve service. So, at the age of 37, too old to be trained on new tanks and too young to be released altogether, the army assigned him to the unit that notifies next of kin about the death of a soldier. The unit, established during the 1973 War, is made up of relatively older men who were never trained for the job, hardly any come from the profession of caregivers (nobody is a licensed psychologist), all are married, and for whom this is the last job they will have in the Reserves. My husband returned home late from his first call. It was a young officer who had died in an auto accident. The father of the soldier, whom he notified, reminded my husband of his own father. They belonged to the same social milieu. It is never easy to knock on a door and announce a death. It is even harder when it feels as if one is announcing one's own. My husband told me about this first-time experience. Like with any other couple, the spouse listens, supports, tries to understand and sympathizes. In fact, this is one of the reasons the army insists that only married men perform this job. But in our case, that spouse was also a sociologist who studied such heart-breaking moments. So, after listening, trying to be supportive and being horrified by the intimacy of death, I wondered if anybody had ever studied this topic. The following morning I went to the library and discovered that very little – in fact nothing – was ever written about this subject. Nobody ever interviewed those who announce death: those who forever and ever will be remembered by the devastated family.[3]

The essence of my research has been mostly around and about difficult moments, ones that took place at the level of the individual or the collective: the emotional turbulence of the high-school reunion in the United States, the commemoration of an assassinated prime minister in the context of the fractured collective identity of Israeli society, and the knock on the door that announces the worst news of all. Each instance is an autobiographical occasion of immense importance at the individual, the organisational or the national level, and with it come questions of memory and identity, the management of emotion and the search for meaning within the constraints and opportunities afforded by social structures and culture.

I did not set out to exemplify the phenomenon of 'a generation' by my own experience. Only minor parts of my work were directly generated by Mannheim's theory. In fact, my work refined his thesis by showing the power of the state as an intervening variable in the social construction of the generations (Shuman, Vinitzky-Seroussi and Vinokur 2003). No less important are the theoretical contributions made by Marianne Hirsch's work on postmemory (2008) and Alison Landsberg's work on prosthetic memory (2004). Both push the borders of Mannheim's experience far beyond those who went 'through the mud' to the effect of stories, images and behaviour that transmit the traumas of parents to their children (Hirsch), and to the power of technologies of mass culture to construct shared memories among people who never experienced the past they are now consuming (Landsberg). Nor did I turn to Mannheim because I thought only he could explain my or anybody else's journey through life, collective memory or any other research question for that matter. But, Mannheim illuminated the role of experience, coincidence, opportunities, moments, historical luck or lack of it in forging our life, and, as in my case, our curiosity, our research trajectories, our questions, thinking and writing. While Mannheim was mainly concerned with macro social knowledge and consciousness constructions, and one should not mix macro and micro levels of social analysis, I still feel that Mannheim inspired me more than

---

3   See Vinitzky-Seroussi and Ben-Ari 2000.

others did. He did so because I let history (micro and macro, small and large, collective and personal) touch me, knock on my door and call my attention. Then, of course, came the readings, the concepts, the theory, the scholars and what constitute the social sciences. My take on Mannheim may look simplistic, almost technical, but we are all born into a historical moment and go through time – whether as part of a generation or a nation or a gender or an ethnicity or a family or a class – only to know and experience what we can. I could write about my generation, wondering if we were a generation to begin with and if so what defined us. Instead, I took Mannheim more literally, acknowledging the impact of experiences, locations, changes, historical events, tiny moments that ended up forming the kind of scholarly work I have done in the past 20 years, work that first and foremost dealt with the notion of difficult past and challenging moments.

Let me end this chapter by recalling Danny Boyle's movie *Slumdog Millionaire*, a heart-breaking and telling film about many things, not the least of which is about the way we know things. And the way in which we, and the protagonist Jamal Malik, know things is through experiences. The 2008 British drama narrates the story of a young man from the slums of Mumbai who appears on the Indian version of *Who Wants to be Millionaire?* In front of a stunned crowd, worried producers, suspicious investors and other agents whose business is making money through commercial television, this young working-class man knows too much for the historical, social and economic class he came from: so much that everybody suspects he is cheating. As the movie moves forward (and backward) and the despair grows more intense, one is convinced that we are (or what we know is) what we experience. This is what Mannheim told us many years ago in 'The Sociological Problem of Generations', and, with a little help from Marx and Weber, he shaped not only scholars of collective memory but everybody else, whether they acknowledge his contribution to their life, professional and personal, or not.

References

Amery, J. 1980. *At the Mind's Limits: Contemplations by a Survivor on Auschwitz and Its Realities*, trans. S. Rosenfeld and S.P. Rosenfeld (Bloomington: Indiana University Press).

Erll, A. 2011. 'Travelling Memory', *Parallax* 17/4: 4–18.

Eyerman, R., and B.S. Turner 1998. 'Outline of the Theory of Generations', *European Journal of Social Theory* 1/1: 91–106.

Fussell, P. 1979. *The Great War and Modern Memory* (New York: Oxford University Press).

Hirsch, M. 2008. 'The Generation of Postmemory', *Poetics Today* 29/1: 103–28.

Karacsony, A. 2008. 'Soul-Life-Knowledge: The Young Mannheim's Way to Sociology', *Studies in East European Thought* 60/1–2: 97–111.

Landsberg, A. 2004. *Prosthetic Memory: The Transformation of American Remembrance in the Age of Mass Culture* (New York: Columbia University Press).

Mannheim, K. 1952 [1925]. 'The Sociological Problem of Generations', in *Essays on the Sociology of Knowledge*, ed. P. Kecskemeti (London: Routledge and Kegan Paul), pp. 286–320.

Mosse, G.L. 1991. *Fallen Soldiers: Reshaping the Memory of the World Wars* (New York: Oxford University Press).

Olick, J. (ed.) 2003. *States of Denial: Continuities, Conflicts and Transformation in National Retrospection* (Durham, NC: Duke University Press).

— — V. Vinitzky-Seroussi and D. Levy (eds) 2011. *The Collective Memory Reader* (New York: Oxford University Press).

Schuman, H., and W.L. Rodgers 2004. 'Cohort, Chronology and Collective Memories', *Public Opinion Quarterly* 68/2: 217–54.

—— and J. Scott 1989. 'Generations and Collective Memories', *American Sociological Review* 54/3: 259–381.

—— V. Vinitzky-Seroussi and A. Vinokur 2003. 'Keeping the Past Alive: Memories of Israeli Jews at the Turn of the Millennium', *Sociological Forum* 18/1: 103–36.

Vinitzky-Seroussi, V. 1998. *After Pomp and Circumstance: High School Reunion as an Autobiographical Occasion* (Chicago: University of Chicago Press).

—— and E. Ben-Ari. 2000. 'A Knock on the Door: Managing Death in the Israeli Defense Forces', *Sociological Quarterly* 41/3: 391–411.

Winter, J. 1995. *Sites of Memory, Sites of Mourning: The Great War in European Cultural History* (Cambridge: Cambridge University Press).

Wohl, R. 1979. *The Generation of 1914* (Cambridge, MA: Harvard University Press).

Zussman, R. 1996. 'Autobiographical Occasions', *Contemporary Sociology* 25/2: 143–8.

Semiotic Theory of Cultural Memory: In the Company of Juri Lotman

Marek Tamm[1]

Introduction: The 'Cultural Turn' in Memory Studies

Over the last decade, memory studies has undergone a significant transformation which could, in a somewhat hackneyed way, be called a 'cultural turn'. While in the twentieth century, the study of collective memory took shape and evolved mainly within the framework of sociology, in the twenty-first century the field has been increasingly dominated by cultural historians and theorists. As a result, the concept of 'cultural memory' has risen meteorically, overshadowing the formerly popular 'social memory' as well as 'collective memory' itself. The change is not only disciplinary and conceptual – but substantial. While the study of memory within the social framework emphasised social interaction and the role of mnemonic communities, the cultural approach focuses on the media that carry and shape memory. The concept of 'cultural memory' is more ambitious and broader than 'social' or even 'collective memory': it is largely synonymous with the concept of 'culture' itself, stressing its mnemonic function.[2]

The choice of intellectual forefathers and sources of inspiration has also changed as a result of the cultural turn: instead of sociologists like Emile Durkheim and Maurice Halbwachs, students of cultural memory look to the work of cultural theorists like Aby Warburg and Walter Benjamin. Undoubtedly the work of Aleida Assmann and Jan Assmann, credited with the very concept of cultural memory, has been most instrumental in the cultural turn of memory studies. The term 'cultural memory' was introduced by Jan Assmann in his article 'Collective Memory and Cultural Identity': 1988

> The concept of cultural memory comprises that body of reusable texts, images, and rituals specific to each society in each epoch, whose 'cultivation' serves to stabilize and convey that society's self-image. Upon such collective knowledge, for the most part (but not exclusively) of the past, each group bases its awareness of unity and particularity (J. Assmann 1988: 132).

---

1   This chapter was written during my stay as a Kone Foundation Research Fellow at the Helsinki Collegium for Advanced Studies. The study was also supported by the European Union through the European Regional Development Fund (Centre of Excellence in Cultural Theory) and by the Estonian Research Council: grants IUT3–2 and IUT18–8. I am grateful to Peeter Torop for his comments.
2   For recent overviews of cultural memory studies, see Erll 2011; Erll and Nünning 2008; Tamm 2013 (with further bibliography). The point that 'cultural memory' is actually a more ambitious and broader term than 'collective memory' was recently made by Etkind (2013: 40).

In his book *Das kulturelle Gedächtnis* (1992), Jan Assmann gave a more thoroughgoing and systematic discussion of cultural memory, this was later elaborated and developed by Aleida Assmann in her book, *Erinnerungsräume* (1999).[3] Their approach rests on the understanding that shared memories of the past are not accidentally produced by interacting social groups, but a consequence of cultural mediation, primarily of textualisation and visualisation. While collective memory circulates orally too (a process called 'communicative memory' by Jan Assmann), its character is definitively shaped by all kinds of cultural mediation channels, such as texts, images, objects, buildings and rituals. Although Assmann and Assmann's theory of cultural memory is not the topic of this chapter, it is important to note how their research is inspired and influenced by the work of Juri Lotman (1922–93) and other researchers of the Tartu–Moscow school of semiotics. Jan Assmann, discussing the origins of the concept of cultural memory in his *Das kulturelle Gedächtnis*, admitted this openly: 'Out of this concept of the extended situation emerged what Aleida Assmann and I – continuing the research of Juri Lotman and other culture theorists – have called cultural memory in our work' (J. Assmann 2011: 7; cf. A. Assmann 2011: 10).[4] Since much of Lotman's work is only available in Russian, his early influence has unfortunately been overlooked by subsequent students of cultural memory. The main aim of the present chapter is to present Juri Lotman as a companion to formative theorists of cultural memory. By placing the work of Lotman and his Russian colleagues before the cultural turn of memory studies, one can trace the importance of Lotman's theory for the advancement of the study of cultural memory.[5]

Lotman's Semiotic Theory of Culture

Although some observations on the general mechanism of culture (specifically literary culture) can already be found in Lotman's earlier writings from the 1950s and 1960s, the year 1970 may be regarded as an important point after which the theoretical analysis of culture becomes the main theme of his research.[6] The first, exploratory ideas were published in *Studies in the Typology of Culture* (1970) and were more systematically developed in a subsequent paper written in cooperation with Boris Uspensky, 'On the Semiotic Mechanism

---

3   Both books were recently and simultaneously published in English: A. Assmann 2011; J. Assmann 2011.

4   Aleida Assmann mentioned the important role of Renate Lachmann, professor of general literary theory and Slavonic literatures at the University of Konstanz, in introducing and mediating the work of Lotman (personal communication). Lachmann made active use of Lotman's work in her own research, to develop her theory of intertextual cultural memory (see Lachmann 1990; cf. Lachmann 1993, 2004, 2012).

5   This undertaking is justified in turn by the fact that even in the relatively rich literature dedicated specifically to the study of Lotman and the Tartu–Moscow school, little attention is paid to the concept of cultural memory. For some recent attempts, see Arán and Barei 2002: 52–5, 130–34; Avtonomova 2009: 203–56; Portis-Winner 1994: 171–9; Semenenko 2012: 100–109; Tsaryova 2010: 100–102; Żyłko 2009: 104–5. Since many of Lotman's key articles, including those where he elaborated his theory of cultural memory, remain unavailable in English, I have purposely included in my text a substantial number of quotations from his works.

6   Russian speakers are provided with a good survey of Lotman's life and work by his close friend and long-time colleague Boris Yegorov (1999). A rather good systematic English overview of his views on the semiotics of culture is Semenenko 2012. Shukman 1977 remains a valuable introduction to Lotman's earlier creative period. Also worth mentioning are the interesting discussion of Andrews (2003) and the two edited volumes dedicated to Lotman (Schönle 2006; Frank, Ruhe and Schmitz 2012). The most recent insight into the beginnings of the cultural semiotics of Tartu–Moscow school is Salupere, Torop and Kull 2013.

of Culture' (J.M. Lotman and Uspensky 1971). However, the birth of cultural semiotics as a new discipline can be dated to 1973, when the programmatic text 'Theses on the Semiotic Study of Cultures' was conceived, on Lotman's initiative in collaboration with other semioticians of the Tartu–Moscow school. Although the main foundations of the semiotic theory of culture had thus been established, Lotman continued to elaborate and develop this collectively defined model for analysis, as demonstrated by numerous articles and several books, primarily *Universe of the Mind: A Semiotic Theory of Culture* (1990), *Culture and Explosion* (1992a) and the posthumously published *The Unpredictable Workings of Culture* (written in 1990–92, published in 2010).

Lotman's cultural semiotics departs from the basic premise that culture and semiotics are not mutually independent phenomena – culture is essentially semiotic and semiotics evolves in a cultural environment. Therefore semiotics is primarily the semiotics of culture, and the source for other branches of semiotics (see M. Lotman 2013: 262). Lotman's conception of culture was born in the 1960s, under the rising star of cybernetics and information sciences, which is why he conceives of culture first and foremost as an extensive and elaborate system of processing information. In 1970, he proposed a preliminary definition of culture as 'the sum of all nonhereditary information and the means of its organisation and preservation' (J.M. Lotman 1970a: 395).[7] Even this early formulation reveals that, from a semiotic perspective, the preservation of information is as important in a culture as its transmission and organisation. The view was explicitly stated in 1971, when Lotman and Uspensky wrote:

> We understand culture as the nonhereditary memory of the community, a memory expressing itself in a system of constraints and prescriptions. ... Furthermore, insofar as culture is memory or, in other words, a record in the memory of what the community has experienced, it is, of necessity, connected to past historical experience. Consequently, at the moment of its appearance, culture cannot be recorded as such, for it is only perceived ex post facto. (J.M. Lotman and Uspensky 1971: 487–8; Eng. trans. 213–4)

Thus, we can already see how the idea of collective memory as a crucial mechanism for the operation of culture springs from Lotman's general theory of cultural semiotics.

Conceiving of culture as a communication system, Lotman, however, added an important dimension that is lacking in traditional communication theories but is key to understanding the mnemonic character of culture – namely the ability of autocommunication. In Lotman's view, autocommunication is the dominant mode of communication in culture, as well as the basis of its mnemonics. Lotman believed culture to have a natural ability of self-description and self-interpretation at the meta-level (J.M. Lotman 1989: 641; Eng. trans. 10). Self-description enables culture to construct self-models and to include in its memory a concept of itself that ensures its structural unity and largely defines its characteristics as a reservoir of information (J.M. Lotman 1970a: 420). Lotman emphasised in particular the great value of self-models in the workings of cultural memory: '[an] extremely important role in cultural memory is played by the meta-models (the self-descriptions of culture's previous experience)' (J.M. Lotman 1977a: 567). A distinction relevant for our present purposes is the one Lotman made between the two main spheres of autocommunication: first, autocommunication of the mnemonic type that essentially informs itself of what was already known; and second, communication of the type of 'discovery' or 'inspiration', where 'my informational input correlates with previous information fixed in my memory, organises it, and produces a noteworthy quantitative increase of information as output' (J.M. Lotman 1970a: 426).

---

7   All translations from Russian, unless otherwise noted, are my own.

Alongside culture as a system of communication, another characteristic of Lotman's theory of culture is his conception of culture as a bounded unity.[8] Although Lotman saw culture as a complex, heterogeneous and multilingual phenomenon, he argued that all its elements are mutually isomorphic and make up a coherent unity. This cultural unity is ensured, on the one hand, by the fact that culture is bounded, on the other, by the isomorphism of its elements. Lotman expressed this idea well in the final paragraph of his *Conversations about Russian Culture*: 'History, reflected in one person, in his life and gesture, is isomorphic to the history of mankind. They are reflected in one another and are comprehended through one another' (J.M. Lotman 1994: 389).

Lotman's view of culture as a bounded and organised unity enabled him to reduce it to a linguistic mechanism: 'Defining culture as a sign system subjected to structural rules allows us to view it as a *language*, in the general semiotic sense of the term' (J.M. Lotman 1970a: 396). Thus, from a semiotic perspective, culture is a multilingual system in which, side by side with natural languages, there exist cultural languages or secondary modelling systems (secondary to natural language as a primary modelling system) based on the former.[9] Cultural languages are split into two main types by Lotman: discrete and continuous (iconic-spatial) ones. While discrete languages give pride of place to the sign, and meanings are created through the meanings of signs, continuous languages give pride of place to the text and meaning is generated through the text as a whole that integrates even the most heterogeneous elements (cf. Torop 2005: 168).

'Yet culture includes not only a certain combination of semiotic systems [languages], but the sum of all historically existent messages (texts) in these languages', Lotman found it necessary to add (1970a: 397). This is why, as the last central characteristic of Lotman's model of cultural theory, we can bring out the notion of culture as a text or a sum of texts. A text must, of course, be understood here in the broadest semiotic sense as a message that 'has integral meaning and integral function' (Ivanov et al. 1973: 508; Eng. trans. Uspensky et al. 1973: 38; cf. J.M. Lotman 1970b: 59–66) regardless of whether it is a ritual, piece of art, or musical composition. For Lotman, a text was the basic element of culture and culture itself. He distinguished two aspects of the text: linguistic and artistic. While the first plays an important role in communication, the other plays an important role in autocommunication. The prominence of the text proves the spatial character of Lotman's model of analysis, since the text refers to the boundedness of the object of analysis and its division into smaller bounded wholes. At the same time, Lotman immediately emphasised that the textual character of culture did not mean that culture is inherently static: 'Culture can be presented as an aggregate of texts; however, from the point of view of the researcher, it is more exact to consider culture as a mechanism creating an aggregate of texts and texts as the realization of culture' (J.M. Lotman and Uspensky 1971: 492; Eng. trans. 218). Thus, culture constitutes a kind of giant mechanism of text generation that constantly translates non-cultural messages into cultural texts, thus contributing to the shaping of cultural memory. Lotman himself expressed this principle in more abstract terms: 'The translation of a certain part of reality

---

8   Hence also the clearly spatial character of Lotman's semiotic model of culture – culture (as well as memory and text) was described by him primarily in spatial categories, allowing him, on the one hand, to underline the importance of the boundary as a semiotic mechanism of translation in culture and, on the other, to see the relations between centre and periphery as a mainspring of cultural dynamics. On this point, see Randviir 2007.

9   More specifically, Lotman distinguished three types of secondary modelling systems or cultural languages: First, language as a higher sign system (myth, literature, poetry); second, language as meta-language or part of meta-language (art, music, dance, etc.; criticism and history); and third, language as a model or analogue (language of film, dance, music, painting, etc.). See Torop 2012: 290–91.

into one or another culture language, its conversion into a text, that is, into information fixed in a certain way, and the introduction of this information into collective memory – this is the sphere of everyday cultural activity.' And he added: 'Only that which has been translated into a system of signs can be appropriated by memory; in this sense, the intellectual history of mankind can be regarded as a struggle for memory' (J.M. Lotman 1970a: 397).

Departing from Ferdinand de Saussure's well-known distinction between *langue* (language) and *parole* (speech), but borrowing his terms from Roman Jakobson, Lotman analysed culture on two levels: that of the code and that of the text (or message) (e.g. J.M. Lotman 1970a: 36; 1970b: 27). In order for communication to succeed in culture, it must be possible to code and decode each message (or text) in some way. But unlike Saussure, whose work centred on language (code), Lotman was even more interested in the particular expressions of language – that is texts (messages). And for him, the text was not merely a realisation of some specific code, but 'a complex device that preserves various codes, capable of transforming received messages and generating new ones' (J.M. Lotman 1981a: 161). The notion also plays an important role in Lotman's discussion of cultural memory, since this, too, as we shall see below, is based on the distinction between code and text: 'The memory common to a given cultural space is guaranteed, first, by the existence of certain constant texts and second, by either the unity of codes, or their invariance, or the unbroken and lawful character of their transformations' (J.M. Lotman 1985: 673; cf. J.M. Lotman 1986: 621).

In addition to the distinction between code and text, Lotman's model of cultural theory also assigns great importance to the distinction between static and dynamic aspects of culture, based on Saussure's well-known distinction between synchronic and diachronic aspects of semiotic systems. Whereas from a static point of view, one can study culture as a text (or aggregate of texts) and analyse its inner architectonics of discrete entities, from a dynamic aspect, culture appears as a process and a text-generating mechanism, which due to its continuous character, can only be analysed as a whole, not in its several parts. The dynamic aspect of culture became increasingly important for Lotman, particularly in his later work, culminating with his views on the importance of unpredictable mechanisms and explosive situations in the development of culture. And naturally each cultural explosion, that is the clash of 'own' and 'foreign' cultural languages or texts, brings about a change of collective memory – or a retrospective re-evaluation of the culture's historical past (J.M. Lotman 1992a: 25; Eng. trans. 16–17; 1992b: 348–9).

In the early 1980s, Lotman's holistic theory of culture evolved into a general model of a semiotic continuum surrounding the human society that he called the 'semiosphere' (on analogy with the term 'biosphere' coined by Vladimir Vernadsky): 'The semiosphere is that same semiotic space, outside of which semiosis itself cannot exist' (J.M. Lotman 1984: 13; Eng. trans. 208). In a sense, the semiosphere can be understood as an elaboration of the notion of 'culture' to its logical limits, resulting in an isomorphic chain: text–culture–semiosphere. An important development worth noting, however, is that while speaking about culture, Lotman had mainly used mechanical metaphors ('device', 'mechanism', 'system' and so on), whereas the semiosphere he described in biological terms, such as 'organism' (see Alexandrov 2000; Mandelker 1994, 1995; Torop 2005).

Lotman's Theory of Cultural Memory

An important premise of Lotman's semiotic theory of culture is his distinction of the three functions of culture (e.g. J.M. Lotman 1990: 11–19). First, there is the communicative function that secures the adequate transmission and reproduction of messages (texts) in a culture.

Second, there is the creative function that performs the task of generating new texts and codes. And finally, there is the mnemonic function that takes care of recording texts and codes. Yet this distinction, as Lotman underlined, is merely methodological, since in reality all of these functions are inseparably intertwined and incapable of operating on their own.

Lotman's important contribution to the development of semiotics consists, in fact, in the highlighting of the mnemonic function of culture and its placement at the core of the semiotic analysis of culture. He argued compellingly that memory, both individual and collective, is first and foremost a semiotic phenomenon. What memory records, processes and puts out are signs, not objects signified by these signs. Lotman was one of the first semioticians to see memory as a collective phenomenon and to associate it directly with culture. A programmatic instance of this statement can be found in 'Theses on the Semiotic Study of Cultures':

> *If we regard the collective as a more complexly organized individual, culture may be understood by analogy with the individual mechanism of memory as a certain collective mechanism for the storage and processing of information. The semiotic structure of culture and the semiotic structure of memory are functionally uniform phenomena situated on different levels. (Ivanov et al. 1973: 516; Eng. trans. Uspensky et al. 1973: 17)[10]*

Many years later, in 1987 Lotman still wrote in the same spirit: 'Just like individual consciousness has its mechanisms of memory, so collective consciousness, upon discovering the need to fix something shared in common by the whole collective, creates the mechanism of collective memory' (J.M. Lotman 1987a: 103; cf. J.M. Lotman 1987b: 199).

The term 'cultural memory' (память культуры) first appeared in Lotman's article 'Binary Models in the Dynamics of Russian Culture' (1977), written with Boris Uspensky: 'The essence of culture is such that the past contained in it does not "depart into the past" as in the natural flow of time; it does not disappear. It becomes fixed in cultural memory, and acquires a permanent, if background, presence' (J.M. Lotman and Uspensky 1977: 116; Eng. trans. 65). More specifically, however, Lotman formulated his idea of cultural memory in two articles written in the mid-1980s, 'The Concept of Memory from a Cultural Perspective' (1985) and 'Cultural Memory' (1986). While the latter focused mainly on analysing text-generation in cultural memory,[11] the former shorter but more comprehensive article presented in six theses the general principles of the functioning of culture as memory.

'The Concept of Memory from a Cultural Perspective' opens with a thesis that resumes what I have tried to explain above:

> *From the viewpoint of semiotics, culture constitutes collective intellect and collective memory, that is, a supra-individual mechanism for the preservation and transmission of certain messages (texts) and the generation of new ones. In this sense, cultural*

---

10   But the same idea had appeared already in 1970: 'Above, culture was defined as the sum of nonhereditary information, the shared memory of mankind or a certain more narrowly bounded collective – a nation, a class, etc.' However, Lotman at once specified: 'Memory is understood here in the same sense as that used in information theory and cybernetics: as the ability of certain systems to record and accumulate information' (Lotman 1970a: 400).

11   In this article, Lotman also defined his research position most clearly, distinguishing between two general types of cultural memory: external and internal, with the former referring to mankind's earlier experience as a whole (which might be called the static aspect of cultural memory) and the latter to its earlier particular states (the dynamic aspect). It is precisely these states that Lotman considered the main objects of his research (see J.M. Lotman 1986: 616).

space can be defined as the space of general memory, that is, a space in which certain general texts can be preserved and actualised. And their actualisation takes place within the framework of a certain conceptual invariant, allowing us to say that despite the variance of interpretations, the text preserves identity with itself in the context of a new era. (J.M. Lotman 1985: 673)

Next, Lotman suggested a provisional distinction between the two types of cultural memory: 'informative memory' on the one hand and 'creative memory' on the other. The former is characterised by its focus on recording as precisely as possible the result of knowledge – the final text: 'this type of memory is planar by nature, located in one temporal dimension and subject to the law of chronology. It evolves in the same direction with the flow of time, and is congruent with this flow' (J.M. Lotman 1985: 674). In the second type of memory, however, 'the whole depth of texts' proves active: the result is no more important than the process – the actualisation of certain texts – and it is not governed by the formula 'the newest is the most valuable'. Unlike informative cultural memory, creative cultural memory is not just panchronic, but even opposed to time: 'It preserves what once was as what currently is. From the viewpoint of memory as a mechanism that works throughout its whole depth, the past is not past' (ibid. 674–5). From this, Lotman drew the important epistemological conclusion that traditional literary and cultural history which is based on the idea of progress is deeply misleading: 'Therefore, in the study of literature, historicism in its original form, as shaped first by the Hegelian theory of culture and then by the positivist theory of progress, is in fact anti-historicist, since it ignores the active role of memory in the generation of new texts' (ibid. 675). Lotman's distinction between informative and creative cultural memory is quite similar to the distinction made by Aleida Assmann and Jan Assmann between 'storage memory' and 'functional memory', in which the task of the former is to record a maximum amount of information in a culture and of the latter to create new connections, constellations of these messages, thereby providing them with a new meaning and actuality (J. Assmann 1988: 130; A. Assmann 1999: 123–32; 2006: 54–8). A companion to Lotman's typology is the further distinction made by Aleida Assmann between 'cultural working memory' (the canon) and 'cultural reference memory' (the archive), whereby the first type represents the active aspect of cultural memory that records primarily works of art that are meant for recurrent use, while the second type represents the passive aspect that records de-contextualised cultural messages that have lost their original meaning (A. Assmann 2008).

Although Lotman distinguished two aspects of cultural memory as informative and creative, he was convinced of its principally dynamic and creative character. This conviction runs like a thread through his whole work. On the figurative level, the conviction is expressed in the struggle against the storehouse metaphor of memory that he waged in numerous articles. Already in 1970, he emphasised that 'culture, however, is not a storehouse of information. It is an extremely complex mechanism which preserves information while constantly working out the most efficient means to do this; it receives new information, encodes and decodes communications and translates them from one sign system into another' (J.M. Lotman 1970a: 395; Eng. trans. 215). And he restated it again, lapidarily, in 1986: 'Memory is not a storehouse of information, but a mechanism generating it' (J.M. Lotman 1986: 618; cf. J.M. Lotman and Uspensky 1977: 116; Eng. trans. 65; J.M. Lotman 1977a: 567; 1985: 675; 1990: 272). As noted above, Lotman attached particular importance to the view that culture is not subject to the logic of linear time: it is not necessarily orientated from the present toward the future, but frequently toward the past. Together with Uspensky, he noted: 'Culture, united with the past through memory, generates not only its future, but also its past, presenting, in this sense, a mechanism that works against natural time' (J.M. Lotman and Uspensky 1977: 116; Eng. trans. 65).

The dynamic of cultural memory is modelled by Lotman as primarily the interaction of codes and texts: creative memory generates not only new texts, but also new ways of interpreting and encoding them. Furthermore, the texts not only record information, but are capable of accumulating earlier interpretations of them, as well as of actualising certain aspects of it at the cost of suppressing others (see J.M. Lotman 1981a: 160; 1981b: 583; cf. J.M. Lotman 1977b: 169, 174; Eng. trans. 81, 86). This allowed Lotman to speak about 'text memory' as a distinct cultural phenomenon (or even about text as a 'thinking unit').[12] He illustrated this with reference to Shakespeare's *Hamlet*: 'Nowadays *Hamlet* is not just a play by Shakespeare, but it is also the memory of all its interpretations, and what is more, it is also the memory of all those historical events which occurred outside the text but with which Shakespeare's text can evoke associations' (J.M. Lotman 1990: 18–9; cf. J.M. Lotman 1964: 242).[13] Rapid cultural changes as a rule bring about a reorganisation of cultural memory, including the generation of new codes which allow for old texts to be provided with new meanings: 'Under the influence of new codes employed for deciphering texts stored in the cultural memory in times long past, a shift in the meaningful and meaningless elements of the text's structure takes place' (J.M. Lotman 1985: 675). The extent to which cultural memory is transformed depends on the degree of the semiotic shift. Cultural history knows several radical turns which Lotman termed 'cultural explosions'. The latter can be broadly split into two types: the ones caused by an intensive onslaught of new cultural texts (Lotman exemplified this with the way classical sculpture or Provençal poetry flooded the Italian cultural memory of the late Middle Ages), the others rising from a situation in which 'new texts are introduced into cultural memory that are structurally remote from its immanent organization and for the deciphering of which its internal tradition has no adequate codes' (ibid.). As an illustration of the latter, Lotman cited the massive invasion of Christian texts into Russian culture in the eleventh and twelfth centuries and of West European texts after the reign of Peter the Great. This kind of explosive mechanism was described by Lotman in some detail:

> First, a pause occurs in text generation (culture switches to reception, as it were, the capacity of memory increases much faster than the possibilities of deciphering texts); then the explosion occurs, and renewed text generation takes on a particularly stormy, productive character. In this situation, the evolution of culture assumes a semblance of extraordinarily bright, almost spasmodic flashes. And while undergoing a period of flash, a culture formerly located in the periphery of the cultural area frequently converts into its centre and itself actively translates texts in the smouldering craters of the former centres of text generation processes. (J.M. Lotman 1985: 676)

The dynamic model of cultural memory clearly demonstrates that forgetting is an integral part of collective remembering. This fact was first highlighted by Lotman in 'On the Semiotic Mechanism of Culture' (1971), written with Uspensky, where they distinguished three types of recording into collective memory: First, a quantitative increase in the amount of knowledge; second, a redistribution in the structure of the nodes of the coding system; and third, forgetting. The last type is explained as follows:

---

12   Lotman's concept of 'text memory' is, of course, directly influenced by Bakhtin's earlier idea of 'genre memory', elaborated in *Problems of Dostoevsky's Poetics*: 'A genre lives in the present, but always *remembers* its past, its beginning. Genre is a representative of creative memory in the process of literary development. Precisely for this reason genre is capable of guaranteeing the *unity* and *uninterrupted* continuity of this development' (Bakhtin 1984: 106).

13   The example of *Hamlet* provided by Lotman has been thoroughly elucidated and further elaborated in Semenenko 2007; cf. Semenenko 2013.

> *The conversion of a chain of facts into a text is invariably accompanied by selection; that is, by fixing certain events which are translatable into elements of the text and forgetting others, marked as nonessential. In this sense every text furthers not only the remembering process, but forgetting as well. (J.M. Lotman and Uspensky 1971: 489–90; Eng. trans. 216)*

Later, Lotman elaborated on the same idea in different terms, focusing more on the dynamic relations between remembering and forgetting:

> *Each culture defines its paradigm of what must be remembered (that is, preserved) and what must fall into oblivion. The latter is cast out of the collective memory and, in a way, 'ceases to exist'. But with the change of time, of the system of cultural codes, the paradigm of memory and oblivion changes, too. That which had been declared 'really existent' may turn out to be 'as though nonexistent' and doomed to oblivion, whereas the nonexistent may become existent and meaningful. (J.M. Lotman 1985: 675)*

While earlier, Lotman reduced the mechanism of cultural memory to the interaction of codes and texts, in 'Cultural Memory' (1986), he introduced a new category, the 'symbol', destined to become the most important element of the unity and dynamicity of cultural memory in his subsequent analysis. Although he never explicitly defined the interrelationship of the code, the text and the symbol, we may presume that he considered the symbol as a kind of 'over-semiotised' text that had gained a certain invariant meaning in the culture. In 'Cultural Memory' he noted: 'The function due to which a meaningful element can play a mnemonic role, we call *symbolic*; and henceforward we describe as symbolic all such signs as have the ability of concentrating in themselves, preserving and reconstructing *memory* of their earlier contexts' (J.M. Lotman 1986: 617). In greater detail in 'The Symbol in the Cultural System', published a year later, he highlighted the symbol as the stablest constituent part of culture and the main guarantee of its coherence:

> *Since symbols are important mechanisms of cultural memory, they can transfer texts, plot outlines and other semiotic formations from one level of a culture's memory to another. The stable sets of symbols which recur diachronically throughout culture serve very largely as unifying mechanisms: by activating a culture's memory of itself they prevent the culture from disintegrating into isolated chronological layers. (J.M. Lotman 1987b: 192; Eng. trans. J.M. Lotman 1990: 104)*

Lotman saw the symbol as having a double nature: on the one hand, it realised its invariant nature by penetrating the various layers of culture; on the other, however, it actively correlated with new cultural contexts and in the process of influencing them was itself transformed. 'Its invariancy is realized in variants,' as Lotman put it (J.M. Lotman 1987b: 193; Eng. trans. J.M. Lotman 1990: 104). As a rule, symbols belong to the more archaic, deeper layers of culture, accumulating in themselves old messages that can be discharged in a new shape in each new cultural situation – 'coming to life in a new text like a grain in fresh soil', to borrow an image from Lotman himself (ibid. 194; Eng. trans. 105). Summarily it thus can be said that within the context of cultural memory, the symbol appears as a 'semiotic condenser' that plays the role of the mediator between different spheres of semiosis, but also between semiotic and non-semiotic reality and between the synchrony of the text and the culture's memory (ibid. 199; Eng. trans. 111).

The last important distinction in Lotman's theory of cultural memory concerns the typology of culture: he saw cultural memory as operating in a fundamentally different manner in the two contrasting types of culture, oral or pre-written and written (see J.M. Lotman 1977a: 567; 1978; 1987a; J.M. Lotman and Mints 1981: 727–31). This distinction is not to be seen as a historical but rather, indeed, as a typological one – which in Lotman's view is ultimately reduced to the bipolar structure of human consciousness. The first of these types Lotman also described as mythological, characterised by iconic-spatial thinking, whereas the second he called historical, characterised by verbal and linear thinking. The clearest elaboration of this distinction within the theory of cultural memory is presented in 'Some Observations on the Typology of Culture' (1987a). Having first outlined our habitual attitude towards memory which presumes that only extraordinary and unexpected events are recorded in a culture, Lotman went on to propose a mental speculation: 'let's imagine the possibility of a different type of memory – one that aspires to preserve messages of order, not of its breaches; of laws, not of excesses' (J.M. Lotman 1987a: 103) and continued: 'a culture orientated not at increasing the quantity of texts but at the repeated reproduction of certain texts that have been given once and for all, requires a different organisation of collective memory' (ibid.) This type of culture has no use for writing but employs in its stead 'mnemonic symbols' which can be either natural (landmarks, stars, etc.) or man-made (idols, grave monuments, buildings, as well as rituals). Oral culture is characterised by a closed and cyclical notion of time and orientation towards the past, whereas written culture relies on a linear-temporal mental paradigm orientated towards the future. Therefore, as Lotman incisively put it:

> It must be kept in mind that all the myth texts we know have reached us as transformations – translations of mythological consciousness into verbal-linear language (live myth is iconic-spatial and realised as a sign in activities and in the panchronic existence of drawings in which, as in cave and rock art, for instance, there is no prescribed linear order) and onto the axis of linear-temporal historical consciousness. (J.M. Lotman 1978: 571)

Written culture produces an increasing mass of text, is interested in causal relations and the results of actions, and has an increasingly acute sense of time, giving rise to a notion of history. 'It can be said that history is one of the side effects of the emergence of writing' (J.M. Lotman 1987a: 103). Oral culture, however, is governed by 'the universal law of the resemblance of everything to everything, the main structural relationship being that of homeomorphism' (J.M. Lotman 1978: 570); for mythical thinking, such events that have no counterparts in the mythical world are non-existent and therefore ignored. Contrary to our habitual idea of written cultures being semiotically more complex, Lotman concluded by saying that 'the emergence of writing did not complicate, but simplified the semiotic structure of culture'. Explaining further: 'Mnemonic-sacral symbols represented by material things are not implanted into verbal text, but into that of a ritual. Furthermore, they preserve a certain independence even of that text; their material existence continues beyond the observance, and being part of many different observances provides them with a wide range of ambivalent meanings' (J.M. Lotman 1987a: 106).

Concluding Remarks

Juri Lotman developed his semiotic theory of cultural memory under Soviet totalitarianism, where an in-depth study of culture and memory was no mere academic pursuit but inevitably entailed an ethical and political stance. Maxim Waldstein (2008) has rightly noted that in order to understand adequately the work of the Tartu–Moscow school of semiotics, one must not overlook the social and political context of the times. The inevitability of culture for human existence is a leitmotif of Lotman's work. In 1970, for instance, he wrote unequivocally:

> One may assume ... that the life of a collective, no matter which collective, is not possible without some kind of culture. For any collective, culture is not merely an optional addition to the minimum requirements for life but a necessary condition for the collective's very existence. (J.M. Lotman 1970a: 394; Eng. trans. 214)

The precondition for the existence of culture, however, is memory, as Mikhail Lotman has written, following his father's lead: 'Without memory there is no culture, nor a personality that could be the subject of culture. *Homo culturalis* is inevitably *homo memor*' (M. Lotman 2013: 264).

As we noted at the outset, in Lotman's view, semiotics (and science in general) is inseparable from culture. Any analysis of culture is also that culture's self-analysis, and its main *raison d'être* is to ensure for that culture the ability of self-cognition and dynamic development. Let us, for example, recall the very last statement from the 'Theses on the Semiotic Study of Cultures':

> Scientific investigation is not only an instrument for the study of culture but also part of its object. Scientific texts, being metatexts of the culture, may at the same time be regarded as its texts. Therefore any significant scientific idea may be regarded both as an attempt to cognize culture and as a fact of its life through which its generating mechanisms take effect (Ivanov et al. 1973: 525; Eng. trans. Uspensky et al. 1973: 28).

When we add to this declaration another of Lotman's central ideas, according to which the development of cultural memory is directly linked to social and political processes ('social decline, as a rule, is accompanied by an ossifying of the mechanism of the collective memory and by an increasing tendency to contract' [J.M. Lotman and Uspensky 1971: 490; Eng. trans. 217]), it becomes clear that Lotman expected his semiotic study of culture not only to contribute to the development of science, but also to enrich the surrounding cultural environment. I do not think we can be mistaken in assuming that Lotman's constant emphasis on the autonomy and creativity of culture and cultural texts throughout his work was not merely a theoretical stance but was also political. Quoting Bulgakov's famous words that 'manuscripts don't burn', he noted in a newspaper article that the resistance of cultural texts is huge: 'If such forces were applied to the destruction of a tank, it would have been reduced to rubble long ago' (J.M. Lotman 1993: 293). Lotman's own texts undoubtedly constituted a very important mechanism of resistance in Soviet society, helping to ensure the creative independence of thinking and remembering in the face of political and ideological power.

Yet when we look at Lotman's role in the 'disciplinary memory' of contemporary memory studies, the unfortunate fact is that the main part of his work has been forgotten or remains undiscovered, and only a small part of its potential has been actualised. Thus, we do not find Lotman's texts included in English anthologies of memory studies. Nor can we find contemporary readers or overviews of memory studies entering into dialogue with him. At best, sporadic references to his work can be found.[14] The two fundamental texts opening

---

14   See e.g. Erll 2011: 12, 102. A good example is the recently published *Collective Memory Reader*, whose introduction briefly refers to the contribution of Lotman and his Russian colleagues to the study of collective memory, but refrains from discussing it because 'their work has not been

Lotman's conception of cultural memory, 'The Concept of Memory in Cultural Perspective' (1985) and 'Cultural Memory' (1986), let alone numerous other important articles on the theory of culture, have not yet been translated into English.[15] However, as I attempted to demonstrate, Lotman was one of the first to identify memory as a major subject of cultural studies, the first to propose a general theory of 'cultural memory', and an important source of inspiration for the Assmanns' influential theory of cultural memory.

References

Alexandrov, V.E. 2000. 'Biology, Semiosis, and Cultural Difference in Lotman's Semiosphere', *Comparative Literature* 52: 339–62.

Andrews, E. 2003. *Conversations with Lotman: Cultural Semiotics in Language, Literature, and Cognition* (Toronto: University of Toronto Press).

Arán, P.O., and S. Barei 2002. *Texto/Memoria/Cultura: El pensamiento de Iuri Lotman* (Cordoba: Universidad Nacional de Córdoba).

Assmann, A. 1999. *Erinnerungsräume: Formen und Wandlungen des kulturellen Gedächtnisses* (Munich: C.H. Beck).

—— 2006. *Der lange Schatten der Vergangenheit: Erinnerungskultur und Geschichtspolitik* (Munich: C.H. Beck).

—— 2008. 'Canon and Archive', in Erll and Nünning 2008: 97–108.

—— 2011. *Cultural Memory and Western Civilization. Functions, Media, Archives* (Cambridge: Cambridge University Press).

Assmann, J. 1992. *Das kulturelle Gedächtnis: Schrift, Erinnerung und politische Identität in frühen Hochkulturen* (Munich: C.H. Beck).

—— 1988. 'Collective Memory and Cultural Identity', trans. J. Czaplicka, *New German Critique* 65: 125–33.

—— 2011. *Cultural Memory and Early Civilization. Writing, Remembrance, and Political Imagination* (Cambridge: Cambridge University Press).

Avtonomova, N. 2009. *Открытая структура: Якобсон – Бахтин – Лотман – Гаспаров* [Open Structure: Jakobson – Bakhtin – Lotman – Gasparov] (Москва: Российская политическая энциклопедия).

Bakhtin, M. 1984. *Problems of Dostoevsky's Poetics*, trans. C. Emerson (Minneapolis: University of Minnesota Press).

Erll, A. 2011. *Memory in Culture* (Basingstoke: Palgrave Macmillan).

—— and A. Nünning (eds) 2008. *Cultural Memory Studies: An Interdisciplinary Handbook* (Berlin: De Gruyter).

Etkind, A. 2013. *Warped Mourning: Stories of the Undead in the Land of the Unburied* (Stanford, CA: Stanford University Press).

Frank, S.K., C. Ruhe and A. Schmitz (eds) 2012. *Explosion und Peripherie: Jurij Lotmans Semiotik der kulturellen Dynamik revisited* (Bielefeld: Transcript).

Ivanov, V.V., et al. 1973. Тезисы к семиотическому изучению культур (в применении к славянским текстам) [Theses on the Semiotic Study of Cultures (as Applied to Slavic Texts)], in J.M. Lotman 2000: 504–25.

---

widely integrated into contemporary discussions' (Olick, Vinitzky-Seroussi and Levy 2011: 28). In the context of contemporary memory studies, Wertsch (2002) has paid the most attention to Lotman's work.

15 For an exhaustive list of Lotman's works translated into English by 2011, see Kull 2011.

Kull, K. 2011. 'Juri Lotman in English: Bibliography', *Sign Systems Studies* 39/2–4: 343–56.

Lachmann, R. 1990. *Gedächtnis und Literatur: Intertextualität in der Russischen Moderne* (Frankfurt: Suhrkamp Verlag).

—— 1993. 'Kultursemiotischer Prospekt', in A. Haverkamp and R. Lachmann (eds), *Memoria: Vergessen und Erinnern* (Munich: Wilhelm Fink), pp. xvii–xxvii.

—— 2004. 'Cultural Memory and the Role of Literature', *European Review* 12/2: 165–78.

—— 2012. 'Jurij Lotman: Die vorexplosive Phase', in Frank, Ruhe and Schmitz 2012: 97–118.

Lotman, J.M. 1964. Лекции по структуральной поэтике [Lectures on Structural Poetics], in *Ю. М. Лотман и тартуско-московская семиотическая школа* [J.M. Lotman and the Tartu–Moscow School of Semiotics], ed. A.D. Koshelev (Москва: Гнозис, 1994), 11–263.

—— 1970a. Статьи по типологии культуры [Studies in the Typology of Culture], in Lotman 2000: 391–459; Eng. trans. of Intro.: 'Culture and Information', trans. S. White, *Dispositio: Revista Hispánica de Semiótica Literaria* 1/3 (1976): 213–5.

—— 1970b. Структура художественного текста [The Structure of Artistic Texts], in J.M. Lotman 1998: 14–285.

—— 1977a. Культура как коллективный интеллект и проблемы искусственного разума [Culture as Collective Intellect and the Problems of Artificial Intelligence], in J.M. Lotman 2000: 557–67.

—— 1977b. Текст и структура аудитории, in Lotman 2002: 169–74; Eng. trans.: 'The Text and the Structure of Its Audience', trans. A. Shukman, *New Literary History* 14/1 (1982): 81–7.

—— 1978. Феномен культуры [Phenomenon of Culture], in J.M. Lotman 2000: 568–80.

—— 1981a. Семиотика культуры и понятие текста [Cultural Semiotics and the Notion of the Text], in J.M.Lotman 2002: 158–62.

—— 1981b. Мозг – текст – культура – искусственный интеллект [Brain–Text–Culture–Artificial Intelligence], in J.M. Lotman 2000: 580–9

—— 1984. О семиосфере, in J.M. Lotman 1992c: 11–24; Eng. trans.: 'On the Semiosphere', trans. W. Clark, *Sign Systems Studies* 33/1 (2005): 205–29.

—— 1985. Память в культурологическом освещении [The Concept of Memory in Cultural Perspective], in J.M. Lotman 2000: 673–6.

—— 1986. Память культуры [Cultural Memory], in J.M. Lotman 2000: 614–21.

—— 1987a. Несколько мыслей о типологии культур [Some Observations on the Typology of Cultures], in J.M. Lotman 1992c: 102–9.

—— 1987b. Символ в системе культуры [The Symbol in the Cultural System], in J.M. Lotman 1992c: 191–9.

—— 1989. Культура как субъект и сама-себе объект, in Lotman 2000: 639–47; Eng. trans.: 'Culture as a Subject and an Object in Itself', *Trames* 1/1 (1997): 7–16.

—— 1990. *Universe of the Mind: A Semiotic Theory of Culture*, trans. A. Shukman (London and New York: I. B. Tauris).

—— 1992a. Культура и взрыв, in Lotman 2000: 12–148; Eng. trans.: *Culture and Explosion*, trans. W. Clark (Berlin and New York: Mouton de Gruyter, 2009).

—— 1992b. Изъявление Господне или азартная игра? (Закономерное и случайное в историческом процессе) [The Expression of the Lord or a Gamble? (Regularity and Randomness in Historical Process)], in J.M. Lotman 2002: 342–9.

—— 1992c. *Избранные статьи. Т. I. Статьи по семиотике и типологии культуры* [Selected Works, vol. 1: Studies in the Typology of Cultures] (Таллинн: Александра).

—— 1993. Нам все необходимо. Лишнего в мире нет [We Need Everything: Nothing is Redundant in the World], in J.M. Lotman, *Воспитание души* [Education of the Soul] (Санкт-Пэтэрбург: «Искусство-СПБ», 2003), 287–95.

—— 1994. *Беседы о русской культуре. Быт и традиции русского дворянства (XVIII-начало XIX века)* [Conversations about Russian Culture: Everyday Life and Traditions of the Russian Nobility (18th to early 19th century)] (Санкт-Пэтэрбург: «Искусство-СПБ»).

—— 1998. *Об искусстве* [On Art] (Санкт-Пэтэрбург: «Искусство-СПБ»).

—— 2000. *Семиосфера* [Semiosphere] (Санкт-Пэтэрбург: «Искусство-СПБ»).

—— 2002. *История и типология русской культуры* [History and the Typology of Russian Culture] (Санкт-Пэтэрбург: «Искусство-СПБ»).

—— 2010. *Непредсказуемые механизмы культуры* (Таллинн: Издательство Таллиннского Университета); Eng. trans.: *The Unpredictable Workings of Culture*, trans. B.J. Baer (Tallinn: Tallinn University Press, 2013).

—— and Z.G. Mints 1981. *Литература и мифология* [Literature and Mythology], in J.M. Lotman 2002: 727–43.

—— and B.A. Uspensky 1971. О семиотическом механизме культуры, in J.M. Lotman 2000: 485–503; Eng. trans.: 'On the Semiotic Mechanism of Culture', trans. G. Mihaychuk, *New Literary History* 9/2 (1978): 211–32.

—— and —— 1977. *Роль дуальных моделей в динамике русской культуры (до конца XVIII века)*, in Lotman 2002: 88–116; Eng. trans.: 'Binary Models in the Dynamics of Russian Culture (to the End of the Eighteenth Century)', trans. R. Sorenson, in A.D. Nakhimovsky and A. Stone Nakhimovsky (eds), *The Semiotics of Russian Cultural History: Essays by Iurii M. Lotman, Lidiia Ia. Ginsburg, Boris A. Uspenskii* (Ithaca, NY, and London: Cornell University Press, 1985), 30–66.

Lotman, M. 2013. 'Afterword: Semiotics and Unpredictability', in J.M. Lotman, *The Unpredictable Workings of Culture* (Tallinn: Tallinn University Press), pp. 239–78.

Mandelker, A. 1994. 'Semiotizing the Sphere: Organicist Theory in Lotman, Bakhtin, and Vernadsky', *Publications of the Modern Language Association* 109: 385–96.

—— 1995. 'Logosphere and Semiosphere: Bakhtin, Russian Organicism, and the Semiotics of Culture', in Amy Mandelker (ed.), *Bakhtin in Contexts Across the Disciplines* (Evanston, IL: Northwestern University Press), pp. 177–90.

Olick, J.K., V.Vinitzky-Seroussi and D. Levy (eds) 2011. *The Collective Memory Reader* (Oxford: Oxford University Press).

Portis-Winner, I. 1994. *Semiotics of Culture: 'The Strange Intruder'* (Bochum: Universitätsverlag Dr. Norbert Brockmeyer).

Randviir, A. 2007. 'On Spatiality in Tartu–Moscow Cultural Semiotics: The Semiotic Subject', *Sign Systems Studies* 35: 137–59.

Salupere, S., P. Torop and K. Kull (eds) 2013. *Beginnings of the Semiotics of Culture* (Tartu: Tartu University Press).

Schönle, A. (ed.) 2006. *Lotman and Cultural Studies: Encounters and Extensions* (Madison: University of Wisconsin Press).

Semenenko, A. 2007. *Hamlet the Sign: Russian Translations of Hamlet and Literary Canon Formation* (Stockholm: Almqvist & Wiksell).

—— 2012. *The Texture of Culture: An Introduction to Yuri Lotman's Semiotic Theory* (Basingstoke: Palgrave Macmillan).

—— 2013. Гамлет, Мариа Магдалина и меланхолия. О некоторых механисмах коллективной памяти [Hamlet, Mary Magdalene, and Melancholy: On Some Mechanisms of Collective Memory], in *Случайность и непредсказуемость в истории культуры: материалы Вторых Лотмановских дней в Таллиннском университете* [Change and Indeterminism in Cultural History: Materials of the Second Juri Lotman Days in Tallinn University] (Таллинн: Издательство Таллиннского Университета), 208–21.

Shukman, A. 1977. *Literature and Semiotics: A Study of the Writings of Yu. M. Lotman.* (Amsterdam: North-Holland Publishing Company).

Tamm, M. 2013. 'Beyond History and Memory: New Perspectives in Memory Studies', *History Compass* 11/6: 458–73.

Torop, P. 2005. 'Semiosphere and/as the Research Object of Semiotics of Culture', *Sign Systems Studies* 33: 159–73.

— — 2012. 'Semiotics of Mediation: Theses', *Sign Systems Studies* 40: 286–95.

Tsaryova, E.A. 2010. Ю.М. Лотман: символический фактор в культурной динамике [J.M. Lotman: The Symbolic Factor in the Dynamics of Culture]. *Вестник Московского государственного областного университета. Серия «Философские науки»* [Bulletin of Moscow State Regional University: Philosophical Sciences] 3: 99–104.

Uspensky, B.A., et al. 1973. 'Theses on the Semiotic Study of Cultures (as Applied to Slavic Texts)', in J. van Eng (ed.), *Structure of Texts and Semiotics of Culture* (The Hague and Paris: Mouton), 1–28.

Waldstein, M. 2008. *The Soviet Empire of Signs: A History of the Tartu School of Semiotics* (Saarbrüchen: VDM Verlag).

Wertsch, J.V. 2002. *Voices of Collective Remembering* (Cambridge and New York: Cambridge University Press).

Yegorov, B.F. 1999. *Жизнь и творчество Ю. М. Лотмана* [Life and Work of J.M. Lotman] (Москва: Новое литературное обозрение).

Żyłko, B. 2009. *Semiotyka kultury: Szkoła tartusko-moskiewska* (Gdańsk: Słowo/Obraz terytoria).

PART III
Acts and Places of Memory

Travel Companions

Mieke Bal

Along the Way: Meandering Through Memory Thought

My work has been one long journey, going from discipline to discipline to establish connections ('inter-ships') between them, turning corners without cutting them and looking for ever-new ways of testing my ideas. As a result, I have encountered and temporarily journeyed with too many companions to count. The relationship between thinking about memory and companions has been particularly intense, manifold and inspirational. When, more than 15 years ago, I first began to work on memory, it was at the request of other people. Although I had written on memorialists such as Proust, memory had not been a concept that preoccupied me particularly. But when two professors at Dartmouth College, Leo Spitzer and Jonathan Crewe, invited me to work with them in a six-week long seminar, 'Cultural Memory and the Present', their title immediately made me think about each of its terms. These two colleagues and the other participants – among whom noted memory scholars such as Marianne Hirsch, Ernst van Alphen, and Susan Brison, to name but a few whose work has inspired me especially – became, thus, my first companions. The resulting publication, *Acts of Memory*, appeared in 1999. Another result of this initial and initiating experience was that I proposed the title 'Cultural Memory in the Present' (note the change from conjunction to preposition) for a book series I was asked to co-edit with philosopher Hent de Vries for Stanford University Press, within the framework of the Amsterdam School for Cultural Analysis (ASCA) Hent and I had then-recently co-founded and of which I was the academic director and Hent the chair.[1]

Along the way, interacting with students whose critical enthusiasm also greatly helped my thinking, I had embarked on the project that resulted in the book *Travelling Concepts in the Humanities*. This book came out of my practice as a teacher at the doctoral and postdoctoral level. With an interdisciplinary group, conceptual confusion is always threatening, and finding a way to a satisfactory solution led to the book. In this context, the question is, can 'memory' be considered such a travelling concept? Significantly, there is no chapter devoted to memory in the book. In my view, concepts may be fluid, and memory certainly is, but with 'travelling' as well as with 'concepts' I meant something else. Rather than fluid, open and malleable, travelling concepts are precise, but transform as they move from one period, discipline or cultural domain to another. The concept of memory is used in so many contexts that the idea of travelling becomes redundant, since there is no 'home' where it would begin its journey. According to my distinction in that book, it is a word, rather than a concept. The difference is that words may have various meanings and connotations and may be used in different contexts but are not concepts in that they do not offer a mini-theory

---

1   I co-edited Cultural Memory in the Present from its beginning in 1997 until 2012.

that helps in the analysis of objects, situations, states and other theories. If explicit, clear and defined, they can help to articulate an understanding, convey an interpretation, check an imagination-run-wild and enable a discussion on the basis of common terms and in the awareness of absences and exclusions. Only when memory is qualified, as, for example, 'collective' memory – based on community (Halbwachs) – 'public' memory – dominated by media – or 'cultural' memory does it begin to approach the status of concept. But, as the title of our 1999 volume indicates, the true concept is 'acts of memory.' For, this phrase-concept harbours a set of characteristics that, together, form a mini-theory that makes the concept suitable for analysis.[2]

With the phrase 'acts of memory' I seek to unpack that mini-theory. Memory, this theory says, is a verb, a transitive one, and its mode is active. It is something we do. It has a subject and an object. And, as the change to the preposition 'in' in the title of our book series indicates, that act takes place in the present. The phrase thus encapsulates a theory of memory. This twofold characteristic – activity and present tense – in turn imports into the concept aspects of cultural utterances such as performativity and duration. The former implies that the act of memory has consequences for its 'second persons' – which may be the memorising subject herself or others who are affected by the memory; the latter, that it takes, occupies, or gives time. And with this conception of the act of memory a whole new world of companions opens up. For, there is no better place to seek inspiration for this thought-on-the-move than the world of art. Indeed, along with inspiring philosophers and scholars I find in the process of analysing artworks that the refinements, the assessments of the consequences and potential, and the politics of memory come to the fore.[3]

A few years after I came to this insight, I made yet another turn in my work. Wishing to get more direct access to the culture of the present, the culture 'in becoming' as Deleuze would have it, I began to make films. The subject of these films invariably turned out to be acts of memory. The films I characterise as 'experimental documentaries' concerned issues of migratory culture: the culture in which migrancy is a normal way of life, the culture we all share, whether we ever move or not; in short, present cultures around the world and, in particular, in the West; issues of not having legal papers; of identity becoming a burden; of not being admitted into your own country; and of being boxed into categories that never fit. Most importantly in this context, from 2006 to 2011, I made a video installation, *Nothing is Missing*, in which a group of women never talked about, not documented, completely erased from our cultural awareness, perform their own acts of memory. These women are mothers of migrants. They talk about the memories of the child who left, from birth, childhood, to the departure and its aftermath (Figure 10.1). It became clear from the first film that they were appreciated more in the art world than, say, for television. Thus, willy-nilly, I became an artist. Now and then, I also curated exhibitions on similar subjects.[4]

---

2   See Bal 2002: esp. Intro., ch.1. With the term 'mini-theory,' I mean that the concept harbours the elements and the syntax that form a theory; the concept can be seen as a summary of a theory. This makes it possible to use it for analysis in precise ways that simple words cannot. 'Acts of memory' also seeks to be more specific that the larger term 'mnemonic practices' (Olick and Robbins 1998), which does not foreground the subjective-singular nature of memory.

3   This is also how *Travelling Concepts in the Humanities* is arranged: theorizing through art. A companion in this conviction is Andreas Huyssen, whose recent book on the subject demonstrates that his thinking about memory converges in many respects with mine (including his interest in these two artists) (Huyssen 2013).

4   For information on the films, photographs and clips, see <http://www.miekebal.org/artworks/films/>. On *Nothing is Missing*, see Bal 2012a. The exhibition '2MOVE' was also devoted to subjects of migratory culture as intertwined with considerations of the moving image. See the catalogue (with DVD): Bal and Hernández-Navarro 2008.

Figure 10.1 **Mieke Bal,** *Nothing is Missing,* **multi-channel video installation**
 (Zuiderzeemuseum, Enkhuizen, 2007–8)
 Photo: **Astrid van Wijenberg**

The last phase (for now) of this development was the making of fiction films and video installations derived from them. The first of these, *A Long History of Madness*, is based on a book, *Mère folle* by French psychoanalyst Françoise Davoine (1998). In this book the author develops a theory of the analytical treatment of psychosis – something Freud claimed to be impossible – using fiction as a mode of thinking. We – co-director Michelle Williams Gamaker and I – call the resulting film a 'theoretical fiction'. This term is reminiscent of Freud, who used it, to defend his strangely speculative *Totem and Taboo*. Davoine's book, and the film based on it, has acts of memory at its heart: the memories of old, medieval traditions of revolutionary street theatre; the memories of violence, in wars and within homes, sometimes going back several generations; failed memories, in the acts of negligence called forgetting; and memories of dreams and delusions that help insight to become possible when social companions listen, believe, and support. As an act of trans-temporal dialogue, we installed a version of this work as an exhibition in the Freud Museum London, where a monitor at the foot of Freud's iconic couch performed a visual dialogue with the master of psychoanalysis. As we visually argue, the condition of proving Freud wrong and setting past wounds right is that the analyst behaves like a *therapôn*, or companion (Figure 10.2).[5]

---

5   In the video at the foot of the couch, the analyst and patient are sitting side by side on a
     couch. The importance of the companion in Davoine's book is a striking convergence with the
     present volume on memory (see Davoine 1998, 2014). On our film and related projects, see
     <http://www.crazymothermovie.com/>; on the film in relation to the book, see Landa 2012; on film
     and exhibition, see Bal 2012b; Hannula 2010; Morra 2012.

Figure 10.2   Mieke Bal & Michelle Williams Gamaker, *Saying It* **(Freud Museum, London, 2012)**
Photo: **Paul Hubalek**

Thus, from colleagues and students, to artworks, to the people who appear in my own artworks, to the fictionalised characters whose memories of history had been blocked by madness, I was able to theorise acts of memory that could touch upon, activate and overcome the blocked memory we call trauma. Through the experiment of making this film, I attempted a theorisation of memory that takes as its starting point the active performance of acts of memory in the present, and encompasses the different kind of such acts from unreflective, routine memories, sense memories to narrative memories and the impossible memories that cause trauma, as well as the moods that colour memories – nostalgia being one of these. Enabling such a theorisation is the insight that memory is, in addition, also dialogic, hence, social. What makes an act of memory capable of overcoming traumatic incapacitation is the social process that enables psychotic people to be heard, believed and socially accepted.[6]

A second fiction film enacts yet another act of memory, also thoroughly cultural albeit in a somewhat different way. Our recent project – again with Michelle – is an updated version of Flaubert's masterpiece *Madame Bovary*. Taking quotation as the basic mode of our filming, we propose that the combination of capitalism and patriarchy that disables the main character Emma is still rampant today. This entails not so much an actualisation of the nineteenth-century novel but, instead, working with the novel's own fundamental contemporaneity. Flaubert wrote from and for his own time, and that horizontal temporality is what underlies the idea of acts of memory in the first place. Radicalising this aspect, we install an immersive exhibition of eight installations, together made of 19 screens. Thus, visitors are positioned

---

6   Davoine makes this point forcefully. For more on this approach to psychosis, see Davoine and Gaudillière 2004; Hernández 2006. On trauma as 'after-affect' in art, see Pollock 2013. Although I am not on the exact same wavelength as Pollock's theoretical framework, her analyses are very convincing. The most lucid, concise and conceptually rigorous analysis of trauma in relation to discourse is Van Alphen 2004.

in a confrontational, as well as empathic position, surrounded by screens on which what we have come to call 'emotional capitalism' is acted out and leads to the demise of a talented and beautiful young woman. This installation entails yet another layer of contemporaneity: that of each museum visit, where content is absorbed – or rather, constructed – in the present, while the classic story is also present in its durative contemporaneity.

Encouraged by the installations to actively engage with the characters, visitors literally perform acts of cultural memory in the present, recalling, through the old masterpiece, the current situation of economic anxiety, the ongoing illusions of romantic love and the deceptive promise of that impossibility, permanent excitement, with which emotional capitalism keeps luring us all and destroying many of us. This temporal reversal, which I have called 'preposterous' and that more usually goes by the name of 'anachronism', is perhaps the most literal enactment of the theoretical concept of acts of memory in the present. And, since they are not alone in the galleries where the installation confronts, surrounds or interpolates them, visitors also enact the social aspect of such acts.[7]

After thus sketching the itinerary I have followed since 1997 when I first started thinking about memory, in what follows, I will invoke work by two artists who have greatly enabled my thinking in this matter, Eija-Liisa Ahtila and Doris Salcedo. One makes representational work, the other refrains from representation. Both emphatically choose the present tense for their works that perform acts of memory. Both address violence and attempt to make art relevant for dealing with it. Both seem to heed the warning by Walter Benjamin that for me, condenses the mini-theory of the concept and its political relevance in the most convincing way possible: 'every image of the past that is not recognized by the present as one of its own concerns threatens to disappear irretrievably' (1968: 255). Putting the philosopher's statement and the artworks in dialogue, I attempt to refine and further flesh out the concept as I have so far articulated it.[8]

Responsibility in the Present

Video installation artist Eija-Liisa Ahtila is among those who work with Benjamin's caution. Her six-screen installation *Where is Where?* from 2008 attempts to establish a strong connection between a past that happened long ago and elsewhere and a present here-and-now. Her endeavour as I interpret it is to enable cultural memory to be active and politically productive by distinguishing between guilt and responsibility. She thus eliminates an unproductive postcolonial guilt and replaces it with contemporary responsibility in and for the migratory culture that is an 'after-affect' (Pollock 2013) of colonialism. I learned this from her work, and this distinction helped me understand the political aspect of acts of memory as based on responsibility in the present. Her work consists of an imaginative installation that presents viewers with the possibility of immersion in a temporal-audiovisual-political cacophony. Her tool for achieving political agency for art by means of acts of memory is affect. Positioning the Algerian War of Independence as an issue for, even a creation of, the present, the work is programmed to produce a dynamic intensity in the space between images and viewer. But the creation – rather than reconstruction – of history in the here and

---

7 See <http://madamebproject.com/>. The project was first installed in the Muzeum Sztuki in Łódź, Poland, and traveled in different forms in 2014 to Estonia, Switzerland, Finland, Colombia and Malta. For video tours of the exhibitions see http://www.miekebal.org/artworks/exhibitions/.

8 I have written on both these artists, along with a third, Ann Veronica Janssens, in a trilogy on political art (Bal 2010, 2013a, 2013b).

now does not let us escape into fiction. Instead, she deploys different ways of authenticating the created history through acts of cultural memory. The most obvious of these is the use of archival footage, recalling both the war and early cinema, but the citation of authoritative intertexts is another. Both constitute acts of memory, recalling the recorded reality and the fictional imaginings of a past contemporaneity. Both contribute to the build-up of a cultural network, a spider web of responsibility in which we are caught.[9]

This leads to the inquiry the work's title solicits, the question of location – geographical, social, psychic, political. The retrospectivity of the approach goes hand in hand with a retrospective engagement of the medium. Primarily, a dissociation of image from sound, staged in a dissociative 'syndrome' of the character of one of the earlier works, *The House* (2002) keeps medium and politics bound together. Finally, it is in the genre of tragedy – alluded to, staged, and yet held at bay, that the unique combination of videography, the writing of visions, takes place.

The final image of the central part of the installation is a close-up of a young Algerian boy who has killed a friend, simply because the friend was European (Figure 10.3). The anecdote comes from Frantz Fanon's *Les Damnés de la terre* from 1961. The image is an extreme close-up which, projected on the huge screen of the installation, is as imposing as it is impressive. Filmed in the context, set in Algeria, the face may have an 'Arab effect.'

Figure 10.3   Eija-Liisa Ahtila, *Where is Where?* (2008). HD installation for 6 projections with sound. Final image of middle part, Adel's last sentence
**   *Photo*: Marja-Leena Hukkanen. Courtesy of Marian Goodman Gallery, New York and Paris. © 2008 Crystal Eye – Kristallisilmä Oy**

---

9   Space constraints do not allow me to develop these recollections here. They include Camus' *L'Étranger* and poems by T.S. Eliot. See Bal 2011, 2013b.

Cinematographically, the close-up creates an 'affection-image' to use Gilles Deleuze's term in reference to a category of movement-images. The affection-image is the one that suspends time; that intensifies duration.[10]

In a very useful book on Deleuze's philosophy of cinema, Paola Marrati points at the crucial function of the affection-image – the closest to both the materiality of the image and to the materiality of subjectivity. She writes tersely: 'Between a perception that is in certain ways troubling, and an action still hesitant, affection emerges.' 'It is this image', she continues, 'that transforms the movement of translation into a movement of expression', 'in pure quality' (Marrati 2008: 35). This is why the affection-image is an image in the present, which also has the temporal density needed to make contact possible, or to establish an 'inter-face,' both with other people, such as viewers, and with other times. This property makes the affection image an ideal vehicle for a memory enacted to be shared. Its typical incarnation is the close-up. An image with an 'Arab effect' is an affection-image and stops time: the combination alone is worth dwelling on.[11]

What the affection-image does is provoke a confluence, even if conflicted, between subject and object, without cancelling out the heterogeneity and without falling into a deceptive harmony. Affect, in this conception, is a medium, not a message. The dynamic intensity that is affect enables viewers to 'have' – to perform the act of – other people's memories. This is how they can become companions of people who suffered in the past: not to help those victims, now long gone, but potentially similar victims or, at least, be alert to potential repetitions of the violence.[12]

The affective force of the image is enhanced by the acting style. The young actor, Allaedin Allaedine, suspends all emotion. While in Fanon's passionate anti-colonialist text the interview is a transcription of psychiatric expertise, so the psychiatrist implicitly interprets the lack or suspension of emotion as a particular disturbance we now call traumatic, in Ahtila's visual work it signals avoidance of the pathetic. The addressee in Fanon is the psychiatrist whose questions the boy is answering. In the installation, the addressee is the spectator, invited to re-socialise the traumatised boy.[13]

At some point, by subtle visual allusion, under the guidance of the enigmatic figure of a female priest we are also momentarily in an immigration office. The priest character now floats above the ground, dressed in the red of a Jan van Eijck Madonna or donor or the red of devils (Figure 10.4). The allusion to red queuing ropes also suggests museums. Curious, how immigration offices and museums share this crowd control tool to keep people at bay. We are confronted by this image: two Algerian boys are plucked from the 1950s, pushed forward by a figure – a guardian angel or a devil – as in the Christian religious tradition, passing along the queues of contemporary immigration offices, 'Where is where?' then becomes the question about where the work is situated in space and in time, in something between literal and extended sense, so that multitemporal and multidirectional acts of memory become possible.[14]

---

10   The most succinct formulation of these three types of 'movement-images' is Deleuze 1986: 66–70.
11   On the affection-image, see Pisters 2003: 66–71; on temporality in the movement-image, see Rodowick 1997.
12   For the idea that affect can function as a medium, see Hansen 2003. 'Having the memory of others' is a phrase coined by Kaja Silverman in her superbly stimulating book in which she develops an ethics of vision (1996).
13   The careful and subtle way Ahtila has reworked the text is most obvious when it is compared with the original French (Fanon 2002: 259–61): The quoted sentence – 'faites ce que vous voulez', 'do what you have to do' – is on page 261. Fanon does act as a psychiatrist, but his diagnosis concerns the colonial situation, not the 'patient'.
14   Multidirectional memory evokes an intellectual companion who greatly impacted on my thinking about memory: Michael Rothberg. See Rothberg 2009.

Figure 10.4   Eija-Liisa Ahtila, *Where Is Where?* (2008). HD installation for 6 projections with sound. The Priest ('Guardian Angel') leads the boys through the queuing ropes
Photo: Marja-Leena Hukkanen. Courtesy of Marian Goodman Gallery, New York and Paris. © 2008 Crystal Eye – Kristallisilmä Oy

The complex work with memory usefully complicates the question of political art. This work may seem overly political, because it is so explicitly focused on the Algerian war, suggesting that, 50 years later, this war is still present. It is as if the work was accusing us, people living innocently of all that in the present, of still bearing guilt for it. This is the misunderstanding this work sets itself up for, in order to trouble us more effectively into the insight that guilt and responsibility are sharply distinct, in that denying the former does not dispense us from the latter. Or is it not political enough when the poet sings a religious song and all four screens turn sky blue? This scene would almost be skirting kitsch, if it was not too troubling, with the military march music to which the poet sings. This marching music is literally drummed up by a visible drummer. It is set in the same melody as the earlier whistle, when the Poet calls up Satan, braving the Priest, in a crucial discussion about guilt, forgiveness, and responsibility. The drumming that accompanies the singing brings in, through yet another act of cultural memory, Brecht's political theatre, especially his anti-war play *Mutter Courage* from 1939. Thus, this highly aestheticized scene refers to the history of the attempt to articulate how art, specifically theatre, can be political. The emphatic aesthetic, thus, is not an escape from the political but, on the contrary, a foregrounding of it, an argument in the discussion. Its tool: the multidirectional act of memory.

The merger of fiction and documentary in this work leans on theatricality. This work is also a tragedy. The term implies tradition, death and theatre. Of all literary genres, tragedy is the most long-standing and prestigious: it is truly traditional. The tradition of art, especially politically resonant art, is doubly emphasised: in the many references to literary and cinematic masterpieces, as well as in self-reflexive references to the media of both arts. And to the art that binds the two: theatre. Theatricality is visible in the relentless passage of time, which theatre shares with cinema. At key moments, the setting is a podium with folding chairs around it. This is a visual topos at the ending of *Where is Where?* when Adel's final sentence is spoken to three screens of such empty chairs. The figure of Death, in theatrical costume, illuminated so that we barely ever see anything more than his mouth, keeps us aware of Samuel Beckett's theatrical reductions. And while most of the speeches directly address the spectator, the scene where Death and the Poet sit together at the breakfast table recall amateur theatre performances in small town venues so as to involve us all. Finally, it is precisely because most of the speeches seem performances of poetry-like philosophy, or philosophical poetry, never drama, the moments where the boys in the prison hospital talk to the doctors on the other screens foreground theatricality in the four-screen disposition.[15]

However, the notion that the disposition of *Where is Where?* in four screens is a theatrical setting must be immediately qualified. For, with four screens disposed in a square, theatre is reversed: the work does not take place in front of us but surrounds and absorbs us. In relation to the work, we, its spectators, are on stage. Although the work is based on an implacable logic, it is impossible to follow this logic 'logically'. The environment of four screens one cannot simultaneously observe embodies this impossibility. From this paradox another one emerges: far from contradicting or mitigating it, the very theatricality of this piece, including its emphatic artificiality constitutes its political force. The work is able to make history enter art and, thus, end the unfortunate and damaging opposition between fiction and reality. In-between, memory is situated: acts of memory can achieve performativity.

Ending that opposition, even as a non-polarised distinction is a condition *sine qua non* for political art. Not to establish a preferred presence of 'reality' but to literally suspend the distinction and thus keep fiction present in a never-resolved dialectic. Precisely on the basis of the indispensable co-presence of fiction and reality as not distinguishable – fiction is part of reality and so is language – it becomes possible to approach 'art' beyond the fatigue of an all-pervasive, powerless habit of critique. To make the case for the political force of Ahtila's work, as well as, below, for Salcedo's, we first need to resituate the political in and of art. For, we cannot avoid the great aporia put forward by Adorno in his essay 'Commitment' (2003a): art that seeks to speak of politics becomes propaganda and ceases to be art – it loses any political efficacy – but art that only wishes to be art is political in its refusal of politics.

Taking this aporia as a starting point, we know that neither rhetoric nor thematic focus work, for both pertain to 'propaganda'. Hence, they cannot be art. Resituating the political in art happens where we least expect it: in the avowed, self-conscious artifice of the theatrical. This is, in my view, what *Where is Where?* sets out to do. Theatre, writes Maaike Bleeker, 'presents a *staging* of the construction that is also constitutive of the real' (2008: 9). Theatricality is a vision machine that stages possible forms of looking around us from a culturally and historically specific consciousness, on the basis of a destabilization of the relationship between the act of looking and what is staged.

---

15   On tragedy, see Loraux 2002; on its relation to modernity, see Taxidou 2004; see also the recent, incisive critique of the concept Marx 2013.

Around us: *Where is Where?* once again takes this phrase literally, surrounding us with images that we look at with a sharp awareness that we cannot see them all. It imposes a certain physical restlessness on spectators and makes the acts of memory they are invited to perform literally multidirectional. It forces them to turn around so that their bodies are implicated in the act of looking. To understand how this literal embodiment of theatre works in conjunction with Ahtila's other aesthetic engagements, we only need to realise what cinema and theatre have in common. This work is emphatically cinematographic, with its breath-taking beauty as well as its recalls of earlier cinema. But in its theatrical disposition it is also emphatically opposed to the illusionism of theatre and cinema encouraged when the spectator comfortably sits in the dark, looking straight ahead and forgetting his (her) body. To this illusionism it opposes a 'critical habitat'. We sit or stand there, physically unable to remain abstract and distant, and hence, whatever our critical reflections, we cannot disentangle ourselves from what we critique.[16]

The main character, who is a poet, sets the tone of this multiple memory of the tragedy of the trans-generational transmission of violence. She is a woman who seems real, but whose interlocutor is an allegorical figure. Cinematographically, the memory of Ingmar Bergman is visible here. In a theatrical dialogue, she conducts a discussion with Monsieur la Mort, who asks her to give him words. Later, words fly from a page freshly printed. One wonders where they go, and where that where is. For, boundaries between the Poet and Death, between her and the boys, the watertight boundaries of the individual, as well as of periods and countries, have melted under the spell of multidirectional memory. One gets the feeling that these words, which have flown away, enable this sort of shamanistic communication. The graphic disposition of the words on the page looks more like a script than a poem. A script of a play, enhancing the theatricality of that destabilisation of even the printed word – or is it the script of the work we are watching, in a self-reflexivity that foregrounds the Poet's, the artist's endorsement of her complicity?

I believe it is both – the play that destabilises and the script of *Where is Where?* that puts us in the presence of that destabilisation. For, at stake in this deconstruction of boundaries is responsibility in the present. This is both the temporality of video installation, and the temporality of the close-up that suspends linear time and positions affect instead. Affect is the glue that makes such acts of memory contagious. Therein lies the relevance of art.[17]

Death and Green Grass

Ahtila deploys representation to do her multidirectional memory work, and her central theme here is death. But the actual performance of memory – the act achieving performativity – is due to her chosen format of the surrounding video installation. Doris Salcedo is another contemporary artist committed to keeping the memory of violence alive or even to make such memories accessible where trauma-inducing violence had erased them. Death is also at the heart of her work. But she shuns representation. Salcedo is consistently exploring imaginative ways of invoking violence, indicting it, countering the erasure of its memories

---

16 Apter defines a critical habitat as 'art informed by geopolitics; by an ecologically engaged conceptualism … that critiques the relationship between media and environment and explores forms of global identification' (2002: 22). Her work also requires reflection on installation as art form, which cannot be addressed in the scope of this paper. See Bal 2013b.

17 Ahtila is one of the artists of video installation whose work has persuaded me to embark on that mode myself. For the specific political relevance of the mode, or if you prefer genre, of video installation, see Bal 2013b.

and thus enabling traumatised survivors to reconnect to the social world, without representing it. Like Ahtila but in a very different artistic and memorial mode, she does through art what Davoine and her colleagues do through analysis. In doing so both artists make a strong claim for the relevance of art as a suitable site for acts of memory, but Salcedo does this through problematising representation. She makes sculptures, creating images containing – in more than one sense of the verb – past violence, but not depictions of the violence. I will again limit myself to one work, and on its basis I will add to my mini-theory of the act of memory, the 'palimpsestic' memory put forward by another contemporary companion, Max Silverman (2013).

'Each unit is approximately the length and width of a standard coffin', Doris Salcedo wrote in the artist statement for her 2011 work *Plegaria muda* (Figure 10.5). The word 'coffin' stuck in my throat. When I read this, I had just had my own experience with coffins. For the film *A Long History of Madness*, I had travelled to Seili Island, Finland, to a former psychiatric hospital, a pinkish building amidst green meadows. On Seili, a former leper colony had been converted into a 'madhouse' – something that, as Michel Foucault has told us, had been done in many cases. The disappearance of leprosy marked the invention of the madhouse, or psychiatric hospital (Foucault 2006).[18] On Seili, patients were admitted on one condition: they had to bring their own coffin. This chilling fact turned the mere fact of our filming on that location into a historically layered, palimpsestic act of memory that I qualify as 'political'.

Figure 10.5   Doris Salcedo, *Plegaria muda*, installation (2011)
  Photo: **Studio Doris Salcedo**

Each unit consist of such a coffin-size table, a layer of soil, and another table on top, legs in the air. Through carefully drilled tiny holes, tender stalks of grass pierce the table (Figure 10.6). Salcedo not only uses the dimensions ('approximately') of coffins but also the

---

18   Foucault over-generalises his point somewhat.

Figure 10.6   Doris Salcedo, *Plegaria muda*, installation (2011). Detail
             Photo: Studio Doris Salcedo

material: wood and the colour or discoloration. The size of the tables and their (non-)colour evokes death caused by human hands: victims de-humanized when their bodies could not be retrieved, buried, mourned, because the violence was denied. Mass graves hidden in green pastures, where the hiding is like a second killing, parallel with but opposed to the traditional second burial. In *Plegaria muda*, those killing grounds themselves become visible – barely, piercing through their attempts to stay hidden – for the first time. Green, growing grass, life: it is almost shocking to see those tiny bits surface from between the grey, dead slabs.

Like the coffins of the history of Seili that sentenced, without trial, the allegedly mad to life imprisonment, never to be seen again, the coffin-size sculptures do not explicitly refer to any violence at all. They do not tell stories; they just 'are', touching the visitor with hair-raising horror while remaining mute, immobile, silent as the grave. As we have seen with Ahtila's work, acts of memory in installation settings are effective through the glue of affect that binds what is seen to the viewer who sees it. Such seeing-in-space is sense-based, in the present and makes its content known on the level of experience. This is art – not committed journalism, not politics, not propaganda. Yet there is a reality behind them, or inside them: the reality of mass murder, of which the palimpsestic superposition of other acts of mass violence enables us to have the memories of others. That is the reality of the history of the present, in the aftermath of which we live and enjoy great works of art. This reality is invoked in a manner that is both absolutely inevitable and yet indirect. The numerous units, working together to constitute a mass – as in 'mass graves' – cannot avoid working together to convey or touch us with the horror that inspired them. But nowhere can any representation of violence be seen. Even the grass of the killing fields is modest, small, growing shyly from between two layers of wood that evoke but do not represent the coffin. It is as subtly present as the coffins whose presence on Seili we imagine, even though they are hidden in the past.

From within that present in which Salcedo shows her work, small bits of grass pierce through the layers of attempts to keep life under a lid. I think back of the earlier work I have seen so often (but not often enough), and by which I have been touched so often, through Salcedo's primary medium: affect. I have never seen that work through those shades of green. Green goes very well with grey, but the beauty of a colour scheme matters here only ironically. Instead, it is the struggle of those small green elements that touches me, with the contradictory combination of two meanings. They conceal the place of violence, the invisible grave, by overgrowing it. This makes the grass guilty by omission, complicit with the cruelty that not only killed but also concealed the killing, thus preventing mourning and acts of memory: causing trauma. Yet, they also indicate the perseverance of life, thumbing their noses at those who think killing can erase life. This multi-layeredness makes the acts of memory the work compels us to perform into palimpsestic memories.

The social and cultural relevance of such artistic acts of memory as Ahtila and Salcedo perform fits Benjamin's caution like a glove. His powerful fifth thesis quoted above stipulates that an image of the past only matters for the present when it is seen 'as one of its own concerns'. If it is not identified as such, the image will disappear. Since extinction is forever, the question that needs to be raised could be phrased as follows: How can art prevent the extinction of the past so that the present can make it matter for itself? First of all, through images of it, images that represent the past, that come to us from the past and that make the past matter for the present. Those are the three meanings of the preposition 'of' that resonate in Benjamin's sentence. The operative verb in his urgent warning is 'to recognise'.

The images of the past must be recognised – and recognised in their relevance for the present – so that we can effectively bring them to bear on the present, with all their palimpsestic layers. The penalty for failing to do so is the irretrievable loss not simply of the past but of its images – hence, also of the three forms of relevance that the preposition 'of' suggests they have. The two meanings of recognition, one cognitive – to know again – and one social – to give acknowledgement to, to recognise something 'as' – are bound up together. This is, according to Davoine's book and our film, the double condition of the overcoming of trauma's mad-making blocking of memory. In both senses, recognition pertains to the dialectic of similarity, or repetition, and of difference, or innovation, that constitutes representation. The cognitive sense insists on similarity in the new act, hence, on similarity and innovation as two distinct moments in time, whereas the social sense intimates similarity-in-difference between self and other as both equipped to take the roles of first and second person in turns. Intertemporality and intersubjectivity are, thus, at issue in the concept of recognition: as they are, too, in Benjamin's statement, in Salcedo's work and in the space of its installation. Salcedo's works are entirely visual: they use no words other than their titles, and the only sound they emit is that of an emphatic and empathic silence. Yet, the art's very visuality – its forms, colours and matter – also carries out conceptual work, all the while making its viewers do the same. Now, with *Plegaria muda*, we cannot avoid seeing the conceptual work in the dimensions as well. The allusion to that ultimate private space, the bed – a space of joy and of illness – is also present in our acts of memory. While never representing a human figure, Salcedo does not allow us to forget that figure, if only by the dimensions. Nor can we forget the trace of life, the grass tells us. Forbidding one to forget is an attempt to make trauma potentially curable. Ahtila achieves the same result – the promise of a possibility – by other means. Whether representation is deployed or not is immaterial: the address to the viewer through affect, enhanced by installation-ness, is what makes these acts of memory performative.

The Performativity of Memory

According to the performative conception of art, art participates in the political – it does not simply represent it, and, rather than merely critiquing, it intervenes. For such interference to be possible, art needs to possess as well as bestow agency. The sculpture reflects on the place that representation has in such a search for art's political agency. It helps us to articulate possible ways of making cultural interventions, such as art practices, concretely relevant without the need to resort to representation and its drawbacks of repetition, reduction and distancing – 'stylising', for which Theodor Adorno indicted it in his famous critique of culture and its studies (2003b).[19]

I understand 'relevant' in the sense of being incisive for that domain where differences of opinion are recognised and treated as antagonisms and antagonism as the alternative to enmity. Salcedo does not simply refuse, disavow or reject those artistic and intellectual strategies she seeks to question. Therefore, representation retains a place – however problematical, minimal, and subverted that place may be. In *Plegaria muda*, we can observe it in the dimensions.[20]

Negativity is necessary in order to avoid the moralising talk of 'dominant ideology' and instead to endorse inevitable complicity, as Gayatri Spivak has recommended repeatedly (1999). But one further step is needed, and this step will restore the need for political art, albeit perhaps through the back door. In an essay on the predicament of the compulsion and impossibility of defining 'culture' in anthropology, Johannes Fabian offers a convincing

---

19   This text is often alleged as an indictment of art 'after Auschwitz', a negativity Adorno himself withdrew when it was taken up a bit too easily.
20   For my conception of the political, I draw on Mouffe 2005.

plea for a rigorously negative (non-)definition of this concept. He contends that it is helpful to invoke confrontation and negotiation as the moments in which 'the cultural' emerges (Fabian 2001). This formulation both avoids positive, reifying definitions that are inherently 'othering' and foregrounds process as the domain of culture. Thus it involves temporality, agency and plurality, without falling into the traps of self-congratulatory celebrations of multiplicity and freedom, of idealisations of the possibility of democracy and of the insidious imposition of particular values as universal. Here lies, perhaps, the crucial importance of acts of memory: multidirectional, palimpsestic and including the memories of others. I model my conception of concepts as indefinable because travelling, yet containing mini-theories, on Fabian's view and its refusal to define.

Acts of memory occur in the present. But they cannot occur without a multiple past, indispensable for living. One of the tools of the constant bond between mass violence and the singular suffering it causes is the deployment of time. The growing of grass, its slow yet relentless return to life, focuses on the slow temporality of living against the fast one of killing. Human life can be destroyed faster than grass can grow, yet time is elongated in the face of torture and death. Time loses its meaning. In terms of time, the paradox is that most of Salcedo's work is still. Technically, it is still because it does not move and because it is silent, but it is also still in terms of mood. Yet, it is moving – not primarily emotionally but politically – because of the strong affective impact that compels agency without prescribing what the agent must do.

As a consequence, Salcedo's work, which is committed to stillness, is able to overcome the formal opposition between 'still' and 'moving' images. It also negotiates the gap between an object and its affective charge or, in other words, between the object perceived at a distance and the viewer whose act of viewing affects her. The small patches of grass, different in each unit, need a moving visitor in order to be perceived. While the radical incommensurability between looking at a distance and looking up close is a theoretical issue, Salcedo turns this incommensurability into a literal and experiential aspect of vision. Among the consequences of this paradoxical 'state' is a complex relationship, not only with representation, figuration and space, but also with another aspect of 'human nature': its existence in time. The temporality of human existence precludes stability and warrants constant transformation. This effect keeps the singularity from falling back into (anecdotal) particularity. Finally, the enormous scale of *Plegaria muda* that inflects a gigantic space with greyness, combined with the green grass, brings our attention back to the installation aspect, crucial to all of Salcedo's work. It is in this aspect of installation that, in spite of the many differences, Ahtila's and Salcedo's work join forces. They both entice their visitors to respond to the question 'Where is Where?' with a temporal-spatial intensity that allows memory to be socially productive and helpful as a companion.

Studying acts of memory in contemporary artistic practices has made me aware of the companionship they proffer. More than sources of knowledge, the artworks, as well as the scholarship – in other words, with Benjamin's caution about why images matter, *Where is Where?*, *Plegaria muda*, as well as Rothberg's *Multidirectional Memory* and Silverman's *Palimpsestic Memory*, to name but a few – have functioned as interlocutors, buddies in conceptualisation, fellow travellers in the adventure of growing insight in the importance of cultural acts of memory. Multidirectional and palimpsestic, audio-visual, sculptural, discursive: at first sight all these acts of memory constitute an apparent cacophony of cultural voices. But if we try too hard to harmonise and streamline them, we lose the conceptual mini-theory and fall back onto simple words. And words, besides being the tool of rhetoric as well as of communication, are also sources of self-evident, unquestioned confusions. Memory – its acts, its presentness, its layeredness and its affective load – is too important for that. For, underlying such acts is the multidirectional and durative nature of time, against the strictures of chronology, for which we are responsible – now.

References

Adorno, T.W. 2003a. 'Commitment', in Adorno 2003c: 240–58.
— — 2003b. 'Cultural Criticism and Society', in Adorno 2003c: 146–62.
— — 2003c. *Can One Live After Auschwitz? A Philosophical Reader*, ed. R. Tiedemann, trans. R. Livingstone et al. (Stanford, CA, Stanford University Press).
Apter, E. 2002. 'The Aesthetics of Critical Habitats', *October* 99: 21–44.
Bal, M. 2002. *Travelling Concepts in the Humanities: A Rough Guide* (Toronto: University of Toronto Press).
— — 2010. *Of What One Cannot Speak: Doris Salcedo's Political Art* (Chicago: University of Chicago Press).
— — 2011. 'Losing It: The Politics of the Other (Medium)', *Journal of Visual Culture* 10/3: 372–96.
— — 2012a. 'Facing: Intimacy Across Divisions', in G. Pratt and V. Rosner (eds), *The Global and the Intimate: Feminism in Our Time* (New York: Columbia University Press), pp. 119–44.
— — 2012b. 'Spatialising Film', in J.F. Hovden and K. Knapskog (eds), *Hunting High and Low*, Festschrift for Jostein Gripsrud (Oslo: Scandinavian Academic Press).
— — 2013a. *Endless Andness: The Politics of Abstraction According to Ann Veronica Janssens* (London: Bloomsbury).
— — 2013b. *Thinking in Film: The Politics of Video Installation According to Eija-Liisa Ahtila* (London: Bloomsbury).
— — and M.Á. Hernández-Navarro 2008. *2MOVE: Video, Art, Migration* (Murcia, Spain: Cendeac).
— — J. Crewe and L. Spitzer (eds) 1999. *Acts of Memory: Cultural Recall in the Present* (Hanover, NH: University Press of New England).
Benjamin, W. 1968. 'Theses on the Philosophy of History', in *Illuminations*, ed. H. Arendt, trans. H. Zohn (New York: Schocken Books), pp. 253–64.
Bleeker, M. 2008. *Visuality in the Theatre: The Locus of Looking* (Basingstoke: Palgrave).
Davoine, F. 1998. *Mère Folle: Récit* (Strasbourg: Arcanes).
— — 2014. *Mother Folly*, trans. Judith H. Miller. (Stanford, CA: Stanford University Press).
— — and J.-M. Gaudillière 2004. *History Beyond Trauma*, trans. S. Fairfield (New York: Other Press).
Deleuze, G. 1986. *Cinema I: Movement Image*, trans. H. Tomlinson and B. Habberjam (Minneapolis: University of Minnesota Press).
Fabian, J. 2001. *Anthropology with an Attitude: Critical Essays* (Stanford, CA: Stanford University Press).
Fanon, F. 2002. *Les Damnés de la terre* (Paris: La Découverte/Poche).
Foucault, M. 2006. *History of Madness*, ed. J. Khalfa, trans. J. Murphy and J. Khalfa (London: Routledge).
Freedman, B. 1991. *Staging the Gaze: Postmodernism, Psychoanalysis, and Shakespearean Comedy* (Ithaca, NY, and London: Cornell University Press).
Hannula, M. (ed.), 2010. 'Landscapes of Madness' [exhib. cat.], Aboa Vetus and Ars Nova Museum, Turku, 20 Oct. 2010–29 Jan. 2011.
Hansen, M.B.N. 2003. 'Affect as Medium, or the Digital-Facial-Image', *Journal of Visual Culture* 2/2: 205–28.
Hernández, A. Montoya. 2006. *Paisajes de la locura* (Mexico City: Paradigma).

Huyssen, A. 2013. *William Kentridge, Nalini Malani: The Shadow Play as Medium of Memory* (Milan: Charta).

Landa, E. (ed.) 2012. *Cinéma et psychoanalyse*, special issue of *Le Coq-Héron* 211 (Dec.).

Loraux, N. 2002. *The Mourning Voice: An Essay on Greek Tragedy*, trans. E. Trapnell Rawlings (Ithaca, NY: Cornell University Press).

Marrati, P. 2008. *Gilles Deleuze: Cinema and Philosophy*, trans. A. Hartz (Baltimore, MD: Johns Hopkins University Press).

Marx, W. 2013. *Le Tombeau d'Oedipe: Pour une tragédie sans tragique* (Paris: Editions de Minuit).

Morra, J., (ed.) 2012. 'Saying It' [exhib. cat.], Freud Museum, London, 20 Sept–19 Nov.

Mouffe, C. 2005. *On the Political* (London and New York: Routledge).

Olick, J.K., and J. Robbins. 1998. 'Social Memory Studies: From "Collective Memory" to the Historical Sociology of Mnemonic Practices.' *Annual Review of Sociology* 24: 105–40.

Pisters, P. 2003. *The Matrix of Visual Culture: Working with Deleuze in Film Theory* (Stanford, CA: Stanford University Press).

Pollock, G. 2013. *After-Affects, After-Images: Trauma and Aesthetic Transformation in the Virtual Feminist Museum* (Manchester: Manchester University Press).

Rodowick, D.N. 1997. *Gilles Deleuze's Time Machine* (Durham, NC: Duke University Press).

Rothberg, M. 2009. *Multidirectional Memory: Remembering the Holocaust in the Age of Decolonization* (Stanford, CA: Stanford University Press).

Silverman, K. 1996. *The Threshold of the Visible World* (New York: Routledge).

Silverman, M. 2013. *Palimpsestic Memory: The Holocaust and Colonialism in French and Francophone Fiction and Film* (New York and Oxford: Berghahn).

Spivak, G.C. 1999. *A Critique of Postcolonial Reason: Toward a History of the Vanishing Present* (Cambridge, MA: Harvard University Press).

Taxidou, O. 2004. *Tragedy, Modernity and Mourning* (Edinburgh: Edinburgh University Press).

Van Alphen, E. 2004. 'Symptoms of Discursivity: Experience, Memory and Trauma', in M. Bal (ed.), *Narrative Theory: Critical Concepts in Literary and Cultural Studies* (London and New York: Routledge), vol. 3, pp. 107–22.

'Forked no Lightning':
Remembering and Forgetting in the
Shadow of Big Ben

Stuart Burch[1]

My mother died on Monday 30 January 2012. When I reached out to shut her sightless eyes the time was exactly 11:55am. Of this I can be sure thanks to the large clock that I could see through the hospital window. This timepiece had been my constant companion during the three days I had spent at my mother's bedside. And, five minutes after her final breath, it tolled twelve times. The bell that provided this public pronouncement of a private tragedy is a familiar landmark on the skyline of London and is known the world over as 'Big Ben'. The metaphorical shadow cast by the Clock Tower of the Houses of Parliament serves as the inspiration for the following essay. It, like a number of other chapters in this book, can be understood as an instance of *ego-histoire*: the deployment of personal experiences as a means of considering 'a collective enterprise' (Popkin 1996: 1140), namely memory studies.

Memory Companions

'We are never alone.' So says Maurice Halbwachs in the opening chapter of *The Collective Memory* (1980: 23). He illustrates this claim by recounting his first visit to London. During his stay Halbwachs was shown around by various friends, including an artist, a historian and a businessman. Seeing the world through their eyes drew his attention to aspects that might otherwise have gone unheeded: noteworthy attractions, striking vistas and aesthetically interesting details. Later on Halbwachs retraced his steps, only this time without these companions. Yet, he adds, 'only in appearance did I take a walk alone'. The words of his friends rang in his ears and mingled with information gleaned from all manner of other sources (cf. Bobbio 2001: 30–31). Thus it is that, even when there is no one physically at our side, 'we always carry with us and in us a number of distinct persons' (Halbwachs 1980: 23).

For Halbwachs, the fact that one of these 'distinct persons' happened to be an artist meant that he was able to appreciate 'the lines of the palaces and churches, and the play of light and shadow on the walls and façades of Westminster and on the Thames' (Halbwachs 1980: 23). A prominent feature of this impressive riverscape both during Halbwachs' lifetime and now

---

1   Thanks to Mick Atha of the Chinese University of Hong Kong for his initial encouragement as well as invaluable comments from my Nottingham Trent University colleagues, Ruth Griffin, Patrick O'Connor, Neil Turnbull and, especially, Roy Smith.

is the Houses of Parliament or, to give it its proper name, the New Palace at Westminster. This nineteenth-century neo-gothic edifice is built on what remained of the old palace following a devastating fire in 1834. The resulting palimpsest provides an asymmetrical silhouette, the most recognisable feature of which is the Clock Tower, completed in 1859. Its colloquial name – Big Ben – refers in fact to the great bell inside, and it was this that rang out beyond the window of St Thomas' Hospital on that mournful day in January 2012.

During my vigil the friendly, familiar form of 'Big Ben' functioned like a huge stopwatch, counting down the hours of my mother's life. Its illuminated face was particularly comforting at night. And it was no mere solitary supporter. The clock came with other companions, some of whom stretch back to my formative years. Halbwachs would have understood this. For, wandering the streets of central London, his thoughts returned to the literature of his youth: 'I took my walk with Dickens' (Halbwachs 1980: 23). For my part, I shared my vigil with Virginia Woolf. Among my books is the battered volume of *Mrs Dalloway* that I read as a schoolboy. It is covered in immature annotations which give an insight into my thinking as I sought to get to grips with a novel unlike any I had read before. The key to my understanding was Big Ben. The clock and its chimes accompany the events of the novel as they unfold over the course of a single day in June 1923. This is particularly evident in the short story that Woolf later developed into the book. Entitled 'Mrs Dalloway in Bond Street' the eponymous protagonist is introduced stepping out into the metropolis just as Big Ben strikes eleven. As the 'leaden circles dissolved in the air' we gain access to her thoughts (Woolf 2012: 3). By the time of the tenth stroke we get to see her outward appearance as the stream of consciousness shifts to another character, a Mr Scrope Purvis, a neighbour of Clarissa Dalloway. Whilst hurrying to his office he catches sight of the 'poised, eager, strangely white-haired' woman (ibid. 4). The reverberations of Big Ben connect them – and link to other clocks in their lives. One such example is 'the late clock', so called because it runs two minutes behind Big Ben. Whilst the latter is associated in Clarissa's mind with solemnity, majesty and 'laying down the law', this tardy clock's chimes come 'shuffling in with its lap full of odds and ends' – acquaintances to contact, items to collect, errands to run (Woolf 1976: 137–8).

A recent study of time in the Victorian period begins with Big Ben as 'a monument to standardized [public] time', a new concept deployed to exert control over 'an increasingly disciplinary industrial world' (Ferguson 2013: 1). Hence the scurrying figure of Scrope Purvis for whom the tolling of Big Ben chides him for being late for work.

In *Mrs Dalloway*, Woolf uses the chimes as a device to signal shifts in the narrative between characters and locations. They are also used as a means of distinguishing internal and external time, or as Woolf put it in *Orlando: A Biography*, the 'extraordinary discrepancy between time on the clock and time in the mind' (Woolf 2006: 72). This has much in common with the difference that Henri Bergson draws between *temps* and *durée* (Hasler 1982: 147). For Bergson, 'inner' or 'true duration' differs from so-called clock time or what he refers to as time 'outside of me, in space' (Bergson 1950: 107–8). Whereas inner time is 'the melting of states of consciousness into one another', when it comes to time on a clock face, 'there is never more than a single position of the hand and the pendulum, for nothing is left of the past positions' (ibid. 108). Despite this disparity 'a kind of exchange takes place' between inner and outer time. It occurs in the form of 'a conscious spectator who keeps the past in mind and sets the two oscillations or their symbols side by side in an auxiliary space' (ibid. 109).

This was borne out by my experience of seeing Big Ben from the vantage point of St Thomas' Hospital on the banks of the River Thames. I became all too aware that our lives are made up of joyful 'days of speed' and 'slow time Mondays' (Weller 1981) – like that day of the week when my mother died. Although I could literally see the hands of time, they were slowed by my inner clock and the agonies of death: 'An hour, once it lodges in the queer element of the human spirit, may be stretched to fifty or a hundred times its clock length' (Woolf 2006: 72). Now, much later, as the hours have turned into months and soon years since her demise, inner time is proving just as elastic. For example, 18 months later I happened to be in Boston Massachusetts. Browsing a bookstore I came across a toy model of Big Ben. And suddenly my inner clock reset itself and I was back at my mother's death-bed.

That inconsequential occurrence in a Boston bookstore underscored for me the extent to which Big Ben numbers among the 'iconography of things' – a mnemonic device rooted in a specific memory place but transportable through image and rhetoric (Samuel 1994: 36). One does not need to be on the spot, however: an image alone is sufficient to cause 'a piercing inner vision' (Yates 1999: 4). That said, physically being back in a memory place can make this experience even more penetrating. This was confirmed when I was next obliged to return to central London some months after my mother's death. Revisiting a familiar place after an interval of time triggers remembrances of things that took place there (Cicero, in Yates 1999: 4, 22; Bachelard 1994: 8; Halbwachs 1980: 22). In this regard Westminster is a particularly evocative memory place, a *lieu de mémoire* (Yates 1999; Nora 1996: xvii).

I, like countless visitors before me, own a little relic of this realm of memory in the form of a souvenir. Thus, as I write, I can see my schoolboy copy of *Mrs Dalloway* on a shelf alongside that yet-to-be-built Boston Big Ben plus another such model bought during my earlier trip to London. I now find that I own a collection of Big Bens. Why? Do they equate to a coming to terms with loss, a retranscription, a screening or an effort to control the past? (Kermode 2001; Gaddis 2002: 136–7). Whichever is the case, with all such groupings of things and their constellations into collections, meaning is never inherent in the objects themselves but 'attached' by the collector (Benjamin 1999: 207). Walter Benjamin identified collecting as a form of 'practical memory' – the drawing together of otherwise disparate items 'into a new, expressly devised historical system: the collection' (ibid. 205). Regarding my miniature Big Bens, I can appreciate that they function as souvenirs of London as well as vicarious memorials to my late mother. These Lilliputian Clock Towers enable me to possess a 'trace' of the real thing whilst also allowing me to get 'near' to the person whose memory they invoke (cf. ibid. 447, 848, 883).

It is appropriate that all my Big Bens happen to be models made up of hundreds of tiny fragments. Memory is a jigsaw: the more pieces and the older the puzzle, the more likely there are to be missing parts (Bobbio 2001: 26). On the other hand, these multiples in my collection undermine Bergson's argument: yes, the clock hands show single positions – but it is 4:45 on one model; 10:10 on other; and 11:40 on a third. The problem is that my internal clock keeps changing the time to 11:55.

A common trope of the models in my collection is that they each form one element in a range of diminutive monuments. A case in point is Ravensburger's series of 3D Puzzle buildings (Figure 11.1). This consists of famous structures from various cities around the world. Big Ben's inclusion confirms its status as an icon – both of the sonic and solid variety. The chimes of the bell have been broadcast by the BBC since 1923 (Cannadine 2000: 21). As such it plays an important role for those far away from the capital city and, indeed, beyond even the United Kingdom (Ferguson 2013: 8). As such it is a sensory sign that works at multiple levels: the individual, the local, the national and the global. It is a synecdoche, a part that stands for a whole: in this case 'Westminster', a metonym of the British government. This in turn is promoted as a symbol of democracy, with the New Palace at Westminster held up as the 'mother' parliament – a maternal association that resonates with my own personal reading.

Figure 11.1   Big Ben 3D Puzzle
Image courtesy of © Ravensburger Ltd. All rights reserved

The tower is therefore both a private and collective landmark. Big Ben is a literal instance of 'temporal anchoring' (Huyssen 1995: 7). Modern nation-states seek to sustain themselves 'materially in the everyday lives of their subjects and citizens by associating the iconic inheritance of a national past with the present state and its objectives' (Agnew, in Roca, Clavel and Agnew 2011: 39). This is rendered all the more pressing in an era of unprecedented demographic change, rapid technological development and anxieties about terrorism. An encapsulation of these concerns is to be found in New York's vanished Twin

Towers. Despite – or, perhaps, because of – its physical absence the World Trade Center, like all such landmarks, represents a 'fixed point' (Welzer 2008: 285). The absent towers still cast very long shadows (Spiegelman 2004). The day of their destruction constitutes 'an epoch', that is, a defined moment in time deemed to designate the beginning of a new era (*OED* 2013). Such landmarks are sought out amidst the 'trifles' of everyday life (Woolf 1976: 138; Gosse 1907: 36). These markers are then used to impose coherence on narrative accounts of the past, be they concerned with individual lives or the massed ranks of people through history (Halbwachs 1992: 61; Gaddis 2002: 19). Professional historians and other such 'conscious spectators' mould time. Their actions represent another of those temporal discrepancies, such as that which exists between memory and history. This prompts Gaddis to compare historians with science fiction writers. Both manipulate space and time in their writings (Gaddis 2002: 21–2). And, as we shall soon see, it is thanks to science fiction that we know that Big Ben will endure, even if all else is lost to memory.

Remembering and Forgetting

Iconic landmarks are frequently used in films to establish location. The merest glimpse of Big Ben tells us that we are in London. Developed further it can be used as a device in the drama, as with the 1978 film adaptation of John Buchan's *The Thirty-Nine Steps*. Its denouement sees the hero hanging from the minute hand of Big Ben in a desperate attempt to prevent the detonation of a bomb that has been fiendishly connected to its mechanism. The threat to this much-loved symbol is magnified by its wider ramifications: the destruction of a metonym of democracy would endanger our 'iconic inheritance' and the sense of shared ownership with which it is invested. The dramatic potential of this is used to the full in the film, *It Happened Here* (1964). The movie poster advertising this counterfactual 'story of Hitler's England' shows Nazi soldiers marching past Big Ben. Thanks to the *sotto in sù* angle the metal helmets of these gargantuan warriors reach almost as high as the clock face itself.

These are far from the only occasions that Big Ben has graced the silver screen. Indeed, in 2007 the Clock Tower came top in a poll of most iconic film locations in London (BBC 2007). Third place in the same vote came Westminster Bridge. The two combine to deadly effect in *The Dalek Invasion of Earth* (1964). These armoured cyborgs gliding across the Thames are the extra-terrestrial equivalent of the Nazi soldiers seen in *It Happened Here*. Daleks are the most hated enemy of the time-travelling *Doctor Who*, the eponymous hero of a long-running British science-fiction television series that features heavily in the popular imagination of many Britons. One of the events marking the show's fiftieth anniversary in 2013 recreated the scene on Westminster Bridge by lining up four generations of dalek beneath the shadow of Big Ben.

I watched *Doctor Who* as a child, and again as an adult following its regeneration in 2005. Early on in the first series of the contemporary era the unfortunate Big Ben is struck by a crash-landing spaceship. Meanwhile, in the third season attention shifts to the opposite bank of the Thames when Royal Hope Hospital – a fictional establishment on the site of St Thomas' Hospital – is suddenly transported to the moon.

Doctor Who also exists in the parallel world of fiction writing. One of the volumes that I read as a child was *Doctor Who and the Dalek Invasion of Earth*. Its cover features Big Ben in the year 2164. A dalek in the foreground portends the fall of civilisation. The absence of Big Ben's chimes is used to reinforce the 'dead silence' of London (Dicks 1977: 11). This closely mirrors Alfred Noyes' novel *The Last Man* (1940) where, again, the muting of the bell is a silent siren of disaster. Big Ben is also used as a means of 'temporal anchoring' in M.P. Shiel's

The Purple Cloud (1901). Volcanic eruption has released a gas that has annihilated all life on earth (Bulfin 2013: 153). The miasma has also settled on the world's clocks, which have all ceased at precisely the same time, their 'weird fore-fingers, pointing, pointing still, to the moment of doom' (Shiel 2004: 136). This first becomes apparent on the clock face of Big Ben. Its frozen hands stop the clock on Bergson's theory of time: there is indeed just 'a single position of the hand' – for not only is nothing left of the past, the future has vanished too. In an effort to avoid creating a generation of traumatised children, the author of *Doctor Who and the Dalek Invasion of Earth* announces the return to normality through 'a sound once familiar to every Londoner, one that had been missing for a very long time – the chimes of Big Ben' (Dicks 1977: 122).

One further future projection of Big Ben charts a middle way between continuity and change. In William Morris' *News from Nowhere*, the Palace of Westminster still stands but the nature of the 'strange game' that used to be played there is preserved only in the pages of history books. In Morris' prophetic vision the Houses of Parliament are used as 'a storage place for manure' (Morris 1891: 34). And it transpires that the building was only saved from demolition thanks to the campaigning of an antiquarian society. Its principal function is to serve as a foil for the far better buildings constructed in Morris' socialist utopia.

These fanciful examples are revealing of Westminster's day-to-day 'struggle with forgetfulness' (Forty and Küchler 1999: 16). For its status as a realm of memory replete with historical associations and commemorative devices entails a constant battle to guard against forgetting the things that need to be remembered whilst at the same time marginalising the things that the memory 'authorities' would much prefer us to forget (De Certeau 1984: xv).

Big Ben is exemplary of this dichotomy. Even a monument whose name is known to everyone is bedevilled by amnesia. Why 'Big Ben'? Is it a reference to the politician and engineer, Sir Benjamin Hall (1802–67)? Or was it named after the bare-knuckle boxer Benjamin 'Big Ben' Caunt (1815–61)? Who cares anyway given that even the epithet Big Ben is habitually misapplied, referring as it does to the bell and not the tower.

With this in mind, there is much truth in Michel de Certeau's assertion that memory is not localizable, and – when it does get tied-down – it becomes subject to decay (1984: 86–7, 108; Forty and Küchler 1999: 7, 59). Commemorative associations fade, as do the monuments to which they are attached. And that 'little world of space' on which a life is mapped is similarly transitory: for 'houses, roads, avenues are as fugitive, alas, as the years' (Proust, quoted in Olick, Vinitzky-Seroussi and Levy 2011: 456).

Equally fugitive are statues. Wrongly assuming that our monuments can do the remembering, society at large is sanctioned to forget (Gillis 1994: 16). An eloquent example of the slow diminution of memory are the bronzed Victorian gentleman that cast furtive glances at what was once the arena for their 'strange game'. Originally Peel, Palmerstone, Disraeli and Derby occupied pride of place at the centre of a petrified pantheon of politicians in Parliament Square. Following the Second World War they were shifted to the periphery: a spatial manifestation of their declining significance (Burch 2003: 290).

Another eloquent example of remembering and forgetting in the shadow of Big Ben concerns the contested legacy of Oliver Cromwell. He, together with members of his family and generals in his service, were laid to rest in Henry VII's Chapel of Westminster Abbey adjacent to the Palace at Westminster. Their corpses were disinterred in 1661 following the restitution of the monarchy. Samuel Pepys records that Cromwell's grisly skull, alongside that of his son-in-law, Henry Ireton and John Bradshaw, president of the High Court of Justice, were hoisted upon poles facing New Palace Yard. These admonitory memento mori remained *in situ* for over 20 years (Burch 2003: 234).

Cromwell continued to pose problems following the fire that ripped through the old palace in 1834 (Burch 2003: 228–89). The replacement building has rightly been described as more of 'a royal residence than a democratic legislature' (Cannadine 2000: 15). The façades are richly decorated with royal insignia and statues of the country's kings and queens through the ages. This sculpted history gave rise to a commemorative dilemma: what should be done about Cromwell? For the sake of historical accuracy and completeness he ought to have been slotted in between Charles I (executed in 1649) and his son, Charles II (restored to the throne in 1660). But placing a regicide in a royalist pantheon proved to be a commemorative step too far. Cromwell was sculpturally excised from Westminster's history. Not until the very end of the nineteenth century was the Lord Protector rewarded with a statue. He stands there to this day: at one remove, deep in thought and with his back turned to a parliament building that is festooned with a 'royal line that still salutes him and will salute him forever' (Morrissey 2004).

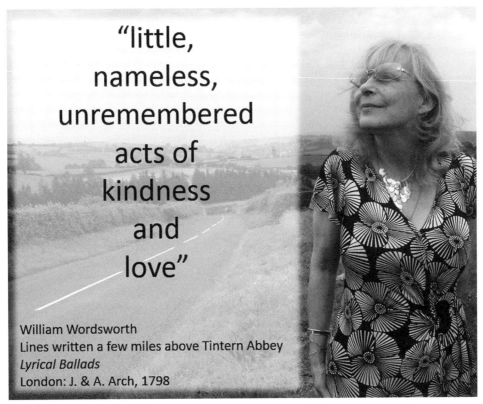

"little, nameless, unremembered acts of kindness and love"

William Wordsworth
Lines written a few miles above Tintern Abbey
Lyrical Ballads
London: J. & A. Arch, 1798

Figure 11.2 William Wordsworth, 'Lines Written a Few Miles above Tintern Abbey' (1798), *Lyrical Ballads*, vol. 1, 4th edn (London: Longman, Hurst, Rees & Orme, 1805), p. 193
Photo: Stuart Burch

For the British obsession with the hereditary principal is in rude health. In 2012, 'Big Ben' was renamed the Elizabeth Tower to mark the diamond jubilee of the present monarch. This is despite the fact that each face of the tower already carries a Latin inscription to her forebear,

Victoria. This renders it doubly regal. These maternal figures act as universal mothers – substitutes for all those other common women consigned to oblivion together with their 'little, nameless, unremembered acts of kindness and love' (Wordsworth 1919: 86) (Figure 11.2). One commoner, however, does manage to vie for public attention, but not for acts of love or kindness. She is Margaret Thatcher, the longest serving British prime minister of the twentieth century and the only woman so far to have held the post. Thatcher's death at the age of 87 left Big Ben speechless. On 17 April 2012 the chimes fell silent as her horse-drawn gun carriage bier trundled past the Houses of Parliament on its way to St Paul's Cathedral.

Big Ben was not the only bell to be muted by the corroding Iron Lady. Those who reviled rather than revered her memory mounted a social media campaign urging people to download 'Ding-Dong! The Witch is Dead', a jaunty tune from the 1939 film *The Wizard of Oz*. The hope being that it might attain Number 1 status to coincide with Thatcher's militaristic funeral. This posed a problem for the BBC over whether to broadcast the song on the *Official Chart* of UK singles. In the end it opted for compromise: rather than censor it completely Tony Hall, director-general of the BBC, decided to treat it 'as a news story' by 'playing a short extract to put it in context' (quoted in Reynolds 2013).

The absence of 'Ding-Dong! The Witch is Dead' from the *Official Chart* is significant. This programme is broadcast on BBC Radio 1, which caters mainly for 15–29 year olds: a generation for whom Margaret Thatcher is largely a figure of history. She was ousted as prime minister in 1990 and dementia in later life meant that she had not been seen in public for many years. The manner of her funeral was thus crucial in securing her legacy. A desire to shape the future was what motivated both the pro- and anti-Thatcher camps. For those who adulated her there was a risk that playing the full song on Radio 1 might result in it being the sole thing for which she was associated in the minds of the younger generation. This was, therefore, not just a storm in a tea cup. Being relegated to a song of ridicule would have been a fate worse than being reduced to, say, a nice cup of tea – as is the case with Charles Grey, the 2nd Earl Grey who was prime minster at the time of the Reform Act of 1832, just prior to the old Palace of Westminster going up in smoke.

The ostensible reason why 'Ding-Dong! The Witch is Dead' was not played in full by the BBC was on the grounds of taste and propriety (Reynolds 2013). Similarly, parliament's decision to silence Big Ben for Thatcher's funeral was as a mark of 'profound dignity and deep respect' (John Bercow, Speaker of the House of Commons, quoted in Hall 2013). But it also facilitated a crucial objective by shifting attention to a famous precedent. Aside from repairs, the last time Big Ben fell silent was for the funeral of Winston Churchill in 1965. The muffling of the bell was therefore part of a clear strategy: to establish Margaret Thatcher in an ongoing chain, the preceding link of which was formed by a man habitually lauded as 'the greatest Briton' (Wyatt 2002).

That the metaphor of the chain is a widespread phenomenon is apparent in *The Collective Memory Reader*, where notions of the 'chain of memory' appear frequently, either in terms of breaking, establishing or maintaining links – and ensuring that other associations are marginalised or erased (Olick Vinitzky-Seroussi and Levy 2011: 77, 102–3, 133, 165, 211, 233, 378, 382).

This has ramifications for the monumental landscape of Westminster. The statues there are officially endorsed. Popular protest is tightly curtailed within a one kilometre radius of parliament. This is legally enforced by the Serious Organised Crime and Police Act (2005). This and other efforts to limit demonstrations in the vicinity of the Houses of Parliament were closely linked to the campaigner, Brian Haw (1949–2011) (Figure 11.3). In June 2001, he erected a peace camp in Parliament Square and, despite repeated attempts to evict him, Haw remained there until his death a decade later. Because his protest began prior to subsequent legislation he was allowed to stay – but with his passing, no-one else will be able to do as he did.

Figure 11.3   Brian Haw in Parliament Square (7 July 2007)
Photo: **Stuart Burch**

Today there is no physical or commemorative trace of Brian Haw in Parliament Square. For the authorities, Haw is in death, as in life, a *persona non grata*. In the monumental landscape he is a nobody.

Nobody History

The echelons of statues and plaques, monuments and memorials that constitute 'London's immortals' occlude 'the infinite others whose memory is lost without trace' (Blackwood 1989; Bobbio 2001: 22). The latter are what the cartoonist, Will Eisner refers to as 'invisible people' (2006: 305–415). This graphic artist is one of those 'distinct persons' that I carry about in my head, sharing and shaping experience as Dickens did for Halbwachs during his visit to London. Eisner's images depict a specific city – New York – but his aim was to use them to reveal truths about metropolitan life the world over (ibid. 3). In *The Building* (1987), for example, the demolition of a block of flats means that the ghosts of four former occupants are all that remains of an 'invisible accumulation of dramas' (ibid. 145). Eisner's spectres mirror any given city's living population of invisible people. Exiting St Thomas' Hospital that day in early January 2012, I numbered myself among them. The previous days' travails were etched on my exhausted face. Nevertheless, this inner turmoil remained 'unnoticed [to] the people who streamed past me' (ibid. 307). Yes, I shared the same space as these strangers, but we were each lost in our own mental landscapes of joy or despair (cf. Roca, Clavel and Agnew 2011: 367). Alone in my grief in the midst of a crowd it was as if I had become a character in the cartoon world of Will Eisner.

Compounding my sense of loss was the realisation that, with the death of my mother, my family would become atomised. She was the centre to which we gravitated in order to share our group memories – and forge new ones. This has been dealt a fatal blow. Without our mother it would be far harder to retrieve or reconstruct the shared recollections of our family unit and those 'peculiar memories' that only we commemorate (Halbwachs 1992: 52, 59, 63). Nor would the laying of future memories be so easy given that opportunities for exchange would arise with far less frequency (ibid. 54). Be in no doubt, this is the death knell of memory. 'The dead retreat into the past' when 'nothing remains of the group in which they passed their lives'. As a consequence 'names slowly become obliterated' (ibid. 73). Other groups, however – those that are more resilient, better connected and empowered – succeed in establishing a cult. Calling the Clock Tower of the Houses of Parliament after the first name of a hereditary monarch is a means of enforcing memory by causing it to 'symbolize [something] beyond the material sign' (ibid. 72).

In contrast, my family, with its paltry connections do not provide access to those 'elite circles' that can secure posthumous renown (Coser in Halbwachs 1992: 31). We number among those 'families of no importance – so much is lost, entire histories, there is no room for it all. There are only the generations surging forward like the tide, the years filled with sound and froth, then being washed over by the rest. That is the legacy of the cities' (Salter 2007: 8).

It is a sad truth that we live and die in a world made up of 'somebody people' and 'nobody people' (Bowie 1972). I find myself firmly ensconced in the latter camp. The moment my mother died is merely a 'trifling incident' (Gosse 1907: 36) for all but a handful of individuals. In contrast, the demise of 'somebody people' is met with such wailing and gnashing of teeth that others are obliged to pay attention, even if the deceased person in question was unknown and uncared for. This is because guardians of memory seek to promote their vision through their dead heroes. If amnesia is a virus (Huyssen 1995: 7), some are in possession of a vaccine promising immunity. Inoculation is, however, a difficult and laborious process, fraught with complexity and danger (Burch 2012a).

The inequalities of the living are mirrored by the exclusions of the dead. It has been noted that 'historical figures, heroes, great men of war no less than artists shelter themselves from death in this way: they enter the memory of peoples; they are examples, active presences' (Blanchot 1982: 94). But this is no benign refuge. Memory is parasitical; a cuckoo-like planting in another's nest – whether the host likes it or not (cf. De Certeau 1984: 86). For we are all hosts to countless memory parasites. Some hosts are receptive to their symbionts, especially if they happen to hold them in high esteem. Even those that do not, however, may still be obliged to carry these 'distinct persons' in their mental baggage. Dislodging a memory parasite that has gained a foothold can be very tricky, not least when myth-making leads to such levels of obsession that the hero effectively controls those in his or her thrall (Bergson 1935: 166). This is particularly unfortunate in the case of heroes who turn out to be despicable hangers-on: like an all-conquering sportsman who is later revealed to be a drug cheat or a popular celebrity whose charitable work transpires to have been simply a means of facilitating terrible sexual crimes. In such circumstances an elaborate process of *damnatio memoriae* is necessary in a futile attempt to expunge a grotesquely alluring anti-hero (Burch 2012c).

In the literature on collective memory forgetting is a firmly accepted idea and, indeed, seen as a very positive thing. This has given rise to notions of 'productive forgetting' (Huyssen 1995: 7) and 'blissful blindness' (Nietzsche 2007: 103). We are told that, in order for museums and archives to make sense, 'a great deal of forgetting must happen first' (Sterne 2009: 57). One of the best studies on forgetting is Bradford Vivian's *Public Forgetting: The Rhetoric and Politics of Beginning Again*. But before we get to read about public forgetting we are provided with an instance of private remembering: the book is dedicated to the author's 'unforgettable' wife with additional acknowledgments to both his parents and his son (Vivian 2010: x).

That this act of intergenerational remembering should serve as a prelude to an exploration of forgetting is what makes the study of memory so fascinating (cf. Forty and Küchler 1999: 2, 16). Vivian's decision to deploy his publication as a textual memorial is appropriate. Arguably the objects that 'best image our being' are books: 'A book in one's own library is in a sense a brick in the building of one's being, carrying with it memories, a small block of one's personal intellectual history, associations unsortable in their profusion' (Aristides, quoted in Tuan 1977: 187).

Authors, as we have seen, can feature as 'distinct persons' in our lives. And books – even when dog-eared and mass-produced – can themselves become cherished objects. This is especially the case when they are inscribed with a dedication or scrawled all over by a puzzled schoolboy like my copy of *Mrs Dalloway*, onto the inside cover of which I have stapled the receipt. Dated 2:13pm Friday 29 March 1991, it is a fragile memorial to an unrecalled purchase on an unremarkable day.

The destiny of such books is the purgatory of the charity shop. Fortunately this fate has not yet befallen the only material possessions that I have inherited from my mother: her small collection of books, most of which are by or about the Welsh poet, Dylan Thomas (1914–53). His words were an immense comfort to me in the days following my mother's death, particularly the poem 'Do not go Gentle into that Good Night'. Thomas dedicated this work to his father, but the message is universal. It urged all those whose 'words had forked no lightning' to 'rage against the dying of the light' (Thomas 1990: 208). One person who fell into this category was my mum. Beyond those lucky enough to be related to her or live next door, few people got to know her. She did not attract attention like lightning does – she was far too modest for that. And for this she is consigned to oblivion, like all those 'obscure heroes' (Bergson 1935: 38) whose words do not shriek for attention.

One of my mother's books was a gift from me following a trip to New York. John Brinnin's 'intimate journal', *Dylan Thomas in America* ends with the tragic account of how Thomas drank so much alcohol that he was admitted to St Vincent's Hospital in New York where he slipped into a coma. Brinnin's description of his bedside vigil is painfully familiar. In a phrase that encapsulates the disparity between inner and outer time, the author recalls the Friday before Thomas died as the 'longest night of all, when every clock stood still' (Brinnin 1955: 282). By the morning of Monday 9 November 1953 Brinnin took one look at Thomas and realised 'that, somewhere in the night, he had gone into his final phase' (ibid. 291). A few hours later he was dead.

Whilst in Manhattan, I bought Brinnin's book and took it on a pilgrimage to the White Horse Tavern on Hudson Street – one of Dylan Thomas's most favourite haunts – and then walked up 11th Street to the hospital where he died. Nowadays my memories of seeing the main entrance of St Vincent's Hospital merge with the look of fear I saw on my mother face as she arrived at St Thomas' Hospital and stared up at its cliff-like façade. She knew instinctively that this imposing building would be where she was to die.

It is easy to dismiss hospitals as 'non-places', just another of those 'transit points and temporary abodes' that do not qualify as anthropological places (Augé 1997: 77–8). This is perhaps especially true of the concrete walls and white-tile cladding of Yorke, Rosenberg and

Mardall's St Thomas' Hospital building (1962–76). Its Brutalist style has all the hallmarks of a non-place. Not to be valued – or, at least, not by today's aesthetic standards, even if there are signs that we are beginning to be more appreciative of our post-war concrete inheritance (Murray 2013).

Heritage is inherently selective, determining the sorts of places that merit preserving: just like the hierarchies and exclusions of collective memory (Burch 2012b). Its workings function as a filter determining what future generations will and will not inherit. The decision to preserve or demolish a building is a political act – as is evident from responses to the destruction of the Edwardian wing of Jessop Hospital in Sheffield. This was the first such establishment where women in labour could be treated outside the home (Williams 2013). With its removal goes the 'accumulated memories' of a building that was 'barnacled with laughter and stained by tears' (Eisner 2006: 144).

A means to revive these annihilated associations is to adopt Gaston Bachelard's approach to 'the localization of memory' (1994: 8). His deployment of topoanalysis as 'the systematic psychological study of the sites of our intimate lives' can and should be extended to a 'non-place' such as St Thomas' Hospital. In doing so we will quickly become aware of the memories that mount in every humdrum corner. It was fitting, for example, that my mother should finally be defeated in a little patch of St Thomas' Hospital that will be forever Wales: the Coronary Care Unit of St Thomas' is dedicated to the Welsh-speaking cardiologist, Evan Jones who died in 1969 (Matthews 1970).

The plural possessive of 'St Thomas' Hospital' indicates it to be a double memorial, invoking as it does both St Thomas Becket and Thomas the Apostle (Clark 1871). Its history stretches back far further than appearances might suggest. One illustrious character in this institutional story is Florence Nightingale, whose nurses' training school opened there before the hospital relocated to the banks of the Thames. Parts of it serve as a living memorial to the First World War. Its dramatic history during the Second World War are recounted by one of the few employees to remain working there throughout the conflict, the surgeon Frank B. Cockett (born 1916). Following a particularly devastating attack he looked across from the bomb-damaged hospital to see that Big Ben had sustained 'three large holes in the clock face' (Cockett 1990: 1466). And as I read those words today I merge this factual event with a fanciful recollection of that scene in *The Thirty-Nine Steps* when the hero kicks his way out to dangle from the hands of time. I wonder if my mum ever saw that film? It is too late to ask her now.

To End at the Beginning

This chapter was written as a memorial to my mother such that, 'printed, her memory will last' (cf. Barthes 1993: 63). There is an onus on me to keep her memory alive (Bobbio 2001: 64). On these pages this invisible, nobody person vies for attention with monarchs and ministers of state. For me, the Clock Tower of the Houses of Parliament is in reality 'the Barbara Tower'. And, should London be afflicted by some future apocalypse and only a scrap of paper from this book survive, historians of tomorrow will struggle in vain to piece together a plausible explanation. Why was it so called? In honour of Saint Barbara who was locked in a tower? Perhaps. After all, there are many statues of the saint with this attribute clutched in her martyred hand.[2] Or maybe it was named after one Barbara Ann Burch? That

---

2   See e.g. 'St Barbara' (carved panel, painted and gilt alabaster, English, 15th century), Victoria & Albert Museum, A.136-1946.

much seems clear from the fragment of a book on memory that appears to date from roughly the same period (Figure 11.4). Not much is known about this person, but she was evidently held in high esteem given that a tower appears to have been named in her honour. Alas, only fragments of this monument remain – and its purpose is now impossible to discern.

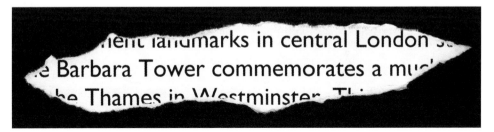

Figure 11.4 Text Fragment
Photo: **Stuart Burch**

Meanwhile, back in the here-and-now, I cannot exert the influence necessary to dominate public space and impose my values on others. But there is one act of naming that I have been able to enact. For the same hands that held my mother as she died, nine months later cradled a new-born baby girl. Her middle name is Barbara. A name by which to 'anchor' her and attach her to a grandmother she was never lucky enough to meet (Halbwachs 1992: 71–2). But, as Halbwachs reminds me, we are never alone. And there is every chance that Barbara Burch née Prince will be a 'distinct person' in my daughter's future life.

References

Augé, M. 1997. *Non-Places: Introduction to an Anthropology of Supermodernity*, trans. J. Howe (London: Verso).
Bachelard, G. 1994 [1958]. *The Poetics of Space*, trans. M. Jolas (Boston, MA: Beacon).
Barthes, R. 1993. *Camera Lucida: Reflections on Photography*, trans. R. Howard (London: Vintage).
BBC 2007. 'Big Ben Tops Film Location Poll', *BBC News* (21 Oct.), <http://news.bbc.co.uk/1/hi/england/london/7055067.stm>.
Benjamin, W. 1999. *The Arcades Project*, trans. H. Eiland and K. McLaughlin (Cambridge, MA: Harvard University Press).
Bergson, H. 1935 [1932]. *The Two Sources of Morality and Religion*, trans. R.A. Audra and C. Brereton (London: Macmillan).
— — 1950 [1910]. *Time and Free Will: An Essay on the Immediate Data of Consciousness*, trans. F.L. Pogson (London: George Allen).
Blackwood, J. 1989. *London's Immortals: The Complete Commemorative Outdoor Statues* (Oxford: Savoy Press).
Blanchot, M. 1982 [1955]. *The Space of Literature*, trans. A. Smock (Lincoln: University of Nebraska Press).
Bobbio, N. 2001. *Old Age and Other Essays*, trans. A. Cameron (Cambridge: Polity).
Bowie, D. 1972. 'Five Years', on *The Rise and Fall of Ziggy Stardust and the Spiders from Mars* [LP] (RCA).

Brinnin, J. 1955. *Dylan Thomas in America* (Boston, MA: Little, Brown & Co.).

Bulfin, A. 2013. '"The End of Time": M.P. Shiel and the "Apocalyptic Imaginary"', in T. Ferguson (ed.), *Victorian Time: Technologies, Standardizations, Catastrophes* (Basingstoke: Palgrave Macmillan), pp. 153–77.

Burch, S. 2003. 'On Stage at the Theatre of State: The Monuments and Memorials in Parliament Square, London' (Ph.D. thesis: Nottingham Trent University).

—— 2012a. 'Introducing Mr Moderna Museet: Pontus Hultén and Sweden's Museum of Modern Art', in K. Hill (ed.), *Museums and Biographies: Stories, Objects, Identities* (Woodbridge: Boydell Press), pp. 29–44.

—— 2012b. 'Past Presents and Present Futures: Rethinking Sweden's Moderna Museet', *Future Anterior* 9/2: 97–111.

—— 2012c. 'Jimmy Savile and *damnatio memoriae*', <http://www.stuartburch.com/1/post/2012/10/jimmy-savile-and-damnatio-memoriae.html>.

Cannadine, D. 2000. 'The Palace of Westminster as Palace of Varieties', in C. Riding and J. Riding (eds), *The Houses of Parliament: History, Art, Architecture* (London: Merrell), pp. 11–29.

Clark, F. 1871. 'Introductory Address Delivered at St. Thomas's Hospital, London', *British Medical Journal* 2/562 (7 Oct.), 397–400.

Cockett, F. 1990. 'The Bombing of St Thomas's', *British Medical Journal* 301/6766 (22–9 Dec.): 1464–6.

De Certeau, M. 1984. *The Practice of Everyday Life*, trans. S. Rendall (Berkeley: University of California Press).

Dicks, T. 1977. *Doctor Who and the Dalek Invasion of Earth* (London: Target).

Eisner, W. 2006. *Will Eisner's New York: Life in the Big City* (London: Norton).

Ferguson, T. 2013. 'Introduction', in T. Ferguson (ed.), *Victorian Time: Technologies, Standardizations, Catastrophes* (Basingstoke: Palgrave Macmillan), pp. 1–15.

Forty, A. and S. Küchler (eds) 1999. *The Art of Forgetting* (Oxford: Berg).

Gaddis, J. 2002. *The Landscape of History: How Historians Map the Past* (Oxford: Oxford University Press).

Gillis, J. (ed.) 1994. *Commemorations: The Politics of National Identity* (Princeton, NJ: Princeton University Press).

Gosse, E. 1907. *Father and Son: A Study of Two Temperaments* (New York: Charles Scribner's Sons).

Halbwachs, M. 1980. *The Collective Memory*, trans. F.J. Ditter Jr and V. Yazdi Ditter (New York: Harper & Row).

—— 1992. *On Collective Memory*, trans. L.A. Coser (Chicago: University of Chicago Press).

Hall, M. 2013. 'Chimes of Big Ben to be Silenced out of Respect during Maggie Funeral', *Daily Express* (16 April): 5.

Hasler, J. 1982. 'Virginia Woolf and the Chimes of Big Ben', *English Studies* 63/2: 145–58.

Huyssen, A. 1995. *Twilight Memories: Marking Time in a Culture of Amnesia* (London: Routledge).

Kermode, F. 2001. 'Palaces of Memory', *Index on Censorship* 30/1: 87–96.

Matthews, M. 1970. 'Obituary: Evan Jones', *British Heart Journal* 32: 559–60.

Morris, W. 1891. *News from Nowhere* (London: Reeves and Turner).

Morrissey. 2004. 'Irish Blood, English Heart', on *You Are the Quarry* [LP] (Sanctuary/Attack).

Murray, C. 2013. 'Brutalism's Return to Favour', *Architects Journal* 238 (27 Sept.): 5.

Nietzsche, F. 2007. 'On the Uses and Disadvantages of History for Life', in M. Rossington and A. Whitehead (eds), *Theories of Memory: A Reader* (Edinburgh: Edinburgh University Press), pp. 102–8.

Nora, P. 1996. 'Preface to the English Language Edition', in *Realms of Memory: Rethinking the French Past*, vol. 1: *Conflicts and Divisions* (New York: Columbia University Press), pp. xv–xxiv.

Noyes, A. 1940. *The Last Man* (London: Murray).

OED [*Oxford English Dictionary*] 2013. 'Epoch', <http://www.oed.com/view/Entry/63645>.

Olick, J., V. Vinitzky-Seroussi and D. Levy (eds), 2011. *The Collective Memory Reader* (New York and Oxford: Oxford University Press).

Popkin, J. 1996. 'Ego-Histoire and Beyond: Contemporary French Historian-Autobiographers', *French Historical Studies* 19/4: 1139–67.

Reynolds, R. 2013, 'BBC Refuses to Play Thatcher Death Song', *The Scotsman* (13 Apr.): 1.

Roca, Z., P. Clavel and J. Agnew (eds), 2011. *Landscapes, Identities and Development* (Farnham: Ashgate).

Salter, J. 2007. *Burning the Days* (London: Pan Macmillan).

Samuel, R. 1994. *Theatres of Memory: Past and Present in Contemporary Culture* (London: Verso).

Shiel, M.P. 2004 [1901]. *The Purple Cloud* (Leyburn: Tartarus Press).

Spiegelman, A. 2004. *In the Shadow of No Towers* (New York: Viking).

Sterne, J. 2009. 'The Preservation Paradox in Digital Audio', in K. Bijsterveld and J. van Dijck (eds), *Sound Souvenirs: Audio Technologies, Memory and Cultural Practices* (Amsterdam: Amsterdam University Press), pp. 55–66.

Thomas, D. 1990. *The Poems*, ed. D. Jones (London: Dent).

Tuan, Y. 1997. *Space and Place: The Perspective of Experience* (Minneapolis: University of Minnesota Press).

Vivian, B. 2010. *Public Forgetting: The Rhetoric and Politics of Beginning Again* (University Park: Pennsylvania State University Press).

Weller, P. 1980. 'That's Entertainment', on *Sound Affects* [LP] (Polydor).

Welzer, H. 2008. 'Communicative Memory', in A. Erll and A. Nünning (eds), *Cultural Memory Studies: An International and Interdisciplinary Handbook* (Berlin: De Gruyter), pp. 285–98.

Williams, C. 2013. 'The Demolition of the Edwardian Wing of Jessop Hospital: Does Heritage Matter?', *History Matters* (8 Aug.), <http://www.historymatters.group.shef.ac.uk/demolition-edwardian-wing-jessop-hospital-heritage-matter>.

Woolf, V. 1976 [1925] *Mrs Dalloway* (London: Grafton).

—— 2006 [1928]. *Orlando: A Biography* (Orlando: Harcourt).

—— 2012 [1923]. *Mrs Dalloway's Party* (London: Vintage).

Wordsworth, W. 1919. *The Complete Poetical Works of William Wordsworth*, vol. 2 (Boston, MA: Houghton Mifflin).

Wyatt, P. 2002. 'Best of British', *Mail on Sunday* (26 May): 24.

Yates, F. 1999. *The Art of Memory* (London and New York: Routledge).

Written in Stone:
Monuments and Representation

Siobhan Kattago

Contrary to Robert Musil's infamous claim that 'there is nothing so invisible as a monument' (1995: 61), they seem to be very visible in many parts of the world – most notably in Eastern Europe. While monuments tend to valorise significant events or individuals, memorials are primarily places of mourning and reflection. Influenced by the fall of the Berlin Wall, my interest in collective memory began with three interlinked questions: What can we learn from the recent past? How should societies deal with difficult pasts? Why do certain monuments seem to represent the past more powerfully than others?

Like many others of my generation, academic interest in memory studies began with Germany and expanded to comparative and interdisciplinary study within a rapidly changing Europe. Beginning from my graduate studies at the New School for Social Research, New York, I was fortunate enough to be part of informal memory workshops conducted by Jeffrey Olick at Columbia University and to benefit from visiting lecturers and former dissidents from Eastern Europe. Links between past and present were in the foreground of numerous symposia and conferences devoted to the end of Communism and the collapse of the Soviet Union. Given its origin as a 'university in exile', the New School was ideally suited for comparative studies of contemporary philosophy, politics and sociology. It was, however, in the work of Tony Judt that I truly found a larger understanding of the complexity of memory and forgetting. With his distinction between memory and 'mis-memory', Judt has been a constant companion in my academic work. In 'The Past is Another Country' (2002) he coined a very useful term that helps us to understand part of the confusion in how the past is remembered. A mis-memory is not necessarily forgetfulness, nor is it an outright lie. However, a mis-memory borders dangerously on mythology by dividing the world into perpetrators and victims, good and evil.

In his last book, *Thinking the Twentieth Century*, posthumously published with Timothy Snyder (2012), Tony Judt describes the difficult, familial relationship between memory and history:

> *They are step-siblings – and thus they hate one another while sharing just enough in common to be inseparable. Moreover, they are constrained to squabble over a heritage they can neither abandon nor divide. Memory is younger and more attractive, much more disposed to seduce and be seduced – and therefore she makes many more friends. History is the older sibling: somewhat gaunt, plain and serious, disposed to retreat rather than engage in idle chit-chat. And therefore she is a political wallflower – a book left on the shelf. (Judt with Snyder 2012: 266–7)*

Granted Judt was a historian and sensitive to the current popularity of memory studies. But, he does make a very serious point that warrants careful consideration – particularly for those interested in the relationship between memory and representation. In paying excessive attention to monuments, docudramas and films about a single event, one runs the risk of turning historical events into myth. By engaging more profoundly with emotions, aesthetic appeals to memory – whether individual or collective – tend to be more powerful than history exhibits that are more difficult to render into images. Memorials and museums focus on events that are to be represented aesthetically in a public space. In side stepping the larger perspective, events might be lifted out of context. As Judt notes, both aesthetic appeals to memory and historical research are necessary, the trick is not to confuse one with the other.

> *But I profoundly believe in the difference between history and memory; to allow memory to replace history is dangerous. Whereas history of necessity takes the form of a record, endlessly rewritten and re-tested against old and new evidence, memory is keyed to public, non-scholarly purposes: a theme park, a memorial, a museum, a building, a television program, an event, a day, a flag. (Judt with Snyder 2012: 277)*

Both memory and history are important ways of remembering the past, however they should not replace one another. 'Without history, memory is open to abuse. But if history comes first, then memory has a template and a guide against which it can work and be assessed' (Judt with Snyder 2012: 278). Judt's nuanced writing on post-war Europe (2005) and careful distinction between memory and mis-memory balance my long-standing interest in how memory is represented in public spaces and monuments.

One of the first signs of regime change is the tearing down of statues and monuments. This symbolic break with the old regime and beginning of a new one leads to a myriad of other questions. What should be done with the old statues? Should memorial sites be renovated or left alone as a historical reminder of bygone times? In Eastern Europe, responses have varied between removal, reconstruction and relocation. In Hungary, some communist monuments have been given a new home in Budapest's Memento Park.[1] In Moscow, there is a vast Communist Sculpture Park (formerly the Park of Fallen Heroes) with over 700 sculptures.[2] Other fallen idols rest at the back of the Tallinn History Museum, as they wait for a place in the forthcoming Estonian Park of Monuments (Figures 12.1, 12.2).[3] One of the strangest reconfiguration of communist monuments is Grutas Park in Lithuania. Comprising statues, museum, Soviet-era playground, zoo, shop and restaurant, Grutas Park combines didactic history with a theme park.[4]

---

1   See <www.mementopark.hu>.
2   See <http://www.muzeon.ru/pages/museum>.
3   See <http://www.ajaloomuuseum.ee/en/estonian-history-museum/park-of-monuments>. As the website states, the 'homeless monuments' will find a new home and a new context in a museum setting. 'The Estonian History Museum aims to collect these monuments as part of the memories of an era and to place these in a new context. We want to set up an outdoor exhibition in the park of Maarjamäe Palace to tell the story of the Soviet occupation through the monuments. The museum's idea to assemble all the so-called homeless monuments, mostly made by well-known Estonian sculptors, into one outdoor exhibition, has gained a lot of attention. Anything associated with Soviet ideology is painful and thus there are dissenting opinions about preserving the monuments. The monuments will find their place in the museum as a unique art collection, a symbol of one era of Estonia's past.'
4   See <www.grutoparkas.lt>.

Figure 12.1   Soviet monuments behind the Estonian History Museum (2013)
    Photo: Siobhan Kattago

With words and gestures literally 'written in stone', the intended meaning of the monuments changes when the regime falls (Levinson 1998). In addition to the fact that many statues have been moved from their original location to a new one, they were typically built to glorify the life and deeds of a single individual – Stalin, Lenin, Dzerzhinsky or local communist leaders – who is no longer hailed as a hero. War memorials, however, are rarely moved from their original location and pose even more difficult questions because they commemorate the death of ordinary soldiers and civilians.

Although there are many aspects that one might consider, I have been drawn to the aesthetic, philosophical and political interplay of how monuments and memorials represent the past. In particular, the study of war and Holocaust memorials offers a glimpse into the emotional power of symbols and sacred spaces in everyday life. In the growing literature, Pierre Nora, Reinhart Koselleck and Jay Winter have been exemplary companions in my research. While there are others who have also contributed greatly to the study of memorials and monuments, these three thinkers are pivotal for understanding how past experience is literally written and re-written in stone.[5] Nora's study of *lieux de mémoire* provides an original way of thinking about the material and symbolic power of particular places. Koselleck's

5   Among the key books, Rudy Koshar (2000) is insightful with respect to German monuments. Kirk
     Savage has analysed American monuments in Washington DC (2011). For war memorials and
     the war experience, see Mosse, 1990. On the sacred origins of national identity, particularly his

genealogy of war memorials distinguishes genres of memorialisation with respect to modernity. In addition, Winter's analysis of war memorials and commemorative ceremonies as sites of mourning introduces important distinctions between the sacred and the profane.

Figure 12.2   Head of Lenin, Estonian History Museum (2013)
        Photo: **Siobhan Kattago**

chapter on 'the glorious dead', see Smith 2003: 218–53. P. Reichel's study (1995) of German sites of memory about the Nazi past is also very helpful.

Symbolic Places and Traces

In many ways, Pierre Nora's *Lieux de mémoire* (1984–93) draws upon Frances Yates's *Art of Memory* (1966) and Maurice Halbwachs's 'The Legendary Topography of the Gospels in the Holy Land' (1992).[6] While his work focuses on French national memory, it has also been adapted to sites of national memory in Germany, Italy, the Netherlands and Austria. Moreover, three volumes mapping European *lieux de mémoire* have recently been published.[7]

As editor of the seven-volume project, it is striking how Nora focuses on places or sites 'in which the collective heritage of France was crystallized, the principal *lieux*, in all senses of the word, in which collective memory was rooted, in order to create a vast typology of French symbolism' (Nora 1996: vol. 1, xv). Hence, heritage, crystallisation, typology and symbolism become key words in his project (Nora 1984–93, 1996–98). Divided into three parts: *La République, La Nation* and *Les Frances*, there have been two separate translations into English which have been arranged differently from the original French editions.[8] Nora defines a place or site of memory in the following way:

> *If the expression lieu de mémoire must have an official definition, it should be this: a lieu de mémoire is any significant entity, whether material or non-material in nature, which by dint of human will or the work of time has become a symbolic element of the memorial heritage of any community (in this case, the French community). (Nora 1996: vol. 1, xvii)*

In English, *lieu* has either been translated as 'place', 'site' or 'realm'. Given the semantic difficulty of translating the symbolism of *lieu*, it is often left in the original French. Although Nora's project has been criticised as nostalgic, one should also be aware that his research intends to dismantle the traditional linearity of national history because it is 'an attempt to subvert as well as to exemplify and magnify that traditional genre known as the "history of France"' (Nora 1996: vol. 1, xix).

Like Jay Winter, Nora argues that: 'Memory situates remembrance in a sacred context' (Nora 1996: vol. 1, 3). Influenced by Halbwachs' distinction between memory and history, he associates memory with life and history with reconstruction. Rapid technological change and the democratisation of history affect how individuals understand their relation to the past. Sites of memory are transformed into 'vestiges' that recall an earlier age of the nation (ibid. 6). *Lieux* such as anniversaries, festivals, monuments and museums are 'relics of another era, illusions of eternity' (ibid.). A *lieu de mémoire* is material, symbolic and functional. Without a complex combination of all three aspects, it is merely an ordinary object or spatial location (ibid. 14). Nora's choice of sites are diverse: a song, flag, ceremony, calendar, schoolbook – but why is he important for studies of memorials and monuments? And, why are memorials considered to be exemplary *lieux de mémoire*? 'Certain broad categories of the genre stand out: anything having to do with the cult of the dead, the national heritage, or the presence

---

6   For important discussions of Yates and Halbwachs, see Hutton Ch. 1 above; Passerini Ch. 5 above.
7   For German sites of memory, see François and Schulze 2001; for European sites of memory in German, see P. Boer et al. 2011–12. For an overview of a European *lieux de mémoire* and the application of Nora's methodology, see Majerus 2014; for Italian, central European and American sites of memory, see Boer 2010; Hebel 2010; Isnenghi 2010; Le Rider 2010.
8   I am referring to Arthur Goldhammer's translation of Nora's *Realms of Memory*, 1996–98. This translation re-arranges the original seven volumes into three. In an effort to come up with a structure for an American audience, Nora decided to use the third part, *Les Frances*, as the basis for all three volumes in English. An alternative four-volume edition and different translation is available as *Rethinking France* (Nora 1999–2010).

of the past can be considered a *lieu de mémoire*' (ibid. 16). Moreover, a *lieu de mémoire* is a pure sign that refers not only to an event, but also to itself. 'Unlike historical objects, *lieux de mémoire* have no referents in reality: or, rather, they are their own referents – pure signs' (ibid. 19). Such a place is a kind of *templum* because it breaks with the passing of time for a brief moment. 'A *templum*: something singled out within the continuum of the profane [whether in space, time or both]' (ibid. 20).

Nora's *Realms of Memory* contains three interesting chapters devoted to memorials commemorating death.[9] These chapters analyse the Pantheon, Verdun and war memorials as French national *lieux de mémoire*. Mona Ozouf writes that the Pantheon is a 'temple of the void' (1998: 326). Built as a place where 'the great men' could co-exist in death without conflict, the entrance bears the inscription: 'Aux grands hommes la patrie reconnaissante'. The Pantheon symbolises the memory of the revolution, writers and scholars. But is it a cemetery or a monument? Ozouf concludes that it is 'neither a cemetery nor a church nor a museum … nor a garden … nor an archive' (ibid. 337–8). Although filled with coffins and ashes of the dead, it is more than a cemetery. Moreover, Ozouf asks: 'Was the Pantheon a monument *of* the Revolution?' (ibid. 339). The statues, grand design and symbolism confirm that the Pantheon memorialises a 'learned assembly of scholastic prizewinners … the École Normale of the Dead' (ibid. 345). In another chapter, Antoine Prost considers how the battlefield of Verdun has been transformed into a national symbol, arguing that it serves to crystallise French national memory of enormous loss and sacrifice (Prost 1998: 377). Because nearly the entire French army took part in the battle from 1916 to 1917, 'Verdun became a sacred place: a place of sacrifice and consecration' (ibid. 383).

In an additional chapter, 'Monuments to the Dead', Prost argues that while the building of monuments to the dead might not have originated with the First World War, 'no other war spawned so many' (Prost 1997: 307). In this sense, he complements the work of Jay Winter and Reinhart Koselleck. Hardly a French township is without a monument to the Great War (ibid.). Prost asks whether these monuments should be considered as 'monuments to the dead or monuments to victory?' (ibid. 308). As early as 1919, a law established subsidies to local governments enabling them to build First World War monuments. However, commemorations held at the war memorials attest to their changing character. Prost argues that such memorials were symbols of a secular cult of the dead and a kind of civil religion. 'In truth, this was a religion in which citizens celebrated themselves. It was a cult in which citizens paid heartfelt homage to those of their fellow citizens who had done their civic duty. In preserving their memory, the monument became a civic site' (ibid. 328). The commemorations of Armistice Day serve as an example of the civic duty to remember the dead. Moreover, such ceremonies employ Catholic imagery related to the cult of the dead. 'To that end it mobilized religious customs borrowed from a Catholicism that was still familiar to most Frenchmen, creating a distinctive ritual that orchestrated movement and immobility; silence and song, symbols, gestures, and words' (ibid. 330). Indeed, one might argue that what unites the various authors in Nora's seven edited volumes is that *lieux de mémoire* have a kind of aura or symbolic magic surrounding them, much like Walter Benjamin described with respect to art. It is precisely this symbolic aura that I have been drawn to in my studies on memory and representation.

---

9   In the original French version of vol. 1, Nora also included two chapters on death and French national memory: Jean-Clément Martin's 'La Vendée, region-mémoire' and Madeleine Rebérioux's 'Le Mur des Fédérés'. I am grateful to Marek Tamm for calling my attention to this.

War Memorials: Commemorating the Dead

While Nora casts a very wide net over the French symbolic landscape, Koselleck narrows his analysis to that of war memorials. In particular, he distinguishes First World War memorials from those commemorating the Second World War and the Holocaust. The crux of his analysis is existential and strongly influenced by Heidegger: Why is death a fundamental question for human existence?[10] What was the intended meaning of a particular war memorial? How might the original meaning change with time? My interest in Tombs of the Unknown Soldier and national memory has been shaped by both Koselleck and Winter. In particular, Koselleck was central for my understanding of the controversy surrounding the reconstruction of the Neue Wache in Berlin (Kattago 2001: 129–41), the reconfiguration of military cemeteries in Estonia and the multiple meanings of the Bronze Soldier memorial in Tallinn (Kattago 2010; 2012: 77–96).

All war memorials provide a way for individuals to identify with the dead. 'The war memorial does not only commemorate the dead; it also compensates for lost lives so as to render survival meaningful' (Koselleck 2002: 287). Unlike monuments recalling natural disaster, war memorials commemorate violent death at the hands of other human beings. The task for a war memorial is to give meaning to the survivors. 'Dying happens alone: killing another takes two' (ibid. 288). Koselleck argues that over time the meaning of a particular monument may change dramatically. 'What is certain is that the meaning of "dying for …" as it is recorded on memorials is established by the survivors and not by the dead' (ibid.). He reflects on the fact that the original meaning is not really written in stone at all. Instead, it might be remembered completely differently later on or become the unexpected site of controversy. The memorial might even become invisible and unnoticed. Hence war memorials reveal what he calls a 'double process of identification' contained in the difference between the actual death and the visual interpretation of it that a memorial offers. One hopes or assumes that the dead died for the same reason for which they are memorialised. Koselleck, however, is doubtful. Their meaning changes, as individuals forget what the monument was intended to represent. 'More than anything else, memorials erected permanently testify to transitoriness' (ibid. 288).

Initially, war memorials represented death as transcendence. In the pre-Revolutionary period, death was not an end, but a 'passageway' (Koselleck 2002: 289). Moreover, Koselleck links war memorials to modernity and the modern experience of time. 'The shift to modernity can likewise be conceptualised in two ways. First, while the transcendent sense of death fades or is lost, the innerworldly claims of representations of death grow' (ibid. 291). While all war memorials commemorate national death, he divides them into three periods. Generally those built before the First World War commemorate leaders who died in the name of the nation. After the First World War, the proliferation of memorials and building of Tombs of the Unknown Soldier represented the democratisation of death by commemorating ordinary soldiers who died for the nation. After the Second World War, negative or counter-monuments were built to visualise loss without justifying a national cause. Soviet war memorials, on the other hand, continued the heroic transformation of death in the name of the Soviet Union or greater cause of Communism.

As a former German soldier and Soviet prisoner of war, opposed to the controversial reconstruction of the Neue Wache in 1995, Koselleck argued that the sculpture of Käthe Kollwitz's private grief changed when it became the central symbol of German memory at the reconstructed Neue Wache (Figure 12.3). Originally sculpted to reflect Kollwitz's grief

---

10   For a philosophical discussion of death and ancestrality influenced by Heidegger and Derrida, see Ruin Ch. 4 above.

when her son was killed in the First World War, the enlarged pietà by Hans Haacke became the symbol of German national grief. This transformation from private grief to symbol of national mourning was not intended by the artist. Moreover, the mother's face is that of Kollwitz herself. The deeply personal and figurative image of maternal grief at the loss of her son works on two levels. Firstly, the pietà is a Christian symbol of sacrifice and death for the sake of redemption. Secondly, Kollwitz's grief focuses on the survivor – on the mother who has lost her son. This attention to those who are left behind, to the survivors, is exactly what the Neue Wache monument achieves, particularly, as it is intended as a place for all the dead – soldiers and civilians, concentration-camp victims, those from bombed cities and battlefields. The inscription on the exterior of the Neue Wache – 'To the Victims of War and Tyranny' – was, however, not without controversy. Koselleck criticised the use of Kollwitz's sculpture and the inscription because both equated the dead without distinguishing them from one another. 'Victimhood in a national monument implies a lack of agency and that all Germans were in some way victims of a hegemonic amorphous regime. Victims in a national monument does not introduce the question of perpetrators but rather induce an institutionalized forgetfulness' (Koselleck 1993: 33).

Figure 12.3   Neue Wache Memorial
        Photo: **Siobhan Kattago**

For him, the desire to grant death meaning is transformed, when the context changes from a religious to secular one. 'The decline of the Christian interpretation of death thus creates a space for meaning to be purely established in political and social terms' (Koselleck 2002:

291). Tombs of the Unknown Soldier are of particular interest to him because they represent 'a democratization of death' (ibid. 317). After the First World War, the memorialisation of the ordinary citizen as an unknown was a remarkable change from the commemoration of leaders and nobility. 'The tombs of the "unknown soldier" – one for all – are the last step in this democratization of death' (ibid.). Because the remains of unknown soldiers are buried in or near the memorial, they continue the medieval tradition of relics (Robinson 2011). Just as every Catholic altar contains the relic of a saint, so Tombs of the Unknown Soldier require the remains of one who is unnamed. Some even include an eternal flame and rotating guard of soldiers.

Soviet War Memorials

The reconstruction of monuments to the Great Patriotic War (1941–45) in post-Communist countries challenges their original intended meaning. Such revision with the intent to update them for a more democratic, and often national, reading of the past renders monuments such as the Soviet World War II Memorial, or 'Bronze Soldier' in Tallinn a kind of palimpsest with multiple layers of inscription, ranging from military sacrifice to identification with the soldier as occupier or liberator (Figure 12.4).[11] Since its original inception as 'Monument to the Liberators', it underwent changes from a wooden obelisk to a sculpture of a Red Army soldier with the addition of an eternal flame and remains of unknowns buried beneath it. The controversial relocation of the monument to an Estonian military cemetery sparked demonstrations in 2007. In many ways, the riots were an example of the difficulties that monuments face in changing societies. Sanford Levinson's slim book, *Written in Stone* captures the totemic importance of symbols. 'We do indeed live by symbols, whether they are tangible pieces of colored cloth or marble depictions of those the culture wishes to honor, or the more intangible messages granted by days of commemoration and celebration' (1998: 130).

Given the dramatic social and political change in Eastern Europe, the study of post-Communist monuments is a rapidly growing field. Katherine Verdery was one of the first to raise important questions for the memorial landscape in Eastern Europe in *The Political Lives of Dead Bodies*. As an anthropologist, she examined the relationship between regime change, symbolism and death. 'Why has the postsocialist period been accompanied by so much activity around dead bodies, and what does the politics concerning them signify?' (Verdery 1999: 3). For some, the Bronze Soldier represents Soviet victory over Fascism; for others, it represents the occupation of Estonia by the Red Army. When most of the unknowns were named and the statue was moved from a public park to the Defence Forces Cemetery in Tallinn, the primary message of the monument signified reverential mourning, rather than victory. Moreover, the inscription, 'To Those Killed in the Second World War', in both Estonian and Russian leaves the interpretation of death as liberation or occupation open. Only the deaths of those individuals killed in the Second World War are memorialised.

---

11   For discussion on the Bronze Soldier controversy, see Brüggemann and Kasekamp 2008; Ehala 2009; Leggewie 2011; Lehti, Jutila and Jokospila 2008; Münch 2008.

Figure 12.4   Bronze Soldier
        Photo: **Siobhan Kattago**

Holocaust Memorials

In addition to Second World War memorials commemorating military death, Holocaust memorials reflect on death, as well as the very limit of what can be represented aesthetically and politically (Friedlander 1992; Young 1993). As memorials, they do not commemorate valorous death but are places of mourning and warnings against future genocide. In debates surrounding the design of the Jewish Museum and Monument for the Murdered Jews of Europe in Berlin, many have called for a different sort of memorial than traditional ones (Figure 12.5). Eschewing figurative design, negative or counter-monuments serve to warn against human aggression without positing a transcendent higher meaning. In reflecting on Holocaust memorials, Koselleck noted a fundamental difference between war memorials and Holocaust memorials.

> *The annihilation not only of the living but also of physical bodies during air raids and even more in the German concentration camps necessitates the renunciation of the old arsenal of forms of war and victory memorials. Victims condemned to senselessness required, if at all, a kind of negative monument. (Koselleck 2002: 322)*

After the Second World War, it was more difficult for monuments to express or create a clear meaning. Rather the task was to search for meaning. An awareness of the limits of representation led to a tendency to design abstract memorials rather than traditional figurative ones (Koselleck 2007: 121). In this sense, Maya Lin's Vietnam Veterans Memorial (1982) in Washington DC conceptualised ways in which to remember individual death without reference to an ideological or national cause.

Figure 12.5   Memorial to the Murdered Jews of Europe
        Photo: Johanna Söderholm

James Young's *Texture of Memory* was one of the first to compare Holocaust memorials in various countries: Germany, Austria, Poland, the United States and Israel. His attention was more on 'collected memory' than on collective (Young 1993: xi). Like Winter and Koselleck, Young was interested in how individuals interact with memorials.[12] A memorial is a 'node' in a 'typographical matrix that orients the rememberer and creates meaning in both the land and our recollections. For like narrative, which automatically locates events in linear sequence, the memorial also brings events into some cognitive order' (ibid. 7). Just as Young's metaphor of textured memory captures the many layers and meanings of a monument, so Andreas Huyssen's metaphor of the palimpsest suggests multiple inscriptions. 'The trope of the palimpsest is inherently literal and tied to writing, but it can also be fruitfully used to discuss configurations of urban spaces and their unfolding in time without making architecture and the city simply into text' (2003: 7).[13]

Since war memorials are created after the fact, they are designed by survivors to recall events of the past. Koselleck makes the important distinction between how the past and future are perceived in the present. The past is understood as the space of experience and the future as the horizon of expectation. Although the 'space of experience' (*Erfahrungsraum*) is broader than Nora's *lieux de mémoire*, the metaphor of a topology is similar. Influenced by Yates, Halbwachs and Nora, it is difficult to think about the past without locating it in places, symbols, texts, frameworks and people. 'It makes sense to say that experience based on the past is spatial since it is assembled into a totality, within which many layers of earlier times are simultaneously present, without, however, providing any indication of the before or after' (Koselleck 1985: 273). The future, in contrast, is unknown because it has not yet been experienced. It can be a dream or a vision, full of fear, hope or anxiety. The future is full of unknown potential.

> An experience might contain faulty memories, or new experiences might open other perspectives. Time brings with it counsel; new experiences are collected. Thus, experiences had once in the past can change in the course of time. The events of 1933 have occurred once and for all, but the experiences which are based upon them change over time. (Koselleck 1985: 274–5)

Past experience leaves traces and residues with unpredictable meanings. War memorials inscribe traces of the past into stone for those who were fortunate enough not to experience such violence.

'Sites of Memory, Sites of Mourning'

Jay Winter argues that the memory boom is 'a re-statement of sacred themes' (2012). Many sites of memory in the twenty-first century are 'modern cathedrals' linking individuals with larger meaning. Secularisation does not mean that the sacred has vanished from everyday life, rather that it is reframed or 'reconfigured'. 'The sacred simply moves out of the churches and inhabits other public spaces' (ibid.). Battlefields, former concentration camps, Tombs of the Unknown Soldier, war cemeteries and history museums are imbued with sacred reverence formerly associated with religious sites. One visits them in silence and reflects

---

12 For a recent study of how individual interact with the Holocaust Memorial in Berlin, see Dekel 2013.

13 For a comparison of German and French Holocaust memorials, see Carrier 2005.

on loss of life. The sacred is not disappearing from modern life, but is transformed into increasingly public sites of memory. In a word, secularisation entails a new configuration of the sacred (ibid.). Hence, the building of new monuments and contestation surrounding older ones reflect fundamental changes in how individuals think about symbols and questions of loss and mourning.

Throughout his many years of research, Winter examines traditional motifs of bereavement and mourning after the First World War – especially the war memorials that were built throughout European towns and cities. 'Their message was to remember the sacrifice, the suffering, the slaughter, the names of the fallen' (Winter 2006: 26). Ranging from letters to novels, poems, films, museums and monuments; he is interested in 'cultural codes and languages of memory' (Winter 1995: 7). Like Nora, he highlights location, as indicated in the title of his seminal book, *Sites of Memory, Sites of Mourning*. Complementing Koselleck, he focuses on memorials that commemorate death and loss. Winter is careful to avoid Nora's reverential tone towards the past. As he notes, 'my "sites of memory" are other than Nora's. First, they are international; secondly, they are comparative; thirdly, they are there for their value in answering specific historical questions' (ibid.). Winter's sites of memory are sites of mourning: 'War memorials were places where people grieved, both individually and collectively' (ibid. 79). Moreover, they express a sense of civic or national indebtedness to those who died in war: 'The living can go about their lives in freedom because of the selflessness and dedication of the man who fell' (ibid. 95).

Tracing changes in the aesthetic design of war memorials after the Second World War, he notes: 'From roughly 1970 onwards the politics of remembrance shifted in such a way to make war a landscape of horror at the center of which are not the heroes, the resister or even the soldiers but the innocent civilians who were massacred in its wake' (Winter 2009: 31). He concurs with Annette Wieviorka that the emergence of the witness as a central figure, history from below and changing technology enabled the video recording of testimony. Memorials were far less about heroic victory and more focussed on 'those who were crushed by the forces of history' (ibid.).[14] He emphasises how the history of war is no longer the history of victory and defeat; it is the history of survivors and those who did not survive, that is the basic change in my lifetime' (ibid. 32).

One common feature of commemorations and visitation at war memorials is silence. Winter argues that such behaviour draws from rituals of liturgical silence when one is in the presence of the sacred. Political silence, however, is more akin to 'social compacts, contracts, not to talk about something that can destroy "the cohesion of society"' (Winter 2009: 34). Silence is not merely the absence of meaning, but also has a performative quality. Likewise, silence is not the equivalent of forgetting, any more than speech denotes remembering. Rather, silence is a particular form of remembrance. Winter is interested in the following paradox: all sacred acts involve silence, but not all silences are sacred (ibid.). 'Silence is always part of the framing of public understanding of war and violence, since they touch on the sacred, and on eternal themes of loss, mourning, sacrifice and redemption' (Winter 2010: 4). Such sacred silences are 'liturgical' because they are related to theodicy and the attempt to explain God's existence along with evil in the world. 'Political silence' is a social construction designed to prevent social conflict. Here, the hope is that silence will heal social and political wounds. Moreover, silence can also be 'essentialist' and pose the question of who has the right or the privilege to speak on behalf of others.

Whether silence is liturgical, political or essentialist, it is still a performative act. In particular, Winter emphasises the power of commemorative silences as sites of memory.

---

14   For reflections on post-Stalinist memory, see Etkind Ch. 17 below. In particular, his distiction between hardware, software and ghostware.

Beginning on Remembrance Day or Armistice Day, 11 November at 11 o'clock, the first commemorative silence occurred in 1919 to commemorate the dead of the First World War. This two-minute or sometimes one-minute silence has been observed in the UK and in the Commonwealth: 'the eleventh hour of the eleventh day of the eleventh month' to commemorate the time when the guns fell silent. In Israel, moments of silence are held on Yom HaShoah in memory of the Holocaust and on Yom HaZikaron in memory of fallen soldiers and victims of terror. The Israeli minute of silence is signalled by the sound of sirens throughout the country. In Winter's analysis, commemorative silence enables private remembrance within a collective. Moreover, this silence is linked to sacred themes of death and loss. 'The social notation of silence was secularized prayer. It forced people to remember, by suspending all other activities for a brief moment' (2006: 143). What is remarkable about the two-minute silence is that it comprises a 'mediation on absence' (ibid. 142).

Similarly to Koselleck, Winter is drawn to the work of Käthe Kollwitz. However, it is not the posthumous enlargement of her pietà that he discusses, but the sculpture of parents grieving for their son. Kollwitz's son, like many of his generation was enthusiastic about enlisting for the army. 'The Elders' presents Kollwitz and her husband grieving for their son. Originally placed in a German military cemetery in Roggevelde in Belgium, the figures were moved to Vladso in the 1950s, along with their son's grave. Kollwitz's memorial expressed familial loss not only of a child but also of an entire generation. Winter suggests that 'The Elders' represents the original insight of Halbwachs, namely that it is within the framework of the family where collective memory truly begins (Winter 2006: 150). Hence, the communicative practices, rituals and designs that began in the First World War provided the template for the subsequent design of war memorials in Europe. 'I suspect that the activity of remembrance, and the creation of the topoi of collective experience which it entails, are irrepressible. They express some fundamental truths about which the tendency of ordinary people, of many faiths and of none, to face the emptiness, the nothingness of loss in war, together' (ibid. 153).

Conclusion

As the proliferation of memorials demonstrates, the study of monuments and sites of memory is a growing field. However, as Winter suggests, it did not emerge from nowhere. Rather it has distinct origins in the reconfiguration of the sacred. As he notes, 'to a degree, the study of memory, the performance of memory is a pilgrimage to the past' (Winter 2012). Sites of memory, particularly war memorials are places where sacred questions that were previously raised in churches are now asked in places of public commemoration. Again, the important emphasis is on 'the reconfiguration of the sacred'. Like Nora, Winter is attentive to the symbolic power of certain sites or *lieux* that link individuals (even if only briefly) to the past. Monuments and war memorials tend to re-present past experience and sacrifice written in stone. By seeking to make present that which is absent, monuments face an almost impossible task. 'All political and social identifications that try to visually capture and permanently fix the "dying for …" vanish in the course of time. For this reason, the message that was to have been established by a memorial changes' (Koselleck 2002: 289). Instead, war memorials are modern palimpsests with multiple layers of meaning and inscription as their meaning changes with the passing of time. Koselleck's argument is a powerful one: 'The history of European war memorials testifies to a common visual signature of modernity' (ibid. 324). Tombs of the Unknown Soldier reflect the democratisation of death in the name of the nation, while Holocaust memorials commemorate death and the enormity of loss, without offering any kind of justification. As Koselleck reminds us, the only thing that we may be certain of is that a war memorial commemorates death and loss of life. 'What remains is the identity of the dead with themselves; the capability of memorializing the dead eludes the formal language of political sensibility' (ibid. 324). Once a memorial has been built, it takes on a life of its own. The original, emotional meaning of suffering and sacrifice may even completely vanish in time.

References

Boer, P. 2010. 'Loci memoriae – lieux de mémoire', in Erll, and Nünning 2010: 19–26.
— — et al. (eds) 2011–12. *Europäische Erinnerungsorte*, 3 vols (Munich: Oldenbourg).
Brüggemann, K., and A. Kasekamp. 2008. 'Politics of History and "War of Monuments" in Estonia', *Nationalities Papers* 36/3 (June): 425–48.
Carrier, P. 2005. *Holocaust Monuments and National Identity Cultures in France and Germany since 1989* (New York: Berghahn).
Dekel, I. 2013. *Mediation at the Holocaust Memorial in Berlin* (Basingstoke: Palgrave).
Ehala, M. 2009. 'The Bronze Soldier: Identity Threat and Maintenance in Estonia', *Journal of Baltic Studies* 40/1 (Mar.): 139–58.
Erll, A., and A. Nünning 2010. A *Companion to Cultural Memory Studies* (Berlin: De Gruyter).
François, E., and H. Schulze (ed.) 2001. *Deutsche Erinnerungsorte*, 3 vols (Munich: C.H. Beck).
Friedlander, S. (ed.) 1992. *Probing the Limits of Representation: Nazism and the Final Solution* (Cambridge, MA: Harvard University Press).
Halbwachs, M. 1992. 'The Legendary Topography of the Gospels in the Holy Land', in *On Collective Memory*, trans. L.A. Coser (Chicago: University of Chicago Press), pp. 193–235.
Hebel, U.J. 2010. 'Sites and Memories in US-American Histories and Cultures', in Erll and Nünning 2010: 47–60.
Huyssen, A. 2003. *Present Pasts: Urban Palimpsests and the Politics of Memory* (Stanford, CA: Stanford University Press).
Isenghi, M. 2010. 'Italian luoghi della memoria', in Erll and Nünning 2010: 27–36.
Judt, T. 2002. 'The Past is Another Country: Myth and Memory in Post-War Europe', in J.-W. Müller (ed.), *Memory and Power in Post-War Europe: Studies in the Presence of the Past* (Cambridge: Cambridge University Press), pp. 157–83.
— — 2005. *Postwar: A History of Europe since 1945* (London: Penguin).
— — with T. Snyder 2012. *Thinking the Twentieth Century* (New York: Random House).
Kattago, S. 2001. *Ambiguous Memory: The Nazi Past and German National Identity* (Westport, CT: Praeger).
— — 2010. 'Commemorating Liberation and Occupation: War Memorials along the Road to Narva', in J. Hackmann and M. Lehti (eds), *Contested and Shared Places of Memory: History and Politics in North Eastern Europe* (London: Routledge), pp. 53–70.
— — 2012. *Memory and Representation in Contemporary Europe: The Persistence of the Past* (Farnham: Ashgate).
Koselleck, R. 1985. *Futures Past: On the Semantics of Historical Time*, trans. K. Tribe (Cambridge, MA: MIT Press).
— — 1993. 'Stellen uns die Toten einen Termin?', in W. Jens (ed.), *Streit um die Neue Wache: Zur Gestaltung einer zentralen Gedenkstätte* (Berlin: Akademie der Kunst), pp. 27–34.
— — 2002. 'War Memorials: Identity Formations of the Survivors', in *The Practice of Conceptual History: Timing History, Spacing Concepts*, trans. T.S. Preser et al. (Stanford, CA: Stanford University Press), pp. 285–326.

—— 2007. Interview with M. Tamm, in *Kuidas kirjutatakse ajalugu? Intervjuuraamat* [How to Write History? A Book of Interviews] (Tallinn: Varrak).

Koshar, R. 2000. *From Monuments to Traces: Artifacts of German Memory 1870–1990* (Berkeley: University of California Press).

Le Rider, J. 2010. 'Mitteleuropa as a lieu de mémoire', in Erll and Nünning 2010: 37–46.

Leggewie, C. 2011. *Der Kampf um die Europäische Erinnerung: Ein Schlachtfeld wird besichtigt* (Munich: C.H. Beck), 56–80.

Lehti, M., M. Jutila and M. Jokospila 2008. 'Never-Ending Second World War: Public Performance of National Dignity and the Drama of the Bronze Soldier', *Journal of Baltic Studies* 39/4 (Dec.): 393–418.

Levinson, S. 1998. *Written in Stone: Public Monuments in Changing Societies* (Durham, NC: Duke University Press).

Majerus, B. 2014. '*Lieux de mémoire*: A European Transfer Story', in S. Berger and B. Niven (eds), *Writing the History of Memory* (London: Bloomsbury), pp. 157–71.

Mosse, G. 1990. *Fallen Soldiers: Reshaping the Memory of World Wars* (Oxford: Oxford University Press).

Münch, F. 2008. *Diskrimierung durch Geschichte? Der Deutungsstreit um den 'Bronzenen Soldaten' im Geschichtspolitischen Diskurs des postsowjetischen Estland* (Marburg: Tectum-Verlag).

Musil, R. 1995. 'Monuments', in *Posthumous Papers of a Living Author*, trans. P. Wortsman (New York: Penguin), pp. 61–4.

Nora, P. (ed.) 1984–93. *Les Lieux de mémoire*, 7 vols (Paris: Gallimard).

—— (ed.) 1996–98. *Realms of Memory: Rethinking the French Past*, 3 vols, trans. A. Goldhammer (New York: Columbia University Press).

—— 1999–2010. *Rethinking France: Les lieux de mémoire*, 4 vols, ed. D.P. Jordan, trans. M. Seidman Trouille (Chicago: University of Chicago Press).

Ozouf, M. 1998. 'The École Normale of the Dead', in Nora 1996–98: vol. 3, pp. 325–48.

Prost, A. 1997. 'Monuments to the Dead', in Nora 1996–98: vol. 2, pp. 307–32.

—— 1998. 'Verdun', in Nora 1996–98: vol. 3, pp. 377–404.

Reichel, P. 1995. *Politik mit der Erinnerung: Gedächtnisorte im Streit um die nationalsozialistische Vergangenheit* (Munich: Carl Hanser Verlag).

Robinson, J. 2011. *Finer than Gold: Saints and Relics in the Middle Ages* (London: British Museum Press).

Savage, K. 2011. *Monument Wars: Washington DC, the National Mall and the Transformation of the Memorial Landscape* (Berkeley: University of California Press).

Smith, D. 2003. *Chosen Peoples: Sacred Sources of National Identity* (Oxford: Oxford University Press).

Verdery, K. 1999. *The Political Lives of Dead Bodies: Reburial and Postsocialist Change* (New York: Columbia University Press).

Winter, J. 1995. *Sites of Memory, Sites of Mourning: The Great War in European Cultural History* (Cambridge: Cambridge University Press).

—— 2006. *Remembering War: The Great War between Memory and History in the Twentieth Century* (New Haven, CT: Yale University Press).

—— 2009. Interview with S.M. Kalayci, *Tarih* 1/1: 29–36; available at <http://graduatehistoryjournal.boun.edu.tr/papers/ISSUE1.2009.REPRESENTATION/2. SuzanMeryemKalayci.Interview.JAY.WINTER.pdf>.

—— 2010. 'Thinking about Silence', in E. Ben-Ze'ev, R. Ginio and J. Winter (eds), *Shadows of War: A Social History of Silence in the Twentieth Century* (Cambridge: Cambridge University Press), pp. 3–31.

—— 2012. 'The Memory Boom and Human Rights', speech for the 'Memory Marathon', Serpentine Gallery, 12–14 October [video], <http://vimeo.com/61087233>.

Yates, F. 1966. *The Art of Memory* (Chicago: University of Chicago Press).

Young. J.E. 1993. *The Texture of Memory: Holocaust Memorials and Meaning* (New Haven, CT: Yale University Press).

Theories of Memory and the Imaginative Force of Fiction

Julie Hansen[1]

Literature has always explored the possibilities and limitations of memory. Odysseus' return to Ithaca after 20 years away is as much about the uncertainty of recognition as it is the story of the hero's homecoming. In the twentieth century, Anna Akhmatova's masterpiece *Poem Without a Hero* (*Poèma bez geroia*, 1965), begun during the Stalinist period, evoked the ghosts of a lost generation of Russian modernists. In our own century, Karl Ove Knausgård's six-volume memoir-novel *My Struggle* (*Min kamp*, 2009–11) mines memory to record the minutiae of the 40-something author's life-to-date. Throughout the centuries, literary works have evoked, provoked, ransacked and interrogated memory in myriad ways.

Memory is unpredictable, even unruly. It can arise unbidden when we least expect, yet it can also elude us when pursued. It is difficult to conceive of memory without her cousin oblivion lurking around the corner. Total recall is impossible (at least humanly), yet we fear memory loss – especially the diagnoses of amnesia and dementia. If memory is located, as John Locke, David Hume and later philosophers have taught us, at the core of our identity, then memory loss is tantamount to loss of the self.

Many thinkers describe memory and forgetting as two, mutually dependent, sides of the same coin. In classical Greece, Edward S. Casey writes, memory and forgetting formed 'an indissociable pair … given explicit mythical representation in the coeval figures of Lesmosyne and Mnemosyne, who are conceived as equals *requiring* each other' (2000: 12). Problems seem to arise when memory and forgetting are out of balance. Paul Ricoeur explains one of the motivations for his study *History, Memory, Forgetting* (*La mémoire, l'histoire, l'oubli*, 2000) thus: 'I continue to be troubled by the unsettling spectacle offered by an excess of memory here, and an excess of forgetting elsewhere' (2004: xv). Richard Terdiman identifies a similar sense of unease in Europe after the French Revolution, when 'disquiet about memory crystallized around the perception of two principal disorders: *too little memory*, and *too much*' (1993: 14). The current 'memory boom' is thus not the first, nor is it likely to be the last – so central is memory to human experience.

1   I am grateful to the Swedish Research Council and the Birgit and Gad Rausing Foundation for Humanities Research for grants that made work on this chapter possible. Thanks also to Siobhan Kattago for insightful comments on a draft of this chapter.

Memory and the Potential of Fiction

Enlightenment philosophers drew a connection between individual memory and identity; Ricoeur calls this connection 'the invention of John Locke at the beginning of the eighteenth century' (2004: 97). Collective memory came into focus in the early twentieth century, with Maurice Halbwachs' seminal works on the social aspects of remembrance. Much recent work within the field of memory studies has examined relations between commemorative practices, museums and monuments, on the one hand, with collective memory and identity, on the other. Arguably, literary fiction also plays a considerable role in memory processes, leading Renate Lachmann to call literature 'the mnemonic art par excellence' (2010: 301). Literature can be seen to comprise its own system of memory in the form of intertextuality, through which texts revisit, rewrite and reinterpret other texts (ibid.). Wolfgang Iser went so far as to liken intertextuality to cultural memory itself, arguing: 'As culture can never be encompassed, especially since it is continually emerging, the memory of the literary text offers an idea of how to visualize this basically ungraspable emergence' (1997: xviii).

But what can fiction tell us about memory that we do not already know, especially in light of the latest advances in neurological and cognitive science? Memory is linked to both identity and the imagination, and therein lies the potential of fiction to help us understand the past and define our relation to it. Literature resides in a grey zone between history and memory, lived and imagined experience. Although it reflects and refracts the real world, fiction frees us from definitive truth claims about reality. Imagined pasts allow us to contemplate alternative interpretations, to question accepted historical truths and to problematise the relationship of society and individuals to past events and even memory itself. Thus, fiction can serve as a catalyst and forum for critical self-reflection. In this and other ways, books are ideal memory companions.[2]

It is most often individual memory that fiction puts under the microscope, but through the reading process, literature also has the potential to shape collective memory. This, as Mary Warnock argues, is true of all art, due to the close connections between memory, imagination and identity.

> The imagination, especially as it is exercised in the creative arts, is that which can draw out general implications from individual instances, can see, and cause others to see, the universal in the particular. The value we attach to recollection is understandable at precisely the point where memory and imagination intersect. Physical and biological continuity and self-identity, ensured and asserted by memory, can be converted into permanence and universality by the attempts we may make to turn memory into art. (Warnock 1987: viii)[3]

Memory is dependent on imagination, yet – unlike fiction – it makes a truth claim at the same time. This duality compromises it in the eyes of some and offers possibilities in the eyes of others.

Literature has always conceptualised memory in its own ways, which have developed not only parallel to, but in interaction with, philosophical and scientific models of the human

---

2   Individual memories can become intertwined with literary ones, as memories from our own lives become associated with the books we happened to be reading at the time. A favourite novel can trigger memories and lead us to revisit our own past in the course of re-reading.

3   Similarly, Lachmann observes that the 'bond between mnemotechnics and literature is grounded in the double meaning of *imago* as an image of memory and as the product of imagination, the creative stimulus of literature. The image-producing activity of memory incorporates poetic imagination' (2010: 303).

mind. Walter Benjamin observed that Proust put 'Bergson's theory of experience to the test' (quoted in Rossington and White 2007: 93). Anne Whitehead holds that 'memory's history is as firmly embedded in Augustine, Wordsworth, and Proust as in Plato, Freud, or Bergson' (2009: 12). Literary representations of memory have also influenced philosophical and scientific conceptions of memory – St. Augustine's 'memory palace' and Proust's famous madeleine are just two instances of literary descriptions that have become iconic. This long-standing symbiosis between philosophy and fiction makes memory theory particularly fruitful for the study of literature.

Recent Fiction from Central and Eastern Europe

The current academic memory boom, ushered in during the 1980s by Yosef Yerushalmi's seminal study *Zakhor: Jewish History and Jewish Memory* and Pierre Nora's seven-volume *Les lieux de mémoire*, is not the first. Whitehead argues that it is 'simply the latest of a series of preoccupations with memory which have punctuated Western culture' (2009: 3). The themes of memory and forgetting are especially interesting against the background of the end of Communism in Central and Eastern Europe. Forgetting, Paul Connerton argues, 'appears in its most brutal form … in the history of totalitarian regimes' (2008: 60). Here the state enforced a kind of historical amnesia (ibid. 69), using the age-old practice of *damnatio memoriae* to remove public traces of events and individuals who did not conform to the reigning ideology.[4]

The Czech writer Milan Kundera used the example of a retouched photograph to illustrate state-sponsored attempts to revise the past in the opening passage of his novel *The Book of Laughter and Forgetting* (*Kníha smíchu a zapomnění*, 1981). Here Kundera describes a photograph of the Communist leader Klement Gottwald after the coup in February 1948. He is surrounded by party comrades, one of whom – Vladimír Clementis – has lent Gottwald his fur cap. The text explains that when Clementis fell from political grace and was executed four years later, his image was airbrushed out of the photo. The only remaining trace of Clementis was his hat on Gottwald's head (1981: 9). Kundera's depiction of the manipulation of a photograph touches upon two aspects of memory and forgetting in Communist Czechoslovakia: first, the regime's organised attempt to manipulate the collective memory, an example of what Ricoeur calls an abuse of memory (2004: 56–92); and second, the persistence of a memory trace (represented by Clementis' hat) nonetheless.

In the wake of glasnost and the fall of the Berlin Wall, the societies of the former Eastern Bloc began to revisit historical events that were previously taboo. 'In a world of change, memory becomes complicated', Terdiman observes, and 'any rapid alternation of the givens of the present places a society's connection with its history under pressure' (1993: 3). In Central and Eastern Europe during the 1990s, this process led to the opening of archives and the publication of previously banned books.[5] At the same time, the field of memory studies was gaining ground as an academic discipline at Western European and North American universities.

---

4   Tony Judt makes a somewhat different argument, delineating distinct relations to the past in Western and Eastern Europe, respectively: 'If the problem in Western Europe has been a shortage of memory, in the continent's other half the problem is reversed. Here there is too much memory, too many pasts on which people can draw, usually as a weapon against the past of someone else' (2002: 172).

5   For a discussion of the effects of glasnost on Soviet society, see Etkind Ch. 17 below.

Now, a quarter of a century after the fall of the Berlin Wall, much literary fiction from Central and Eastern Europe explores the past and how we remember it. While fictional depictions of the Communist period exhibit a variety of forms and approaches, many recent works indicate a new turn. They do not seek primarily to set the historical record straight, nor do they express a nostalgic longing for a lost world. Rather, much recent fiction about the Communist period interrogates memory itself, reflecting critically upon its functions and limitations. In this way, these works of fiction offer a commentary not only on the Communist period, but also on post-Communist Europe and its relation to the past.

The Role of Forgetting

John Frow, in his study *Time and Commodity Culture*, faults the predominant conception of memory for 'its inability to account for forgetting other than as a fault or as decay or as a random failure of access' (1997: 227). Forgetting seems to be getting more scholarly attention lately, however, leading Whitehead to speak of 'a discursive shift … from memory to forgetting' (2009: 154). Aleida Assmann declares that 'when thinking about memory, we must start with forgetting' (2010: 97). Marc Augé's *Oblivion* puts forgetting into focus, describing it in decidedly positive terms. He declares, as if in challenge to Locke and Hume, 'tell me what you forget and I will tell you who you are' (2004: 18). Nonetheless, Augé views forgetting as intricately connected to memory. Employing a metaphor of ocean waves shaping a shoreline, he describes memory as 'crafted by oblivion as the outlines of the shore are created by the sea' (ibid. 20).

The disturbing effects of short-term memory loss are vividly depicted in Christopher Nolan's suspense film *Memento* (2000).[6] The protagonist Leonard Shelby, traumatised by the murder of his wife, suffers from anterograde amnesia. He can recall events prior to the murder but is unable to retain new information for more than a few minutes at a time, which makes his search for his wife's killer difficult at best. Shelby's condition is mirrored by the film's narrative structure, consisting of two alternating storylines divided into segments not longer than a few minutes each. One consists of flashbacks in chronologically ordered, black-and-white segments. These alternate with colour segments from the other storyline, which is told in reverse chronological order. This complex narrative structure challenges viewers to piece together the plot into a comprehensible whole, just as Shelby struggles to make sense of information he has gathered but no longer remembers. He compensates for his mnemonic handicap by recording new information on Polaroid photos, post-it notes and tattoos on his body. I will return below to the idea of writing as a substitute for memory, for it has been central to philosophical reflections on memory from Plato to Jacques Derrida.

A very different affliction – an excess of memory – is depicted in Jorge Luis Borges' short story 'Funes, the Memorious' from 1942. Here an accident renders the eponymous protagonist Funes incapable of forgetting. Unable to filter out insignificant information, his memory is 'like a garbage disposal' (1993: 88), leaving him overwhelmed with details. As James E. Young observes, our capacity to forget is essential to memory, for without it 'there is no space left by which to navigate the meaning of what one has remembered' (2004: viii).

---

6   *Memento*, starring Guy Pearce, Carrie-Anne Moss and Joe Pantoliano, is an adaptation of a short story entitled 'Memento Mori' by Jonathan Nolan, the brother of the film's director and screenwriter Christopher Nolan.

Thus, if writing can serve as a mnemonic aid, Borges's story shows that selective editing is also necessary in order for memory to be of any use.[7]

My own theoretical interest in memory and forgetting began several years ago, while on extended parental leave after the birth of my second son. Those days at home with a baby and a toddler did not leave much time for scholarly work, but I could at least read while they napped. I decided to use these stolen moments to acquaint myself better with the latest literature from Central and Eastern Europe. A decade and a half had passed since the fall of the Berlin Wall, a new generation of writers had come of age, and I was curious about the concerns of literature from these new, post-Communist countries. I cast a broad net, reading works published after 1995, reasoning that, during the early 1990s, authors, publishers and readers alike were busy catching up with previously banned and unpublishable works. (If books were not good memory companions, governments should not go to such trouble to censor and ban them.)

As I worked my way through a stack of novels, I discovered history and memory to be prevalent and recurring themes. These can, of course, be counted among the perpetual preoccupations of Western literature, but here the theme of memory was thrown into sharp relief, depicted as it was against the background of enforced amnesia during the Communist period.

During those intensive, special days at home with my little boys, a broader research project slowly but surely took shape. This project (now nearing completion) applies memory theory to contemporary fiction from post-Communist Europe in order to elucidate the ways this new body of literature portrays, reimagines and seeks to come to terms with the Communist past.[8] My primary interest is not in how accurately fiction represents life in a Communist system, but rather how it uses the theme of memory to explore the Communist period retrospectively, not only reflecting – but reflecting upon – different ways of understanding it. In the process, these works say at least as much about memory as about history.

Conceptualizing Memory through Metaphors

It is difficult to get a perspective on memory because it is so intricately bound up with cognition and identity. As Terdiman writes, memory is 'so omnipresent, so fundamental to our ability to conceive the world that it might seem impossible to analyze it at all' (1993: 8). A.S. Byatt holds that 'humans have always needed metaphors to think about memory' (2009: xiii), and, indeed, a variety of metaphoric constructs for memory appear in scientific, philosophical and literary texts. Metaphors thus comprise a good starting point for an exploration of literary representations of memory.

The historian of psychology Douwe Draaisma traces the historical development of prevalent Western memory metaphors, arguing that they have been influenced by various technological advances, ranging from wax impressions to digital documentation (2000: 3).[9] Yet there is a continuity among these metaphors in Western literature and philosophy

---

7   For another discussion of the depiction of memory in Borges' story, see Frow 1997: 227–8.

8   This project, entitled 'History through the Prism of Memory: Post-Communist Novels from Central and Eastern Europe', was funded by the Swedish Research Council for three years between 2010 and 2013.

9   Draaisma argues that 'over the centuries memory aids provided the terms and concepts with which we have reflected on our own memory' (2000: 3). Byatt also notes a mutual influence between invented memory aids and ways of conceptualising human memory: 'We invent machines to

that is more striking than the differences between them (Rossington and Whitehead 2007: 4; Draaisma 2000: 4). The two most enduring metaphors are of memory as writing and storage, both of which appear in Plato's dialogue *Theaetetus*. Here, the faculty of memory is first likened to a wax block on which specific memories are recorded. Socrates explains: 'whenever we want to remember something we've seen or heard or conceived on our own, we subject the block to the perception or the idea and stamp the impression into it, as if we were making marks with signet-rings' (Plato 2004: 99–100). Later in the same dialogue, Socrates likens memory to an aviary: 'Earlier we constructed a kind of block of wax in our minds; now let's equip each mind with an aviary for all sorts of birds, some in exclusive flocks, some in small groups, and some flying alone, here, there and everywhere among all the rest' (ibid. 109).

While the wax metaphor represents memory as a form of inscription, the aviary is a spatial metaphor. According to this conception, humans fill the space of their minds with memories, just as a bird-keeper fills an aviary with birds. As Draaisma notes, Plato's two metaphors in *Theaetetus* have become highly productive cultural archetypes of memory (2000: 27). Other well-known examples of spatial metaphors for memory include Quintilian's 'the treasure-house of eloquence', Augustine's 'memory palace' and Locke's 'Store-house of our Ideas'. Classical and medieval *ars memoriae* used the visualization of specific buildings as a memory aid (Yates 1966), giving rise to more specific architectural metaphors. William James and Sigmund Freud both compared the faculty of memory to a house (Roediger 1980: 234). Warnock speaks of memory as a kind of closet 'in which things that may come in handy later are put away: a kind of attic or junk-room' (1987: 6).[10]

Equally prevalent is the metaphor of inscription (Whitehead 2009: 40). The idea of memory as a wax impression, expressed in Plato's *Theaetetus*, also appears in Aristotle's *On Memory and Recollection*. Here memory is conceived of as past experience transformed by the senses into an image (*eikon*) impressed upon the mind. Much later, in the nineteenth century, the concept of inscription appeared in metaphors likening memory to technical inventions of the time: photography (1839), which recorded visual images (Draaisma 2000: 110–25), and the phonograph (1877), which recorded and replayed sound by pressing a needle into wax (Draaisma 2000: 85–93).[11]

Spatial and inscriptive metaphors for memory, which John Frow calls 'the two major metaphors through which European culture has conceptualized memory over the last two and a half millennia' (1997: 225), have sometimes merged into one. For example, Cicero exemplifies, in his advice to orators, the art of memorisation with two 'eminent people with almost superhuman memories', who 'recorded what they wanted to remember by means of images in the localities that they had chosen, just as if they were writing them out by means of letters on a wax tablet' (2001: 212). Spatial and inscriptive metaphors are particularly suggestive and productive within the context of literature. During the Middle Ages, memory was often represented as a book, and later as a library, which as a repository for books, embodies the two archetypal metaphors of inscription and storage (Draaisma 2000: 30). The image of an archive also unites the two metaphors through the 'logic of the inscription (or deposit) and the storage of information in systematically articulated space'

---

assist and fortify our memories, and then use these machines as metaphors for thinking about how memory works' (2009: xiii).

10   Memory has also been visualised as a subterranean space. Walter Benjamin employs an archaeological metaphor in *A Berlin Chronicle*: 'He who seeks to approach his own buried past must conduct himself like a man digging' (1986: 26).

11   For a discussion of medieval views of the relation between writing and memory, see Mary Carruthers' *Book of Memory* (2008).

(Frow 1997: 225). From wax impressions and birds to books and digital archives, the ideas of space and writing have remained central to Western understandings of memory.

Freud and Derrida on Memory and Writing

Inscriptive metaphors have been employed by Sigmund Freud and Jacques Derrida to conceptualise memory in ways that link it inextricably to writing and texts. Freud opens his short essay 'A Note upon the "Mystic Writing-Pad"' (1925) with an account of his search for an apt metaphor for the memory faculty. He observes that humans often 'supplement' their memory by writing things down, and gives two examples of how this can be done. The first is by making notes on paper (like Leonard Shelby in *Memento*), the second by writing on a chalkboard. However, Freud rejects both of these memory aids as inadequate representations of human memory. Paper and pen can leave a 'permanent trace', yet their capacity is limited by the size of the paper. Chalkboards, by contrast, can be erased and reused, but do not allow for permanency. Instead, Freud seeks a model of memory that includes both unlimited capacity and permanency of memory. He finds this in what was, at the time, a new children's toy: the *Wunderblock*, or 'mystic writing pad' (sometimes called a 'magic slate' in English).[12] Simpler than it sounds, this toy consists of two connected parts: a wax slate (often cardboard coated with a thin layer of wax) and an overlaying cellophane sheet. A stylus is used to write on the cellophane, which creates an impression in the wax. Because the cellophane sticks to the wax when pressed, marks made by the stylus become visible in contrast to rest of the cellophane sheet. When the cellophane is pulled up and away from the wax, the writing disappears from the cellophane surface. However, the careful eye can still detect a palimpsest-like trace in the wax, which Freud likens to a 'permanent memory-trace' in the mind (1984: 430). The essay concludes with an image of the mind as two hands working simultaneously, one writing on the mystic writing pad, the other periodically lifting the cellophane to erase the writing and clear space for new impressions. In this way, the relation between memory and forgetting is represented not as one of opposition, but of interchange.

Freud's six-page essay on memory and writing inspired a much longer essay by Derrida entitled 'Freud and the Scene of Writing'. It offers a reading of Freud's use of the writing metaphor with the aim of challenging logocentrism and the precedence it gives to spoken language over written language, presence over absence. Derrida argues:

> *From Plato and Aristotle on, scriptural images have regularly been used to illustrate the relationship between reason and experience, perception and memory. But a certain confidence has never stopped taking its assurance from the meaning of the well-known and familiar term: writing. The gesture sketched out by Freud interrupts that*

---

12 Having last seen one of these toys several years ago, I cannot help but wonder if they have been superseded by digital tablets such as the iPad. Draaisma wonders what model Freud would have chosen for the digital age: 'An appealing fantasy would be to transport Freud to the present day and ask ourselves what metaphor he would have used now in order to express the mysterious combination of permanent traces and an unlimited surface area for new notes' (2000: 21). Draaisma argues that a computer is not an apt model because it is more reliable, consistent and predictable than human memory (ibid. 161). Derrida asks: 'Does it change anything that Freud did not know about the computer? And where should the moment of suppression or of repression be situated in these new models of recording and impression, or printing?' (1995: 26).

> *assurance and opens up a new kind of question about metaphor, writing and spacing in general. (2001: 250)*

Derrida's essay (like Freud's) begins with an account of Freud's search for an apt metaphor for memory's seemingly paradoxical 'permanence of the trace and ... the perennially intact bareness of the perceptive surface' (2001: 251). According to Derrida, this search began as early as Freud's *Project for a Scientific Psychology* (1895), continued in a letter dated 6 December 1896 and in *The Interpretation of Dreams* (1900), and finally culminated 25 years later with 'A Note upon the "Mystic Writing-Pad"'. Derrida notes that the metaphor of writing became increasingly central to Freud's thought, arguing that in the 'Mystic Writing-Pad', Freud 'performs for us the scene of writing' (2001: 288). For Derrida, this scene represents not merely psychology, but the world, in which the spoken word is unjustly privileged over the written word because it is uttered in the presence of the speaker, whereas the written word entails a temporal delay and the absence of the speaker. He argues:

> *The Freudian concept of trace must be radicalized and extracted from the metaphysics of presence which still retains it (particularly in the concepts of consciousness, the unconscious, perception, memory, reality, and several others). The trace is the erasure of selfhood, of one's own presence, and is constituted by the threat or anguish of its irremediable disappearance, of the disappearance of its disappearance. (2001: 289)*

Derrida draws a distinction between writing as phonetic script – that is, the transcription of spoken language – and what he calls 'psychic writing', consisting of non-verbal signs, 'metaphonetic, nonlinguistic, alogical' (2001: 259), such as those found in dreams. He argues that in Freud's letter, 'verbal phenomena are assigned a place within a system of stratified writing which these phenomena are far from dominating' (ibid. 258–9).

Derrida focuses on Freud's concept of breaching, or pathbreaking (German *Bahnung*), which 'presupposes a certain violence and a certain resistance to effraction' (2001: 252). A memory trace is created when a perception breaches, or overcomes, resistance in the psyche. Inherent in breaching is deferral:

> *The metaphor of pathbreaking, so frequently used in Freud's descriptions, is always in communication with the theme of the supplementary delay and with the reconstitution of meaning through deferral, after a mole-like progression, after the subterranean toil of an impression. This impression has left behind a laborious trace which has never been perceived, whose meaning has never been lived in the present, i.e. has never been lived consciously. The postscript with constitutes the past present as such is not satisfied, as Plato, Hegel and Proust perhaps thought, with reawakening or revealing the present past in its truth. It produces the present past. (2001: 269)*

Derrida argues that writing always entails deferment, because it comes after the moment it describes, and that this is true for all forms of perception: 'Writing supplements perception before perception even appears to itself. ... "Memory" or writing is the opening of that process of appearance itself' (2001: 282). This last sentence equates memory and writing, at the same time according writing precedence by placing qualifying quotation marks around memory. Derrida sees the faculty of memory as 'not a psychical property among others; it is the very essence of the psyche: resistance, and precisely, thereby, an opening to the effraction of the trace' (ibid. 252). It follows from this argument that our only access to perception is retrospective, after-the-event. The writing of memory, according to Derrida, calls into question the very possibility of presence:

There is no present text in general, and there is not even a past present text, a text which is past as having been present. The text is not conceivable in an originary or modified form of presence. The unconscious text is already a weave of pure traces ... a text nowhere present, consisting of archives which are always already transcriptions. ... Everything begins with reproduction. Always already: repositories of a meaning which was never present, whose signified presence is always reconstituted by deferral. (2001: 265–6)

Derrida returns to Freud in his long essay *Archive Fever*. Like writing, Derrida argues, an archive comprises a 'mnemotechnical supplement or representative, auxiliary or memorandum' (1995: 11). As such, the archive paradoxically carries the potential for destruction as well as conservation of memory, because what is stored there is no longer part of living memory, 'but rather a certain hypomnesic and prosthetic experience' (ibid. 25). As a result, 'the archive always works, and *a priori*, against itself' (ibid. 12).[13] Just as Leonard Shelby in the film *Memento* resorts to writing notes on paper and even on his own skin in the absence of a functioning memory, the archive can be seen as a symptom of memory loss. Nora expressed a similar sentiment when he proclaimed, in the introduction to *Lieux de mémoire*: 'We speak so much of memory because there is so little of it left' (1989: 7).

Derrida argues further that the very content of archives is influenced by the space and form in which it is stored: 'the technical structure of the *archiving* archive also determines the structure of the *archivable* content even in its very coming into existence and in its relationship to the future' (1995: 16). Thus, archives are not solely means of recording the past; according to Derrida, they also produce it. The same can be said to be true of memory itself. As Whitehead states, 'memory simultaneously transforms, so that a memory represents not a copy of an original but more precisely a version of it' (2009: 51). As these essays by Freud and Derrida show, age-old metaphors of storage and inscription continue to inspire new ways of theorising and problematising human memory. The digital age promises to generate new ways of conceptualising writing, storage and memory, and – not least of all – the complex connections between them.

The Acts of Editing and Reading

Frow proposes what he calls a textual model of memory as an alternative to models of inscription and space. This model emphasises 'the non-existence of the past, with the consequence that memory, rather than being the repetition of the physical traces of the past, is a construction of it under conditions and constraints determined by the present' (1997: 228). According to this conception, the past is open-ended, subject to revision and new interpretations. Memory, according to Frow's model, follows the logic of narrative and reading:

In such a model the past is a function of the system: rather than having a meaning and a truth determined once and for all by its status as event, its meaning and its truth are constituted retroactively and repeatedly; if time is reversible then alternative stories are always possible. Data are not stored in already constituted places but are arranged and rearranged at every point in time. Forgetting is thus an integral principle of this

---

13   Whitehead maintains that Plato's 'opposition to writing can be traced in a lasting and persistent distrust of the archive as constituted by written records, in contrast to living memory' (2009: 22).

>   *model, since the activity of compulsive interpretation that organizes it involves at once selection and rejection. (Frow 1997: 229)*

Memory and reading are, indeed, related in significant ways. The ability to follow and make sense of narratives is dependent on memory – hence the challenge presented by the analeptic plot of *Memento*. At the same time, the ability to interpret narratives – and memories – through ordering and contextualising requires a degree of forgetting. In these and other ways, the memory process resembles the reading process.

The inscriptive and spatial metaphors for memory can be extended to include other text-related activities. Editing is a suggestive metaphor for attempts to erase or revise memories of historical events, particularly within the context of repressive Communist regimes. For example, the eponymous protagonist of Olga Grushin's novel *The Dream Life of Sukhanov* is editor-in-chief of a Soviet art journal, and his work is described as tantamount to ideological censorship: 'Going through other people's texts as through dirty laundry, deleting every avoidable reference to God and lowercasing all the unavoidable ones, ferreting out the names of all the blacklisted artists, always sticking these Lenin quotes everywhere' (2005: 207). Significantly, the novel is set in the late-Soviet, early glasnost period, during which censorship was gradually lifted and archives were opened. Over the course of the narrative, Sukhanov begins to remember his own repressed past as a non-conformist artist, and he also comes to despise what he is expected to do as an editor.[14]

The act of reading serves as a fitting metaphor for recollection and interpretation. In the Russian novel *The Stone Bridge* (*Kamennyi most*, 2009) by Aleksandr Terekhov, a detective revisits a cold murder case from the Stalinist era, an undertaking which, significantly, entails a lot of reading. The plot is based on a historical occurrence in June 1943, when two teenage children were killed on Moscow's Great Stone Bridge. Six decades later, during the post-Soviet period, the narrator–protagonist reinvestigates the crime, interviewing three generations of Soviet citizens, tracking down relatives and friends of the victims, former diplomats, government officials, historians and writers, all of whom offer differing versions of events. The investigation leads the narrator to museums and graveyards, which not only offer clues, but are symbolic as spatial repositories of the past.

However, among all the investigative methods employed, the activity of reading occupies a special place. Over the course of the 829-page novel, the detective delves into a variety of texts, including archival material, love letters, newspaper articles, diary excerpts, witness testimony, interview transcripts, email correspondence, internet sites, biographies, memoirs and historical works. In the end, the solution to the crime remains unclear at best, buried in documents and subject to conflicting interpretations.

The novel ultimately poses more questions than it answers – about circumstances surrounding the tragic deaths on the bridge and the original investigation by the NKVD, as well as broader questions about the nature of historiography, human memory and understandings of the Soviet past. By bringing into play an abundance of texts, Terekhov's novel constantly reminds the reader that understandings of historical events are constructed through narratives. In the end, the novel draws merely tentative conclusions about the crime committed in 1943, while highlighting the vulnerability of texts and the unreliability of memory.

'Our present is still not on easy terms with how the past endures, with how it continues to occupy and preoccupy us', wrote Terdiman in his preface to *Present Modernity and the Past Memory Crisis* (1993: vii). If recent and ongoing struggles to come to terms with traumatic historical events are any indication, it is perhaps not realistic to expect that we will ever be

---

14   For an in-depth analysis of the theme of memory in Grushin's novel, see Hansen 2012.

on easy terms with the past. It seems more likely that memory and forgetting will continue to preoccupy philosophers, writers and readers and that literature will continue to imagine and question the past, as well as memory itself. And fiction will continue to serve as a memory companion in every sense.

References

Assmann, A. 2010. 'Canon and Archive', in Erll and Nünning 2010: 97–107.

Augé, M. 2004. *Oblivion*, trans. M. de Jager (Minneapolis: University of Minnesota Press).

Benjamin, W. 1986. 'A Berlin Chronicle', in *Reflections: Essays, Aphorisms, Autobiographical Writings*, ed. P. Demetz, trans. E. Jephcott (New York: Schocken Books), pp. 3–60.

Borges, J.L. 1993. 'Funes the Memorius', trans. A. Kerrigan in *Ficciones*, (New York: Knopf), pp. 83–91.

Byatt, A.S. 2009. 'Introduction', in H. Harvey Wood and A.S. Byatt (eds), *Memory: An Anthology* (London: Vintage), pp. xii–xx.

Carruthers, M. 2008. *The Book of Memory: A Study of Memory in Medieval Culture*, 2nd edn (Cambridge: Cambridge University Press).

Casey, E.S. 2000. *Remembering: A Phenomenological Study*, 2nd edn (Bloomington: Indiana University Press).

Cicero. 2001. *On the Ideal Orator*. trans. J.M. May and J. Wisse (Oxford: Oxford University Press).

Connerton, P. 2008. 'Seven Types of Forgetting', *Memory Studies* 1: 59–71.

Derrida, J. 1995. *Archive Fever: A Freudian Impression*, trans. E. Prenowitz (Chicago: University of Chicago Press).

— — 2001. 'Freud and the Scene of Writing', in *Writing and Difference*, trans. A. Bass (London: Routledge), pp. 246–91.

Draaisma, D. 2000. *Metaphors of Memory: A History of Ideas about the Mind*, trans. P. Vincent (Cambridge: Cambridge University Press).

Erll, A., and A. Nünning (eds) 2010. *A Companion to Cultural Memory Studies* (Berlin: De Gruyter).

Freud, S. 1984 [1925]. 'A Note upon the "Mystic Writing-Pad"', in *On Meta-Psychology: The Theory of Psychoanalysis*, ed. A. Richards, trans. J. Strachey (London: Penguin), pp. 427–34.

Frow. J. 1997. *Time and Commodity Culture: Essays in Cultural Theory and Postmodernity* (Oxford: Clarendon Press).

Grushin, O. 2005. *The Dream Life of Sukhanov* (New York: G.P. Putnam's Sons).

Hansen, J. 2012. 'Memory Unleashed by Perestroika: Olga Grushin's *The Dream Life of Sukhanov*', *Die Welt der Slaven* 57: 161–77.

Iser, W. 1997. 'Foreword', in R. Lachmann, *Memory and Literature: Intertextuality in Russian Modernism*, trans. R. Sellars and A. Wall (Minneapolis: University of Minneapolis Press), pp. vii–xviii.

Judt, T. 2002. 'The Past is Another Country: Myth and Memory in Post-War Europe', in J.-W. Müller (ed.), *Memory and Power in Post-War Europe: Studies in the Presence of the Past* (Cambridge: Cambridge University Press), pp. 157–83.

Knausgård, K.O. 2009–11. *Min kamp* [My Struggle] 6 vols. (Oslo: Oktober).

Kundera, M. 1981. *Kníha smíchu a zapomnění* [Book of Laughter and Forgetting] (Toronto: Sixty-Eight).

Lachmann, R. 2010. 'Mnemonic and Intertextual Aspects of Literature', in Erll and Nünning 2010: 301–10.

Nolan, C. (dir.) 2000. *Memento* [film] (Newmarket Films).

Nora, P. 1989. 'Between Memory and History: *Les Lieux de Mémoire*', trans. M. Roudebush, *Representations* 26: 7–24.

Plato 2004. *Theaetetus*, trans. R.A.H. Waterfield (London: Penguin).

Ricoeur. P. 2004. *Memory, History, Forgetting*, trans. K. Blamey and D. Pellauer (Chicago: University of Chicago Press).

Roediger, H.L. 1980. 'Memory Metaphors in Cognitive Psychology', *Memory and Cognition* 8: 231–46.

Rossington, M., and A. Whitehead (eds) 2007. *Theories of Memory: A Reader* (Edinburgh: Edinburgh University Press).

Terdiman. R. 1993. *Present Modernity and the Past Memory Crisis* (Ithaca, NY: Cornell University Press).

Terekhov, A. 2009. *Kamennyi most* [The Stone Bridge] (Moscow: AST/Astrel´).

Warnock, M. 1987. *Memory* (London: Faber & Faber).

Whitehead, A. 2009. *Memory* (London: Routledge).

Yates, F.A. 1966. *The Art of Memory* (Chicago: University of Chicago Press).

Yerushalmi, Y.H. 1982. *Zakhor: Jewish History and Jewish Memory* (Seattle: University of Washington Press).

Young, J.E. 2004. 'Foreword', in Augé 2004: vii–xii.

PART IV
Politics of Memory, Forgetting and Democracy

Memory and Methodological Cosmopolitanism: A Figurative Approach

Daniel Levy

Memory Studies and Its Trajectories

When the authors of this volume were asked 'to reflect on [y]our own work through the prism of [y]our companions', I was somewhat apprehensive. The social sciences never had the kind of personal awakening like say 'new journalism' or some of the humanities driven by a more subjective approach to writing, even if most of the research questions we pose involve some form of subjectivity and their intellectual sublimation. Yet this rarely detracts from the 'scientific' expectations heeded by most academics, to refrain from inserting themselves into their narratives. Detachment, *Wertfreiheit* and other tales from the scientific crib remain the standards that confer legitimacy on our work. So how to go about this unfamiliar genre without giving in to the temptations to unleash one's narcissistic *homo academicus*? I do not claim to have a satisfactory answer to this conundrum. What I will say though is that having to address the topic of memory (or any other substantive intellectual engagement for that matter) from this personal perspective carries the potential yield of an increase in reflexivity. So I hope that the following comments will generate productive insights on memory and its study. Accordingly, I want to take the chronology of my memory work as a trigger for some broader reflections on the field of memory studies.

I would like to map my deliberations onto the tripartite division Astrid Erll (2011) recently proposed in her essay 'Travelling Memory'. She distinguishes three periods in the study of (cultural) memory. Her starting point is the claims and impulses that the works of Maurice Halbwachs (1980, 1992) and Aby Warburg (Gombrich 1986) generated since the 1930s.[1] This initial phase is marked by a focus on how memory works in society and culture, followed by the 'memory boom' of the 1980s.

> *The focus thus shifted from the dynamics of memory in culture to the specific memories of (allegedly stable and clearly demarcated) cultures – the most popular social unit being the nation-state, which was then swiftly seen as isomorphic with*

---

1   The reception story, that is the diffusion of these French thinkers into the English-speaking realm is a crucial aspect of the development of the memory field. For a good overview see *The Collective Memory Reader* (Olick, Vinitzky-Seroussi and Levy 2011). Suffice it to point out here that the delayed yet successful introduction of Halbwachs during the 1990s in the Anglo-Saxon context was crucial (earlier attempts during the 1950s remained largely without any resonance). The work of Aby Warburg has yet to assume Halbwachs' status for memory scholars outside of Europe.

national culture and a national cultural memory. Memory studies thus entered the stage of 'national memory studies', which characterized much of the work done in the 1990s. (Erll 2011: 6)

As globalisation processes came into sharper relief, the pervasive and persistent explanatory power of 'methodological nationalism' in the social sciences in general, and memory studies in particular, appeared if not anachronistic certainly limited. Thus a third phase, trying to escape the national container, emerged. Erll labels this latest shift 'transcultural memory studies' suggesting:

For memory studies, the old-fashioned container-culture approach is not only somewhat ideologically suspect. It is also epistemologically flawed, because there are too many mnemonic phenomena that do not come into our field of vision with the 'default' combination of territorial, ethnic and national collectivity as the main framework of cultural memory – but which may be seen with the transcultural lens. (Erll 2011: 8)

It is this last and on-going phase in the development of memory studies which this essay will be focused on. There are numerous rationales for this. For one, despite constructive moves during this third phase, sifting through the countless case studies on memory reveals that the national remains the empirical and conceptual focus of most scholars. Plus, asked to reflect on my intellectual undercurrents, my own scholarly efforts of the last 15 years have revolved around and contributed to situating the study of memory in an interdependent global world.

Before addressing the global-memory nexus, I must mention Jeffrey Olick who introduced me to memory studies in the mid-1990s. I was fortunate to meet him at a time when interest in memory was still somewhat rare in mainstream sociology (some would contend that it still is). It was our shared interest in the political culture of West Germany that set the foundations for an ongoing conversation. His near encyclopaedic command of the literature coupled with a sharp analytic mind and a passion for theory made him a formidable companion. We quickly delved into a series of discussions. Before long we started our first research project, resulting in a joint publication in 1997 about the ways in which different modalities of collective memory (distinguishing between taboos and prohibitions) constrain political claim-making (Olick and Levy 1997).

Aside from the case specific findings, our main conceptual point centred on the processual quality of memory-making and the importance of historical trajectories in general. We argued that 'conceiving of collective memory as part of a political-cultural process thus remedies the presuppositional tendency to view it either as an unchanging and definitive past or as pure strategy, always malleable in the present' (Olick and Levy 1997: 923). Our endeavour was squarely situated within the national container characteristic of the second phase. It also underscored the path-dependent and historicising approach to memory. This processual approach is also evidenced in our latest joint publication, namely the conceptualisation and introduction to *The Collective Memory Reader* where we (together with Vered Vinitzky-Seroussi) put forward a somewhat revisionist view of the genealogy of memory studies (Olick, Vinitzky-Seroussi and Levy 2011). After nearly two decades, Olick remains my interlocutor on all matters mnemonic.

Cosmopolitan Memories and the Critique of Methodological Nationalism

It is my decade long collaboration with Natan Sznaider, however, which carries the greatest impact on my recent scholarly trajectory. His originality, historical sensibilities and deep knowledge of social and political theory have left indelible traces on my intellectual biography. Since the late 1990s we have been discussing and developing our thoughts on memory in the global age. We started exploring the impact of globalisation on memory cultures, which were hitherto examined within the context of bounded structures, primarily the nation. We asked: What happens when the self-understanding of an increasing number of people, primarily (but not solely) in the West, is no longer determined exclusively through references to the nation? How do memory practices shape collective orientations outside national boundaries? What role do emerging forms of memory have for the reconfiguration of national sovereignty?

The pursuit of these questions culminated in our first joint monograph in 2001, *Die Erinnerung im Globalen Zeitalter: Der Holocaust*.[2] The book explores the historical and theoretical foundations for the emergence of what we refer to as 'cosmopolitan memories'. The national container, we contended, has been in the process of being slowly cracked resulting in the emergence of cosmopolitan memory-scapes. Processes of 'internal globalisation' during the last three decades suggest that issues of global concern are able to become part and parcel of everyday local experiences and moral life-worlds of an increasing number of people.

National and ethnic memories are transformed in the age of globalisation rather than erased. They continue to exist, of course, but globalisation processes also imply that different national memories are subjected to a common patterning. They begin to develop in accord with common rhythms and periodisations. But in each case, the common elements combine with pre-existing elements to form something new. In each case, the new, global narrative has to be reconciled with the old, national narratives, and the result is always distinctive (Levy and Sznaider 2002: 89).

Since then the critique of nation-centric assumptions has spread and numerous scholars have made important contributions to studying memory beyond the exclusive purview of the nation-state.[3] By now the concept of cosmopolitan memories has become a standard reference point and has been applied productively to different contexts, both Western and non-Western.[4] We also observed how the proliferation of cosmopolitan norms has resulted in

---

2   The book was conceived during the late nineties. A revised English version *The Holocaust and Memory in the Global Age* was published in 2006. To the best of my knowledge, and in a bit of shameless self-promotion, we were among the conceptual progenitors of this third (memory) wave. Jeffrey Alexander's 2002 article 'On the Social Construction of Moral Universals' added valuable insights to this emerging field. Another contributor to this initial interest in the impact of globalization on memory was Andreas Huyssen. His 'Present Pasts' (2000) is an important contribution as were his expanded thoughts in a later book (Huyssen 2003). Together we were at the forefront criticising the nation-centric fallacy of memory studies. Our respective critiques were conceived around the same time and set the stage for ensuing and ongoing discussions about transnational, transcultural and related global manifestation of mnemonic practices.

3   Among the theoretically most generative are Michael Rothberg's concept of 'multidirectionality' (2009); Astrid Erll's notion of 'traveling memory' (2011) and earlier elaborations (Erll and Nünning 2008); and the work of Richard Crownshaw (Crownshaw, Kilby and Rowland 2010). Ann Rigney also takes a decisively global turn (2012). Alison Landsberg's master concept of 'prosthetic memories' (2004) was another earlier entry. These are but a few whose work implies a forceful critique of a prevailing methodological nationalism.

4   The corpus of memory related works including globalised modes of memory practices is by now vast. To get a sense of its extent see 'Memory Studies Bank' which contains over 4,000 memory related references and is growing rapidly: <http://www.stonybrook.edu/mid/msb/about.html>.

the re-nationalisation of memory discourses. These findings have misled some to reproduce the binary suggesting that the cosmopolitan contradicts the national. I will address this misperception in the next section.

Cosmopolitanism and Its Discontents

Reservations about the impact of globalisation and the concomitant 'cosmopolitan turn' involve the aforementioned juxtaposition of the national and the cosmopolitan. As indicated above, some also tend to misinterpret the cosmopolitan analysis of memory cultures as a quasi-teleological instance of linearity and related charges of a homogenising universalism.[5] What these critics share is a resilient methodological nationalism, marked by a lack of reflexivity toward established conceptual categories. In the following I demonstrate that cosmopolitan figurations are characterised by non-linear contingent manifestations and the validation of particularism. And that methodological cosmopolitanism is no longer related to the normative Kantian vision of cosmopolitanism, but refers to an analytical tool kit exploring processes of cosmopolitanisation, including the transformation but not the transcendence of the nation.

The conventional concept of collective memory remains embedded within the container of the nation-state assuming that memory community and geographical proximity, belong together. Some consider globalisation as something that dissolves collective memory and sets up inauthentic and rootless substitutes in its stead. Anthony Smith typifies this view: 'A timeless global culture answers to no living needs and conjures no memories. If memory is central to identity, we can discern no global identity in the making' (1995: 24). Why can it conjure no memories? Because timelessness is of its essence: 'This artificial and standardized universal culture has no historical background, no developmental rhythm, no sense of time and sequence. … Alien to all ideas of "roots," the genuine global culture is fluid, ubiquitous, formless and historically shallow' (ibid. 22). Smith's statement is emblematic of two fallacies: the restriction of memory to the symbolic boundaries of the nation and a view that juxtaposes real lived experiences and inauthentic mediated representations.

Pierre Nora, the doyen of the memory boom is perhaps the most influential exponent of this view. His book *Les lieux de mémoire* is a touchstone in the literature.[6] Nora distinguishes between the social environments, or milieu, of memory and the sites that have been set up to preserve the memory of events. He sees the latter as a substitute for living traditions. 'Memorial sites exist because the social environment of memory exists no longer, the surroundings in which memory is an essential component of everyday experience' (1996–98: vol. 1, p. 1), echoing Smith's distinction between authentic memories and their substitutes. Implied here is the assumption that impersonal representations are mere ersatz and not connected to

---

5   A representative example of this kind of 'universalistic (mis)reading' of our arguments can be found in a 2010 volume edited by Aleida Assmann and Sebastian Conrad entitled *Memory in a Global Age. Discourses, Practices and Trajectories*.

6   Nora's influence on American memory studies can be dated to the publication of his 1989 article in *Representations*. Followed by the English publication of the multi-volume work *Realms of Memory* in 1996–98. This magnum opus was not merely translated into many languages but also applied to numerous countries documenting key national memorial sites. Paradoxically, though probably not unintended considering Nora's stern Republicanism, the scholarly production of the monumental *Realms of Memory* itself was a factor for the reproduction of the memory–nation link. It sought to reinforce the solidity and meaningfulness of national sites of memory. And indeed, one of the reasons that Nora was so adamant about the project was his realization that the centrality of the nation had diminished.

our 'real' emotions and identities. The actual history of the nation-state and its formation is instructive for debunking this essentialised argument. Nora's view essentially restates the sentimental nineteenth-century antagonism between *Gesellschaft* and *Gemeinschaft*, which opposed the new, nation-wide structures to those of local communities. It claimed that larger structures were soulless. And part of this soullessness lay in their impersonal means of communications, like newspapers. But the argument turned out to be a romantic and nostalgic one. Mechanical representations did not stand in the way of strong identifications but facilitated them. The centrality of collective means and modes of communication for the nascent nation-state was already addressed by Karl Deutsch and Richard Merritt (1953). Two pivotal works during the so-called 'constructivist turn' during the 1980s confirmed this. Benedict Anderson's *Imagined Communities* (1983) and Eric Hobsbawm and Terence Ranger's equally influential notion of 'invented traditions' (1984). Together they pretty much quelled attempts at essentialising the nation and attendant conceptions of groupness.[7]

Our critique of methodological nationalists like Nora is thus directed against their implied normative claims and the (static) fixation on the nation-state as the sole possible (and imaginable) source for the articulation of collective memories. The ideological tenor of Nora's national conceptual vocabulary is accentuated by the fact that he recognises and regrets the impact of global transformations and the de-coupling of state and society along with the diminishing returns of the national. Hence he laments that 'the acceleration of history, then, confronts us with the brutal realization of the difference between real memory and history, which is how our hopelessly forgetful modern societies, propelled by change, organize the past' (Nora 1989: 8). Along with this transformation, Nora notes that the transmission of memory has expanded to social forces outside the realm of the state. 'The coupling of state and nation was gradually replaced by the coupling of state and society' (ibid. 11). No longer is the nation-state the uncontested privileged site for the articulation of collective memories. Nora points to and deplores the erosion of the state's ability to impose a unitary and unifying framework of memory. He constructs an opposition that is reminiscent of the *fin de siècle* syndrom, based on the abstract assumption that modernity destroyed tradition. While Nora bemoans the demise of nation-state dominance, we are underscoring the significance these changes have empirically and for our conceptual tool kits.

Let me briefly return to some bones of contention with the critics of cosmopolitan analysis. They view it as being teleological, too optimistic and underwritten by a universalistic Kantian understanding of cosmopolitanism. This cartoonish straw-man version is counterproductive. Especially since the field of cosmopolitan studies is increasingly characterised by its attentiveness to contingency, path-dependent validations of the particular and transformations (and not transcendence) of nationhood. All of these components are already manifest in our early work on Holocaust memory.

In *The Holocaust and Memory in the Global Age* we illustrated some of these transformative dynamics through an examination of how the Holocaust has been remembered in Germany, Israel and the USA during five decades between the 1940s and the late 1990s. Our central argument was:

> *The Holocaust has been confronted by various forces, which have attempted to universalize it, to particularize it, and to nationalize it. But recently this memory has continued to exist on a global level. Its strength as a global collective memory has been powered and maintained precisely through the fiery interaction between the local and the global. We argue that this dual process of particularization and universalization has produced a symbol of transnational solidarity that is based on a cosmopolitanized*

---

7   For a poignant critique of categorical and ahistorical group attributions, see Brubaker 1996.

> memory – one that does not replace national collective memories but exists as their horizon. (Levy and Sznaider 2002: 93)

The cosmopolitanisation of memories then should not be situated in the context of either universal or particular orientations.

> Instead of reducing these terms to their ideological assumptions, we treat them as an important object in our investigation. We historicize notions of particularism and universalism, thereby de-moralizing them while retaining them as valuable sociological tools. Our primary objective is to disentangle these terms from their conventional 'either–or' perspective and understand them in terms of 'as well as' options. … Consequently speaking about the cosmopolitization of Holocaust memory does not imply some progressive universalism subject to a unified interpretation. The Holocaust does not become one totalizing signifier containing the same meanings for everyone. Rather its meanings evolve from the encounter of global interpretations and local sensibilities. … The cosmopolitanization of memory does not mean the end of national perspectives so much as their transformation into more complex entities where different social groups have different relations to globalization. (Levy and Sznaider 2002: 92)

In other words, it is the very encounter between the global and the local and the universal and the particular (whereby the latter pairing does not necessarily map onto the former) that is reflective of and contributes to cosmopolitanisation. On this view, the West might be dominant in terms of its capacity to diffuse world cultural models, but it does so neither inevitably nor in a homogenising fashion. Gerard Delanty puts it succinctly:

> Despite the western genealogy of the word cosmopolitanism, the term is used today in a 'post-western' register of meaning. Cosmopolitanism, as used here, does not assume the generalizability of western historical experiences and instead takes experiences that are relevant to all societies and for which there may be different conceptual genealogies. In this sense, cosmopolitanism is a 'post-western' orientation that is located neither on the national nor global level, but at the interface of the local and the global (Delanty 2012b: 335–6).

Staking out the broader theoretical and methodological agenda of cosmopolitan studies, Ulrich Beck and Natan Sznaider sought 'to overcome the naive universalism of early Western sociology. Methodological cosmopolitanism implies becoming sensitive and open to the many universalisms, the conflicting contextual universalisms' (Beck and Sznaider 2006b: 13).[8] Delanty has referred to this as post-universal, in the sense of

> a relativatization of universalism that the epistemological framework of cosmopolitanism is a post-universalism since it stands for a universalism that does not demand universal assent or that everyone identifies with a single interpretation. Depending on the social context or historical situation, social actors will interpret universal rules differently and put them to different use. … By this is simply meant that statements of truth and justice etc. are not absolute, immutable or derivable from an objective order of universal values, but nonetheless it is still possible to make

---

8   An excellent historical–sociological case study for the pertinence of the particular within the universal is Sznaider 2011.

judgments and evaluations, the universalistic strength of which will vary depending on the context of application. (Delanty 2012b: 337)

It would be easy to dismiss these positions as relativistic, but as the empirical works of neo-institutionalists show there is broad consensus on world cultural models (e.g. rationality, education). At the same time they identify significant discrepancies among countries, that is a de-coupling of intended goals and actual applications (Meyer et al. 1997). I will address both trajectories, that is, the global diffusion of cosmopolitan values and practices, on the one hand, and the local appropriation of these scripts, on the other. Cosmopolitan scales are a crucial characteristic of methodological cosmopolitanism stressing processual, relational and situational dimensions.

This scaled approach also stands at the centre of our second monograph addressing the intersection of human rights and memory (Levy and Sznaider 2010). We examined how memories of the Holocaust have evolved into a universal code synonymous with an imperative to address past injustices (both legally as well as in commemorative terms). Although the 'memory imperative' originated with the centrality of Holocaust memories during the 1990s, it has become a decontextualised code for human-rights abuses as such. Nation-states engage (or are expected to) with their own history in a sceptical fashion. This dynamic, we argued, explains both the importance of human-rights norms as a globally available repertoire of legitimate claim making and the differential appropriation of this universal command..

We demonstrated how, at different historical junctures and through the proliferation of memories of past injustices, the discourse of human rights and memories of past human-rights abuses have developed into a powerful idiom vested with legitimacy. The discourse of human rights and its legal inscriptions has grown into a cultural and political force substantially re-configuring the basis of legitimate sovereignty the scope of political responsibility, and forms of belonging. The accretion of political, cultural, and institutional capital through the human-rights regime has resulted in a substantial reconfiguration of state sovereignty (Levy and Sznaider 2006a), an extension of political responsibilities and new forms of cosmopolitan solidarity (Beck and Levy 2013). Rather than start from an abstract notion of political interests we probed how, once institutionalised, human-rights idioms themselves constitute political interests. Memory politics of human rights have become a new form of political rationality and a prerequisite for state legitimacy. Sovereign rhetoric is increasingly evaluated by the extent to which it is related to the legal recognition of human rights. Memory clashes abound and provide ample evidence that the prominence of human rights does not imply the end of the national and, at times, even raise the spectre of exclusionary renationalisation or re-tribalisation. We are thus not suggesting that this global context implies an end of the nation. On the contrary, perceptions of globalisation are frequently the main trigger for nationalistic rhetoric. And clearly the identification with non-national realms is nothing new. However, the contemporary intensity, extensity and volatility of these processes is unparalleled and has become part of a self-conscious reflexive approach among many political elites around the world as their legitimacy frequently depends on their commitment to such cosmopolitan tropes.

Cosmopolitan Memory Studies

Let us now move from this defensive terrain (on which scholars pursuing epistemological correctives frequently find themselves) and advance a cosmopolitan framework. This brings me to Ulrich Beck, my third companion, who coined the term 'methodological cosmopolitanism'. We have collaborated for over a decade and his theoretical ingenuity has been nothing short of inspirational. Together we are systematising the conditions for such a cosmopolitan framework.

What is at (empirical and conceptual) stake is not the transcendence of the nation-state but its transformation. As indicated above, the cosmopolitan memory thesis has frequently been misunderstood as a description in which the nation-state is overcome. Two presuppositions inform this misperception: one views cosmopolitanism in a Kantian fashion and conflates the aspirational language of a normative cosmopolitanism with the sociological approach towards cosmopolitanisation; the other refers to the binarism that views nationalism and cosmopolitanism as antithetical.

The difference between the propagation of cosmopolitanism as an ideal and the study of cosmopolitan realities is quite telling. Reflected in the renewed interest political theorists have shown in the concept since the 1990s, the initial focus revolved around its normative potential in a global age. It was Martha Nussbaum's (1996) revival of a universalistic Kantian understanding of the term, which triggered a wide range of critical response. For the most part, the ensuing debates have centred, around the question of whether it is possible to expand solidaristic fellow-feelings beyond the national. Potential scenarios range from utopian notions of world citizenship to visions in which universal orientations and particular attachments co-exist (Appiah 1997). While these debates have no doubt contributed to the burgeoning field of cosmopolitan studies, they also have reinforced the misperception that cosmopolitanism is primarily a normative stance and an elite phenomenon. This limited purview is further compounded by the fact that cosmopolitanism is frequently treated as a concept with categorical qualities reflected in a static 'ism' (Fine 2003).

Scholars have responded by attempting to ground cosmopolitanism sociologically. At the forefront of these efforts, Beck has redirected attention to a process-oriented notion of cosmopolitanisation and its attendant realities.[9] Whereas cosmopolitanism refers to a philosophical-normative theory, cosmopolitanisation is a factum and a social-scientific research programme beyond the confines of methodological nationalism (Beck 2002, 2006; Beck and Sznaider 2006). Unlike older philosophical engagements with cosmopolitanism as a universalistic principle, the sociological dynamics of cosmopolitanisation imply an interactive relationship between the global and the local. It is a 'non-linear, dialectical process in which the universal and particular, the similar and the dissimilar, the global and the local are to be conceived not as cultural polarities, but as interconnected and reciprocally interpenetrating principles' (Beck 2006: 72–3).

The proliferation of cosmopolitan studies among social scientists has shifted the focus away from normative approaches. Instead explorations of cosmopolitan realities and practices have taken centre stage. This is not the place for a literature review: suffice it to say that much of this research has been driven by a common perception about the crisis of the hitherto hegemonic national mode of belonging. And indeed, the concept of the national is often perceived, both in public and academic discourse, as the central obstacle to the realisation of cosmopolitan belonging. Consequently, debates about the nation misleadingly revolve around its persistence or its demise and not only among those who adhere to methodological nationalism.[10]

---

9   The list of conceptual works tackling issues of methodological cosmopolitanism is too exhaustive to be detailed in this essay. For good overviews, see Beck and Sznaider 2006b; Delanty 2012a; Skrbiš and Woodward 2013.

10   Incidentally, this binary fallacy epitomises the ahistorical bias among scholars who fail to distinguish between earlier processes of nationalisation and later manifestations of nationalism. As Eugen Weber (1976) has shown for France, while nationalism eventually became a potent idea

> *Regardless of their understanding that the nation is a constructed category, most cosmopolitan scholars accept that it is or was the natural and rational form of socio-political organization in the modern age, i.e. that it is or was the organizing principle of political modernity. This curiously re-natured view of the nation-state mirrors the modernism it opposes (Fine and Chernilo 2004: 36).*

The presuppositions of nationhood and statehood, as well as, the histories through which both have been linked (as the composite noun 'nation-state' suggests), remain largely untouched. Cosmopolitanism too is often articulated in opposition to this conventional (i.e. naturalised) and inevitable version of the nation.[11] Accordingly, nationalism and cosmopolitanism are frequently conceptualised as part of an unchanging zero-sum game.

Some scholars have moved away from this 'either–or' perspective and emphasised how cosmopolitan orientations can complement the national (Skrbiš and Woodward 2013). 'In the contemporary world, human beings often combine profound local, ethnic, religious or national attachments with a commitment to cosmopolitan values and principles that transcend those more local boundaries' (Kymlicka and Walker 2012). This view of cosmopolitanism as complementary to nationalism represents an important step forward. However, it does not sufficiently focus on how cosmopolitan processes are intersecting and potentially transforming the idea of the national itself. After all, 'because nationhood – both conceptually and in practice – is malleable, there is no reason to believe that nations will not be perpetually imagined, even though such imaginings will change in content and form' (Croucher 2003: 2). It is therefore not sufficient to recognise that the nation is a historically constructed category, but essential to explore how this malleability and contingency of nationhood evolves in a global context. Whereas the constructed nature of nationalism is widely recognised, the national is now naturalised in the sense that the future of nationhood is too often no longer addressed from a constructivist perspective. Beck and Levy, therefore, warn that 'rather than deploying cosmopolitanism as a normative desideratum, or as antithesis to an essentialized version of the national, [we contend that] cosmopolitanization is a constitutive feature for the reconfiguration of nationhood itself and emerging features of orientation, identification and belonging' (2013: 5).

To understand how past and present narratives of nationhood are related to each other and how the universal and the particular are crystallised into processes of cosmopolitanisation, I propose to think about cosmo-national imaginaries in Norbert Elias's figurative terms of a 'continuum of changes' (1992). Meaningful political and cultural premises are informed by significant pasts, presents that are being transformed and different horizons of future expectations.[12] On this view, collective modes of identification and memory that are perceived as legitimate may change over time; however, their respective meanings remain linked 'by

---

and basis for solidarity, much time and ideological labour was required until real existing national structures trickled down and became dominant. At the beginning of the twenty-first century we are witnessing several (partly concentric) circles of real existing cosmopolitanisation, which may or may not, culminate in the internalisation and emergence of cosmopolitanism. Conversely, and continuing the historical analogy with the national, cosmopolitanisation may spur strong anti-cosmopolitanism – as much as nationalism initially triggered strong resistance (e.g. early twentieth-century cosmopolitanism).

11   A notable exception can be found in the work of Gerard Delanty. He suggests that cosmopolitanism and nationalism, while in tension, are nevertheless linked, producing nations without nationalism in the contemporary global environment (2006: 358).

12   A shared sense of the past becomes a meaning-making repository, which helps define aspirations for the future. In his historical analysis of times and temporalities Reinhart Koselleck points out that the present is situated between past experiences which is 'present past, whose events have been incorporated and can be remembered' and a horizon of expectations which refers to 'the

a long continuum of changes'. Elias' methodological deliberations on historical processes seem particularly beneficial for the study of epochal changes and emerging mnemonic figurations, which form by mixing old and new elements. Hence the persistence of older structures (and norms) cannot be interpreted as a mere anachronism – as modernisation theorists did with religion and ethnicity. Rejecting any kind of self-sustaining logic of development, Elias instead focuses on the historical and institutional conditions through which cultural and political claims are established and inscribed as foundational meaning systems. Their respective dominance is largely a function of changing figurations.

Among scholars who are attentive to the processual and relational requirements of a thorough methodological cosmopolitanism, Delanty's views are of particular value for our understanding of the cosmopolitanisation of memory cultures. Delanty describes 'four main kinds of cosmopolitan relationships, which together constitute the social ontology of cosmopolitanism. These are the relativisation of identity, the positive recognition of the other, the mutual evaluation of cultures, and the creation of a normative world culture' (2012b: 333). He develops a framework 'that distinguishes between the preconditions of cosmopolitanism, its social mechanisms and processes (of which three are specified: generative, transformational and institutionalizing) and trajectories of historical change' (ibid.).

This framework has numerous virtues. For one, it pre-empts the kind of universalistic (and at times linear) assumptions that have guided methodological nationalism. Early forms of modernisation theory are perhaps the most flagrant example for this. For a variety of reasons, a processual–relational perspective underwriting methodological cosmopolitanism is less susceptible to accusations of ethno-centrism and universalism. To be sure, early articulations of cosmopolitan sociology were drawn largely from the Western and even more limited European experience. There is, of course, nothing wrong with that historically, considering the origins of the term and its diffusion, yet it has become apparent that the conditions of possibility for the spread and expressions of cosmopolitanism reveal a great degree of variety. While the contemporary origins of cosmopolitanism are European, research about non-European settings cannot assume a universalised cosmopolitan model, implying a particular developmental path and presupposing political and cultural flows from the centre to the periphery.[13]

Another important analytic move to avoid the categorical fallacy of a homogenous and static notion of cosmopolitanism refers to the significance of the situational properties of cosmopolitanization. Needless to say this situational dimension is not unique to cosmopolitanism but also applies to the historical trajectories of nationalism. Both operate on a continuum that involves strong, weak and, no less important, self-contradictory manifestations. The incorporation of a situational perspective is indispensable when we consider that cosmopolitan practices are circumscribed by temporal, spatial and material structures (Woodward and Skrbiš 2013). Thus instead of categorizing cosmopolitan

---

future made present, it points to the not-yet, to that which has not been experienced, to that which can only be discovered' (1985: 272).

13   Elsewhere I have shown how the relationship between core and periphery itself is subject to a recursive relationship (Levy 2010). To capture the tension of 'synchronicity' and 'path-dependency' I introduced the notion of 'recursive cosmopolitanisation'. The concept refers to an open-ended process in which centre and periphery stand in a recursive relationship that is reflected, among other things, in the intercrossings of global normative expectations and their local appropriations. Moreover, recursive cosmopolitisation also reveals how local articulations are inscribed into global norms. By unpacking a variety of cosmopolitan iterations, Beck and Edgar Grande too are providing a corrective for teleological temptations, which tend to generalise a Western path. 'The idea of cosmopolitan modernity must be developed out of the variety of modernities, out of the inner wealth of variants of modernity' (Beck and Grande 2010).

memories as ideal-typical formations, we concur with Ian Woodward and Zlatko Skrbiš who theorise cosmopolitanism 'as [a] flexible, available set of cultural practices and outlooks which are selectively mobilized depending on social and cultural contexts' (ibid. 129). This approach looks not for 'fixed and stable attributes, but to the performative, situational and accomplished dimensions of being cosmopolitan. That is, it understands cosmopolitanism as an expression in particular social contexts and settings' (ibid.). Woodward and Skrbiš suggest:

> *Cosmopolitanism is never an absolute or fixed category that resides simply within some individuals more than others, but a dimension of social life that must be actively constructed through practices of meaning making in social situations. ... While claiming to be a universal position of cultural inclusiveness and generosity, it is in fact a culturally located and environmentally enabled viewpoint, which is itself based in a regime of value-attribution. (Woodward and Skrbiš 2013: 132)*

This situational dimension then is a crucial component underscoring how, depending on the situation, people can weave in and out of particular memory constellations.

Outlook

In conclusion, studying memory from a cosmopolitan perspective is part of a larger epistemological project. Reflecting on our critique of methodological nationalism underscores how the resilience of national-methodological categories is obfuscating our grasp of the cosmopolitanisation of global mnemonics. It also sheds light on the propensity for how both observers (scholars) and actors are prone to engage in reductionism by way of reification. While the actor's attempts at naturalising collective identities are valuable data, the observer's tendencies to essentialise categories should be treated as preventable professional deformations. Despite the fact that it is commonplace to recognise the constructivist aspects of concepts, de-naturalise the categories we use as observers and recognise the malleability characterising how people ascribe meanings to their memory practices, reification remains a potential hazard for our analysis. Put differently, there is a tendency (driven partly by a lack of reflexivity as well as practical considerations of deploying familiar – that is, non-controversial – terms) among scholars to reify and ultimately ossify the categories they use. Which is one of the reasons for methodological nationalism to remain the privileged taken-for-granted perspective. No doubt, it owes some of its scholarly success (or longevity) to turning the malleable process of nationalism into variable-oriented categories and other practices privileging static over process. Unless we explicitly address these traps common to knowledge production, methodological cosmopolitanism too might fall prey to this kind of categorical thinking and attendant modalities of essentialising.

A case in point illustrating these predicaments and the opportunities that a more reflexive-cosmopolitan approach affords is Halbwachs' key concept of 'social frameworks'. Enabling and restraining collective memories, the historical, relational and situational facets of social frameworks themselves must be part of our analytic and empirical focus. Put differently, the salience and composition of particular social cadres and their normative validation is in flux before becoming a stable mnemonic framework of reference. Halbwachs, for instance, referred to professional organisations as powerful sources for collective memory production. Clearly these institutions have been profoundly transformed since, raising questions about their mnemonic impact. Membership of a guild encompassed sentiments of trust, loyalty and other aspects transcending the mere functionality of a 'job'. This cannot be said of the tenuous professional environments most people are embedded in today.

Neither cosmopolitanism nor nationalism provides an adequate interpretive framework when treated in isolation. This is also evident when we interrogate the alleged stability of 'cultural memory' as defined by Jan Assmann.

> *Just as the communicative memory is characterized by its proximity to the everyday, cultural memory is characterized by its distance from the everyday. Distance from the everyday (transcendence) marks its temporal horizon. Cultural memory has its fixed point; its horizon does not change with the passing of time. These fixed points are fateful events of the past, whose memory is maintained through cultural formation (texts, rites, monuments) and institutional communication (recitation, practice, observance). (Assmann 1995: 128–9)*

While this might hold true for religious practices (and even here 'fixed points' are subject to contestation), arguably this can not be applied to, say, 'national myths', which are subject to different generational experiences, to name but one aspect of non-fixity. To be sure, I am not questioning the potency some events have for collective memory, but I do not see any compelling conceptual reason to transform them into fixed points. That, after all, remains the contested terrain on which memory entrepreneurs seek to privilege their respective frameworks.

A cosmopolitan perspective, I hope to have shown, provides a more appropriate analytic perspective for a globally interconnected world in tune with processual, relational and situational dynamics. Supported by, among others, the proliferation of travelling trans-national, trans-cultural and multidirectional approaches to the study of memory. My point here then is not (only) to challenge the accepted (conceptual) wisdom of our fields of knowledge but, rather, to issue a call for a continuous reflexive engagement with our vocabulary of motives (frequently masquerading as timeless theories). If methodological nationalism had its merits in the context of post-feudal and post-imperial nation-state formation, methodological cosmopolitanism provides the appropriate heuristic for the global age.

References

Alexander, J. 2002. 'On the Social Construction of Moral Universals: The "Holocaust" from War Crime to Trauma Drama', *European Journal of Social Theory* 5/1: 5–85.

Anderson, B.R. 2006 [1983]. *Imagined Communities: Reflections on the Origin and Spread of Nationalism* (London: Verso).

Appiah, K.A. 1997. 'Cosmopolitan Patriots', *Critical Inquiry* 23/3 (Spring): 617–39.

Assmann, J. 1995. 'Collective Memory and Cultural Identity', trans. J. Czaplicka, *New German Critique* 65 (Spring/ Summer): 125–33.

— — and S. Conrad 2010. *Memory in a Global Age: Discourses, Practices and Trajectories* (Basingstoke: Palgrave Macmillan).

Beck, U. 2002. 'The Cosmopolitan Society and Its Enemies', *Theory, Culture and Society* 19/1–2: 17–44.

— — 2006. *The Cosmopolitan Vision* (Cambridge: Polity Press).

— — and D. Levy 2013. 'Cosmopolitanized Nations: Re-imagining Collectivity in World Risk Society', *Theory, Culture and Society* 30/2: 3–31.

— — and E. Grande 2010. 'Varieties of Second Modernity: The Cosmopolitan Turn in Social and Political Theory and Research', *British Journal of Sociology* 61: 409–43.

— — and N. Sznaider 2006a. 'A Literature on Cosmopolitanism: An Overview', *British Journal of Sociology* 57: 153–64.

— — and — — 2006b. 'Unpacking Cosmopolitanism for the Social Sciences: A Research Agenda', *British Journal of Sociology* 57: 1–23.

Brubaker, R. 1996. *Nationalism Reframed: Nationhood and the National Question in the New Europe* (Cambridge: Cambridge University Press).

Croucher, S. 2003. 'Perpetual Imagining: Nationhood in a Global Era', *International Studies Review* 5: 1–24.

Crownshaw, R., J. Kilby and A. Rowland (eds) 2010. *The Future of Memory* (New York: Berghahn).

Delanty, G. 2006. 'Nationalism and Cosmopolitanism: The Paradox of Modernity', in G. Delanty and K. Kumar (eds), *The Sage Handbook of Nations and Nationalism* (London: Sage), pp. 357–68.

— — 2012a. *The Routledge Handbook of Cosmopolitanism Studies* (London: Routledge).

— — 2012b. 'A Cosmopolitan Approach to the Explanation of Social Change', *Sociological Review* 60: 333–54.

Deutsch, K., and R. Merritt 1953. *Nationalism and Social Communication: An Inquiry into the Foundations of Nationality* (Cambridge, MA: MIT Press).

Elias, N. 1992. *Time: An Essay*, trans. E. Jephcott (Oxford: Oxford University Press).

Erll, A. 2011. 'Travelling Memory', *Parallax* 17/4: 4–18.

— — and A. Nünning (eds) 2008. *Cultural Memory Studies: An International and Interdisciplinary Handbook* (Berlin: De Gruyter).

Fine, R. 2003. 'Taking the "ISM" out of Cosmopolitanism: An Essay in Reconstruction', *European Journal of Social Theory* 6: 451–70.

— — and D. Chernilo 2004. 'Between Past and Future: The Equivocations of New Cosmopolitanism', *Studies in Law Politics and Society* 31: 25–44.

Gombrich, E.H. 1986. *Aby Warburg: An Intellectual Biography* (Chicago: University of Chicago Press).

Halbwachs, M. 1980. *The Collective Memory*, trans. F.J. Ditter Jr. and V. Yazdi Ditter (New York: Harper & Row).

— — 1992. *On Collective Memory*, trans. L.A. Coser (Chicago: University of Chicago Press).

Hobsbawm, E.J, and T.O. Ranger (eds) 1984. *The Invention of Tradition* (Cambridge: Cambridge University Press).

Huyssen, A. 2000. 'Present Pasts: Media, Politics, Amnesia', *Public Culture* 12: 21–38.

— — 2003. *Present Pasts: Urban Palimpsests and the Politics of Memory*, Cultural Memory in the Present (Stanford, CA: Stanford University Press).

Koselleck, R. 1985. *Futures Past: On the Semantics of Historical Time*, trans. K. Tribe (New York: Columbia University Press).

Kymlicka, W., and K. Walker 2012. *Rooted Cosmopolitanism: Canada and the World* (Vancouver and Toronto: University of British Columba Press).

Landsberg, A. 2004. *Prosthetic Memory: The Transformation of American Remembrance in the Age of Mass Culture* (New York: Columbia University Press).

Levy, D. 2010. 'Recursive Cosmopolitanisation: Argentina and the Global Human Rights Regime', *British Journal of Sociology* 61: 579–96.

— — and N. Sznaider 2001. *Die Erinnerung im Globalen Zeitalter: Der Holocaust* (Frankfurt: Suhrkamp Verlag).

— — and — — 2002. 'Memory Unbound: The Holocaust and the Formation of Cosmopolitan Memory', *European Journal of Social Theory* 5: 87–106.

— — and — — 2006. *The Holocaust and Memory in the Global Age*, trans. A. Oksiloff (Philadelphia: Temple University Press).

— — and — — 2010. *Human Rights and Memory* (University Park: Pennsylvania State University Press).

Meyer, J.W., et al. 1997. 'World Society and the Nation-State', *American Journal of Sociology* 103: 144–81.

Nora, P. 1989. 'Between Memory and History: Les Lieux de Mémoire', *Representations* 26 (1 Apr.): 7–24.

— — (ed.) 1996–98. *Realms of Memory: Rethinking the French Past*, 3 vols, trans. A. Goldhammer (New York: Columbia University Press).

Nussbaum, M. 1996. *For Love of Country: Debating the Limits of Patriotism* (Boston, MA: Beacon).

Olick, J.K., and D. Levy 1997. 'Collective Memory and Cultural Constraint: Holocaust Myth and Rationality in German Politics', *American Sociological Review* 62: 921–36.

— — V. Vinitzky-Seroussi and D. Levy (eds) 2011. *The Collective Memory Reader* (New York: Oxford University Press).

Rigney, A. 2012. 'Transforming Memory and the European Project', *New Literary History* 43: 607–28.

Rothberg, M. 2009. *Multidirectional Memory: Remembering the Holocaust in the Age of Decolonization* (Stanford, CA: Stanford University Press).

Skrbiš, Z., and I. Woodward 2013. *Cosmopolitanism: Uses of the Idea* (London: Sage).

Smith, A.D. 1995. *Nations and Nationalism in a Global Era* (Cambridge: Polity).

Sznaider, N. 2011. *Jewish Memory and the Cosmopolitan Order: Hannah Arendt and the Jewish Condition* (Cambridge: Polity).

Weber, E. 1976. *Peasants into Frenchmen: The Modernization of Rural France 1870–1914* (Stanford, CA: Stanford University Press).

Hannah Arendt and Thomas Paine: Companions in Remembering, Forgetting and Beginning Again

Bradford Vivian

I awoke in the middle of the night, not knowing where I was, I could not even be sure at first who I was; I had only the most rudimentary sense of existence, such as may lurk and flicker in the depths of an animal's consciousness; I was more destitute than the cave-dweller; but then the memory – not yet of the place in which I was, but of various other places where I had lived and might now very possibly be – would come like a rope let down from heaven to draw me up out of the abyss of not-being, from which I could never have escaped by myself.
– Marcel Proust, In Search of Lost Time, vol. 1: 'Swann's Way'

Marcel Proust's heavenly rope of personal memory symbolises, in my estimation, the vital sense and value that much interdisciplinary scholarship and many Western institutions assign to the very concept of collective memory. Memory, as commonly defined in such contexts, is a salutary medium of continuity with the shared past, a veritably animate conduit of historical tradition, cultural identity and socio-political values. Memory emerged as a particularly valuable topos in American and European postwar literature and public culture in tandem with a series of dramatic events, including, Andreas Hyussen writes,

> *ever more ubiquitous Holocaust discourse … the historical and current work related to genocide, AIDS, slavery, and sexual abuse; the ever more numerous public controversies about politically painful anniversaries, commemorations, memorials [and] the latest plethora of apologies for the past by church leaders and politicians in France, Japan, and the United States. (Huyssen 2003: 14).*

Social, religious and political communities have long engaged in rites of collective memory as a means of preserving praiseworthy ideals and historical wisdom. But widespread public awareness of horrendous and materially devastating modern developments, such as those that Huyssen describes, typified immediate postwar preoccupations with collective memory and have intensified in the present *fin de siècle*. So much has been destroyed, so many lives and legacies have been forgotten. Practices of collective memory connote, in our time, a critical means of preventing further oblivion, if not of recovering treasured portions of the past from its darkness altogether. Proust's rope of memory rescues him from 'the abyss of not-being', from a loss of his very self; entire communities weave symbolic ropes of remembrance in order to rescue endangered portions of their defining heritage from alleged abysses of historical not-being.

The question of whether communities might elect to ostensibly forget durations or accoutrements of their collective history motivated my previous research on the topos of forgetting and its role within cultures of collective remembrance (Vivian 2009, 2010). This question, however, did not motivate me to pose collective forgetting as a simple antithesis to collective memory. Indeed, I rested dissatisfied with commonplace ways that scholarly as well as public discourse often described events of forgetting in relation to collective practices of remembrance. Forgetting is often, albeit not exclusively, described as a necessarily redactional element of personal and public memory alike, even by authors who elegantly seek to appraise it in favourable terms (see e.g. Augé 2004; Margalit 2004; Mayer-Schönberger 2011; Weinrich 2004). It thus signifies unavoidable gaps in, or periodically discrete losses of, otherwise continuous individual and collective recollections that one must tolerate as a matter of course. I wondered, however, whether and how communities might choose to forget portions of their historical memories and its material emblems for desirable reasons. The possibility of reconsidering ready equations of forgetting with forms of absence, amnesia or negation in the context of collective memory led me to investigate publicly organised practices of forgetting as a social, political or moral good.

I sought scholarly companions for this project, prior researchers on matters of public remembrance and forgetting, who would assist me in disclosing more fully the rhetorical formation and transformation of memory practices. I regard forms of collective remembrance as well as forgetting, in other words, as products of diverse rhetorical arts. Communities and institutions employ an impressive array of rhetorical appeals to communicate, reinterpret, debate or symbolise the past for persuasive purposes in the present. Neither memory nor forgetting in collective forms connote individual, cognitive processes of remembrance (at least not literally or exclusively). Collective memory and its alleged opposite signify, instead, metaphorical constructs – the multifarious body of commemorative beliefs, artefacts and practices that communities invent to organise prolonged and pervasive deliberation, even contestation, over the meaning of the shared past to present-day affairs. I thus examined in my previous research how communities invent rhetorical means to symbolically redact segments of their historical past in the service of contemporary public interests – in order, for instance, to quell hostilities among rival political factions or ethnic groups fuelled by memories of historical animosities.

Hannah Arendt and, more recently, Thomas Paine are foremost among the intellectual companions who have accompanied me in my research on public practices of forgetting. They provocatively explore how members of political communities defined by longstanding historical traditions strive to liberate themselves from lingering recollections of former times that adversely plague present-day civic relations. Arendt and Paine's writings investigate, in this respect, how political agents might join together to declare an end to their former historical existences and announce the advent of a new and freer era. The prospect of political beginnings joins their work, and draws me to them both.

Political movements throughout Western modernity have attempted to begin again both rhetorically and politically – to declare that the end of a historically protracted repressive regime is at hand in language or symbolism that convinces followers to join in the creation of a new political entity. The institution of a French Republican Calendar, Karl Marx and Friedrich Engels' *Communist Manifesto* and Filippo Tommaso Marinetti's *Futurist Manifesto* variously herald the end of repressive epochs and the beginning of dramatically new social, political and aesthetic realities. Revolutionary movements of this sort, which ended millennia of aristocratic rule by agitating for various forms of modern government (from democracy and republicanism to socialism and Communism) inherently shaped the political history of Western societies from the late Enlightenment forward.

The question of historical beginning in this context refers not to absolute or transparent origins but to a critical and formative dynamic in modern political history: beginning again, always in the middle of established historical memory and socio-political hierarchies. Western revolutions of the eighteenth and nineteenth century redefined the very concept of a revolution to connote rejections of a prior time, 'a process of rapid, fundamental, and progressive social and political change', in contrast to its former meaning as a circular, orbital process (Philp 1995: vii; see also Arendt 1965: 42–3). Modern revolutionary movements labour to begin again, to give birth to an entirely new political time of individual freedoms, representative government and accelerating human progress. They seek to replace the ruins of the *ancien régime*, a period of repressive government and obsolete socio-political customs or hierarchies. Modern revolutionary beginnings depend upon rhetorical as well as political effect: spokespersons for and leaders of successful political revolutions attempt to persuade the public to adopt new socio-political identities – to think, speak and act as a new people no longer defined by a cumbrous and seemingly natural historical order.

Arendt's and Paine's respective reflections on rhetorical and political dimensions of beginning initially spurred and continue to shape my analyses of how and why individuals, groups and institutions advocate organised rituals of forgetting in pursuit of enhanced collective freedoms and new forms of civic identity. Arendt's philosophy fascinates because of her distinctive and steadfast commitment to fostering conditions of natality in human affairs as an essential ingredient of freedom – the freedom of thought, speech and action indispensable to the *vita activa*. Paine's *Common Sense* represents a resounding effort to incite such conditions of natality, to move the pre-revolutionary colonial public to think, speak and act as radically new historical and political subjects in language that would influence subsequent political manifestos throughout the Western world. I demonstrate, in the remainder of this chapter, how their individual ruminations on the social and political value of beginning amid timeworn vestiges of hoary regimes combine to form remarkably companionable touchstones for my own research on the new historical realities and commemorative traditions that rituals of forgetting may produce, and not simply destroy.

I

> *The revolutionary spirit of the last centuries, that is the eagerness to liberate and to build a new house where freedom can dwell, is unprecedented and unequalled in all prior history.*
> Hannah Arendt, *On Revolution*

The names for beginning in Hannah Arendt's philosophy are numerous: *principium*, ἀϱχή, natality, birthing, acting, forgiving, promising, creating and more. Her delineations of beginning in the realms of speech and action – or, as an intertwined political and rhetorical prospect evident across the history of Western modernity – are especially critical to my research. 'The organization of the *polis*', according to Arendt, 'consists essentially in 'a kind of organized remembrance' (1998: 198). Public memory is therefore vital not as a ceremonial or lyrical aspect of the political realm but as a medium for transmitting models of excellence, of *aretē* or *virtus*, to successive political generations across historical time. Yet I have never read Arendt's claims that such 'organized remembrance' allows words and deeds to attain 'immortal fame', thereby 'arresting their perishability' so they may 'enter and be at home in the world of everlastingness' (1968: 43, 45), as suggesting that public remembrance constitutes an essentially continuous medium of faithful repetition in either form or effect.

Her recondite vigilance against forms of unalterable, automated processes – including, by implication, those of communal recollection – guards against this interpretation.

Organised remembrance – or tales of historical words, works and deeds worthy of emulation – furnishes the *vita activa* with lasting demonstrations of how excellence may appear in the world. The *polis* is given to remember nothing less than the worldly reality of freedom itself via this medium. 'Men *are* free', Arendt maintains, 'as long as they act, neither before nor after; for to *be* free and to act are the same' (1968: 153). Action in her definition naturally occurs in, or is occasioned by, the *polis*, whose '*raison d'être* would be to establish and keep in existence a space where freedom and virtuosity can appear' (ibid. 153). The *vita activa*, a realm of action and thus freedom *par excellence*, is inconceivable in Arendt's philosophy if not as a forum in which 'events are talked about, remembered, and turned into stories before they are finally incorporated into the great storybook of human history' (ibid. 154–5). I detect a vital pedagogical aspect in these 'stories': they communicate to members of the *polis* examples of how one may act according to principles, rather than with fidelity to automatic processes, and thus preserve the capacity for action (not causal repetition) as a worldly phenomenon. 'The principle of an action', Arendt elaborates, 'can be repeated time and again, it is inexhaustible, and in distinction from its motive, the validity of a principle is universal, it is not bound to any particular person or to any particular group' (ibid. 152). The realm of political affairs commemorates past words and deeds for the express purpose of cultivating among its members the very principle of acting in concert in order to initiate some new process that will evolve along an unpredictable historical path.

Arendt's reflections on the relevance of historical lore to political speech and action provoked my examinations of forgetting as a transformative property of public remembrance. Rituals of communal remembrance commonly cherished as mediums with which to preserve the essence of past events may, under certain conditions, exemplify a version of the 'automatism inherent in all processes' (Arendt 1968: 168). Those vital rituals can evolve into habitual repetitions of engrained commemorative forms that primarily accommodate unreflective reverence for orthodox objects of remembrance. Many scholars have documented how autocratic regimes commonly impel the populations under their control to participate in commanded spectacles of remembrance, thereby manufacturing illusions of popular support for the historical rule of repressive leaders. Arendt's caution against potential tyrannies of uninspected, obligatory traditions first suggested to me the relevance of such claims for normative traditions of public remembrance:

> The end of a tradition does not necessarily mean that traditional concepts have lost their power over the minds of men. On the contrary, it sometimes seems that this power of well-worn notions and categories becomes more tyrannical as the tradition loses its living force and as the memory of its beginning recedes; it may even reveal its full coercive force only after its end has come and men no longer even rebel against it. (Arendt 1968: 26)

Arendt allows one to infer that the grave danger inherent in normative traditions of public remembrance devolves upon questions of rhetorical form. Traditional forms of narrating, representing or debating the meaning of past events can become merely formulaic, cherished by all manner of groups and individuals for the predictable and familiar versions of public history and ceremonial lore they communicate. Form, in this context, refers to far more than simple stylistic ornamentation. Rather, it connotes discursive patterns that communities use to formulate and reify complex systems of belief and institutional modes of judgement. Communities do so rhetorically – that is, selectively or strategically – by perpetuating accepted modes of public remembrance which support cognate distributions of social, political and moral authority.

Arendt's observations about the potential tyranny of a tradition that has lost 'its living force', a tradition that comes to invite merely formal reverence or dutiful acknowledgement, makes her a fellow traveller with figures in rhetorical studies attuned to the shaping power of rhetorical forms on personal and collective thought, speech or action. Kenneth Burke, for instance, argues that 'many purely formal patterns can readily awaken an attitude of collaborative expectancy in us,' such that 'a yielding to the form prepares for assent to the matter identified with it' (1969: 58). A variety of traditional rhetorical forms sustain public memory in the postwar era: cultural institutions employ time-tested oral, textual and material resources to preserve the semblance of substantive connection with former persons, places and events amidst massive wartime calamities, large human migrations, erosions of longstanding ethnic, religious or regional identities and extensive technological, economic and political upheavals.

Arendt's unfailing suspicion of automatism in humanly initiated processes led me to wonder how and why communities might come to disenthrall themselves from traditions of public remembrance – to remember differently, as an act of self-conscious commemorative reinvention rather than preservation. Investigating this phenomenon obliges one to examine how and why communities strive to invent new, substantively altered forms of remembrance that qualitatively transmute the characteristic goods of public remembrance itself: the so-called lessons of history and the models of praiseworthy social, political or moral conduct they disseminate from one generation to the next. I now realise, upon reflection, that Arendt's philosophy allows me to analyse acts of remembrance – or more precisely, remembering anew – as a form of action, according to her distinctive sense of the term. Such action occurs temporally as a broadly recognised event of historical beginning in the chronology of public affairs. Advocates for revolutionary social and political change may adopt radically revised forms of remembrance or invent rituals of forgetting in order to declare fundamentally new civic identities and statuses, norms of association and conditions of deliberative judgment. These actions can persuade members of an embryonic public to conceive of their role in history as initiators of a new epoch, if not of a qualitatively transformed sense of historical time altogether.

The ability of social and political agents to imagine their role in historical time anew corresponds directly with their capacity for exercising the twinned faculties of forgiving and promising. Forgiving, in Arendt's secular appropriation, counteracts forms of automatism, allowing 'redemption from the predicament of irreversibility – of being unable to undo what one has done though one did not, and could not, have known what he was doing' (1998: 237). The nominal sins of the past need not automatically perpetuate divisions and hatreds among those in the present who stand to inherit their debilitating socio-political legacies. To live among one's fellows without the seemingly intractable influences of such past sins would be to live in accordance with a qualitatively altered sense of historical purpose and significance. The faculty of making and keeping promises, as Arendt would have it, provides conditions in which members of a polity might not simply liberate themselves from the shared burdens of their past but also establish socio-political relations appropriate to their new, but fledgling, historical existence. If forgiving 'serves to undo the deeds of the past', then promises made and kept in the wake of that undoing 'serve to set up in the ocean of uncertainty, which the future is by definition, islands of security without which not even continuity, let alone durability of any kind, would be possible in the relationships between men' (ibid. 237). The faculties of forgiving and promising in this account evince inescapable mnemonic, if not commemorative, dimensions. One must first remember, or provide a full account of, past crimes in order to absolve them, and promises made may not necessarily be honoured, kept – in a word, remembered.

Reinventing conditions of public remembrance by collectively exercising these faculties represents a form of action insofar as it engenders opportunities for a new historical beginning. Action, for Arendt, consists precisely in the collective capacity to interrupt apparently unalterable historical processes so as to initiate unpredictable, unexpected consequences. Acting is consubstantial with beginning, and vice versa. 'It is in the nature of beginning', Arendt writes, 'that something new is started which cannot be expected from whatever may have happened before' (1998: 177–8). She also describes the fruits of action, in a telling parallel, as 'something whose end he [the acting agent] can never foretell, if only because his own deed has already changed everything and made it even more unpredictable' (Arendt 1968: 84). Arendt thus suggests that the faculties of forgiving and promising, of acting together in hopes of effecting a new historical beginning, do not result in a utopian condition. They require one, rather, to negotiate ongoing forms of contestation and uncertainty that define social and political plurality and to embrace the fact that fortune and chance will inevitably undo the goods of even the most auspicious beginnings. In the following section, I demonstrate how Thomas Paine in early 1776 sought to rhetorically incite, and provide conditions for politically managing, precisely the sort of unwieldy and pluralistic beginning that represents such an important topos of Arendt's philosophy – and, as a result, my own.

II

> *We have it in our power to begin the world over again.*
> *Thomas Paine, Common Sense*

The leaders who steered the American colonies to declare independence from Great Britain wrote and spoke of their political revolution as a collective achievement wholly separate from war. John Adams insisted, in an 1815 letter to Thomas Jefferson, that war 'was no part of the Revolution; it was only an effect and consequence of it. The Revolution was in the minds of the people', he stressed, long before shots were fired in anger. 'The records of thirteen state legislatures, the pamphlets, newspapers in all the colonies, ought to be consulted during that period to ascertain the steps by which the public opinion was enlightened and informed concerning the authority of Parliament over the colonies' (Adams, quoted in Bailyn 1992: 1). Bernard Bailyn explicates the mechanism of nonviolent revolution that Adams' letter merely implies: the American Revolution was, by his definition, a simultaneously rhetorical and ideological achievement – a labour of mass persuasion conducted in protean representative realms. The leaders of the Revolution, Bailyn reports, 'wrote easily and amply, and turned out in the space of scarcely a decade and a half … a rich literature of theory, argument, opinion, and polemic. Every medium of written expression was put to use' (1992: 1). Such leaders strove to think, write and speak a new people into being, recognisably distinct from their former national identity, so as to interrupt the seemingly destined reign of British rule and thus certify the existence of a novel political compact. Such was the essence of the revolution as its authors understood it: an expression, to adapt Arendt's terminology, of the collective capacity to rebel against the tyranny of tradition and initiate unexpected and unpredictable phenomena in both words and deeds.

The publication of Thomas Paine's *Common Sense* in January 1776 decisively accelerated the process of mass ideological conversion that Bailyn describes. Paine's wildly popular pamphlet significantly galvanised colonial opinion in support of separation from Great Britain. The decision of the Continental Congress in July of that year to establish an independent nation and publicise their actions in Thomas Jefferson's Declaration of Independence benefitted from the transformation in public opinion that Paine notably helped to orchestrate.

Common Sense formally enacts many features of political beginning consistent with Arendt's philosophy. Paine's text speaks of a new time in a novel voice of democratic cosmopolitanism best suited to expressing its allegedly unprecedented political significance. It entails an uncompromising effort to rhetorically induce an entirely new social and political order commensurate with the dramatically changing meaning of the term 'revolution' in the late eighteenth and early nineteenth centuries. Instead of signifying 'a return to the basic principles of the constitution', as it did in political affairs of the mid-eighteenth century, 'revolution' after the age of Paine signified a wholesale rejection of longstanding social and political hierarchies (Philp 1995: vii). Paine implores the reader to witness the emergence of a new time: a time of beginning amid decaying traditions in which an entirely unique *polis* has emerged, bound together by novel rights, duties and customs of association. 'A new era for politics is struck; a new method of thinking hath arisen' (Paine 1995: 20). Such is the meaning of 'revolution' for Paine.

Paine's *Common Sense* is widely acknowledged to have rhetorically effected a wide and deep transformation in American colonists' understanding of their interrelated political and historical conditions. It offered colonists a political language with which they could plausibly imagine and speak of themselves as an independent nation. His depictions of time and its political implications form the guiding threads of his appeals. The disastrous future outcomes of reconciliation with Great Britain, he insists, are predetermined precisely because reconciliation involves acquiescing to the mere conventions of an aged form of government whose simple historical endurance now represents a tyrannical evil. Paine asserts to his fellow colonists that 'if we will suffer ourselves to examine the component parts of the English constitution, we shall find them to be the base remains of two ancient tyrannies, compounded with some new republican materials', namely the 'remains of monarchical tyranny' and 'aristocratical tyranny' (1995: 8). Paine frames his argument against the British crown with a lengthy critique of monarchy writ large. 'There is something exceedingly ridiculous in the composition of monarchy' generally, and, in the specific case of Great Britain, 'the constitution of England is so exceedingly complex, that the nation may suffer for years together without being able to discover in which part the fault lies' (ibid. 9, 8). The exceeding complexity and ridiculousness of monarchy, according to Paine, is a product of its agedness. He synopsises the long historical origins of monarchy, beginning with biblical history, in order to reveal how its defenders have perpetually cited mere vagaries and invented myths of hereditary right to justify its existence. 'For monarchy in every instance', Paine concludes, 'is the Popery of government': an ancient, superstitious, and cumbersome relic of the past (ibid. 25).

The analogy between monarchy and Catholic hierarchy is apt for Paine's purposes. Centuries' worth of accumulated supernatural legends and apocrypha legitimise the authority of monarchs and popes alike. Neither system is appropriate to the modern age of reason and science. Paine contends that monarchy, like 'Popery', perverts human reason and impartial judgement. 'The prejudice of Englishmen, in favour of their own government by king, lords, and commons', Paine writes, 'arises as much or more from national pride than reason' (1995: 10). Indeed, 'reason forbids' reconciliation, much less 'friendship', with Great Britain because it amounts to 'madness and folly' (ibid. 35). Paine's contempt for monarchy, and particularly British monarchs, comports well with Arendt's misgivings about 'the power of well-worn notions and categories' that become 'more tyrannical as the tradition loses its living force' (1968: 26). The ultimate danger of such outworn tyrannies of tradition, according to Arendt and Paine alike, is that individuals may lose their capacity for critical thought and action under the influence of those obsolete customs until 'men no long even rebel against it' (ibid.).

Paine's postulation of an opportune but potentially fleeting moment ripe for rebellion inflects his appeals with particular urgency. Forget your former allegiances to the decaying husks of monarchy, he implores his readers: seize this critical opportunity to begin again, and thereby thwart the allegedly natural perpetuation of 'eternal tyranny' (1995: 35). Such is a precious moment that affords the opportunity, in Paine's reckoning, to not simply to mark the natural advent of a successive historical era but, rather, to interrupt the tyrannous automatism of monarchical rule by pronouncing the emergence of a qualitatively new and different historical and political time – a time of independent American democracy. Hence the relentless immediacy of Paine's appeals: 'Now is the seed time of continental union, faith and honour. The least fracture now will be like a name engraved with the point of a pin on the tender rind of a young oak; the wound will enlarge with the tree, and posterity read it in full grown characters' (ibid. 20). The present juncture is a 'seed time', a time of vital infancy, an irruption whose magnanimous effects are only beginning to appear. 'The birth-day of a new world is at hand' and the colonists who inhabit it stand to 'receive their portion of freedom from the event of a few months' (ibid. 53). The immense stakes of the moment at hand thus warrant immediate judgement and action rooted in the logic of nature itself: 'Every thing that is right or natural pleads for separation. The blood of the slain, the weeping voice of nature cries, "'TIS TIME TO PART"' (ibid. 24). Paine's emphatic appeals to time and historical judgement make clear that his fellow colonists should seize this consequential, but nevertheless fleeting, moment without delay (ibid. 53). 'The present winter is worth an age if rightly employed, but if lost or neglected, the whole Continent will partake of the misfortune' (ibid. 26). *Common Sense* thus represents, in the context of my research, an unusually persuasive example of how one may not only identify conditions for a new political beginning but, more significantly, formulate a political language that so convincingly portrays the historical present as an irreparable breach with the past.

The present 'seed time' that Paine heralds, this 'birth-day of a new world', obliges the colonists to enter into transformed but untested socio-political relations at home and abroad. Paine thus recasts for his readers the meaning of immediate historical and political time in ways reminiscent of Arendt's remarks on the faculties of forgiving and promising. He implores the colonists, in this respect, to not simply renounce their old traditions but also to passionately recognise themselves as a new *polis* endowed with new rights, duties and customs. Paine proposes, for example, that colonists exercise a nominal equivalent to forgiving the whole of Europe. 'Our plan is commerce', he states, 'and that, well attended to, will secure us the peace and friendship of all Europe; because it is the interest of all Europe to have America a *free port*' (1995: 23). Independence, according to Paine, affords an opportunity for perpetual friendship and peaceable commerce with Europe. 'Any submission to, or dependence on Great Britain', he observes, 'tends directly to involve this [North American] continent in European wars and quarrels; and sets us at variance with nations, who would otherwise seek our friendship, and against whom, we have neither anger nor complaint' (ibid. 23). Declaring it entails renouncing colonial complicities in British affairs, particularly protracted and costly wars with European powers – a geopolitical ground for cessation of historical divisions.

Transforming the quality of American relations with European powers as Paine advises also involves the reciprocal effect of occasioning something like forgiveness among divided colonists at home. Paine's deductive logic regarding the antithetical natures of monarchies and republics ensures this effect. 'The republics of Europe', he states, are always 'in peace', and

'Holland and Swisserland are without wars, foreign *or domestic*' (1995: 31, emphasis added) Republics necessarily cultivate pacific, even forgiving, relations among their constituencies. The complexities and confusions that monarchies breed among their subjects explains, by implication, how some American colonists can divisively argue for reconciliation with apparent tyranny. A republic, in Paine's reasoning, will ameliorate such divisions.

Paine's portrait of nascent independence includes gestures of forgiveness as a practical element of national unity and international statecraft rather than as an expressly Judeo-Christian dissipation of metaphysical sin. The prospect of undoing, to use Arendt's wording, existing geopolitical alliances represents a potential 'redemption from the predicament of irreversibility' (1998: 237) – in this case, alliances that automatically involve the colonists, either directly or indirectly, in longstanding European hostilities. Here, the faculty of forgiving, as Arendt would define it, appears as a worldly phenomenon in one's capacity to alleviate the effects of deeds already done, to achieve measures of redemption from seemingly irreversible consequences that one previously unleashed.

Paine asserts that establishing an independent nation will transform socio-political relations and commitments at home in addition to forgiving, so to speak, the nominal sins of war abroad. Independence in this context is not simply an objective territorial status. It constitutes, rather, the essential binding lineament of national solidarity: 'In short, Independence is the only BOND that can tye and keep us together' (Paine 1995: 53). Hence, conditions of independence would exercise, for Paine, the faculty of making and keeping promises as Arendt describes it: as 'the joy of inhabiting together with others a world whose reality is guaranteed for each by the presence of all' – by political plurality as such – instead of the vagaries of hereditary descent or 'an identical will which somehow magically inspires them all' (Arendt 1998: 244–5). The stakes of such nominal promises are paramount. Paine clamours for an independent and republican country as the first salvo in a broader effort to end the baneful reign of Western monarchy itself. 'The sun never shined on a cause of greater worth. 'Tis not the affair of a city, a country, a province, or a kingdom', nor 'the concern of a day, a year, or an age; posterity are virtually involved in the contest, and will be more or less affected, even to the end of time, by the proceedings now' (Paine 1995: 20). Colonists must pledge themselves to the untested mutual declarations of 'continental union, faith and honor' that compose a modern, independent nation in order to seize this precious epochal opportunity (ibid. 20).

These mutual declarations, Paine attests, vitally allow the colonists to pledge themselves to a momentous common pursuit: nothing less than the dawn of a wholly new form of cosmopolitan statehood. *Common Sense* portrays an independent America as a keenly inclusive country, the novel and defining creed of which reflects a radical commitment to democratic plurality:

> *Every spot of the world is overrun with oppression. Freedom hath been hunted round the Globe. Asia and African have long expelled her. Europe regards her like a stranger, and England hath given her warning to depart. O! receive the fugitive, and prepare in time an asylum for mankind. (Paine 1995: 35)*

One can easily call into question the quasi-utopian grandiloquence of such passages throughout Paine's tract. But they nevertheless reveal his concerted and undeniably influential effort to induce the historical birth of something like a new political entity by entreating those who would populate it to promise themselves to each other in novel ways – by together affirming the radical, historically untested principles, for instance, that 'in American the law is king' or that 'a government of our own is a natural right', not the dispensation of a higher authority (Paine 1995: 34). *Common Sense* constitutes, in sum, an ardent rhetorical effort to persuade British subjects in America to annul their prevailing historical and memorial existence as royal subjects so they may recognise and affirm the nascent bonds, the bases of mutual promises and obligations, which band them together as independent citizens pledged to the construction of a new and manifestly freer society.

Paine's celebrated pamphlet represents far more than mere rhetoric. It persuaded scores of colonial subjects to think, speak and act as a new social and political body. *Common Sense* did not prophesy the exact future course of American society and republican government, but its contents have proven prophetic insofar as Paine's vision of distinctive social, religious, political and commercial ideals supplied normative idioms with which Americans of all stripes continue to define their national origins, duties and destiny. Robert Ferguson explains its impact in convincing statistical terms:

> No other text by a single author can claim to have so instantly captured and then so permanently held the national imagination. At a time when the largest colonial newspapers and most important pamphlets had circulations under 2,000, Common Sense reached between 120,000 and 150,000 copies in its first year alone. ... Hundreds of thousands of Americans, perhaps a fifth of the adult population in all, either read Common Sense or had it read to them during the course of the Revolution. (Ferguson 2000: 465–6)

To speak in the language of basic and enduring American ideals – *e pluribus unum*, the law as king, the country as a haven for humankind – is to speak in the language that Paine invented in *Common Sense* (Pütz and Adams 1989: vii; Ferguson 2000: 467). Paine's invention of a dramatically 'new political language' to replace millennia of monarchical wisdom (and not the eventual *fait accompli* of independence) likely represents his most consequential and lasting revolutionary achievement (Foner 1976: xvi).

I regard Arendt and Paine as companion thinkers on the question of political beginnings. Their writings evince, in my estimation, notably harmonious conceptual and pragmatic criteria useful for determining when, at what historical juncture, particular civic traditions, habits and modes of commemoration have lost their initial value as resources of political thought, speech and action. Arendt and Paine share in common an appreciation for the simultaneous rarity and revolutionary character of truly novel political performances. Paine implores his fellow colonists, in language consistent with Arendt's aversion to all forms of automatism, to reject organised modes of remembrance based on their traditional status as British subjects in favour of a dramatically new collective historical consciousness, and thus a new political identity.

Arendt and Paine's similar predilections for beginning manifest highly compatible definitions of political freedom. Both writers provide grounds for understanding freedom as a mode of performance – of 'virtuosity', in Arendt's terms – easily confused with either acts of violence or mere governmental offices and procedures (Arendt 1968: 153). Their most acute point of agreement in this context concerns their respective understanding of the degree to which revolutions preserve conditions of natality – of political freedom as such. Freedom appears in the world, according to Arendt, as 'an element of virtuosity', as a performance initiated and sustained by 'acting men' (ibid.) akin to that of performing artists whose dance, drama or music only exist while artists perform them. Paine likewise defined the essence of political freedom as a form of cooperative action rather than abstract ideals or official documents. 'A constitution', he wrote in *Rights of Man*, 'is not the act of a government, but of a people constituting a government. All power exercised over a nation, must have some beginning' (1995: 240). The capacity for members of the *polis* to gather together in the service of beginning, of acting freely as such, is thus the genuinely constitutive aspect of any popular form of government. Arendt advances essentially the same claim in her analysis of modern political revolutions: 'the American Revolution ... did not break out but was made by men in common deliberation and on the strength of mutual pledges' (1965: 213). One can find the true signature of that revolution, she concludes, in the entirely new 'understanding of power and authority' that it produced (ibid. 155). Paine, of course, significantly contributed to authoring the basic vocabulary of such new power and authority. Freedom, for both thinkers, consists precisely in the pluralistic capacity to initiate – to begin, or to begin again, as such.

I understand Arendt and Paine to coincidentally provide grounds for differentiating productive acts of public forgetting, which engender conditions for natality, from crudely destructive processes that simply appear to initiate new forms of worldly action. Some of the most theatrical displays of alleged forgetting that transpired during the French Revolution, such as the execution of Louis XVI or destructions of aristocratic signs and symbols in public spaces, inevitably authorised abuses of power reminiscent of the *ancién regime*. Arendt argues, in the case of the French revolutionaries, that 'even if their former representatives were denounced', the courses of destruction they waged did not engender true or lasting conditions of socio-political natality but 'almost automatically led the new experience of power to be channelled into concepts which had just been vacated' (1965: 155). Apparent rituals of forgetting can be oppressively commemorative as such. Arendt and Paine would agree with Gordon Wood's contention that the American Revolution produced comparatively radical, unprecedented social and political results: 'Far from remaining monarchical, hierarchy-ridden subjects on the margin of civilization, Americans had become, almost overnight, the most liberal, the most democratic, the most commercially minded, and the most modern people in the world' (1993: 6–7). Wood thus emphasises the salutary public goods that rituals of forgetting can produce, which Paine and Arendt celebrated, in contrast to reactionary violence associated with the French Revolution.

Traditions of public remembrance vitally help to sustain all manner of social, political and moral institutions. But commemoration – or, literally, remembering in the company of others – can further conservative as well as transformative civic ends. Arendt's philosophy of beginning and Paine's *Common Sense* are indispensable to my ongoing research on collective memory because they provocatively show how those modes of organised remembrance which constitute a *polis* may also constrain the capacity of its members to engage in unimpeded thought, speech and action. A venerated past may inhibit as well as inspire forms of political freedom. The prophetic rope of memory can rescue as well as bind. Paine and Arendt offer compelling evidence that one's ability to forget and begin anew as an expression of coordinated political action, to slip the bindings of remembrance when necessary, represents an indispensable (if not constitutive) principle of the *vita activa*, of shared political life as such.

References

Augé, M. 2004. *Oblivion*, trans. M. de Jager (Minneapolis: University of Minnesota Press).

Arendt, H. 1965. *On Revolution* (New York: Penguin).

— — 1968. *Between Past and Future: Eight Exercises in Political Thought* (New York: Penguin).

— — 1998. *The Human Condition*, 2nd edn (Chicago: University of Chicago Press).

Bailyn, B. 1992. *The Ideological Origins of the American Revolution*, enlarged edn (Cambridge, MA: Harvard University Press).

Burke, K. 1969. *A Rhetoric of Motives* (Berkeley: University of California Press).

Ferguson, R. 2000. 'The Commonalities of *Common Sense*', *William and Mary Quarterly* 57: 456–504.

Foner, E. 1976. *Tom Paine and Revolutionary America* (New York: Oxford University Press).

Huyssen, A. 2003. *Present Pasts: Urban Palimpsests and the Politics of Memory* (Stanford, CA: Stanford University Press).

Margalit, A. 2004. *The Ethics of Memory* (Oxford: Oxford University Press).

Mayer-Schönberger, V. 2011. *Delete: The Virtue of Forgetting in the Digital Age* (Princeton, NJ: Princeton University Press).

Paine, T. 1995. *Rights of Man, Common Sense and Other Political Writings* (Oxford: Oxford University Press).

Philp, M. 1995. 'Introduction', in Paine 1995: vii–xxvii.

Pütz, M. and J.K. Adams 1989. *A Concordance to Thomas Paine's Common Sense and The American Crisis* (New York and London: Garland).

Vivian, B. 2009. 'On the Language of Forgetting', *Quarterly Journal of Speech* 95: 89–104.

— — 2010. *Public Forgetting: The Rhetoric and Politics of Beginning Again* (University Park: Pennsylvania State University Press).

Weinrich, H. 2004. *Lethe: The Art and Critique of Forgetting*, trans. S. Rendall (Ithaca, NY: Cornell University Press).

Wood, G. 1993. *The Radicalism of the American Revolution* (New York: Vintage).

Interactions between History and Memory: Historical Truth Commissions and Reconciliation

Eva-Clarita Pettai[1]

Political scientists concerned with memory are usually interested in the ways in which memories and historical narratives are constructed to forge loyalties and collective identification. At the same time we look at how political processes themselves are being shaped by memory, both in its individual and collective forms. The field of 'memory politics' as an area of political science research is still new and remains highly under-conceptualised. Students of memory politics are required to have a sound understanding of both history and political science concepts. Moreover, depending on their specific area of study they often cross further disciplinary boundaries by using ideas and concepts from social theory, education or legal inquiries. The primary research task for political scientists engaging with memory, however, is to look at institutional mechanisms, legislation, state policies and elite discourses in order to identify processes of public-political meaning and decision-making. A rather common approach in these inquiries (though not the only one) is to identify and study specific political actors, their emergence and interactions as well as their relative power to influence public policy and discourses. The current chapter follows this approach by identifying historical truth commissions as interesting semi-state actors that emerge in particular situations of memory-related conflict and operate under specific constraints determined both by power structures and social processes. As this is meant as a contribution to a volume on 'memory studies', my goal here is not so much focused on determining causalities in relation to commissions' emergence or effects. Instead my aim is to propose a memory-based conceptualisation of these interesting actors seeing them as mediators between history, memory and power.

Such an approach indeed nicely brings together a number of different strands of my previous research in the field. Studying history and political science with a focus on Eastern Europe the evolving field of *Geschichtspolitik* within social science research intrigued me as it offered new avenues to understanding social and political processes unfolding in the former Soviet Union. This was the time when old narratives were being challenged and new histories were written all over the former Communist region. Inspired by these events, I turned to the works of historians like E.H. Carr (1961) and Eric Hobsbawm (1998), marvelling

1   I would like to thank Elazar Barkan for his comments on an earlier draft of this chapter. Support for this work came from two important research grants from the Estonian Ministry of Education and Research (Targeted Finance Project no SF0180128s08 and Institutional Research Grant no IUT20-39).

at the power of historians to change narratives and with them political realities. Travelling in Eastern Europe, I witnessed the transformative power of historical truth, of re-discovered memories and historical images in creating a new sense of purpose and mass mobilisation for political change. At the same time I also saw the emergence of newly exclusive, narrowly ethno-centric histories and myths that left little room for alternative versions or experiences. The uses and abuses of history for creating (state) legitimacy, moulding collective memories and forging the political (national) community became the subject of my research, both in theoretical terms and in the analysis of post-Communist democratisation processes. While my first approach was to link these inquiries to theories of national identity and nationalism, these soon failed to provide satisfying answers to the issues arising in the newly democratic societies of Eastern Europe. Thus I started thinking with John Gillis (1996) and others about the democratisation of commemorative processes and about issues of representation and recognition in societies with diverging memories and related claims. Taking much inspiration from theories of collective memory (Assmann 2008; Olick 1999), I thus conceptually explored the interactions between different forms of collective memory and democratic politics (Onken[2] 2010). Underlying these explorations was the normative idea that in open and pluralist societies both history and memory are constantly negotiated and re-negotiated in the public sphere. Following from this, I concluded that the degree of diversity in these negotiations, both with regard to the actors involved and the issues discussed, indicate a certain level of democratic maturity.

With the current discussion of historical truth commissions, I continue to draw on these earlier discussions, yet take a slightly different turn, derived from my more recent interest in questions of retrospective justice and reconciliation (Pettai and Pettai forthcoming). My initial interest in state commissions of historical inquiry was much informed by empirical observations, mostly relating to three parallel international commissions that have operated in the Baltic states of Estonia, Latvia and Lithuania since 1998 (Onken 2007; Pettai 2011). The three commissions emerged from a context of 'memory political conflict' between these young democracies and international actors characterised by controversies and divergent conceptions regarding Nazi-era truth-seeking and commemorative practices in the Baltic States. Despite certain variations in set-up and operation, all three commissions involved international experts and aimed at reconciling interpretive disputes. Thus they raised interesting questions about history in international relations, about historical truth and about the possibilities of rewriting history and changing perceptions against the backdrop of powerful and often mutually exclusive narratives of (collective) victimisation. The commissions' attempts at creating a multi-national dialogue on the complex history of the Second World War and two totalitarian regimes in the Baltic region also raised questions of historical accountability and justice that required further exploration. My thoughts in this direction received inspiration not least from the growing literature on truth commissions in post-regime-change contexts around the world (Freeman 2006; Brahm 2009).

The current attempt at further theorising particular historically focused state commissions in part draws on this literature. However, my main focus will be less on questions of restorative or historical justice. Instead, I return somewhat to my original interest in historical scholarship and historians as creators of narratives as well as memory political actors, asking with Elazar Barkan, whether 'history can … be drawn upon to facilitate reconciliation?' (2005: 229). Or, in my own words, can deep-seated antagonisms, rooted in memories of past violence and suffering, be overcome by the means of critical historical scholarship? If so, how can this be achieved and what are the potential pitfalls in this process?

---

2   Until 2011, I published under my maiden name, Onken.

My suggestion here is that we may find answers to these questions if we look at the work of a historical commission through the conceptual lenses of memory studies. More specifically, I will begin the discussion by proposing a tentative definition of historical truth commissions that stresses the rather academic character of these bodies, which is deeply rooted in the ethical and methodological standards of historical scholarship. Following from this, I will map out various ways in which the historical truth commission process and product involves different kinds of collective memory, both in the form of political myths and in the form of social memories. With this later distinction I draw on the writings of Aleida Assmann, Jeffrey Olick, Duncan Bell and others, who had inspired my earlier thinking about memory and democratic politics. In a concluding discussion of three recent, mainly Holocaust-related, historical truth commissions, I will illustrate my conceptual points and draw preliminary conclusions as to the future study of historical truth commissions.

Towards a Definition of Historical Truth Commissions

Though not a completely new phenomenon, the past two decades have seen a proliferation of state-sanctioned commissions tasked with inquiring into a controversial yet remote past. The establishment of these historical commissions often came in response to re-emerging historical conflicts rooted in claims for recognition by groups or nations whose memories of past injustice had long been neglected by the political and ideological constraints of the Cold War (Barkan 2005, 2009). Indeed, the past three decades have seen a growing number of smaller and larger memory political conflicts in Europe and elsewhere that sometimes resulted in veritable domestic and or foreign policy crises. These conflicts usually involve opposing truth claims with regard to historic injustice or mass rights abuses that put into question longstanding and firmly institutionalised collective historical self-perceptions and narratives of nations and states and thus constitute a challenge to current political leadership and even social cohesion.

Historical truth commissions are thus often established in order to resolve or at least mediate in interpretive disputes and antagonisms by revisiting the historical facts and clarifying existing misconceptions or biases. Endowed with an official mandate and with the authority of historical scholarship, the findings of these commissions can provide a narrative foundation for future dialogue and reconciliation between the estranged groups and/or nations. The direct 'employment' of historians and of historical scholarship for political purposes, however, contains its own specific challenges making the commissions most interesting phenomena for those interested in the politics of history, historical justice and conflict resolution. Indeed, some scholars see historical truth commissions as embodying the growing importance of history in world politics and of the new 'juriprudencial' role of the historian in resolving particular bilateral conflict situations (Barkan 2005, 2009; Engel 2009; Karn 2006).

The growing literature on individual commissions and their work reveals considerable variation among them, not only with regard to their size, composition and length of operation but also in their thematic scope, modes of operation and final outcome. This variation makes it extremely difficult to find a unified definition of these particular truth-seeking bodies and conceptualise them for a more fruitful comparative analysis of their potential and actual impact on processes of historical reckoning or reconciliation.

Some scholars have tried to define historically oriented commissions within frameworks of transitional justice, thus as sub-types of truth commissions (Freeman 2006; Grodsky 2009; Stan 2009). This approach certainly takes account of the fundamentally political character of these commissions, as well as of their basic aim to revisit long-held truths and discover new evidence of past crimes and abuses, thereby contributing to restorative justice. Yet, approaching historically focused commissions from a truth commission angle runs the danger of overlooking a number of fundamental differences in the aims, operative work and outcome of both kinds of official investigations. These differences are not least relevant for our discussion here as they relate to the key concepts of history and memory.

Both kinds of commissions proceed rather differently in the establishment of 'truth' resulting from a fundamentally different understanding of this very concept. Commissions concerned with more proximate human-rights violations take a semi-judicial approach to establishing facts thereby relying heavily on subjective statements by primary eye-witnesses and victims of human-rights violations (Brahm 2009; Hayner 2010). Investigations into patterns of mass crime and abuse committed decades earlier on the other hand see 'truth' as a relative value, grounded in factual reconstruction yet ultimately a result of interpretive processes and embedded in narrative frameworks. In their search for truth, historical truth commissions only occasionally draw on personal accounts of past events and rather rely on a thorough examination and evaluation of written evidence and archival resources, perhaps also on forensic evidence. Moreover, an essential part of historical scholarship and thus a commission's research effort entails a re-evaluation of existing interpretations of historical events, as well as of sometimes longstanding and powerful biases or incomplete collective perceptions and memory.

The distinguishing lines between both forms of official commissions of inquiry may be at times blurred, as not least the titling of many recent commissions concerned with historical crimes or abuses in Canada or Brazil as 'Truth Commissions' indicate. Ultimately, both seek to reconstruct patterns of gross human-rights violations and to develop a narrative of the past that allows the opposing sides to engage in dialogue. Nevertheless, the methodological differences in how these commissions approach their task of finding truth and under what social and political conditions remain important. The tentative definition of historical truth commissions I intend to propose will take these observations into account, inviting further debate on these issues of conceptual differentiation. I have thus come to the point where I may propose the following six core features of a historical truth commission:

First, historical truth commissions are *official* bodies of inquiry, that is, established by state institutions or actors, both on the national and more local levels. They differ from civil society initiatives or academic ventures in that they thus represent an official attempt by the state to address controversial historical questions or to reveal previously neglected aspects of the nation's past. This is not to neglect the important role informal commissions can have in fostering inter-group reconciliation processes. However, for our purposes here the official character is important as it emphasises the more immediate political mandate vested in the truth-finding endeavour. Though usually given considerable leeway and autonomy, these commissions are more directly linked to power and function as distinct political actors within the broader societal processes of public meaning-making and memory-related policy.

Second, historical truth commissions are *ad hoc and temporal* bodies of inquiry, emerging in specific crises situations that require an immediate response by state actors and usually operating for a period of several years. This is an important point as it distinguishes historical truth commissions from more permanent commissions of historians created as some sort of professional association, supporting and carrying out research on specified fields, regions or centuries. In addition the ad hoc character marks historical truth commissions from other official 'truth projects' such as research institutes or documentation centres. These certainly share some features with historical truth commissions by being more academically inclined and/or seeking to shape public discourses and perceptions of the past (Karn 2006; Mink 2013). Moreover, there are a number of cases in which initially temporal commissions eventually merged into more established research institutes or managed to renew their mandates continuously, thus operating under quasi-institutional conditions. Yet, the ad hoc and temporal character of the historical truth commissions entails rather specific dynamics, both within the commission itself (among members), as well as between the commission and the outside world. Moreover organisational and structural matters specific to an ad hoc operation make this a crucial feature of historical truth commissions.

Third, historical truth commissions are *concerned with the historical past*. By this I mean events and developments that took place in the more distant past. This can mean a time-span stretching back between 30 and 100 or even more years, yet the events and social relations that are being investigated are clearly located in the historical past thus bearing no direct links to present political or social constellations. This point has been discussed before as one of the key differences between the more recently focused truth commissions operating in transitional contexts and historical truth commissions as understood here. Moreover, this is perhaps one of the most important aspects to take into account when trying to understand the interactions between history and memory in the work of these bodies, as is the purpose of this chapter.

Fourth, historical truth commissions either consist of or draw on the work of *professional historians* in state and private archives. Their mandate may provide them with the legal powers to consult classified documents, to summon witnesses or to carry out forensic research, if necessary. However, their approach to historical facts is dominated by consulting written documents and is informed by ethical and methodological standards of historical scholarship, rather than by normative criteria or legal concerns.

Fifth, the historical truth commissions' research and negotiations take place mostly *outside the public eye*. This is mainly due to the duration and highly academic character of the average commission's operation and the limited attention span of modern media. The degree of public outreach in the form of conferences or other more public forums may differ from commission to commission, yet it is usually not part of the official mandate of such a commission to involve the wider public in the truth-seeking or interpretive process. This has both positive and negative effects. On the one hand, it gives the commission members more freedom to engage with historical facts and interpretation, on the other hand, the lack of publicity can diminish a commission's ultimate influence on public discourses and perceptions.

Sixth, a historical truth commission's final product comes in the form of an *extensive joint report of the research findings* that covers various questions and areas of the subject investigated and offers a reading of past wrongs that is critical of previous biases and shows respect for the complexity of historical perceptions and memories. Historical truth commission's reports rarely contain concrete policy recommendations.

To summarise, we may say that *a historical truth commission is an ad hoc academically grounded body of inquiry set up by state institutions to revisit historical records and facts about wrongs committed many decades earlier, to engage in research and interpretive negotiations in a rather closed environment and to produce a joint report that offers a more diversified and critical narrative of past events*. It is important to note that this definition does not say anything about the specific timing of the commission's establishment. Thus a historical truth commission can but does not have to be part of a political transition process. Likewise the definition does not include details of a commission's membership composition. Thus, a historical truth commission can but does not have to include state officials or representatives of the opposing parties in a memory political conflict. What is crucial here is that this definition puts critical historical scholarship at the centre of what historical truth commissions do. In what follows I will further elaborate on this point showing how in a state commission context historical scholarship is challenged both by the postulates of politics as well as by alternative truth claims and organised social memory.

Historical Truth Commissions and Memory: Developing the Conceptual Framework

In juxtaposing the historian's work with truth commissions and retrospective judicial investigations, Charles Maier once pointed out that while the latter two investigate and engage with the past in order to 'serve justice', the former have to be rather critical of the evidence compiled by commissions and courts, as they approach 'the truth' from a fundamentally different angle, aiming to 'serve history'. Despite the usually non-judicial character of truth commissions, he maintains, their inquiries into past human rights violations look to establish the truth in order to find closure. The historian's 'truth' on the other hand is never conclusive, but subjected to continuous re-evaluation and possible revision against new evidence and interpretive frameworks (Maier 2000: 264). Coming from a similar normative understanding of the professional historian's task, Duncan Bell concurs that the critical historian has to be 'self-reflexive, aware of the partiality, weak foundations, and fallibility of [his or her] enterprise' (2008: 153). History written in this way can thus only be a suggested version of what happened, based on the broadest possible evidence interpreted against a set of most rigorous standards of ethical and methodological honesty. Though these normative thoughts on the character of history are by no means new or very original, they are not necessarily shared by all those who engage professionally with the past. Moreover, they are essential for theorising the work of historical truth commissions.

Unlike most truth commissions, historical truth commissions deal with the historical past as we determined earlier. Thus Maier's dichotomy becomes less that of 'serving history' versus 'serving justice', than that of 'serving history' in the above described non-conclusive way as opposed to 'serving politics', which aims at closure to interpretive disputes by avoiding ambivalence in the evaluation and presentation of past events. One could argue that this dichotomy is part of the professional reality of any trained historian, and all too often historians have served politics more than they have contributed to explaining historical complexities and opacities. Yet the tension between historical scholarship and politics becomes even more complex in the context of a politically sanctioned historical truth commission. As Barkan reminds us, historians who serve on a state commission are 'explicitly motivated by politics' (2009: 902). Indeed, if a historian wanted to 'stay out of politics' why would he or she join such a commission? But stepping out of the ivory towers of historical scholarship and assuming what Alexander Karn (2006: 32) calls an 'activist historian's' role requires skills that go beyond the familiar paths of factual analysis and interpretation. Historians serving on a state commission need to embrace the ideas of negotiation, advocacy and compromise in dealing with historical facts. Their aim is or should be to create a historical narrative that not only demonstrates factual accuracy but also leaves room for disagreement and compromise in order to allow all sides involved in the process, 'to maintain the claims that are crucial to their identities' (Karn 2006: 42). Last but not least, commissions of historians need to be ready to demonstrate communicative skills in reaching out and explaining the results of this process to broader, non-professional audiences that might have a stake in the commission outcome. In sum, it is the skilful balancing of both assignments, to serve history and to serve politics at the same time, that characterises the work and, indeed, determines the success of the historical truth commission.

The pendulum between both assignments can easily swing to either side resulting in less desirable outcomes. A commission of historians can easily remain stuck in a narrow understanding of historical scholarship that stresses only the need to collect historical facts and present them in the most complete yet technical fashion devoid of any conceptual framework or compelling narrative that is able to penetrate the historical consciousness of broader audiences. The outcome of such a commission process is often an exercise in 'factology', as one might call it, that is, a rather voluminous report that is merely stating facts in a dry and academic fashion incomprehensible to a more general readership. Yet as Kaii maintains, 'if highly technical reports sail above the heads of average readers, then any academic gains are likely to be offset by continued misunderstanding at the grassroot level' (2006: 36). Such a collection of facts thus fails to communicate the commission's findings and at best ends as a reference book for other scholars. Though this may have its uses for subsequent research and investigations, the commission that has produced such a result has not only failed to embrace the possibilities provided by its political mandate and specific organisational settings but also ultimately missed the chance to truly engage with history.

A commission process can, however, also tip in the other direction, serving politics in ways that fly in the face of historical scholarship. If serving politics becomes the primary purpose of a commission, the result is often either a report that defends existing dominant narratives and myths or one that seeks to create a new narrative in order to bolster particular ideological stances or power-political interests. In both cases the historical truth commission becomes an active agent in political-myth-making thus undermining attempts at historical dialogue or reconciliation.

A brief note on what I mean by political myth in this context may be at place here. Used in connection with concepts of collective memory, 'political myth' should not be misunderstood as only negative, as a somehow false or deliberately misleading account of the past. Instead the term rather describes a form of collective memory that is constructed and institutionalised through top-down mechanisms of state policy, public commemoration and elite discourses. Characterised by a simplified narrative – often about a nation's past glory or defeat – the political myth provides larger political communities with an identificatory framework. The political myth can occur in the form of a national myth of origin, ancient heroes and constitutive events. However, in our context political-myth-making usually concerns more recent historical events that are politically and institutionally elevated to provide higher meaning to the political or national community.

In sum, the interactions (and indeed tension) between historical scholarship and politics embodied in a historical truth commission can result in a truly reconciliatory historical narrative able to have an impact on the memory political conflict at hand. This kind of narrative demonstrates respect for the complexities of the past and offers a new reading of the historical past that is compelling yet open enough to encourage critical revision of longstanding myths and further dialogue. The other possible outcome of this core dynamic between historical scholarship and politics is a reduced version of history – either in the form of an inaccessible collection of facts that provides little guidance regarding possible meanings and holds little appeal to the broader readership or in the form of simplified and biased narratives that either neglect or discredit alternative historical narratives and identity-informing memories. Neither is conducive to resolving the memory political conflict and fostering reconciliation.

The factors that determine a commission's ultimate investigative function – as an honest mediator, a fact-finder or a myth-maker – are manifold. Much depends on a commission's original mandate and the self-declared goals of the commission. Moreover, organisational modalities, procedural rules, financial and public support all have an impact on how the investigative work is carried out and to what end. Finally, more idiosyncratic factors such as the attitudes of individual commission members, researchers or political sponsors that are often derived from specific biographical or ideological backgrounds can also influence the truth-seeking process. I will come back to some of these factors in my later discussion of cases. At this point, however, I would like to draw attention to the latter two factors: the support (or pressure) commissions receive from the broader society (from specific interest groups or a broader media discourse) and the social frames of individuals involved in the commission. Both are indeed related to another form of collective, namely social memory.

The question of how historical truth commissions relate to social memory brings me back to my earlier definition of historical truth commissions. As we determined, historical truth commissions do not usually involve victim statements or methods of storytelling. Thus, there is no engagement with experience-based (or embodied) personal memories in their quest for historical truth. Instead they usually investigate acts of wrongdoing, the perpetrators, victims or witnesses of which are either long dead or incapable of providing testimony to their actions or sufferings. This, however, does not mean that their memories are not available to historians or that they do not matter to the truth-seeking process. Quite the contrary, memories of past wrong communicated within families, peers or generational cohorts can remain quite powerful even after the primary carrier of these memories is no longer around. If we follow scholars of collective (social and communicative) memory, then aggregate individual memories as well as memories that are transmitted through social interaction and communication, though temporarily and spatially limited, can generate collective meaning and identification (Assmann 2004; Olick 1999; Welzer 2002). Indeed, generational research shows that children of victims and perpetrators alike often feel deep emotional involvement in their parents' stories and are more relentless and unforgiving towards other truths than the parent generation itself (Buruma 1999; Woolf 2005). Thus social memories of victimisation and trauma but also of guilt and responsibility can constitute a 'social fact' that can be both empowering and constraining.

In returning to the historical truth commission operating in a context of memory-based conflict, social memory in its various manifestations becomes important – whether in the form of shared memories attached to actual experiences or in the form of Halbwachsian 'social frameworks' that create meaning and a sense of group identity beyond experiential boundaries. Members and researchers of historical truth commissions are not immune to the emotional and attitudinal effects of the many social memories that exist in society. 'Memory agents' such as victim organisations or other representatives of particular historical claims can impart considerable influence in public and political discourses, thus directly or indirectly effecting a commission's investigative and evaluation process. Likewise, the personal background of the actors involved in the process, the experiential, autobiographical, generational or ideological frames they live in can become crucial for determining interpretations and/or inter-personal relations, thus effecting a commission's outcome.

In summarising the complex dynamics between history and memory in a state commission context, we may conclude that it is the primary task of the commission to overcome the contradictions and tensions that arise when critical historical scholarship encounters politically motivated requests for truth. Yet its ability to achieve this depends to a large extent on the dynamics between collective, political memory or myths, on the one hand, and collective, social memories both within and outside the commission, on the other. In other words, we need to determine the role of memory in its political and social manifestations in order to estimate the possibilities and limitations of historical truth commissions as mediators in historical conflicts. In the following I will illustrate these conclusions by briefly reflecting on three recent Holocaust and Second World War related historical truth commissions. This is, by no means an exhaustive analysis, but is rather meant as an invitation for further research and comparative analysis of historical truth commissions from a more conceptually informed angle.

Concluding Review of Cases

The focus of the following discussion will be on three cases of historical truth commissions concerned with totalitarian regime crimes, two from post-Soviet Eastern European and one from post-Cold War Western European: the 1996 Swiss Independent Commission of Experts (ICE), the 1998 Estonian International Commission for the Investigation of Crimes against Humanity (usually referred to as the Estonian Presidential Commission) and the 1998 International Commission for the Evaluation of the Crimes of the Nazi and Soviet Occupation Regimes in Lithuania (the Lithuanian Presidential Commission). All three were tasked with clarifying past gross human-rights violations and patterns of state abuse in relation to the Nazi period and the Holocaust. In the two Baltic cases, investigations into Stalinist crimes were equally included to the commissions' mandates. All three were composed of a majority of professionally trained historians or heavily relied on historians' research and were given a political mandate that provided them with far-reaching political and material independence to carry out the investigation and evaluation requested. Yet when it came to the evaluation of these commissions' ultimate outcomes, their ability to arrive at joint conclusions and develop historical narratives that enabled further dialogue and reconciliation, the results were quite diverse. The ICE has been evaluated as having significantly contributed to changing Swiss collective self-perceptions and deconstructing the national myth of wartime 'neutrality' (Barkan 2000; Karn 2006). The Estonian Presidential Commission has been praised for its thorough, though rather technical and legalistic reconstruction of Nazi crimes in Estonia during Nazi occupation. At the same time it has been criticised for its inability to raise public awareness of these crimes among Estonians and to promote an honest dialogue on issues of collaboration and accountability (Weiss-Wendt 2008). Finally, the Lithuanian Presidential Commission has been regarded as an honest effort at research and international academic exchange, yet these efforts never resulted in a joint final report. Instead, the commission's work was discontinued after almost ten years of operation, paralysed by open obstruction from various political and societal actors (Budryte 2012).

The reasons for the divergences in outcome certainly involve a range of factors beyond the realm of memory. Indeed, in each case, organisational or procedural modalities, issues of mandate, membership and mission as well as political support ultimately effected the outcome (Pettai and Pettai forthcoming: ch. 6). Yet, following my previous conceptual elaborations, I would like to focus my attention on the 'memory factor' as a core explanatory variable in understanding variation in commission outcome. My aim is to determine the relative weight of both social memory and political myth in (1) the original conflict situation from which the respective commission emerged and (2) the commission's investigative and deliberative process and final product.

When we look at the situation from which the commissions emerged, we see that they share certain core features. All of them were established in response to external criticism and pressures on governments to confront their country's involvement in Nazi-era crimes. The ICE's task involved historical and legal investigations into the volume and fate of assets moved to Switzerland before, during and after the war. Later it expanded into investigating official policies towards (Jewish) refugees and state concessions made towards the Axis powers during the Second World War (Junz 2003).[3] Expectations were that this commission would finally clarify the accusations of complicity in Nazi crimes and postwar wrongdoing and thus put an end to the recurrent controversies that caused much negative publicity and interfered in Swiss foreign relations (Barkan 2000: 88–111). In both Baltic cases the accusations voiced by international actors regarded the two states' reluctance to confront, both legally and historically, local collaboration with the Nazi occupation authorities and killing squads in the extermination of Jews. By setting up historical truth commissions to research and clarify past events and actions, the Baltic presidents hoped to refute some of these highly simplified narratives of Baltic mass collaboration in the Holocaust that started to interfere in Baltic aspirations towards Western integration. Both commissions moreover aimed at promoting critical dialogue on controversial historical issues and at fostering mutual understanding.

Thus, all three commissions shared essential features with regard to the initial reasons for their establishment. However, a closer look at the dynamics between political myths and social memories in the memory political conflict from which they emerged reveal considerable differences between all three cases.

In the case of Switzerland, we have to look quite far back in time, at a decades-long record of reluctance and obfuscation by both Swiss banks and governments in response to claims by former Jewish refugees and Holocaust survivors regarding undisclosed assets that had found their way into Swiss banks during and after the war. Later these claims for justice were joined by critical questions regarding the so called 'Nazi Gold' – often taken from Jews killed in the Holocaust – and other assets that were deposited in Swiss banks and, not least, support of the German war machine. Instead of responding to the specific accusations and clarifying the claims, Swiss bankers and state officials were reluctant to contribute to more transparency, reacted defensively and 'broadened the dispute into a question of national defence and pride' making it into 'a struggle for historical identity' (Barkan 2000: 89).

By the mid 1990s, the winds had changed. The breaking of ideological chains and new discoveries in archives after the end of the Cold War led to an environment in which the Swiss were losing their high moral ground and critical questions about the country's involvement in Nazi crimes threatened to seriously damage the its international image (Barkan 2000: 88–90). Moreover, ever since the 1980s, a Holocaust-centred narrative had been firmly institutionalised throughout European and Western public policy and discourses that not only stressed the guilt of the Nazis but also that of their local collaborators in the occupied territories as well as of the failure of Western civilisation as a whole to prevent the mass atrocities from being committed. In the 1990s, this international political myth became increasingly translated into what Barkan has called a 'new international emphasis on morality'. Rooted in the experience of the Holocaust, this emerged as a universal framework asserting pressure on nations to 'act morally' and to acknowledge historical wrongs (Barkan 2000: xvi).

The Swiss parliament's decision to establish the ICE has to be seen against this backdrop of contrasting political (mythical) memory frames. Consequently, the commission's main concern was not with making proposals for future redress settlements between Swiss banks and/or government and Jewish claimants – all the more so as a lawsuit against Swiss banks was being launched parallely, resulting in a $1.25 billion settlement between two major banks and Jewish plaintiffs in 1998. Thus, even if there remained much room for additional redress, social memories and resulting claims played less of a role in the ICE's investigations. Instead it aimed to answer broad questions about Swiss 'guilt' and responsibility during the Nazi

---

3   See the official website of the Bergier Commission, including its final report: <http://www.uek.ch/en/>.

period and in the crimes of the Holocaust. In other words, it sought to address the dominant national narratives or national myth of 'neutrality' and of Switzerland as a safe haven for Jewish refugees, the deconstruction of which had already begun in public discourses.

The ICE process of investigation and evaluation took place largely behind closed doors and took five years. The commission members, historians from Polish, American, Israeli and Swiss backgrounds, had a mandate that provided them with sufficient financial resources and legal powers to access private or classified material. Moreover, according to one of the members, the commission enjoyed far reaching political independence (Junz 2003). The result of this was a final report of 22 volumes, altogether around 11,000 pages appearing in 2001 that detailed in a most painstaking, if at time technical, way the degree of 'Jewish despoliation and Swiss complicity'. As Karn points out, it was not so much the ICE's factual revelations or conclusions, most of which were long known to the Swiss public, but the ability to arrive at a synthesised narrative that presented a clear message about the motivations (greed) and degree of Swiss complicity in Nazi crimes thus 'etch[ing it] clearly in public memory' (2006: 36). Moreover, by managing to largely 'institutionalise guilt' yet finding very clear words about the inhuman and in part anti-Semitically motivated refugee policies during the war, the commission report was also acceptable to those, for whom an official acknowledgement of guilt was important (ibid. 36). In sum, the ICE's findings and their presentation managed to penetrate Swiss collective self-perceptions and further rectify national myths, thus providing the grounds for resolving the 'foreign and domestic policy crisis' of the 1990s (Barkan 2000: 89; Junz 2003).

In the Estonian case, both the initial conflict situation that led to the establishment of the commission as well as the subsequent process of investigation and narrative deliberations was quite different in the dynamics between political (national) myths and social memories. First of all, both Estonian and Lithuanian state independence had been achieved in 1991, not least thanks to the empowering and transformative role of social memories of victimisation under Stalinist terror. For decades, these memories of loss and subjugation existed only in the form of family communication and social interaction. As soon as Soviet control decreased in the 1980s, these memories re-emerged and drove people to mass demonstrations and, ultimately, to demand the return to national self-determination. With the re-establishment of national independence, the social memories became institutionalized through laws and declarations, school textbooks and public commemorative practices, turning into a national myth of victimhood and heroism. Accusations of guilt with regard to the Nazi period thus not only challenged this process of institutionalisation, but also challenged Estonian and Lithuanian social memories of their own victimisation.

Still, the situations from which the two historical truth commissions emerged differed in crucial ways. In Estonia there was hardly any memory of the Holocaust in society by 1991 due to the relative small size of the pre-war Estonian-Jewish community, the extermination of which during Nazi occupation happened largely unnoticed by the majority of Estonians (Weiss-Wendt 2008). As a result, in post-Soviet public discourses the voices of those remembering Jewish life in Estonia and the way it ended were absent. Accusations of local Nazi collaboration found no echo in social memory discourses that were dominated exclusively by stories of Estonian suffering under Stalin. Not surprisingly, therefore, a pure Holocaust-related commission, as demanded by Western officials and Jewish organisations, would have found little acceptance in society. In order to satisfy both external and domestic demands for historical truth, President Lennart Meri decided to give the commission a dual mandate to investigate both totalitarian periods. Yet the commission's set-up and operative mode was not very conducive to furthering dialogue between Jews and Estonians on their common past or clarifying existing public misperceptions. Critical exchange was, indeed, only given to the extent that the seven commission members, none of whom were Estonian and without any Estonian investigators involved, discussed the drafting of joint conclusions based on the facts supplied. The final result was a report that combined general 'conclusions' with a series of rather factual and dry historical reports detailing the historical events and repressive structures of both regimes on altogether over 2,000 pages published in 2008. The report indeed offered many hitherto unknown facts and did not shy away from revealing names and determining individual responsibilities (Onken 2007). However, any potential academic gains from this were offset by its highly technical ('factological') and at times legalistic language that failed to provide the kind of diversified and negotiated narrative necessary to further critical debate. The report proved ultimately unable, moreover, to truly penetrate the Estonian historical consciousness of the Holocaust visible in continuous misrepresentations and stereotypes of past events in the public realm.

In contrast to both the Swiss and Estonian cases, in post-Soviet Lithuania the initial situation from which the Lithuanian Presidential Commission emerged involved social memories to a considerable degree. In fact, I would claim that the conflict between two deeply antagonistic and hostile social memories of the Holocaust among native Lithuanians on the one hand and Lithuanian Jews on the other was what determined the memory political conflict in this case. As in Estonia, the 1980s had seen memories of Soviet-era mass deportations, postwar partisan violence and cultural subjugation reclaim the Lithuanian public discursive arena and translate into collective political action. At the same time, however, Jewish memories of suffering at the hands of Nazis and their Lithuanian henchmen also resurfaced after decades of Soviet public and historiographical neglect. In the 1990s, these memories found their representation in a re-established Lithuanian-Jewish community. This was only a shadow of the erstwhile large and flourishing Jewish community that had lived on current Lithuanian territory before the Second World War, yet its demands for historical truth and commemorative activities found much support not only by well-institutionalised and connected international Jewish organisations, but also in foreign governments. Domestic discourses and even statements by Lithuanian state officials soon turned rather defensive, resulting in hostile mutual accusations. Thus the Jewish narratives about the Lithuanians as anti-Semites and willing executors of their Jewish neighbours were countered with the narrative of the Jewish NKVD agent responsible for the killing and deportation of Lithuanians (Budryte 2005).

The Lithuanian Presidential Commission, composed of both Lithuanian and foreign historians, tried to counter these highly emotional controversies and accusatory narratives with the methods of critical scholarship. Through establishing clear procedural rules that guaranteed a critical dialogue between diverse actors and interpretations, the commission sought to overcome potential biases and oversimplified interpretations of the ambiguous and complex historical processes. Yet from the beginning the commission was lacking political support. With its combined mandate, similar to that of the Estonian commission, it raised criticism among both nationally minded Lithuanians and Jews, as both feared the relativisation of their own group's historical suffering (Suziedelis 2007).

In almost ten years, the commission managed to produce a number of intermediate reports and one volume on the early months of the German occupation. These results demonstrated high academic standards and the honest wish to arrive at a 'negotiated historical narrative' (Barkan 2005: 233) that would enable further dialogue. However, the lack of domestic political support, strong opposition by Lithuanian and Jewish 'memory agents' and, not least, memories and social frames of individual commission members themselves ultimately paralysed the investigations (Pettai 2011). The Lithuanian Presidential

Commission was discontinued in 2007, leaving a situation behind that was no less conflict-ridden than at the beginning of its operations.[4]

These have been only three out of a large number of historical truth commissions worldwide concerned with historical injustice. Yet they demonstrate how different the outcome of such official historical inquiries and deliberations can be. In returning to my initial question, can we thus say that historical scholarship provides a key to resolving memory political conflicts? As usual in the social sciences the answer is a conditional 'yes and no'. First of all it requires a kind of historical scholarship that is well aware of its political power and finds a way to use it without losing its academic footing. Second, it requires a kind of historical scholarship that is aware of the power of memory and finds a way to acknowledge subjective truths without betraying its ethical and methodological standards in dealing with historical evidence. In this sense, my discussion here should be seen as an invitation to those interested in issues of historical conflict resolution to focus more attention on the dynamic relationship between different forms of collective memory in a given commission context and on the ways in which they enable or constrain the search for a new reconciliatory historical narrative. This may not only help to better understand historical truth commission processes and their outcomes but also offers a potential analytical tool for avoiding pitfalls and failure in future commission endeavours.

References

Assmann, A. 2004. 'Four Formats of Memory: From Individual to Collective Constructions of the Past', in C. Emden and D. Midgley (eds), *Cultural Memory and Historical Consciousness in the German-Speaking World Since 1500* (Oxford: Peter Lang), pp. 19–37.

— — 2008. 'Transformations between History and Memory', *Social Research* 75: 49–72.

Barkan, E. 2000. *The Guilt of Nations. Restitution and Negotiating Historical Injustice* (New York: Norton).

— — 2005. 'Engaging History: Managing Conflict and Reconciliation', *History Workshop Journal* 59: 229–36.

— — 2009. 'Historians and Historical Reconciliation', *American Historical Review* 114: 899–913.

Bell, D. 2008. 'Agonistic Democracy and Politics of Memory', *Constellations* 15: 148–66.

Brahm, E. 2009. 'What is a Truth Commission and What does it Matter?', *Peace and Conflict Review* 3/2: 1–14.

Budryte, D. 2005. *Taming Nationalism? Political Community Building in the Post-Soviet Baltic States* (Burlington, VT: Ashgate).

— — 2012. 'International Commission for the Evaluation of Crimes of the Nazi and Soviet Occupation Regimes in Lithuania', in L. Stan and N. Nedelsky (eds), *Encyclopedia of Transitional Justice* (Cambridge: Cambridge University Press), pp. 135–8.

Buruma, I. 1999. 'The Joys and Perils of Victimhood', *New York Review of Books* (8 Apr.).

Carr, E.H. 1961. *What is History?* (London: Penguin).

Engel, D. 2009. 'On Reconciling the Histories of Two Chosen Peoples', *American Historical Review* 114: 914–29.

---

4   In 2013, the Lithuanian presidential commission was re-instated with a new, much expanded membership structure, but similar mandate and organisational modalities. Whether this revived commission will be more successful in finding a common voice and contributing to a more constructive historical dialogue between the antagonistic groups within and outside Lithuania remains to be seen.

Freeman, M. 2006. *Truth Commissions and Procedural Fairness* (Cambridge: Cambridge University Press).

Gillis, J. 1996. 'Memory and Identity: The History of a Relationship', in J. Gillis (ed.), *Commemoration: The Politics of National Identity* (Princeton, NJ: Princeton University Press), pp. 3–23.

Grodsky, B. 2009. 'Beyond Lustration: Truth-Seeking Efforts in the Post-Communist Space', *Taiwan Journal of Democracy* 5/2: 21–43.

Hayner, P. 2010. *Unspeakable Truths: Transitional Justice and the Challenge of Truth Commissions*, 2nd edn (London: Routledge).

Hobsbawm, E. 1998. *On History* (London: Abacus).

Junz, H.B. 2003. 'Confronting Holocaust History: The Bergier Commission's Research on Switzerland's Past', *Post-Holocaust and Anti-Semitism* 8 (May), available at <http://www.jcpa.org/phas/phas-8.htm>.

Karn, A. 2006. 'Depolarizing the Past: The Role of Historical Commissions in Conflict Mediation and Reconciliation', *Journal of International Affairs* 60/1: 31–50.

Maier, C. 2000. 'Doing History, Doing Justice: The Narrative of the Historian and of the Truth Commission', in R.I. Rotberg and D. Thompson (eds), *Truth v. Justice: The Morality of Truth Commissions* (Princeton, NJ: Princeton University Press).

Mink, G. 2013. 'Institutions of National Memory in Post-Communist Europe: From Transitional Justice to Political Uses of Biographies (1989–2010)', in G. Mink and L. Neumayer (eds), *History, Memory and Politics in Central and Eastern Europe: Memory Games* (New York: Palgrave Macmillan), pp. 155–70.

Olick, J. 1999. 'Collective Memory: The Two Cultures', *Sociological Theory* 17: 333–48.

Onken, E.-C. 2007. 'The Politics of Finding Historical Truth: Reviewing Baltic History Commissions and Their Work', *Journal of Baltic Studies* 38: 109–16.

— — 2010. 'Memory and Democratic Pluralism: Rethinking the Relationship', *Journal of Baltic Studies* 41: 277–94.

Pettai, E.-C. 2011. 'The Convergence of Two Worlds: Historians and Emerging Histories in the Baltic States', in M. Housden and D. J. Smith (eds.), *Forgotten Pages in Baltic History: Inclusion and Exclusion in History*, Festschrift for John Hiden (Amsterdam: Rodopi), pp. 263–79.

— — and V. Pettai forthcoming. *Transitional and Retrospective Justice in the Baltic States* (Cambridge: Cambridge University Press).

Stan, L. 2009. 'Truth Commissions in Post-Communism: The Overlooked Solution?', *Open Political Science Journal* 2: 1–13.

Suziedelis, S. 2007. 'The Perception of the Holocaust: Public Challenges and Experience in Lithuania', Wilson Center, Meeting Report 341, available at <http://www.wilsoncenter.org/publication/341-the-perception-the-holocaust-public-challenges-and-experience-lithuania>.

Weiss-Wendt, A. 2008. 'Why the Holocaust does not Matter in Estonia', *Journal of Baltic Studies* 39: 475–98.

Welzer, H. 2002. *Das kommunikative Gedächtnis* (Munich: C.H. Beck).

Wolff, S. 2005. 'Historians: Private, Collective and Public Memories of Violence and War Atrocities' in F. Cappelletto (ed.), *Memory and WWI: An Ethnographic Approach* (New York: Berghahn).

Post-Stalinist Russia:
Memory and Mourning

Alexander Etkind

Though terror in Nazi Germany and Communist Russia both resulted in many millions of victims, their memories are different. The popular memory of the Holocaust boomed in the last years of the twentieth century on an industrial scale, but the popular memory of the Soviet terror has not advanced much since the 1960s. The debate over the relationship between German Nazism and Soviet Communism has been a long and fierce one. Hannah Arendt's Cold-War era concept of totalitarianism, positing a metaphorical 'common denominator' shared by the two regimes, was largely rejected by Western academics from the 1960s to the 1980s, later embraced enthusiastically in Russia during the Gorbachev era and has been largely resurrected in the Western scholarship of the new century. However, many Western thinkers, from Freud to Habermas and Derrida, have emphatically rejected the notion that these two regimes should be viewed as symmetrical.[1] Their methods may have been similar, but their purposes were fundamentally different, they say. The Soviet project was at least congruent with the Enlightenment tradition and based on admirable ideals. Historians have often challenged this philosophical argument: from Ernst Nolte who launched the German 'Historians' Dispute' in 1986 to Timothy Snyder's *Bloodlands* (2010), historians demonstrate the comparable scale and mutual dependency of the lethal policies pursued by the Soviet and Nazi regimes.

We can only speculate about what would have happened if Nazi Germany had won the Second World War: would Hitler's successor have denounced the Holocaust? In the Soviet Union, it was the very same institutions and personalities that had organised the mass crimes that later revealed them voluntarily. But under their control, this process of working through could not achieve closure. Ironically, Stalin's major achievement, the military strength of the Soviet Union, created a unique situation in which his regime had to analyse, exculpate and dismantle itself. There was nobody else to do it.

In 1956, the head of the Soviet state, Nikita Khrushchev, started the de-Stalinisation process. There is no doubt whatsoever that he was personally implicated in the 'repressions', that he oversaw, through the decades of his service as the party leader of Ukraine and Moscow, some of the bloodiest of the bloodlands (Snyder 2010). There was nothing coercing Khrushchev to confess other than his own guilty memory of the terror and his fear of the terror's re-enactment. This autonomous, self-imposed character of Khrushchev's revelations makes them unique, even unprecedented in the history of twentieth-century violence.

In 1953, there were 166 labour camps in the Soviet Union, plus a huge number of other penitentiary institutions, from prisons to special settlements. About 10 million people served

---

1   On Freud's thinking about the changing regime in Russia, see Etkind 1997: 225–7.

time in these institutions. Almost all of them were released in 1954–56. The enormous system of the gulag melted away with amazing ease, foreshadowing the collapse of the Soviet Union a few decades later. At the moment of his celebrated confession at the Twentieth Congress of the Communist Party in 1956, Khrushchev was at the height of his power, but, according to his son, Khrushchev was 'ceaselessly returning to Stalin, poisoned by Stalin, trying to expunge Stalin out of himself and failing to do so' (Khrushchev 1994: ch. 4). Whether his incomplete revelations were driven by individual atonement or political calculation, he explained them using the vaguely Hegelian and to some extent, also Freudian, idea that a crime should be acknowledged in order to prevent its repetition. 'Never again' resounded as a leitmotif both in his report to the Twentieth Party Congress and later in his memoirs. Mourning and warning were tightly linked in his rhetoric, with the latter providing political arguments for the former. You may feel no remorse, he kept warning his peers, and you are not required to confess your own crimes; but if you do not mourn your victims, your fate will be the same as theirs. Khrushchev succeeded in transforming his milieu to such an extent that he escaped the worst: deposed in 1964, he was left in peace to live for many more years, dictated his memoirs, and was buried by his family. As the Soviet phrase went, he enjoyed the supreme luxury of dying in his own bed – a luxury that, in his case, was well earned.

From German memorials to Russian memoirs, one can trace a continuum of the cultural genres of mourning, but the contrasts are remarkably sharp. If the Nazi Holocaust was ended and exposed by others, the Soviet terror was ended and exposed by its former perpetrators, who were also its potential victims. Like in the classical Cretan paradox, self-applied concepts present notorious epistemological problems. In the Soviet terror, its agents and targets seem blurred, agency dispersed, purpose uncertain, causality cyclical and renunciation and reconciliation incomplete.

Mourning and haunting have etched their imprints on many products of late Soviet and post-Soviet culture. Striving to understand and appreciate this culture, scholars need a particular sensitivity to the warped, the doubled, the uncanny and the ghostly. According to the trained historian, Soviet dissident and later, the leading post-Soviet human-rights activist, Liudmila Alexeyeva, in 1953, the Moscow public was accustomed to stories like this:

> One night the general was found in a cold sweat, screaming, 'Forgive me, Dmitry Ivanovich!' His wife asked him who he was talking to; he did not respond. After a few weeks, the general started talking to the invisible Dmitry Ivanovich while awake. After they took him to the insane asylum, his wife learned that Dmitry Ivanovich was a man the general shot with his own revolver in 1937. (Alexeyeva and Goldberg 1990: 71)

Within his party, whose members were often found screaming in a cold sweat, Khrushchev failed to rally support for his courageous repentance. His sympathisers were mainly intellectuals in the Russian capitals and provinces, who were numerous and important in the technocratic and still ambitious Soviet Union, but he failed to address them directly. This intelligentsia included scores of gulag survivors and their relatives. A popular writer who outlived Stalinism, Ilia Ehrenburg, called this period the 'Thaw'. De-frosting three decades of Stalinism (1924–53), this remarkable decade ended in 1964, when a vigorous protest from the Communist Party against Khrushchev's capricious reforms led to his dismissal.[2] During the long, dreadful 'Stagnation' that followed (1964–85), the authorities resumed their attempts to

---

2   On the culture of the Thaw, see Condee 2000; Jones 2006, 2008; Plamper 2005; Prokhorov 2008; Reid 2006.

escape from the memory of Stalinism. Playing with the two meanings of 'repression', I would call this dark period of memory 'the repression of repressions'. However, those inconsistent moves revealed as much as they obscured. Banished from politics and transferred to culture, the work of mourning became the most sensitive ideological issue in the late Soviet period.

Tragically incomplete, the Thaw was the most successful of Russia's de-Stalinisation projects. Led by poets and writers, Russia's mourners had their moment of recognition that eventuated in their unprecedented popularity during the Thaw and in the later period. Less than ten years after Stalin's death, Khrushchev staged a performative act of major importance: the removal of Stalin's corpse from the Mausoleum on Red Square (1961). Announced on the television that the Soviet people had only recently obtained, the news about this removal was watched with wonder and relief. I was a child in Leningrad, and I remember watching this news together with my father, who was inexplicably moved by it. Watching my father watching Stalin's removal happened to be the first political experience of my life, though of course I did not know what would follow later.

The periods that within the Soviet Union were called the Thaw and the Stagnation, coincided with what has gone down in global memory as the central phase of the Cold War between the Soviet Union and the Western world. Throughout this period, the memory of the gulag was preserved internationally by American and European historians, activists, writers and politicians and Soviet dissidents and memoirists. As the legacies of Hannah Arendt, Isaiah Berlin and many others testify, the Cold War struggle against Soviet expansion was also a struggle for human rights within the Soviet Union and for the historical memory of its victims. The Cold Warriors smuggled, translated and published manuscripts by Solzhenitsyn, Grossman, Osip and Nadezhda Mandelstam, and many others; they produced magisterial pieces of scholarship such as Arendt's *Origins of Totalitarianism* (1951) or Robert Conquest's *Great Terror* (1968); and they gathered an amazing array of Soviet artworks, such as Norton Dodge's collection that preserved precious pieces of art from the gulag and other places.

Several major factors should be taken into account in comparing the state of the German memory of National Socialism to the Russian memory of Soviet Socialism. First, the Communist regime in Russia lasted much longer than the Nazi regime in Germany. Repairing the damage will probably hence require more time. In addition, Russia is less distant from the collapse of its Soviet state than Germany is from the collapse of its Nazi state. Since the Soviet regime lasted for seven decades, including at least three decades of terror, the concept of generation is less useful here than in the studies of the Holocaust survivors and their descendants. In post-Stalinist Russia, mourning was suspended for several decades, which included an abortive mourning period during Khrushchev's Thaw. Second, the Soviet victims were significantly more diverse than the Nazi victims: their descendants are more dispersed and in some cases, have competing interests, which creates multiple memory conflicts in the post-Soviet space. Third, Germany's postwar transformation was forced upon it by military defeat and occupation, while Russia's post-Soviet transformation was a political choice. No occupation force ruled Russia; it has continuously ruled itself. Instead of a Marshall Plan, the international support for the post-Soviet transition was remarkably inconsistent. Finally, there are substantial differences when it comes to the subjective experiences of victimisation and mourning among the victims of both regimes and their descendants.

In the aftermath of genocides and other catastrophes, global memory has played various roles. Sometimes it has been a supplement to national memories, sometimes a catalyst, and sometimes a substitute. The prominent Holocaust historian, Dan Diner, recently re-examined this problem. Starting with Maurice Halbwachs' classic argument that collective memory requires a remembering collective, Diner comes to the conclusion that nations can preserve memory while some other social groups, such as classes, cannot. Diner states that the Nazi crime 'entered the ethnicized memory' of Germans because the regime eliminated those whom Germans considered to be 'part of a culturally and historically different collective'. In contrast, the Soviet regime defined both victims and perpetrators 'as part of the same historical mnemonic collective' (Diner 2000: 191–2). Therefore, Diner concludes, German guilt and Jewish mourning have been passed down through generations, while the Soviet crimes vanished from memory.[3]

Naturalising ethnic differences, Diner denies the ability of non-ethnic groups to structure 'mnemonic collectives' and remember their dead in a collective way. Even in the German-Jewish case. I find this argument questionable: Germans were not 'fundamentally different' from Jews; it was the Nazis who invested enormous efforts into construing this religious group as the national Other. Unavoidably, the 'thesis of a fundamental difference' between ethnic and other groups underestimates those types of solidarity that transcend and transgress national borders. According to Diner's argument, the repressions of 'kulaks' or 'nepmen' could not and do not remain in the collective memory, either because these groups were ideological fictions created by the Bolsheviks with their theories of class warfare or because these groups were successfully exterminated and did not leave descendants to mourn them. Diner characterises such crimes as historically describable but mnemonically non-transmissible. With some hesitation, Diner makes an exception to this rule for those Soviet groups who suffered from repressions that were (if not in Bolshevik theory, then in their practice) defined by ethnicity. Diner mentions Ukrainians here, but he could give many more examples, for instance, Chechens, Crimean Tatars, or, indeed, Jews after the Second World War. However, my central question addresses not these ethnically defined cases but a more general picture that Diner draws: Is Diner's nationalisation of memory (i.e. the identification of the remembering collective with the nation) historically true and morally defensible? I do not believe so. Diner's concept of collective memory seems to be custom-made for the Nazi Holocaust. Designed to clarify comparisons between the Holocaust and other cases of mass murder, it precludes many of these comparisons. Diner seems to operate within a simplified distinction between two types of human collectives, nations and classes. Marxist efforts to furnish classes with self-conscious identities do not seem convincing to Diner, but the idea that nations have identities, and therefore subjectivities, is something he appears to take as a given.

It is individuals who feel guilt or sorrow. However, these individuals have the ability to pass on, preserve and exchange their feelings, and culture provides them with the instruments for these purposes. Culture allows people to share their experiences without requiring physical encounter. Various media and genres of culture transmit and distort memory, which moves between individuals, communities, and generations. Using cultural means, some individuals and groups are able to shape the feelings of other individuals and groups. With the help of texts, images and other cultural instruments, some individuals even create new groups and collectives. Besides nations and classes, there is a third type of collective: associations, as Alexis de Tocqueville first described them.[4] The post-Soviet transformation has not happened within an undivided – classless, nationless, subject-less – unity. It has been a struggle between myriads of collective subjects, who construct themselves according to a variety of principles, from the ethnic to the political to the generational to the memorial, and shape their identities in this struggle.

---

3   In a similar way, Charles S. Maier contrasted 'hot memory' of the Holocaust to 'cold memory' of the socialist past. It seems that in 2002 when he draw this distinction, he felt this contrast to be intuitively evident. Twelve years later in Eastern and Central Europe, the political temperature of local memories has come to a boiling point, and I doubt that scholars and activists in Tallinn or Sevastopol, Kiev or Moscow would agree with Maier's contrast. See Maier 2002.

4   On associations and democracy in Alexis de Tocqueville, see Putnam 2000; Skocpol and Fiorina 1999; Warren 2001: 29–30.

In the modern world, the cultural communities of those who subscribe to a certain journal or take part in online chat, play the role of such collectives. The concept of cultural memory is close to the concept of collective memory but is significantly broader (Assmann 2011). Cultural memory presumes a remembering 'collective' only in the broadest and loosest sense. The turn from 'collective memory' to 'cultural memory' de-emphasizes the remembering collective and focuses on the materials of which memory is made. It is a turn from the sociology of memory in the tradition of Maurice Halbwachs, to cultural studies of memory in the tradition of Walter Benjamin. 'Multimedia collages' of cultural memory integrate multiple types of signifiers: from memoirs to memorials, from historical studies to historical novels, from family albums to museums and archives, from folk songs to films to the Internet (Kansteiner 2002). The leading role of the Memorial society, a typically Tocquevillian association, in preserving memory of the Soviet victims, monitoring human rights and struggling for Russia's democratisation, exemplifies the post-Soviet type of the 'remembering collective' and testifies to the powerful role of memory in structuring the social space.

In the mid-1980s, Mikhail Gorbachev launched glasnost, a sweeping project of public truth-seeking that revealed more about the Soviet past than about Russia's present. Newly published memoirs, archival findings and popular histories documented the processes, institutions and personalities of the Soviet terror in unprecedented detail.[5] The great texts of the Thaw that remained unpublished at the time – Solzhenitsyn, Shalamov, Grossman – were all published in large print-runs. Hundreds of memoirs and autobiographies published in the 1980s dealt with the sufferings of their authors or their parents under the Soviet regime. In 1993, the literary historian Marietta Chudakova, then an adviser to President Yeltsin, wrote that such writing would fulfil the function of a 'Russian Nuremberg', staged not in the courtroom as in Germany, but on the pages of memoirs (1993: 136).

This hope failed to materialise. Dispersed and marginalised, the intelligentsia of early twenty-first-century Russia has been deprived of its economic or political relevance. Nostalgia for the Soviet past has been purposefully spread by the state-controlled television, and its manifestations have become increasingly frequent on the printed page and the computer screen. Among the historical novels, biographies, films and documentaries that have been disseminated in abundance during this period, a growing share belongs to conspiracy theories and propaganda that effectively deny the crimes of the Soviet period. Often, this 'restorative nostalgia' has more to do with the drive to criticise the current Russian government than it does with any genuine sympathy for the world of communal apartments, collective farms and the gulag,[6] but the booming social media in Russia and their decisive role in political processes in the 2010s testify to the truth of Tocqueville's words that he wrote, with a quill, in the 1830s:

> *Among the laws that rule human societies there is one which seems to be more precise and clear than all others. If men are to remain civilized or to become so, the art of associating together must grow and improve in the same ratio in which the equality of conditions is increased. (Tocqueville 1956: 201–2)*

There is no doubt that the increasingly consumerist and also, sociable, Russian society has become less interested in Soviet guilt than it was 50, or even 20, years ago. However,

---

5   See Merridale 2000; Smith 1996; Toker 2000. In recent years, autobiographical accounts have received more attention than other forms of memory (see Garros, Korenevskaya and Lahusen 1995; Hellbeck 2004; Paperno 2002).

6   For a critical theory of nostalgia, see Boym 2001.

references to this legacy are surprisingly robust in political debates and cultural products of the post-Soviet era. During this decade, the challenging task of making sense of the Soviet past has also produced original and important novels and films. My statistical study of Russian blogs and online media demonstrate that the memory of Stalinism plays an amazingly significant role in the post-Soviet public sphere: for example, Stalin is mentioned by Russian bloggers more often than any living political leader, Russian or foreign, with the exception of Putin and Medvedev.

In 2014, the pro-European revolution in Ukraine caused an incredible intensification of memory wars. Drawing a continual genealogy of this revolution from a Ukrainian nationalist movement of the Second World War, which was led by Stepan Bandera, enemies of this revolution re-interpreted the political and economic discontent of the Ukrainian people in the obsolete terms of the Soviet past. A heroic and controversial figure, Bandera was killed in Munich by Soviet agents in 1959, and no apologies have been given for this crime by Russian authorities. By about 2005 local authorities in Lviv and later, national Ukrainian authorities started a commemorative campaign that turned Bandera in one of many national heroes of the country. But there is no apostolic, ideological or any other kind of continuity between Bandera and the murdered heroes of Maidan, who are now commemorated as the 'Heaven's Hundred'. On many levels, both national and transnational, a passionate memory war has supplanted a more rational and political understanding of the events. However, only those debates in the public sphere that articulate the present and political, not the past and obsolete, dimensions of the crisis could lead to its resolution.

Drawing on Freud's classic formulations, I reject the popular ideas that these manifestations of memory wars in the Russian or Ukrainian public sphere are either 'amnesiac' or 'nostalgic' and argue that there are 'melancholic'. If amnesia prefers the present to the past and nostalgia prefers the past to the present, melancholia fails to distinguish between the past and the present. This condition describes many disturbing manifestations of the public sphere in twenty-first-century Russia (Etkind 2013a, 2014). In this sense, Russia is still not post-Soviet or even post-Stalinist, like many parts of the globe are still not postcolonial or of the developed world is still not postmodern. Commenting on a similar observation, Marianne Hirsch coins a prefix 'posting', which connotes the ongoing, incomplete and tortured character of these 'post-' transformations (Hirsch 2012).

For the Soviet regime, an insistence on its own definition of truth was crucial: as soon as it faltered in this, it collapsed. In the twenty-first century, Russia's authoritarian 'transition' demonstrates the tortured complexity of its post-catastrophic situation, in which the past haunts the citizenry, divides the society and limits political choice. If the second and third generations live on the same territory where the catastrophe happened; if the political regime on this territory, despite having gone through multiple transformations since the catastrophe, remains ambiguous in its treatment of the catastrophic past; if the perpetrators are not condemned, the victims are not compensated, the criminal institutions are not banned, the monuments are not built the postmemory of the catastrophe acquires intense and peculiar forms. The very concept of postmemory is not easily applicable to this situation because strictly speaking, this is not yet a *post*memory. Transforming time in a way that is typical for the post-traumatic condition, the mourned and dreadful event, the subject of remembrance, continues into the present and shapes the future. The memory of the past becomes indistinguishable from the obsessive fear of its repetition, and the dread of the future takes the shape of compulsory repetitions or creative remembrances of the past. Mourning merges with warning, shaping a temporal zone of indistinction, which combines the past and the future in a joint effort to obscure the present.

According to an exhibition of monuments to the victims of the gulag staged in 2007, there were 1140 such monuments and memorial plaques in place on the territory of the former Soviet Union: stones, crosses, obelisks, bells, bas-reliefs, angels. Among these monuments, there are very few realistic sculptures that depict an actual prisoner in a moment of suffering. Interestingly, if anthropomorphic sculptures are found at all, they are usually erected in places like Ukraine, Kazakhstan or Tuva, where a bare, senseless life in the camp is easier to re-imagine as a sacrifice to the nationalist cause. The general rule seems to be that guilt monuments are non-figurative, while pride monuments tend to depict people, on horseback or otherwise. It is easier for postcolonial memory to construct meaning for losses and revolutions than it is for postsocialist memory. The imagining of meaningless suffering requires non human, abstract or monstrous symbols, but monuments to national emancipation, such as one in Tuva, are more human.

Sculptor Ernst Neizvestny became known in 1962 when he confronted Khrushchev during the latter's notorious attack on the artists and poets of the Thaw, whom Khrushchev called 'abstractionists' and 'homosexuals', two words that he believed to be derogatory (Neizvestny 1984: 5). Years later, the dying Khrushchev asked his wife to commission Neizvestny to carve his grave monument, which she did. Made of black and white pieces of marble, the monument symbolised Khrushchev's internal contradictions. The 15m high 'Mask of Death' (1996), a concrete sculpture in Kolyma, is a genuinely impressive monument to the victims of the Soviet terror. It obviously refers to Abraham Bosse's image of Leviathan on the frontispiece of Thomas Hobbes' book of 1651. This imagery is very different from the contemporary German, and especially Israeli, representations of the Holocaust, which search for heroes of the resistance rather than for passive sufferers (Young 2000). Russian monuments do not give any hint of the solidarity of political prisoners, their fights with criminals and with the administration, numerous camp rebellions and escapes. Other than the usual image of prison bars and barbed wire, these monuments do not tell us much about techniques of torture, incarceration or execution. These depoliticised images avoid Soviet emblems and say nothing about the ideology that determined all of these murders. A basic lack of information is typical of all of these monuments, including the most sophisticated ones.

Monuments to Soviet victims have been built by civil society, but the resources that are necessary for these monuments, starting with their sites, are controlled by the state. Interestingly, the most important monuments are erected not on the sites of the former camps, as is true in many German cases, but near them. This pattern demonstrates not the replacement of the old regime by a new one, but rather manifests their quiet coexistence. In a comparative perspective, such localisation is not necessarily exceptional. The obvious analogy is the Berlin Holocaust Memorial near the Reichstag. On the other hand, even such proximate location of memory is far from being the rule in Russia. Near the horrifying building of the Leningrad KGB, there is not a single monument, plaque or inscription commemorating the millions of its victims. Such a monument is notably absent from the vicinity of the Kremlin as well.

In a work that has become exemplary, in the 1980s and 1990s, a group of French historians led by Pierre Nora produced a seven-volume study of French monuments and other sites of historical memory (Nora 1996–98). Shifting the emphasis from the content and functions of cultural memory to its forms and 'sites', Nora interpreted monuments belonging to several epochs of French history as representations of the changing national identity. Erecting these monuments, he argues, the state imprints its own self-representations as they were shaped in time and constructs its own grandeur. This is memory as Pantheon: the selective representation of great personalities and events of the past. For a modern nation-state, immortalising the memory of its victories and great leaders becomes not only an indispensable instrument but, moreover, a part of its internal structure.[7] Such monuments demonstrate the continuity of the political tradition of a nation-state from its great founding fathers. Nora's volumes presented cultural memory as a number of spatially organised sites, which are static, self-contained and unconnected. They contrasted memory and history as if they belonged to two different worlds: memory vanishing and romanticised; history modernising, trivialising and all but colonising. They overemphasised the spatial structures of cultural memory and underestimated its temporal dynamics. They focused on monuments, memorials and museums and depreciated the historical controversies and competing narratives that fuel imaginative novels, academic studies, textbooks and alternative histories. As Pierre Nora's phenomenal success in the France of the 1990s showed, this shift of balance responded to the needs of that society. In his subtle analysis, Tony Judt connected Nora's volumes with François Mitterrand's monumental constructions that were erected during the same decade. I would add that both were created when France shunned the Internet, the deterritorialized and increasingly language-neutral space of memory, and chose instead Minitel, a closed network bound by French language and fixed terminals (Castells 1996). France is special, but in many ways it is also typical, and Judt generalized: 'The Western solution to the problem of Europe's troublesome memories has been to fix them, quite literally, in stone' (2005: 826). It was indeed a Franco-German solution, but in Eastern Europe and Russia, it did not translate into anything close in scale to either German memorials or French historiography. In these Eastern parts of the West, the cultural memory is out of balance, but its trajectory moves in the opposite direction. In Russia and Eastern Europe, novels, films and debates about the past vastly outpace and overshadow monuments, memorials and museums.

I like to compare monuments to crystals that settle in a solution of memory, provided that this solution is strong, stable and not too hot. In Eastern Europe, cultural memory is hot and liquid rather than cool and crystallised.[8] Its structures are temporal rather than spatial. Its units are memory events rather than sites of memory. Contemporary Russian memory barely approaches the minimal conditions of crystallisation. An important condition, analogous to the temperature of the solution, is social consensus. High social consensus encourages the proliferation of monuments, but, since there is not much to debate if everyone agrees, it discourages public debates. We see such a situation in contemporary Germany. In contrast, low consensus suppresses public memory, but can intensify manifestations of memory among the remembering minority. The enthusiastic efforts of solitary individuals, veritable heroes of memory, are vital in this situation. Like catalysers, they help the solution of memory to shape the crystal-like monuments.

The arts of memory are diverse. Awareness of the past may be achieved by the publication of a document or by the erection of a monument, by writing a memoir or by creating a memorial, by launching a discussion or by opening a museum. In culture, as in a computer, there are two forms of memory, which might be likened to hardware and software. Soft memory consists primarily of texts (including literary, historical and other narratives), while hard memory consists primarily of monuments. Of course, the soft and the hard are interdependent. Monuments without inscriptions are mute, while texts without monuments are ephemeral. The monumental hardware of cultural memory does not function unless it interacts with its discursive software. On the other hand, the software – public opinion, historical debates, literary imagery – would pass away with every subsequent generation or even fashion, if it were not anchored by monuments, memorials and museums. The hardening

---

7   Contemporary theorists of nationalism are more interested in other forms of memory and imagination, such as newspapers (Benedict Anderson), education (Ernest Gellner), and invented traditions (Eric Hobsbawm). More sensitive to monuments is Hroch (1985).

8   On hot and cold memories, see Assmann 1992.

of memory is a cultural process with specific functions, conditions and thresholds. It is not the mere existence of the hardware and the software but their interaction, transparency and conflicts that give cultural memory life. Like a computer, culture does not work if either the software or the hardware does not work or if there is no proper interaction between the two.

This intuitive model allows for a range of possible imbalances and imperfections, and I believe that in Eastern Europe these shifts are the opposite of those that Judt noticed in France. Studies of Russian memory and mourning should take full account of the proliferation of cultural texts, from memoirs to novels to films, and the lack of monuments in the region. Monuments are inconspicuous if people are not talking and writing about them; mourning rites are incomplete if they do not crystallise in monuments. It is the interaction between texts and monuments that makes the core of cultural memory, but this interaction has not been adequately explored in memory studies.

Printing and digital technologies have largely deterritorialised cultural memory. Texts such as the Jewish Torah or medieval manuscripts are singular. Located in sacred spaces, they function as hardware monuments as well as software texts. In contrast, the modern arts of memory, from memoir to film to the Internet, are space-neutral. Often describing specific sites, they do not have location themselves: mechanically or electronically reproduced, they are available in many places at once. Still dependent on space and its sites, modern memory is structured by time. Its temporal units are 'memory events', which I define as acts of re-visiting the past that create ruptures with its established cultural meanings (Etkind 2010; Etkind et al. 2012). Memory events are secondary to the historical events that they interpret, usually taking place many years or decades later. Sometimes, a memory event attains the significance of an historical event, therefore blurring the distinction between the two. But there are also a number of differences.

Memory events unfold in many cultural genres, from funerals to historical debates, from museum openings to court proceedings, from the erection or the destruction of a monument to archival findings, films, novels, exhibitions and websites. Historical events tend to be singular while memory events rarely are. They repeat themselves in new, creative but recognizable forms, which circulate in cultural space and reverberate in time. Like waves, these events move across cultural spaces, and they are indeed often carried by waves.

No consensus on the crucial issues of historical memory has been reached in twenty-first-century Russia. Reflecting the moving equilibrium between the competing forces of politics, culture and time, accepted definitions of what is 'right' and 'healthy' in the memory of the Soviet past shift with every new generation. While the state is led by former KGB officers, who are no more interested in apologising for the past than they are in fair elections in the present, the struggling civil society and the intrepid reading public are possessed by the unquiet ghosts of the Soviet era. But the circular time of post-catastrophic experience conflates uneasily with the linear time of history.[9] Whatever the scale of victimisation, mourning remains a personal matter, but collective rituals and cultural artefacts are critical for the process. Sharing sorrow with the community, burial rituals prevent mourning from developing into melancholy. Crystals of memory, monuments keep the uncanny where it belongs, in the grave. The anthropologist Katherine Verdery asserts that 'in many human communities, to set up right relations between living human communities and their ancestors depends critically on proper burials'. Though it is never easy to learn which relations are 'right', wrong relations are universally believed to be unfair to the dead and dangerous to the living (Verdery 1999: 42–3). In the post-Soviet economy of memory, where the losses are massive and the monuments in short supply, the dead return as the undead. The innocent victims turn into uncanny monsters.

---

9   For theoretical discussion of the temporality of collective trauma, see Edkins 2003: ch. 2.

Having distinguished between two forms of cultural memory, the hardware and the software, in Russian memory and mourning, I see the proliferation of a third form, which is impossible to reduce to the first two. I am referring to ghosts, spirits, vampires, dolls and other man-made and man-imagined simulacra that carry the memory of the dead.[10] Usually, ghosts live in texts; sometimes, they inhabit cemeteries and emerge from monuments. Most often, ghosts visit those whose dead have not been properly buried. Three elements of cultural memory, its software, hardware and ghostware, are intimately connected. Texts are symbolic, while ghosts are iconic: as signs, ghosts possess a visual resemblance to the signified; in contrast to monuments, texts and ghosts are ephemeral; and in contrast to texts and monuments, ghosts are uncanny. These ghostly components of memory deserve a detailed analysis and close reading (Etkind 2013b).

For a long time, spectres have been haunting this space that survived Communism. The scholars of the European Enlightenment observe how its rational ordering of the world, which was still full of unpredictable suffering, led to the invention of the uncanny, 'a new human experience of strangeness, anxiety, bafflement, and intellectual impasse' (Castle 1995: 16). By analogy, I argue, Soviet culture, with its combination of bellicose rationalism and absurd violence, generated a veritable explosion of figurative and mystical ways in which people responded to their world. Official culture locked these ghostly ways in the underground of everyday life with its rumours, legends and anecdotes and also in low genres of art and literature that were less susceptible to censorship. Released by the glasnost of the late twentieth century, repressed figures of this hauntic underground returned to their place of origin, high culture, where they became dominant ways of representing history and even politics (Etkind 2013b: ch. 11). Slavoj Žižek suggests that the return of the dead has become 'a fundamental fantasy of contemporary mass culture' (1991: 22).[11] Defeating the ideals of the Enlightenment, this process seems to be especially prominent in Russia, which has inherited and rejected the ideals of the Enlightenment in their perverted Soviet forms. Postsecular politics entails a transformation of 'the state's secularist self-understanding' in various parts of the world, and its historical mechanisms and manifestations are different everywhere (De Vries and Sullivan 2006: 3). In the global world of the twenty-first century, mourning and warning are developing their dual alliance, but their proportions and relations within this alliance differ in different cultures. Some cultures proliferate their ghosts, vampires and zombies in response to the catastrophes of the past; other cultures generate this imagery in anticipation of the catastrophes of the future. Either way, this ghostly perspective on world affairs – hauntological worldliness, I would say – is both realist and humanist. It is only on the hauntological level that Edmund Burke's 'great primeval contract' between the living, the dead and the unborn can be imagined or, for that matter, observed.

Having taught the relevance of ghosts to the interpretative community of his readers, Derrida does not offer much help in understanding their nature, taxonomy or life cycle. As some critics have mentioned, his ghosts are not the same as the sophisticated phantoms of Nicolas Abraham and Maria Torok, which keep the secrets of the past and transmit them, in eternally encrypted form, from generation to generation. Derrida's ghosts could reveal a secret if they wished, but they do not necessarily do that, and the reason behind their

---

10   A proliferation of ghosts and zombies in high and popular cultures has been observed by scholars of postsocialist transformations in Poland, East Germany, Ukraine and Russia. For a similar effect in South Africa after apartheid, see Comaroff and Comaroff 2002. A recent example is a Cuban film, *Juan of the Dead*, described as 'the blood-drenched tale of a slacker who decides to save the island from an invasion of cannibalistic zombies', though the film is also scattered with allusions to traumatic moments in Cuba's recent history (Victoria Burnett in *The New York Times,* 10 Dec. 2011).

11   See also Blanco and Peeren 2010; Castricano 2001.

existence is different from this conspiratorial knowledge. 'It is in the name of *justice'* that Derrida speaks about the ghosts and not in the name of knowledge, but this is a special kind of justice, one that brings the living and the dead together in a single ghostly equation. As for Burke, for Derrida 'present existence … has never been the condition … of justice'. Theirs is the justice of relations between the living and the dead. It needs to be established '*through* but also *beyond* right and law,' though not beyond human comprehension, with its rhetorical devices such as ghosts (Derrida 1994: 221). Practically speaking, this particular 'justice', one of the most frequent concepts in Derrida's late writings, is the debt owed to the dead.

But it is also true that these debts owed the dead can never be repaid and this justice can never be established. I am sure that all our philosophers of mourning, from Tasso to Burke to Siniavsky to Derrida, would agree with this thesis, which gives post-catastrophic mourning its interminable, melancholic character. Having granted these images – ghosts, debts, posthumous justice – all the metaphorical relevance they deserve, one still feels puzzled by them. How can we, the living, redeem our debt to the dead? What kind of justice are we talking about? Can we repay the ghosts? Do we have a currency that is convertible for this task? Can this toolkit of legal and financial metaphors provide any help in carrying out the work of mourning?

Derrida links his hauntology with the idea of retributive justice. In a post-catastrophic situation, we mourners live lives and die deaths that are incomparably better than those of our precursors. This is why to live with ghosts means 'to live otherwise, and better. No, not better, but more justly' (Derrida 1994: xviii). This kind of justice does not require judiciary power, but it does need scholars. As the living and the undead grow more accustomed to each other, they develop an uneasy friendship that needs to be noticed, articulated and recognised. As Derrida urged, the ghostly dimension of our life-world is permanent; we must 'learn to live with ghosts'. This is a departure from a folklore understanding of ghostly apparitions as consequences of improper burial rites, with the implicit promise that re-burial would send the ghosts safely back to their graves. Derrida does not wish this to happen as a general case, and I do not see it happening in Russia. In contrast to laying them to rest, learning to live with ghosts is an open-ended process, which generates the unpredictable and rich variety of 'victim's balls', memory events and cultural innovations.

These mournful experiences need to be summarised, but I feel that justice is a poor concept for doing this work. In my view, ghosts need recognition rather than justice. There is no way to redistribute anything of value between the dead and the living, but there is a very real sense in which unjustifiable deaths can be recognised by the living. Ghosts do not want us to repay our debts; all that they want is recognition.

References

Alexeyeva, L., and P. Goldberg. 1990. *The Thaw Generation: Coming of Age in the Post-Stalin Era* (Boston, MA: Little, Brown & Co.).

Assmann, J. 1992. *Das Kulturelle Gedächtnis: Schrift, Erinnerung und Politische Identität in frühen Hochkulturen* (Munich: C.H. Beck).

— — 2011. *Cultural Memory and Western Civilization: Functions, Media, Archives* (Cambridge: Cambridge University Press).

Blanco, M., and E. Peeren (eds) 2010. *Popular Ghosts: The Haunted Spaces of Everyday Culture* (New York: Continuum).

Boym, S. 2001. *The Future of Nostalgia* (New York: Basic Books).

Castells, M. 1996. *The Rise of the Network Society: The Information Age*, vol. 2 (New York: Blackwell).

Castle, T. 1995. *The Female Thermometer: Eighteenth-Century Culture and the Invention of the Uncanny* (New York and Oxford: Oxford University Press).

Castricano, C.J. 2001. *Cryptomimesis: The Gothic and Jacques Derrida's Ghost Writing* (Montreal: McGill-Queen's University Press).

Chudakova, M. 1993. 'Pod skrip ukliuchin', *Novyi mir* 4.

Comaroff, Jean, and John Comaroff 2002. 'Alien-Nation: Zombies, Immigrants, and Millenial Capitalism', *South Atlantic Quarterly* 104: 779–805.

Condee, N. 2000. 'Cultural Codes of the Thaw', in William Taubman et al. (eds), *Nikita Khrushchev* (New Haven: Yale University Press), 160–76.

De Vries, H., and L.E. Sullivan (eds) 2006. *Political Theologies: Public Religions in a Post-Secular World* (New York: Fordham University Press).

Derrida, J. 1994. *Specters of Marx: The State of the Debt, the Work of Mourning and the New International*, trans. P. Kamuf (New York and London: Routledge).

Diner, D. 2000. *Beyond the Conceivable. Studies on Germany, Nazism, and the Holocaust* (Berkeley: University of California Press).

Edkins, J. 2003. *Trauma and the Memory of Politics* (Cambridge: Cambridge University Press).

Etkind, A. 1997. *Eros of the Impossible: The History of Psychoanalysis in Russia* (Boulder, CO: Westview).

— — 2010. 'Mapping Memory Events in East European Space', *East European Memory Studies* 1: 4–5.

— — 2013a. 'Mourning and Melancholia in Putin's Russia: An Essay in Qualitative Mnemonics', in E. Rutten, V. Zvereva and J. Fedor (eds), *Old Conflicts, New Media: Post-Socialist Digital Memories* (London: Routledge), pp. 32–48.

— — 2013b. *Warped Mourning: Stories of the Undead in the Land of the Unburied* (Palo Alto, CA: Stanford University Press).

— — 2014. 'Post-Soviet Russia: The Land of the Oil Curse, Pussy Riot, and Magical Historicism', in W. Godzich and A. Starosta (eds), *Second-Hand Europe*, special issue of *Boundary 2*, 41/1: 153–70.

— — et al. 2012. *Remembering Katyn* (Cambridge: Polity).

Garros, V., N. Korenevskaya and T. Lahusen (eds) 1995. *Intimacy and Terror: Soviet Diaries of the 1930s* (New York: New Press).

Hellbeck, J. (ed.) 2004. *Autobiographical Practices in Russia / Autobiographische Praktiken in Russland* (Göttingen: Vandenhoeck & Ruprecht).

Hirsch, M. 2012. *The Generation of Postmemory: Writing and Visual Culture after the Holocaust* (New York: University of Columbia Press).

Hroch, M. 1985. *Social Preconditions of National Revival in Europe* (Cambridge: Cambridge University Press).

Jones, P. 2008. 'Memories of Terror or Terrorizing Memories?', *Slavic and East European Journal* 86/2: 346–71.

— — (ed.) 2006. *The Dilemmas of De-Stalinization: Negotiating Cultural and Social Change in the Khrushchev Era* (London: Routledge).

Judt, T. 2005. *Postwar: A History of Europe since 1945* (New York: Penguin Press).

Kansteiner, W. 2002. 'Finding Meaning in Memory: A Methodological Critique of Collective Memory Studies', *History and Theory* 41: 179–97.

Khrushchev, S. 1994. *Nikita Khrushchev* (Moscow: Novosti).

Maier, C.S. 2002. 'Hot Memory … Cold Memory: On the Political Half-Life of Fascist and Communist Memory', *Transit* 22: 153–65, available at <http://archiv.iwm.at/index.php?option=com_content&task=view&id=316&Itemid=48>.

Merridale, C. 2000. *Night of Stone: Death and Memory in Twentieth-Century Russia* (London: Granta).

Neizvestny, E. 1984. *Govorit Neizvestny* (Frankfurt: Posev).

Nora, P. (ed.) 1996–98. *Realms of Memory: Rethinking the French Past*, 3 vols. trans. A. Goldhammer (New York: Columbia University Press).

Paperno, I. 2002. 'Personal Accounts of the Soviet Experience' *Kritika* 3: 577–610.

Plamper, J. 2005. 'Cultural Production, Cultural Consumption: Post-Stalin Hybrids', *Kritika* 6: 755–62.

Prokhorov, A. 2008. *Unasledovannyi diskurs: Paradigmy stalinskoi kul'tury v literature i kinematografe ottepeli* (St Petersburg: Akademicheskii proekt).

Putnam, R.D. 2000. *Bowling Alone: The Collapse and Revival of American Community* (New York: Simon & Schuster).

Reid, S. 2006. 'The Soviet Art World in the Early Thaw', *Third Text* 20: 161–75.

Skocpol, T., and M.P. Fiorina (eds) 1999. *Civic Engagement in American Democracy* (Washington DC: Brookings Institution Press).

Smith, K.E. 1996. *Remembering Stalin's Victims: Popular Memory and the End of the USSR* (Ithaca, NY: Cornell University Press).

Snyder, T. 2010. *Bloodlands: Europe between Hitler and Stalin* (New York: Basic Books).

Tocqueville, A. 1956. *Democracy in America*, Ed.,. R.D. Heffner (New York: Mentor Books).

Toker, L. 2000. *Return from the Archipelago: Narratives of Gulag Survivors* (Bloomington: Indiana University Press).

Verdery, K. 1999. *The Political Lives of Dead Bodies: Reburial and Postsocialist Change* (New York: Columbia University Press).

Warren, M.E. 2001. *Democracy and Association* (Princeton, NJ: Princeton University Press).

Young, J.E. 2000. *At Memory's Edge: After-Images of the Holocaust in Contemporary Art and Architecture* (New Haven, CT: Yale University Press).

Žižek, S. 1991. *Looking Awry: An Introduction to Jacques Lacan through Popular Culture* (Cambridge, MA: MIT Press).

Afterword

Jeffrey K. Olick

Social and cultural memory studies begin from a position at odds with the ideological texture of the modern world. As Louis Althusser so famously put it, in the modern capitalist order, 'ideology hails or interpellates concrete individuals as concrete subjects'. And nowhere is this more true than in the realm of memory, which appears to contemporary common-sense as a paradigmatically individual capacity. Yet notions of collective, social and cultural memory begin from a different starting point, one that presumes the individual's embeddedness in shared contexts and enduring traditions: the individual's memories – both their operations and contents – are the products of these contexts and traditions, not the fixed building blocks of them.

Yet, as is so often the case, we frequently forget to apply the same insights we use to understand the objects of our study when we discuss our own work. Here too it is crucial to remember that, as much as our careers and works are hailed as products of individuals and we as subjects of them, our scholarship too is the embedded product of shared contexts and enduring traditions. And this is why the present volume's many considerations of intellectual and even personal companions in memory scholarship are so important and, indeed, unique.

In many ways, the editor's call itself serves as a spur to memory, a sort of *petite madeleine* leading the scholar to involuntary memories of his or her influences and contexts. For myself, the call brought me immediately back to my first encounter with Halbwachs. As a sociologist-in-training interested in storytelling and its relationship to identity, I found in Halbwachs both a key term – 'collective memory' – as well as a legitimation for my interest in such topics, which were not (and still are not) in the mainstream of sociological research in the 1980s when I was in graduate school: this was a major protégé of the discipline's founder, Emile Durkheim, addressing exactly what was interesting to me, whether or not it was at the top of my discipline's agenda. I also remember the excitement with which I read Patrick Hutton's *History as an Art of Memory*, which so vastly expanded my range of intellectual reference and understanding, as well as Jan Assmann's *Moses the Egyptian*, which provided the concept of 'mnemohistory', which has been a central inspiration for my work.

But intellectual companions – the identification of which is the *raison d'etre* of this volume – are not merely constitutive in this way, namely in shaping one's work from behind. Intellectual companionship also results from one's work in a field, when one finds comrades in arms whose companionship one acquires along the journey. Here just a few of my own are worth mentioning. Perhaps the first, and most important, has been the sociologist Barry Schwartz, who not only did all the things Halbwachs, Hutton and Assmann did for me from a distance – supplying legitimation, erudition and inspiring concepts – but who provided personal mentorship as well.

For American sociologists interested in memory, Schwartz has been a true pioneer and father figure. In the 1980s, just as the memory boom was hitting in European scholarly contexts, Schwartz was the only American sociologist whose work drew directly on Halbwachs and whose research sought to specify, extend and test his insights systematically. Schwartz's paper, 'The Social Context of Commemoration: A Study in Collective Memory', published in 1982, was an extension of his earlier Durkheimian inquiries into the sociology of time. The paper was one of the earliest English-language engagements by an American sociologist with Halbwachs' work on collective memory, ten years ahead of Lewis Coser's well-known translation and critical edition. The paper demonstrated rigorously how the significance of historical events changes from generation to generation, but, contrary to instrumentalist accounts, Schwartz showed how these changes in 'collective representations' are the result of the needs of the culture. In a subsequent paper in 1986, Schwartz and colleagues presented the fascinating case of Masada, the memory of which was strangely recovered in the twentieth century. Since then, Schwartz has produced an enormous body of work that seeks to temper the tendencies to see the past as either entirely malleable or entirely durable, as well as either manipulated or resonant: the remembered past is all of these at the same time, though in complicated balances. There is also no question, at a more practical level, that Schwartz' extensive engagement with the work of younger scholars has decisively shaped the course (and status) of collective memory research in American sociology. It has certainly shaped my own work in countless ways, direct and indirect: in the latter regard, it is probably not incidental that my first sociology teacher, Robin Wagner-Pacifici, was a significant collaborator of Schwartz's, resulting in their landmark 1991 paper on the Vietnam Veterans Memorial.

But, the social structure of companionship is not exhausted only by intellectual forebears and the mentorship one has received. If one is particularly lucky, one might have the pleasure of passing on one's understanding to others. And even better, one might have the joy of seeing those others move from being students to genuine companions. This is certainly true of this volume's editor, Siobhan Kattago, who, as an advanced graduate student at the New School for Social Research in New York, attended a workshop I organised at Columbia University in the mid-1990s, which we called 'the memory collective'. It is true as well of Daniel Levy, who was a student in the first graduate seminar I offered on collective memory, I believe in 1995. Kattago and Levy have both become more than equal companions along the way.

Beyond mentors and students, one also acquires other friendly companions through a career, whose insights and responses shape the work. For me, two in particular are worth mentioning here: Vered Vinitzky-Seroussi, with whom Levy and I collaborated on *The Collective Memory Reader*, and Astrid Erll, whose insights from a different corner – literary and cultural studies – have transformed my view of the enterprise. Vinitzky-Seroussi's own work on reunions illuminated for me the role of memory in personal life alongside the role of memory at the level of the state that had always interested me. She also introduced me to Nachman Ben-Yehuda, another protégé and friend of Barry Schwartz's, whose further work on Masada draws connections between memory politics and deviant behaviour, among other things. For her part, Erll's work on travelling memory is part of what she has rightly identified as a 'third wave' of memory studies, focusing on what Michael Rothberg has called 'multidirectional' memory. While my own work has remained firmly within the second wave, where a number of problems remain to be analysed, it is clear that Erll's and Rothberg's work will bring memory studies into the future.

Depending on one's culture, of course, how one breaks bread – the literal meaning of companionship – depends on specific cultural codes. How strong are the norms of civility? What topics can one bring up over a meal? How heated can the discussion become? For all the emphasis on companionship and collegiality, then, one should not minimise the impact of antagonisms, though I am also lucky enough that most of my intellectual antagonisms have been friendly and constructive (I say 'most' to hedge against the possibility of hurt feelings of which I am unaware).

Indeed, friendly antagonisms were there at the very beginning of systematic work employing the term collective memory, namely in Strasbourg in the 1920s and 1930s, when Halbwachs interacted with the historians Marc Bloch and Lucien Febvre and psychologist and physician Charles Blondel. Halbwachs was very much an active agent of Durkheim's disciplinary imperialism, seeing sociology as incorporating history and opposing at least individualistic psychology. While these antagonisms were friendly ones, they did involve an effort to articulate a sociological perspective in contrast to the historical and psychological. Of course, the intellectual pressures went in both directions. In his review of Halbwachs' 1925 *Social Frameworks of Memory*, for instance, Bloch questioned whether Halbwachs' approach had anything to say about the actual past, and Halbwachs' second book on memory, *The Legendary Topography of the Holy Land*, was in part a response to this challenge. Additionally, the physician Blondel charged Halbwachs with neglecting the 'somatic' bases of memory. Halbwachs in turn made it clear that this was no unintentional oversight but a matter of principle, and his series of essays published posthumously as *The Collective Memory* are filled with direct responses to Blondel and arguments against his charges.

In the contemporary period, Halbwachs himself has stood as a contrast figure in the work of Jan Assmann, who not only rejects the term 'collective memory' but whose articulation of the concept of 'cultural memory' is drawn in contrast to the 'communicative memory' Assmann sees as a more appropriate description of Halbwachs' subject. In order to do this, Assmann develops a contrast between Halbwachs as a progenitor for the sociological study of communicative memory and Aby Warburg as a progenitor for Assmann's own cultural memory studies. And there seems little question as to which enterprise is, in Assmann's view, the more profound, though of course Assmann acknowledges a debt to Halbwachs' contributions to the memory discourse.

For myself, I have found two distinct friendly intellectual antagonists along the way as well. In the first place, my thinking about the differences between what I termed 'collected' and 'collective' memory came in reaction to the survey-based research of the sociologist Howard Schuman. In turn, Schuman has challenged my valuation of the different sides of the distinction. For my part, this exchange – I call it an antagonism only for rhetorical purposes – has been enormously fruitful, helping me to crystallise my position, as well as to dial back my glibber formulations. In turn, the psychologist Bill Hirst takes up in this very volume some of the limitations of my distinction. Arguing with Hirst over the last decade over the differences between, and possible collaborations of, psychology and sociology on issues of memory has been an essential form of antagonistic (in a good way) companionship for me as I work to solve empirical alongside theoretical issues, as well as to contemplate the multiple trajectories of memory studies as a field.

As for the field of memory studies itself – should such a thing exist or be coming about as a more or less coherent enterprise – this too is a source of companionship, and the present volume is an outstanding example of it. The field is indeed many and varied, and the particular stories each of the authors has told in the foregoing pages about their companions contribute to an understanding of the field as a complex set of not-necessarily-overlapping entanglements. As Erll and Rothberg have pointed out, this is now to be expected of memory. This volume helps us expect it – in an exciting way – of memory studies as well.

Index